THE AUTHOR   Kenneth Pearce is the author of *The View from the Top of the Temple: Ancient Maya Civilization and Modern Maya Culture* published by the University of New Mexico Press. The book traces the religious beliefs of the contemporary cultures of Mexico and Guatemala to those of the ancestral Maya. His current project develops the rise and fall of the Aztec Empire from archival documents written by descendants of Mexican royalty and other ruling groups in the Valley of Mexico. He lives in California and visits and stays in Mexico frequently.

SERIES EDITOR   Professor Denis Judd is a graduate of Oxford, a Fellow of the Royal Historical Society and Professor of History at the University of North London. He has published over 20 books including the biographies of Joseph Chamberlain, Prince Philip, George VI and Alison Uttley, historical and military subjects, stories for children and two novels. His most recent book is the highly praised *Empire: The British Imperial Experience from 1765 to the Present.* He is an advisor to the *BBC History* magazine and has reviewed and written extensively in the national press and in journals, and is a regular contributor to British and overseas radio and television.

Other Titles in the Series

A Traveller's History of France
A Traveller's History of Paris
A Traveller's History of Spain
A Traveller's History of Italy
A Traveller's History of Russia
 and the USSR
A Traveller's History of Scotland
A Traveller's History of England
A Traveller's History of London
A Traveller's History of Ireland
A Traveller's History of Turkey
A Traveller's History of Greece
A Traveller's History of India
A Traveller's History of South
 East Asia
A Traveller's History of Japan
A Traveller's History of China

A Traveller's History of North Africa
A Traveller's History of the
 Caribbean
A Traveller's History of Australia
A Traveller's History of the USA
A Traveller's History of Canada

THE TRAVELLER'S HISTORY SERIES

'Ideal before-you-go reading' *The Daily Telegraph*

'An excellent series of brief histories' *New York Times*

'I want to compliment you ... on the brilliantly concise contents of your books' *Shirley Conran*

Reviews of Individual Titles

A Traveller's History of France
'Undoubtedly the best way to prepare for a trip to France is to bone up on some history. *The Traveller's History of France* by Robert Cole is concise and gives the essential facts in a very readable form.' *The Independent*

A Traveller's History of China
'The author manages to get 2 million years into 300 pages. An excellent addition to a series which is already invaluable, whether you're travelling or not.' *The Guardian*

A Traveller's History of India
'For anyone ... planning a trip to India, the latest in the excellent Traveller's History series ... provides a useful grounding for those whose curiosity exceeds the time available for research.' *The London Evening Standard*

A Traveller's History of Japan
'It succeeds admirably in its goal of making the present country comprehensible through a narrative of its past, with asides on everything from bonsai to *zazen*, in a brisk, highly readable style ... you could easily read it on the flight over, if you skip the movie.' *The Washington Post*

A Traveller's History of Ireland
'For independent, inquisitive travellers traversing the green roads of Ireland, there is no better guide than *A Traveller's History of Ireland*.' *Small Press*

A Traveller's History of Mexico

A Traveller's History of Mexico

KENNETH PEARCE

Series Editor   DENIS JUDD
Line Drawings   *JOHN HOSTE*

Interlink Books
An imprint of Interlink Publishing Group, Inc.
New York • Northampton

First American edition published in 2002 by
INTERLINK BOOKS
An imprint of Interlink Publishing Group, Inc.
99 Seventh Avenue • Brooklyn, New York 11215 and
46 Crosby Street • Northampton, Massachusetts 01060
www.interlinkbooks.com

Text copyright © Kenneth Pearce 2002
Preface copyright © Denis Judd 2002

*The front cover shows a detail of a mural from Bonampak, Mexico, courtesy of the
Museum of Anthropology, Villahermosa, Mexico.*

Library of Congress Cataloging-in-Publication Data
Pearce, Kenneth, 1921–
     A traveller's history of Mexico/Kenneth Pearce ; line drawings,
John Hoste.—1st American ed.
          p. cm.
Includes bibliographical references and index.
     ISBN 1-56656-402-6
     1. Mexico—History.   I. Title.
     F1226 .P36 2001
     972—dc21

                    2001004463

Printed and bound in Great Britain

To order or request our complete catalog,
please call us at **1-800-238-LINK** or write to:
Interlink Publishing
46 Crosby Street, Northampton, MA 01060
e-mail: info@interlinkbooks.com • website: www.interlinkbooks.com

Table of Contents

Preface	xi
CHAPTER ONE: **The Land**	1
CHAPTER TWO: **Prehistoric Mexico**	12
CHAPTER THREE: **The Rise of Civilization**	20
CHAPTER FOUR: **The Militaristic States**	46
CHAPTER FIVE: **Conquest**	85
CHAPTER SIX: **The Colonial Period**	125
CHAPTER SEVEN: **The Wars of Independence**	156
CHAPTER EIGHT: **The Texas Rebellion**	177
CHAPTER NINE: **The Mexican–American War**	189
CHAPTER TEN: **The Caste War of Yucatán**	199
CHAPTER ELEVEN: **Juárez and Maximilian**	215
CHAPTER TWELVE: **The Porfiriato**	229
CHAPTER THIRTEEN: **The Mexican Revolution**	250
CHAPTER FOURTEEN: *1920–40* **The Roots of the Modern State**	275
CHAPTER FIFTEEN: **The Modern Era**	288

Epilogue   332

Mexican Heads of State   338

Chronology of Major Events   343

Further Reading   349

Historical Gazetteer   354

Glossary   379

Index   381

MAPS AND   Physical map of Mexico   3
DIAGRAMS

                Cenote distribution in the Yucatán
                Peninsula   11

                Teotihuacán Ceremonial Centre   26

                Maya territories in Mexico and Central
                America   41

                Tribal boundaries in the Valley of Mexico   57

                The Anahuac, 1519   63

                The lineage of the kings of Mexico   65

                The Grijalva expedition   87

                Cortés's march to Mexico   97

                Northern and southern lake systems in the
                Valley of Mexico   101

                Moctezuma's descendants   114

                Guatemala and surrounding countries   128

                The journey of Cabeza de Vaca   132

Northward expansion of the sixteenth century 145

The War of Independence: theatres of operations 161

Texas territory, 1824 179

US–Mexico border dispute 192

The Mexican War 195

The Caste War 204

Revolution: October 1914 267

Modern Mexico 322

Baja California 377

Preface

Historically Mexico has meant very different things to the two largest English-speaking nations. For the British, it is part of a far away, Latin dominated continent with which they have traditionally been very little involved, aside from some trifling scraps of empire, some useful commerce and a complex and often fraught relationship with Argentina and Chile. For the United States however, Mexico is one of only two neighbouring countries with which a frontier is shared. The American interaction with Mexico has had a special, unpredictable and colourful quality, often teetering between peace and war, and beset by all the problems inherent in the interaction between a quasi client state and a continental and global super power.

Mexico's place in history, though, is far more securely based than that. During the great expansion of Europe overseas, beginning in the late fifteenth century and leading to the protracted age of empire, Mexico came to symbolise many things in the imagination of the world. One was the almost disorientating fact that the New World contained completely unknown and sophisticated civilizations. Witness the awe-struck description of one of Cortés's conquistadors on first seeing the great Aztec market place of Tlatelolco: 'We marvelled at the number and variety of wares sold here ... we saw dealers who sold feathers, mantles, precious stones, and finely crafted artifacts of gold and silver ... they sell tiger pelts, otter and beaver fur, and the hides of deer and jackal ... we also found paper and reeds scented with the sap of the sweet gum and filled with tobacco, salt and grain... One cannot see all the merchandise sold in the market place in two days. Soldiers who have been to Constantinople, to Rome ...

swore that had never before seen a market place of this size, nor one so well administered.'

Beyond this, Mexico became part of the avaricious, imperial dreaming of the European conqueror. What could be more alluring than the fantasy of El Dorado made flesh in the plundering of the great South American civilizations of the Aztec and the Inca? Moreover, conquest and conversion could be justified even more easily in the light of the Aztec predilection for constant mass human sacrifice in order to ensure the continuation of their world. And was it not stranger than fiction that Cortés should arrive in Mexico precisely when the Aztec expected the return of the god Quetzalcoatl from the sea seeking to reclaim his kingdom?

Kenneth Pearce recounts this high historical drama with great feeling and flair. The story of Mexico, however, is far more complex and just as fascinating as the history of its conquest. Beginning by carefully describing the country's geographical and physical features, the author goes on to unravel an enormous quantity of historical detail. It is a story set amid great rivers, menacing volcanoes, vast deserts, arid plans, apparently endless mountain chains, sticky sub-tropical forests, deadly malarial swamps and much else.

It is also the story of violent struggles for control, the crash of conflicting cultures, and the survival of old traditions and individual hope despite the arbitrary wielding of power for so long. Mexico eventually threw off its Spanish masters, only to be threatened by the United States' claim to a continental supremacy based on the assertion of 'manifest destiny'. Even when Mexico's frontiers were finally fixed, the country had to face internal revolution, upset and conflict in bewildering sequence.

Mexico is now a great magnet for tourists. They come from all over the world, and in increasing numbers. There is a great deal for them to see and do in a country that is much bigger and more varied than many of them may imagine, and whose history contains many surprises – for instance, how many will know that 'Mexico City is the oldest continuously inhabited city in North America'? After reading Kenneth Pearce's very well researched, comprehensive and thoughtful book, however, they will know far more than this about an exotic, beautiful and amply rewarding country.

Denis Judd, London, 2001

CHAPTER ONE

The Land

The Highlands

North of the twenty-second parallel, Mexico is a vast land of mountains, deserts, arid plateaus, and hot, sterile plains. In the west, the Sierra Madre Occidental stretches for eleven hundred miles to the south. The range is, on the average, a hundred miles wide with no more than three or four passes to the interior. As the sierra moves inland at the twenty-first parallel, the Sierra Madre del Sur rises along the coast, forming a barrier that stretches as far as the Isthmus of Tehuantepec, seven hundred miles to the south. Beyond Tehuantepec the sierra rises once again, paralleling the coast for another two hundred miles before it passes into Guatemala.

In the east, the Sierra Madre Oriental isolates the coastal plain of the Gulf of Mexico from the interior. Six hundred miles to the south, it ends abruptly at a great tectonic seam, an active volcanic range that splits the nation in two from the Atlantic to the Pacific.

Separated from the mainland in the west by the Golfo de California, Baja California parallels the coastline for more than seven hundred miles, reaching from the border of California to the Tropic of Cancer and beyond. The Baja is a dry, barren land, sparsely inhabited save in the extreme north, where the westerlies that cross the United States provide some rain, and at the southern tip, where it enters the tropical rain belt. The Sierra de San Pedro Mártir and the Sierra de La Giganta run down the centre of the peninsula, and the highest point is Pichaco Del Diablo at 10,073 feet (3070 m).

The greater part of the peninsula is no more than eighty miles wide, with but a single road along its entire length.

SONORA DESERT

The Sonora Desert, one of the hottest and most arid regions of the world, lies to the east across the Golfo de California. Two hundred miles wide in the north, it narrows sharply when it reaches the twenty-eighth parallel at Guaymas, squeezed between the coastal plain and the sierra. The monstrous heat of the desert makes travel nearly impossible other than in the winter months, and Hermosillo, the transportation hub of the Sonora, has an average yearly temperature of 91°F.

At Guaymas the coastal plain, fed by rains driven north by tropical storm tracks from the Pacific Ocean, becomes more habitable, giving way to fertile lands in the south, then to tropical jungle north of Cape Corrientes, where the Rio Grande de Santiago flows out into the sea.

RIO GRANDE DE SANTIAGO

The source of the Santiago lies four hundred miles to the southeast in the Valley of Toluca, where it is called the Lerma. The river begins its journey through a narrow gorge into the Bajio, the rich agricultural lands of Michoacán, Guanajuato, and Jalisco. At Lake Chapala, it becomes the Santiago, and at Guadalajara, the river breaks through the western escarpment and flows northwards through Nayarit, dropping five hundred feet to the ocean in a waterway 220 miles long. In 1951 the Lerma Aqueduct was opened, draining off 23 million gallons of fresh water a day for Mexico City, and generating 12 thousand kilowatts of electrical power along the way.

East of the Sonora, the broad triangle of the central plateau encompasses the states of Chihuahua, Durango, Coahuila,and Zacatecas. It begins its gentle rise at an elevation of 4,000 feet along the Texas border, and climbs to an altitude of more than 8,000 feet at San Luis Potosí, 700 miles to the south. The climate of the plateau is moderate to cool, with a yearly variation of approximately 15°F. The average yearly rainfall, however, is so low that it offers poor support for the population.

East of the plateau the land begins its rise into the Sierra Madre Oriental, where rainfall can be as much as 24 inches a year, making eastern Coahuila and Nueva Leon one of the best farming districts of

Physical map of Mexico

0 250 miles
0 500 km

PACIFIC OCEAN

Tropic of Cancer

20°N
30°

Cabo San Lucas

Sonora Desert

Sierra Madre Occidental

Chihuahuan Desert

Bravo del Norte / Rio Grande

Islas Marías
Cabo Corrientes

Balsas R.

Sierra Madre del Sur

Grande de Santiago River

Sierra Madre Oriental

Bolsón de Mapimí

Pánuco R.

U S A

Golfo de California

Golfo de Tehuantepec

Istmo de Tehuantepec

Sierra Madre

Usumacinta R.

GUATEMALA

EL SALVADOR

BELIZE
Gulf of Honduras

HONDURAS

NICARAGUA

Bahía de Campeche

Yucatan Peninsula

Cabo Catoche

Yucatan Channel

G U L F   O F   M E X I C O

CUBA

110°
100°
90°
80°W

Over 5000 metres
500-5000 metres
0-500 metres

Principal volcanoes on a tectonic seam, heights in feet
1 Cofre de Perote............14,049
2 Orizaba......................18,697
3 La Malinche.................14,636
4 Iztaccíhuatl.................17,345
5 Popocatepetl................17,887
6 Nevada de Toluca..........14,854
7 Paracutín.....................9,248
8 Pico de Tancítaro..........11,158
9 Nevada de Colima.........14,121

Mexico. Beyond the sierra, between Brownsville, on the Texas border, and Tampico, the land drops sharply to the sterile plains of the Gulf Coast, a hot and humid region where rainfall exceeds 40 inches a year.

VOLCANOES

In eastern Mexico, at the nineteenth parallel near San Andreas Tuxtla, the great seam of broken land and volcanoes, a hundred miles wide and eight hundred miles long, crosses the nation to Cape Corrientes on the Pacific Coast. A procession of volcanoes, eight of which are more than 11,000 feet high, and scores of smaller ones lie along the seam. At its eastern end, Orizaba, or Citlaltepetl, as the Aztecs called it, soars to an altitude of more than 18,000 feet, and its snow-capped peak can be seen from a hundred miles away in the Gulf of Mexico. Fifty miles east of Mexico City, at an elevation of more than 17,000 feet, Popocatepetl stands between heaven and the underworld of the Aztecs, and three hundred miles to the west lies the Nevada de Colimo, one of the Earth's most active volcanoes.

In February of 1943, in the state of Michoacan, the great forces that

Popocatepetl in the clouds

lie beneath the seam rose in a cornfield near the village of Paricutin. For a month earthquakes rattled the region, then a fissure opened at the foot of the Tanticaro volcano. Six days later, a cone stood 500 feet above the fissure, and in seven months it grew to a height of 1200 feet. Lava flows spread out over an area of seven square miles, completely covering the village of Parangaricutiro and damaging ten others in the vicinity. Nine years later, after a lava flow of more than a billion tons, all activity ceased, leaving Paricutin at its present height of more than 8,000 feet.

The great basin of the Valley of Mexico, more than 7,000 feet above sea level, covers an area of 50,000 square miles. Before the Pliocene Epoch, its rivers flowed southwest into the Balsas River, but as the great seam created mountains and volcanoes to the south, the valley was shut off from the sea, and the trapped waters formed a 500 square mile system of interconnected lakes. The largest of the lakes, Texcoco, was fed by the salty waters of San Cristobal, Xaltocan, and Zumpango to the north, and to the south by Xochimilco and Chalco, fresh water lakes fed by streams flowing from the mountains to the west and north of the valley.

Although located on the Torrid Zone, the climate of the valley has many of the characteristics of the Temperate Zone. The temperature ranges from 30°F to 85°F, but even in the coldest months, the temperature can reach 86°F. The average annual rainfall is 26 inches, most of it falling from May, the begining of the rainy season, to October, reaching a maximum in July or August. Air circulating from the Atlantic and the Pacific brings steady summer rains, but in winter, rainfall is limited to condensation precipitated by northern winds, cooling as they pass over the mountains.

MEXICO CITY

Mexico City is the oldest continuously inhabited city in North America. The city was built upon the ruins of Tenochtitlán, the home of the ancient Aztecs, on a small island near the western shore of Lake Texcoco. After the conquest, the city quickly outgrew the original site, and the lakes were filled in one after another to accommodate a burgeoning population of colonists from Spain.

Surrounded on two sides by mountains, with no outlet to drain off surface water, the city was far from ideal for a growing metropolis. Canals were dug, dykes were constructed, and tunnels bored through the mountains to drain the city of water accumulated from periodic floods, but no satisfactory solution was found until the nineteenth century, when the Tequixquiac tunnel was completed. In time, the tunnel drained all six lakes, but as the floor of the valley dried, the ground began to sink, and with it, the city. At first the sinking was imperceptible, but as more and more homes and public buildings rose on the island, the rate of sinking increased until it reached more than a foot per year in the twentieth century. The city, unfortunately, is still growing and sinking. From 1960 to 1997, the population increased from less than three million people to more than thirteen million.

THE GULF OF MEXICO

Southeast of the Valley of Mexico, high in the mountains of Puebla, Veracruz, and Oaxaca, the Papaloapan River and its tributaries begin a precipitous drop of 5,000 feet to the tropical coastal plain of the Gulf of Mexico. At the base of the escarpment, the tributaries join the lower Papaloapan, and the river begins its hundred-mile journey to the Gulf, discharging thirty billion tons of fresh water a year into the sea.

For years, the towns in the river basin were plagued by destructive floods and swarms of mosquitoes from vast malarial swamps. But the potential for irrigation and hydroelectric power was too great for this source to remain untapped. By 1950, the Miguel Alemán Dam was completed, allowing the river to be aligned to unblock the runoff. The swamps were drained, the mosquitoes controlled, and a dike was built just in time to protect the city of Cosamaloapan from the hurricane of 1950. By 1960, three hundred thousand acres of new farmland were under irrigation, two hundred and fifty thousand kilowatts of electricity was generated by dams along the system, four hundred new schools were built, and the region was opened to commerce by a thousand miles of new roads.

The Lowlands

The wet winds southeast of Veracruz bring heavy rains for nine months of the year, and as the land follows the wide arc of the Gulf of Mexico to the Isthmus of Tehuantepec, rainfall increases from 50 inches a year to 120 inches. Between Coatzacoalcos and the Laguna de Terminos, the Grijalva, Usmacinta, and Candelaria Rivers create a near impassable region of swamps and waterways 5,000 square miles in extent. In pre-Conquest times, this was the territory of the Chontal Maya, a seagoing culture that controlled all commerce between the coast and the interior. The Usmacinta, born in the highlands of Guatemala, joins the Grijalva fifteen miles south of the coastal town of Frontera, and the resulting flow is so powerful that it sends a current of fresh water six miles into the Gulf of Mexico.

The belt of jungle continues southwards until it reaches the uplands that rise towards the Chiapas Plateau and the mountains of Guatemala. The plateau rises to a height of nearly 7,000 feet, where moisture-laden winds from the Gulf and the cool climate of the mountains make it a pleasant though cool region. Below the southern escarpment, however, the Pacific coastal plain is plagued by heat, dust, and flies in the dry season, and heat, mosquitoes, and mud in the wet.

Between the Laguna de Terminos and Campeche, the jungle moves further inland and spreads across the base of the Yucatán Peninsula to the Caribbean Sea. The tropical rain forest extends 80 miles north of the jungle road that crosses the base of the peninsula, and 120 miles south into the Peten region of Guatemala and into Belize. The only access into the territory is by pack roads, trails, and paths.

Water

North of Campeche, the Yucatán jungle gives way to a featureless land without rivers, lakes, or any other topographical features save for the Puuc hills, a low-lying range south of Mérida. The subsurface structure of northern Yucatán consists entirely of porous limestone, which acts like a giant sponge in its ability to soak up the annual rainfall.

In much of the peninsula, the water table is too deep to provide the population with sufficient water during the dry season. The ancient Maya, however, satisfied the needs of large urban populations by storing water in *chultunes*, large bottle-shaped receptacles carved into the bedrock under their plazas, or in *aguadas*, large artificial reservoirs lined with stone. The *chultunes* were approximately equal in size, holding 7,500 gallons, enough to meet the needs of twenty-five to fifty people for six months.

Throughout the northeast corner of Yucatán, however, the Maya developed their earliest settlements around *cenotes*, large natural wells that provide access to a vast network of underground rivers and streams, moving with a current that is barely discernible. In some areas, the *cenotes* connect the subterranean rivers, and their waters rise and fall in unison with the annual cycle of rainfall and drought. In other areas the *cenotes* are isolated from each other, and different species of fish are found in *cenotes* that are only a few miles apart. Strong offshore springs are fed by this complex underground hydraulic system, and far out in the Caribbean, fresh water rises to the surface from enormous ports in the ocean floor with such velocity that the turbulence can be seen far out to sea. These sweet-water ocean springs, called *ojos de agua* by the natives, provided fresh water for Maya coastal craft for centuries before the conquest, and are still used by native fishing boats.

The depth of water below the surface of the land, and the difficulty of reaching it, are best described by John Lloyd Stephens in his travels through the Yucatán *circa* 1840.

... each with a torch in hand, entered a wild cavern, which, as we advanced, became darker. At ... sixty paces, the descent was precipitous.... Here all light from the mouth of the cavern was lost, but we soon reached the brink of a great perpendicular descent, to the bottom of which a strong body of light was thrown from a hole in the surface, a perpendicular depth ... of two hundred and ten feet. As we stood on the brink of this precipice, under the shelving of an immense mass of rock, ... gigantic stalactites and huge blocks of stone assumed all manner of fantastic shapes....

From the brink on which we stood an enormous ladder, of the rudest possible construction, led to the bottom of the hole. It was between seventy and eighty feet long, and about twelve feet wide, made of the rough trunks

The interior of the vast *cenote* at Bolonchen

of saplings lashed together lengthwise, and supported all the way down by horizontal trunks braced against the face of the precipitous rock.

Our Indians began the descent, but the foremost had scarcely got his head below the surface before one of the rounds slipped, and he only saved himself by clinging to another. We attempted a descent with some little misgivings, but, by keeping each hand and foot on a different round, with an occasional crash and slide, we all reached the foot of the ladder.... As yet the reader is only at the mouth of this well....

On one side of the cavern is an opening in the rock, ... entering by which, we soon came to an abrupt descent, down which was another long and trying ladder ... not so steep as the first, but in a much more rickety condition; the rounds were loose, and the upper ones gave way on our first attempt to descend.... At the foot of this ladder was a large cavernous chamber, from which irregular passages led off in different directions to deposites [*sic*] or sources of water.

Moving on by a slight ascent over the rocks, ... we came to the foot of a third ladder ... two or three steps beyond another five feet high, and six paces farther, a fifth.... A little beyond we descended another ladder eleven feet long, and yet a little farther along we came to one – the seventh – the length and general appearance of which induced us to pause and consider.... Holding by the side of the ladder next to the rock, we descended, crashing and carrying down the loose rounds ... we moved on by a broken, winding passage, and, at the distance of two hundred feet, came to the top of a ladder eight feet long, at the foot of which we entered a low and stifling passage; and crawling this on our hands and feet, at the distance of about three hundred feet we came to a rocky basin of water. From the best calculation that I can make, which is not far out of the way, we were then fourteen hundred feet from the mouth of the cave, and at a perpendicular depth of four hundred and fifty feet.

The *cenotes*, according to one theory, were formed by subsurface streams wearing away the bedrock, causing the land above to collapse. A more recent and interesting theory is that they were formed by debris from the outer shell of a giant meteor or a comet that collided with the Earth some sixty-five million years ago. The debris blown into the atmosphere is said to have wiped out the dinosaurs. Satellite images taken in 1995 show that the *cenotes* are distributed in a semicircle some

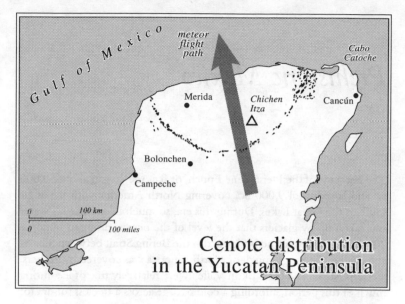

Cenote distribution
in the Yucatán Peninsula

80 miles in diameter somewhere near Punta Arenas, a small fishing village on the north coast. The *cenotes* are believed to mark the outer limit of the crater, which lies off the coast of Yucatán in the Gulf of Mexico. With the passage of millennia, heavy debris from the meteor sank into the earth more rapidly than the surrounding sediment, causing fractures that eventually created the *cenotes*. Efforts are currently underway to locate and map the crater.

CHAPTER TWO

Prehistoric Mexico

The last stage of the Pleistocene Epoch, or Ice Age, began about 50,000 BC and lasted until 9,000 BC, covering North America with ice as far south as the Great Lakes. During this era, so much of the Earth's water was taken up by glaciers that the level of the oceans dropped by some 200 feet, exposing a land bridge across the Bering Strait between Siberia and Alaska. Although much of North America was covered by glaciers, western Alaska and the Yukon Valley were relatively free of ice during much of this period, affording a cold passage across a treeless tundra for early immigrants from northeast Asia to the western world. As they proceeded to the warmer regions to the south, they found great herds of mastodons, woolly mammoths, horses, giant bison, cameloids, sloth, antelope, beaver, and an abundance of small game such as jack rabbits, gophers, rats, turtles, and birds. About 8000 BC, the waters rose with the receding glaciers and the land bridge disappeared, leaving the immigrants to develop their culture and civilization relatively free from Old World influence.

The earliest date for the arrival of man in the New World has never been clearly established. The earliest reliably dated material is found in archaeological sites in South America, with dates fixed at 22,0000 BC. Radiocarbon dates of charcoal found at early campsites in Nevada and Texas indicate occupation before 37,000 BC and 28,000 BC, but the quality of the samples is questionable. The regions nearest Siberia-Alaska and Canada, on the other hand, have not provided any significantly earlier dates than South America.

Nearly all the dated archaeological sites in North America contain projectile points for darts or spears. There are others, however, yet

undated, with only stone tools, such as choppers and scrapers manufactured by more primitive means. The inference has been made that
such sites may represent a much earlier habitation of the New World,
but the sad truth is that the time man first arrived in the New World is
not known within a span of 40,000 years.

HUMAN REMAINS

Before 1992, all human remains from this era in North America were
clearly Mongoloid – no remains of Peking man, Neanderthal, or any
other species from the Old World had ever been discovered.

The skull of a man found in 1997 at Kennewick, Washington,
however, was found to have characteristics not common to American
Indians. The skull was long and narrow with an almost delicate brow,
and had receding cheekbones and an angular jaw more characteristic of
Europeans and south Asians, closely resembling those of the Ainu of
northern Japan and Polynesians from the south Pacific. A later study,
however, published in January 2000, dated the remains reliably at 9,300
years old, and determined them to be those of an American Indian,
even though the cranial features do not match any modern American
Indian population. The skeleton indicates that it was of a man most
likely to have descended from north Asians who migrated across the
Bering Strait 12,000 years ago. But the issue is far from settled. Eight
scientists have filed suit to seek access to the remains, and have filed a
petition to conduct DNA studies to determine that Kennewick man
may have ancestral connections to parts of the world not linked to early
North American migrations. Tribal groups from Washington and
Oregon, however, have demanded a halt to all studies and insist on
reburial of the remains.

A later discovery of a skull in South America, reliably dated to be
11,500 years old, was found to have characteristics similar to people of
the South Pacific. Thigh bones of a woman found on Southern
California's Channel Islands, tentatively dated to be 13,000 years old,
are possibly the oldest human remains found in the Western Hemisphere. The presence of the bones on the islands suggests that the
woman may have arrived by boat from Polynesia or Asia, but there is
no supporting evidence.

A Clovis dart point – the earliest evidence of human presence in Mexico

The earliest evidence of man's presence in Mexico was the find of a Clovis point, a two-inch dart, near Durango, which is associated with archaeological sites of the tenth millennium. In the Valley of Mexico, projectile points and other man-made artifacts found among the remains of a mammoth that had been butchered at Santa Izabel Iztapan, a village some 12 miles northeast of Mexico City, appeared as early as 8000 BC. Remains of another mammoth were found approximately 1000 feet south of the first site, and from the position of the bones, it appeared that the animal had been fleeing from hunters when its hind leg was caught in the heavy mud of the lakeshore. The sites yielded no radiocarbon dates, but charcoal from a campfire at the second site was dated at 7700 BC.

The earliest fossil human remains found in Mexico came from a site at Tepexpan, a village about a mile and a half north of the mammoth sites. The skeleton was that of a woman between the age of twenty-five and thirty, who had been buried face down with her knees drawn up beneath her chest. The skeleton, old as it may be, could easily be mistaken for that of an average Indian from central Mexico. The remains were determined to be ancient, but no specific date could be established. Fluorine and nitrogen tests, however, suggest that they are contemporary with the mammoth sites in the vicinity.

Pre-Columbian cultures possessing the attributes of high civilization in the New World appeared only in South America and Mesoamerica, that part of Mexico and Central America which was civilized at the time of the Spanish conquest. It lies between 10° and 22° north latitude and includes most of central, southern, and southwestern Mexico, the Yucatán peninsula, Guatemala, Belize, and the westernmost regions of Honduras and El Salvador. No other native culture in the New World ever achieved the wealth, urbanization, advancement of the arts, political systems, science, and calendar development found in Mesoamerica and Peru.

With the transition from hunting/gathering to full time agriculture, two pre-eminent cultures rose in Mesoamerica: one in the highlands that culminated in large urban cities; the other in the lowlands of Mexico, Guatemala, and Belize, where smaller, less populated ceremonial centres evolved.

In each of these regions, dissimilar ecological environments dictated their degree of urbanization and cultural development. In the highlands, light rainfall and sparse vegetation allow agriculture of sufficient intensity for dense populations to live in large, nucleated communities. But in the tropical lowlands, rainfall is heavy and vegetation dense and overgrown, restricting agriculture to techniques that set upper limits to the size and population of its communities.

Agriculture and Urbanization

The evolution of the hunter/gatherer to village life in the Mexican highlands can be traced by his progress in agriculture from the time he planted the first seed to the time he could not only feed himself and his family, but provide a surplus to support a ruling class, a priesthood, specialists and craftsmen, and engage in trade with other communities.

The transition of early man's nomadic life, subsisting upon game and wild plants, to village life and full-time agriculture was a gradual process covering a span of eight millennia. Each step of this progress has been traced by excavations in caves and dry-season camps, where foodstuffs, seeds, faeces, human remains, and other perishable artifacts enabled archaeologists to reconstruct the diet and way of life of the early inhabitants.

Prior to 7200 BC, small bands of four to eight people subsisted on wild plants and small game, primarily jack rabbits, gophers, rats, and birds, with a diet that was 40 per cent plants and 54 per cent meat. The bands were nomadic, changing camps three or four times a year. Although they hunted horses and antelope, mammoth kills were rare. Notwithstanding the mammoth kill sites found in the Valley of Mexico, mammoth hunting in Mexico seems to be more the exception than the rule, perhaps because the region lacked the vast grassy plains needed to support the herds.

After 7200 BC, small bands continued to hunt and collect wild plants in the dry season, but in the spring and the wet season they gathered into bands of forty or more to live in areas of lush vegetation.

By 5200 BC, they had domesticated squash, chilli peppers, and avocados, but cultivated plants as yet contributed only five per cent of their diet. Small fragments of blankets, coiled baskets, and darts provide evidence that they had mastered the art of weaving and woodwork.

During this period the bands were most likely to be under the leadership of a male; shamans practiced medicine and led ceremonial rites such as burial and rites of human sacrifice.

It was at about this time that maize, one of the world's greatest cereal crops, was domesticated in the New World. The cobs, though, were only a fraction of the size of modern corn. Whether maize was first domesticated in Mexico or South America has never been clearly established. What is known, however, is that a complex series of genetic changes took place between Mexican varieties and varieties of wild corn found in Peru and Ecuador. The primitive domesticate of Mexico was undoubtedly crossed with a primitive domesticate in South America, and once again with a grass that grows in Bolivia and other parts of the Andes. The result was a dramatic improvement in the size of the ear, the kernel, and other characteristics. The South American maize then returned to Mesoamerica, where it was crossed again with *teosinte,* a native grass, creating the ancestor of modern corn.

By 3400 BC, population in the highlands increased tenfold, and the

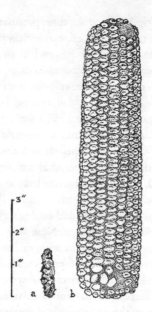

Maize which fuelled the growth of Indian civilization: the picture shows the difference in size between ancient and modern maize. On the left a charred cob from Coxcatlán, Puebla, right: a modern corn

larger bands remained in the same place for longer periods of time. People now had gardens and added more domesticated plants to their diet, including gourds, amaranth, and yellow zapotes. The increasing dependence upon agriculture may have added rituals of planting and harvesting to the duties of the shaman.

After 3400 BC, settlement patterns underwent a significant change. Pit house villages now appeared on river terraces and in the valleys, and agriculture was more efficient. Cultivated plants accounted for 21 per cent of their diet, and a variety of gourds, pumpkins, common beans, and hybrid corn had been domesticated. Cotton and pottery now made their first appearance in Mexico, and wild dogs had been tamed.

By 1500 BC, full-time agriculturists appeared. Thirty-five per cent of their diet now came from cultivated plants, with beans gradually replacing meat as a source of protein. Village life was fully developed, with populations of one hundred to three hundred people living in wattle and daub houses. It is not certain that they built temples, but female figurines attest to a complex religious life, and rich female burials imply matriarchal influence in the community and in property ownership. Pottery shows a marked improvement with the appearance of a few monochromes.

By way of comparison, the same level of agricultural technology, animal domestication, and village life in the Old World developed between 8500 and 5000 BC, approximately half the time it took in the New World. It is to be noted, however, that wheat, the principal cereal crop of the Old World, is more productive than corn in the wild state, and more easily domesticated. Furthermore, animals were available for domestication, and pigs, goats, sheep, and cattle carry considerably more meat than dogs and turkey, the principal New World domestic animals.

Unlike in the highlands, there is no well-defined sequence of agricultural development in the tropical forests of the lowlands that led to village life and eventually to urbanization. In spite of intensive studies by prominent archaeologists and anthropologists, there has as yet been no determination of how the early lowland farmers raised their crops, nor is there any certainty of what their staple foods were. Most reconstructions of lowland Maya agriculture have assumed that maize was the principal crop, and given the adverse environment, that the Maya chose a system that would produce an adequate yield with a minimum of labour.

Slash-and-burn agriculture is the most efficient method for clearing fields. It was practised throughout the rain forests from prehistoric times, and is still in use today in the vicinity of Tikal, the great Maya ceremonial centre in Guatemala.

The technique calls for burning off trees and shrubs, then planting the area by dropping kernels of maize and beans into holes poked in the ground with a pointed stick. After one or two years of cultivation, the plot is abandoned to allow the soil to recover. The number of years the plot lies fallow depends upon the soil and whether it was used for one or two crops each year. Thus a stable rotation system, where each parcel was farmed for two years, can require as many as four parcels, three of which lie fallow for two to six years.

Extensive studies of maize crop yields, however, have clearly established that slash-and-burn agriculture, by itself, is far from adequate to support the known population of the great Maya ceremonial centres of Mexico, Guatemala, and Belize. The technique can support approximately two hundred people per square mile. By comparison, the known population density of the major Maya ceremonial centres was of the order of 1,600 people per square mile.

The lack of urbanization, however, did not limit the cultural and intellectual development of the Maya. They were far more sophisticated than the highlanders in astronomical science and mathematics, and, alone among all New World cultures, they possessed a written language.

CHAPTER THREE

The Rise of Civilization

The Olmec

By 1500 BC agriculture had progressed sufficiently to support fully developed village life throughout Mesoamerica, Central America, and South America. People lived in small communities of wattle and daub houses separated from each other by courts and patios, and maize, beans and squash were their staple foods. Their pottery was relatively well made, with globular neckless jars and flat-bottomed dishes common. The lack of permanent temples or other religious structures suggests that religious rites were focused on the numerous clay figurines of women found throughout Mexico.

In the period, 1500–600 BC, a momentous change took place in one of the most inhospitable regions of Mesoamerica, a crescent of tropical lowlands reaching from southern Vera Cruz to the Pacific Coast of Guatemala. Here 80 to 120 inches of rain per year create vast swamps that are frequently flooded by rivers that flow through a network of marshes, estuaries, and lagoons on their way to the sea.

Early in this period, village life and culture of the region were much like that of greater Mesoamerica. Maize was grown along the river banks where annual floods left rich deposits of silt, the rivers and oxbow lakes providing the people with sufficient protein to allow a sedentary life style, with an occasional wild pig or deer to add meat to their diet.

In some areas of this region, however, monumental sculpture, elegant jade figurines, and civic architecture made an abrupt appearance, and ceremonial centres with a professional priesthood and accomplished craftsmen rose in the rainforest. These centres reached their greatest development at three sites: San Lorenzo, La Venta, and Tres Zapotes, all located in the northern part of the Isthmus of Tehuantepec. The size and complexity of all three are indicative of a well-organized social system supported by a rural peasantry.

The identity of these ancient people has never been established. For lack of a better name, the archaeologist George Vaillant assigned the name 'Olmec' to the people of the Gulf Coast, whom the sixteenth-century scholar Bernardino de Sahagun called the 'rubber people'. Linguists, based upon the fact that Huastec, an isolated Maya tongue, is still spoken in northern Veracruz, postulated that Maya may have once been spoken along the entire Gulf Coast, and that the ancient Olmecs may have been Maya speakers.

Few, if any, antiquarians will argue that the Olmec heartland was not the cradle of Mesoamerican civilization. Here, art made a giant leap from miniature female figurines to life-sized and larger-than-life sculptures of great power, expression, and mobility; from clay statuettes of human forms to grotesque, half-human beings carved from jade; from primitive shapes of the human body to graceful three-dimensional sculptures consistent with human anatomy.

ANCIENT ART

Perhaps the best-known Olmec sculptures are their colossal heads, some of which weigh as much as 20 tons. The features of the individuals portrayed, presumably rulers or members of the élite class, are heavy and Negroid, with wide noses and full lips, and each wears a head-dress resembling a football helmet. All were initially polychrome, and the largest of the sculptures, from San Lorenzo, is now in the Museum of Anthropology in Mexico City.

The hallmark of Olmec sculpture is the were-jaguar figurines that combine the human body with feline characteristics. The creatures have infantile bodies, cleft heads, puffy features, and either toothless gums or curved fangs. All are carved from blue-green jade.

The origin of the were-jaguar probably derives from two badly damaged stone sculptures that show a jaguar copulating with a human female. The were-jaguar is now known to be a heavenly rain spirit that eventually evolved into various guises of the rain god of the later Classic

Giant stone head from San Lorenzo

period. The Olmec themselves are portrayed as tubby people with child-like features and disproportionately large heads.

The earliest Olmec site lies at San Lorenzo (1150–900 BC), 35 miles south of Coatzacoalcos on the Chiquito River. The site contains more than 200 house mounds, which presumably supported thatch-roofed huts similar to those used today in the region. The population of the centre was approximately 1000 people, and their public works are larger and more sophisticated than those of any other contemporary Mesoamerican culture.

The centre collapsed about 900 BC. Wholesale destruction of architecture and mutilated sculptures buried in rows indicate a revolt or an overthrow by outside forces.

La Venta, the greatest Olmec centre, lies on an island in a swamp along the Tonala River. Although many scholars have argued that a civilization so advanced could not have existed before the Classic period (300–900 AD), radiocarbon dates place the centre between 800 and 400 BC, well within the Middle Formative period.

Four colossal heads, like those of San Lorenzo, were also found at La Venta, but the most important artifact found was a miniature setting of sixteen figurines carved from jade. The figurines were between six and seven-and-a-half inches tall, and all were standing in an enclosure formed by six palisades. The scene is thought to represent a meeting of Olmec leaders. The figurines are now in the National Museum of Anthropology in Mexico City, arranged just as they were found at La Venta.

The deliberate mutilation of the sculptured monuments at La Venta marks a violent upheaval that led to the fall of the centre some time between 400 and 300 BC.

The Olmec site of Tres Zapotes lies above the swampy basin of the San Juan and the Papaloapan Rivers, just to the west of the Los Tuxtla Mountains.

Little is known about the site save for its sculpture. A number of jade objects have been found that are inscribed with glyphs that have never been translated but which possess characteristics similar to Maya glyphs of a later date. The Tres Zapote glyphs may mark the beginning of writing in Mesoamerica. A basalt monument carved with an abstract jaguar mask bears one of the earliest dates in Mesoamerica, 31 BC on a linear calendar, called the Long Count, developed and used only by lowland people. (The Aztecs, for example, possessed only a calendar that was repeated in 52-year cycles, with no reference to a beginning date.) The only earlier recorded date found in Mesoamerica, 36 BC, is inscribed on a monument at Chiapa de Corzo in the Grijalva Basin. The Tuxtla Statuette, a small jade figurine found in the Olmec heartland, bears the late Long Count date AD 162. Since both dates fall well within the period 300 BC–AD 300, it suggests that the Olmec, and not the Maya, whose culture developed at a later date, invented the Long Count.

Olmec sculptural themes and artifacts have been found throughout Mexico. Figurines resembling those of the Olmec appear at the Zapotec centre of Monte Albán in Oaxaca; the characteristic baby-face theme of the Olmec is repeated on figurines from pre-Classic sites in Morelos; and small Olmec artifacts have been found as far away as Guerrero, on the Pacific coast. The Olmecs also left their monuments in Chiapas, along the coastal plain of Guatemala, and in El Salvador. There is no strong evidence that the Olmec occupied these territories, however. The prevailing theory is that missionaries spreading the Olmec cult or traders brought the artifacts with them.

Teotihuacán

The great Olmec centre at La Venta had been dead and lifeless for more than a hundred years before the central Mexican highlands emerged from simple village life to communities based around ceremonial centres. Around 300 BC, their temples were crude structures with thatched roofs built upon earthen platforms, not very different from the dwellings of the common people.

Their greatest architectural achievement came late in the period at Cuicuilco, a site south of Mexico City on the *Pedregal,* a vast expanse of broken lava. The central feature was a cone-like structure mounted on a four-tiered platform, and ramps on either side led to the summit, where a temple once stood. Unfortunately, the temple was built at the foot of the Ixtli volcano, and in 150 BC, the volcano erupted, leaving it partly covered with lava. The volcano undoubtedly had a religious significance for Cuicuilco, since many incense burners in the image of Xiutecuhtli, the Fire God of the ancient Mexicans, were found at the site

About the time Cuicuilco was destroyed, foundations for Teotihuacán, the first great city of the New World, were being laid in a valley 27 miles northwest of Mexico City. Neither the origins nor the language of the people who built the city are known. Juan de Torquemada, the sixteenth-century chronicler, credits the Totonacs; some later scholars the Otomies; and others the Olmecs, but the resemblance of Teotihuacan sacred and secular themes with those of the Toltecs and the Aztecs strongly suggests Nahua (highland) origins. They left no decipherable hieroglyphics, and the calendrics of the Olmec and the Maya are rarely in evidence.

In 200 BC, the population of the city was no more than 2000, but by AD 100, when the great religious structures were built, the population had risen to 60,000, and by AD 600, 150,000 people lived in a city that covered eight square miles.

The city's markets, plazas, temples, palaces, and urban residential districts were laid out in blocks of about 230 square feet, and the entire city was paved with plaster tiles. Two thousand of Teotihuacán's 2600 known buildings were single-storied, flat-roofed apartment complexes.

The complexes varied in size from 6,750 to 64,000 square feet; the smaller residences accommodated about 20 people, probably extended families, and the larger ones as many as 100. Each apartment contained a kitchen and an interior patio open to fresh air and sunshine. Large ceramic figures decorated the roof edges of each dwelling, and downspouts from gutters along the eaves carried off rain. Lava rock set into a matrix of clay, gravel, and mortar were the primary construction materials, and highly polished plaster covered the walls, ceilings, and floors. Wooden vertical risers supported the walls, and wooden beams the roof and doorway lintels. Three rooms in the Quetzalpapalotl palace, which measure 26 feet on each side without the use of central supports, stand in evidence to the skill of the early builders.

Religious structures, residences, and palaces provided work for full-time masons, plasterers, and carpenters, and the city's 500 workshops quartered craftsmen who produced obsidian artifacts, stone masks, pottery, feathered costumes, and leather sandals for the élite. Evidence that Teotihuacan society also supported full-time painters, well versed in the exotic iconography of their culture, is seen in murals on the walls of public buildings and houses throughout the city.

On the outskirts of the city, areas were set aside for textile workers from Vera Cruz, potters from the Gulf Coast and the Maya lowlands, and in others, the presence of merchants from Oaxaca is indicated by their tombs, glyphs and funerary urns.

THE STREET OF THE DEAD

The major religious structures lie along the Street of the Dead, a wide thoroughfare nearly a mile in length that runs from the Ciudadela (citadel) to the Pyramid of the Moon. The Aztecs, in the belief that the numerous mounds and structures along the way were tombs of monarchs and high priests, gave the street its name.

The most important structure in the courtyard of the Ciudadela is the pyramid of Quetzalcoatl, one of the most spectacular examples of Teotihuacán architecture. Feathered serpents with their heads protruding from what appear to be flowers are carved in relief along the panels, and masks with huge fangs and goggle eyes, possibly representing the rain god Tlaloc, peer out from between the serpents.

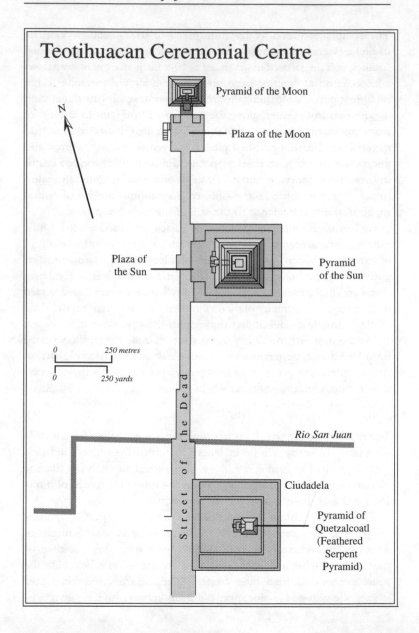

Teotihuacan Ceremonial Centre

N

Pyramid of the Moon

Plaza of the Moon

Plaza of the Sun

Pyramid of the Sun

0   250 metres

0   250 yards

Street of the Dead

Rio San Juan

Ciudadela

Pyramid of Quetzalcoatl (Feathered Serpent Pyramid)

The temple may have been the site of the first mass sacrifice in Mexico. Recent excavations have unearthed 133 skeletons, males and females, in 21 separate graves inside the pyramid and along its edges and corners. Female and male skeletons were arranged in segregated groups of 4, 8, 9, 18, and 20, numbers that appear in the Mexican calendar.

The Pyramid of the Sun, constructed about AD 100, lies half a mile from the Ciudadela on the east side of the Street of the Dead. The base of the massive structure measures 740 feet on each side, only two feet less than the great pyramid of Cheops in Egypt. The height of the original pyramid was approximately 243 feet, whereas Cheops's pyramid is 490 feet high and considerably more sophisticated in its architecture and construction. The exterior of the pyramid was once faced with stone and covered with plaster, and adobe bricks and other rubble filled the interior.

Astronomers have noted that on the day the sun passes over the pyramid, about 18 May, the Pleiades star cluster makes its first predawn appearance, an event that held great religious significance for the early Mexicans,

The Street of the Dead ends at a broad rectangular ceremonial plaza that covers seven acres. The principal structures in the plaza are: the Palace of the Quetzalpapolotl, which may have served administrative purposes; the Jaguar's Palace, so named because of its murals; the Temple of the Feathered Shells, named for its bas-reliefs; the Building of the Altars, a strange quadrangular structure with ten altars in the interior; and the Pyramid of the Moon. The configuration of this pyramid is similar to that of the Pyramid of the Sun, but it is significantly smaller.

The greatest source of information about the people who lived in Teotihuacán comes from brilliant murals found on the interior walls of the more important residences and public buildings of the city.

The general qualities of Teotihuacán art are the use of flat colours, the absence of spatial depth, and the lack of human sexual characteristics. In its earliest phase, zoomorphic representations of religious themes predominated. Murals in the Temple of the Mythological Animals portray feathered serpents and jaguars in different poses, and flying fish and reptiles with large bulges on their bodies, which are allegorical references to the water cult. In the Jaguar's Palace, jaguars on either side of a door jamb wear feather head-dresses, and a row of shells trails down their backs to the tips of their tails. Both are blowing a conch shell adorned with feathers, from which a sound scroll appears. Representations of Tlaloc and the year symbol appear alongside, indicating that the entire presentation is associated with rain and fertility.

Later in the period, we see priests dressed in long cloaks wearing feather head-dresses with a bird's head in the middle and jade masks with circular earflaps. In the Maguay Mural, a speech scroll from the mouth of a priest contains various signs for water, and Tlaloc's head-dress appears along its edges.

The intimate relationship between man, god, and nature is brilliantly displayed in the murals of the Tepantitla complex, located about half a mile from the Temple of the Sun. On the top panel of an interior wall, Tlaloc appears with drops of rain falling upon the scene below. On the lower panel, a great waterspout gushes upwards, lifting people into paradise. The spout is formed by two rivers that flow from springs guarded by jaguars, and irrigated fields of fruit trees border the rivers. People are swimming and playfully splashing water on each other, while those in the fields are busy catching butterflies, cutting flowers, and dancing. In another mural, people are playing a game with long bats and round objects in a large field, and speech scrolls show that they are singing. These are the first known murals without strict religious themes, with a style dictated only by the imagination of the painter.

Late in the history of Teotihuacán, art shifts to themes of war and

The Maya year bearer symbol

sacrifice, as murals now show warriors armed with spear throwers, darts, and shields, and symbols of sacrifice.

At the height of Teotihuacán civilization, its influence was felt throughout Mesoamerica. At Kaminlajuyú, an early Maya ceremonial centre on the outskirts of Guatemala City, archaeological evidence shows clearly that the site was under Mexican rather than Mayan influence. From the evidence, scholars reason that Teotihuacán chose Kaminaljuyú because of its proximity to the Pacific Ocean, where it could control the lucrative cacao trade between Central America and Mexico. Mexican governors ruled the site from AD 300–600, and when Teotihuacán fell, Kaminaljuyú collapsed.

Indication of a Teotihuacán presence in the Maya lowlands is found at Becan, a large centre at the base of the Yucatán Peninsula, and at Tikal, the great Maya ceremonial centre in Guatemala. Mexican artifacts confirm that strong political ties existed between the two cultures in the fifth century, and Mexican motifs engraved on dated Maya stelae show that their presence lasted for sixty years.

Teotihuacán presence in the lowlands has yet to be explained. There were few exportable resources in the region, and it was unlikely that anything of value, such as cacao, existed in the rain forest. A more probable explanation is that Tikal's proximity to the strategic colony at Kaminaljuyú was of some advantage to the Mexicans.

Teotihuacán ceased to dominate Mesoamerica some time between AD 600 and 650. The terminal date is still in doubt, as are the forces that caused the decline, but the city survived in much-reduced circumstances until its physical destruction in 750. A layer of ash and burnt debris covered much of Teotihuacán, but there is some doubt about when the city was put to the torch.

Monte Alban

Monte Alban, the great Zapotec site, lies two miles south of the city of Oaxaca on a series of ridges above the valley. Seven petty states flourished in the valley in 400 BC, but Monte Alban, perhaps because of its strategic location and defensive position, soon dominated the others. The only major structure built prior to 100 BC is a pyramidal platform with boneless figures carved on slabs along the sides that seem to be dancing or swimming in a viscous fluid. All are nude with genitals clearly shown, many appear lifeless, and some are sexually mutilated. The distorted poses and open mouths suggest that the subjects are possibly rival chieftains killed or captured by the early rulers of Monte Alban.

Many of the slabs have calendrical hieroglyphs alongside the figures which show that the Zapotecs observed the Ritual Year of 260 days and the Vague Year of 365 days, which were in common usage throughout Mesoamerica. The Zapotecs may have been the first culture in Mesoamerica to develop a written record of their history. As early as 600 BC, they erected monuments to record the names of defeated enemies and their communities.

What little information exists about the about the early inhabitants comes primarily from pottery and effigy vessels found in burials. Men are seen wearing cloaks, breechcloths, bracelets, helmets, hats, scarves, masks, and false beards. The ubiquitous naked female figurines are also present, and body painting and tattooing is in evidence. Ten male gods can be identified from the effigy vessels.

In the period 100 BC to AD 200, the ridge tops were levelled and terraces carved into the slopes to provide dwellings for a rapidly increasing population. The magnitude of the task indicates that the centre was able to mobilize a large labour force from the surrounding country.

An arrowhead-shaped observatory was the most prominent structure built during this period. Heads with closed eyes, wearing elegant head-dresses in an upside-down position, are inscribed on stone slabs mounted on the exterior. The figures are assumed to be defeated lords, and the accompanying glyphs are interpreted as names of regions or towns they ruled.

Some fifteen male deities and two female deities can be identified from figurines and pottery of this era. Females are now clothed, and male dress is considerably more elegant, with chinstraps, plumes, top-knots, ribbons, and elaborate head-dresses.

Calendrics and writing systems were fully developed, but are as yet poorly understood by comparison with the Maya glyphic systems.

Zapotec inscriptions tend to be short and sometimes incomplete, but only a fraction of the scholarly effort devoted to deciphering the Maya glyphs has been given to those of Monte Alban.

CLASSIC PERIOD

AD 200 to 900 is the Monte Alban Classic period, when ceremonial and public architecture, élite residences, and housing were built to accommodate an urban population of 50,000 people.

Numerous stelae were erected in the Grand Plaza during this period, commemorating important events, new conquests, and religious themes. A stela on the South Platform shows a warrior driving a spear through the name glyph of a town, and others nearby show bound captives standing on the glyphs of their towns. One, carved on onyx, shows a priest or a god standing to the left of the patron deity of Monte Alban. In the earlier part of the period, strong Teotihuacán elements are seen, but after AD 650 and the decline of Teotihuacán influence, they disappear.

One hundred and fifty-three élite tombs have been found in the Grand Plaza and under patio floors of apartments. The more elaborate have an antechamber, niches with offerings for the dead, and wall murals. The most spectacular of the funerary murals, found in Tomb 104 on the northern part of the site, shows a procession of gods moving toward the crypt of the dead lord. Again, the influence of Teotihuacán is seen in the frescoes.

Elegant funerary urns found in the tombs offer insights into Zapotec religion and glimpses of Zapotec life. The urns range in size from seven centimetres to as much as a metre and a half, emphasizing the upper part of the body while diminishing the torso and the limbs. Characteristically, the figure sits with crossed legs and hands placed upon the knees.

Some 39 gods have been identified, 11 of which are female. The principal gods identified to date are Cocijo, the rain god; Pitao Cozobi, the maize god, who sometimes takes the form of a bat; the Fire God; Quetzalcoatl in his guise of the wind god; Xipe Totec, the flayed god; and possibly the Water Goddess. Males generally wear breechcloths and capes, while females wear *huipiles* and skirts, and style their hair in a feminine fashion. Nearly all of these gods were worshipped at the time of the conquest,

The urns and other ceramic sculptures of this period provide a vivid picture of Zapotec life, portraying acrobats, jugglers, ball players, soothsayers, farmers, and porters. There are men with small and large paunches, cleft palates, cataracts, enlarged nipples, sunken cheeks, and toothless grins. Costumes, jewellery, hair styles, and head-dresses are also evident.

The reasons for the collapse of Monte Alban are not clear. After AD 900, building activity came to an end in the Grand Plaza, and the major part of the Monte Alban urban complex fell into ruins. Whatever the cause, the period between AD 650 and 1000 was a time of great upheaval in Mesoamerica, marked by the abandonment of Teotihuacán in 650 and the great Maya centres in the ninth and tenth centuries.

The Lowland Maya

Detailed information about the Maya of the central and northern lowlands before 1000 BC is rather scarce, since most of their dwellings, artifacts, and ceremonial structures lie buried beneath the massive temples, plazas, and palaces constructed during the Maya Classic period. (AD 300–900).

The earliest known occupations in the Maya lowlands lie at the archaeological sites of Seibal and Altar de Sacrificios in Guatemala, dated about 1000 BC. Pottery and other evidence indicate that the first colonists, the little-known Xe people, occupied villages of less than a hundred people along the shores of the Pasión River. None of their pottery indicates ritual and religious life, but their solid clay figurines may signify curing and fertility rites. Jade axes and a blade found in a cache with Olmec characteristics indicate a Gulf coast influence in the region.

Population grew rapidly over the central and northern lowlands during the period 550–300 BC. Large villages are found in Dzibilchaltún on the Yucatán coast; at the Maní *cenote* in northern Yucatán; in the southern lowlands near Tikal; on the Pasión River; and along the lower Usmacinta River. Slash-and-burn agriculture may account for the rapid expansion of villages throughout this region, since the unlimited availability of land would encourage widespread settlement patterns.

The ubiquitous female figurines and a novel form of mushroom-shaped pottery are found at many of the lowland sites. This zone of Mesoamerica is rich in hallucinogenic mushrooms, which shamans still use for curing ceremonies and divination, suggesting that the pots were once used for aboriginal religious ceremonies. Later in the period, formal architecture, religious structures, and ceremonial centres make their first appearance.

The giant step from simple village life to urban life in the ceremonial centre took place in a relatively short period, so short that many scholars once attributed Maya civilization to external influences. The most common theory was that their culture was the result of contacts with early seafarers from the Orient or other distant places across the Pacific or Atlantic. This has been proved not to be the case. No artifacts from the Old World have ever been discovered at any Maya site, and none of the theories of overseas contacts has ever withstood scientific scrutiny.

Some time in the first century AD, large ceremonial structures appeared at Yaxuná in northern Yucatán; at Becan in the south; at Uaxactún, Tikal, and Altar de Sacrificios in the Peten. In this era, the Maya developed their writing and mathematical systems and applied them to astronomical observations.

The flowering of Maya civilization took place during its Classic period, from AD 200 to 850, when the great ceremonial centres flourished throughout the lowlands. The term 'ceremonial centre' was coined to distinguish the Maya centres from true cities, primarily on their relatively low population densities, an ecologically limiting factor for all lowland settlements. The distinction may be moot, since for all purposes, the centres exercised administrative and religious functions for a widely distributed population, and possibly served as a weekly marketplace.

The Tikal Project

An exemplar of a major Maya ceremonial centre of the Classic period is Tikal, located in the Peten, Guatemala, where the University of

The Tikal site in Guatemala

Pennsylvania conducted the most extensive excavations of any Maya site. The thrust of the project was twofold: to investigate the élite structures in the core of the centre, and to excavate house mounds and platforms within the centre and the outlying areas. The latter effort, though not as glamorous as excavating tombs, is more pertinent for a better understanding of the culture.

Maya temples, for the most part, were built upon terraced platforms with no chambers other than tombs that were relatively small compared with the mass of the platform. The rooms on the summit of the temple were high and narrow with corbelled vault ceilings. The corbelled vault, characteristic of Maya architecture, is not the true arch, but a successive series of stones set upon each other in overlapping rows, then stabilized at the top with a capstone. An ornamented wall, or roofcomb, was often built on top of the temple and painted with larger-than-life figures surrounded by symbols of power and divinity. People wearing elegant clothing, serpents, jaguars, and scrollwork with hieroglyphic texts were carved upon lintels above the doorways in the more important temples.

The so-called palaces are multiple-room structures that were used for élite residences and possibly for other purposes, such as storage facilities, administrative functions, and rituals. The rooms tend to be too dark, damp, and small for comfort, which would count against their use as dwellings, but a study of Maya murals and life style, and the presence of paved courts and terraces found in front of them, would argue otherwise.

Sacbes, elevated causeways 15 feet high and 60 feet wide, connected important buildings within the centre. The longest known *sacbe* is 62 miles long, linking the sites of Cobá and Yaxuná in northern Yucatán. The current consensus is that their purpose was ritual, possibly the ancient forerunner of the modern practice of religious parades in the Maya highlands, where the effigy of a saint is carried between neighbouring towns.

From excavations of the house mounds, we learn that they were compounds of three or four houses built on a single platform, suggesting that the basic social unit was an extended family consisting of a mature couple, their children, and their children's families. The modern Maya still use similar configurations to house their families.

Intensive studies have been made of food production in the Maya lowlands, but to date, no explanation of how Tikal's 40,000 people were fed has been found. The house mounds were only about 500 feet apart, which would eliminate slash-and-burn agriculture as a method of producing sufficient maize for a population of this size. One study has shown that the Maya may have depended as much or more upon root crops such as manioc and sweet potatoes, which, with more efficient land usage, yield more calories than maize. The ramon, or breadnut tree, which the Maya planted and cultivated among the house mounds, is another promising source of food. The breadnut is a good source of vegetable protein, the trees require little or no maintenance, and their useful lifetime is nearly a hundred years. Furthermore the nuts, if properly stored, can be preserved for as long as 18 months.

Artifacts unearthed at the house mounds reveal that various occupations existed at Tikal, such as potters, sculptors, painters, and obsidian tool makers. More important, however, burial patterns reveal that a marked social stratification took place between the Maya élite and the middle classes at the beginning of the Late Classic period (AD 600–900).

House mound excavations of the Early Classic period, (AD 300–600) yielded valuable artifacts in the graves of young men, while artifacts found in graves of older men were relatively poor. The inference drawn from this was that young males, regardless of their social status, were given every opportunity to accumulate wealth. Those who survived to old age were presumed to have moved on to prestigious posts in the ceremonial centre, since only older male adults, all accompanied by rich artifacts, were found in temple burials.

During the Late Classic period, however, burial patterns shifted dramatically, both in the ceremonial centre and in the house mounds. Burials in the palace-temple complex were no longer limited to male adults, but included children, adolescents, and adults of both sexes. Wealth, as indicated by funerary offerings, was distributed among all age and sex groups.

A similar distribution of wealth among sexes of all ages was found in house mound burials of the late period, the primary difference being a substantial reduction in the degree of wealth, and the offerings accompanying young adult males were the poorest of all.

The rich offerings found in the temples accompanying children and adults too young to have amassed personal assets indicate that wealth was now passed down along family lines, and that a Maya aristocracy and the lower classes were now segregated.

Astronomy and Mathematics

Glyphs carved upon their stelae and those in their codices testify to the skill of the Maya in astronomical science. Astronomers at Copán, Honduras, the intellectual centre of the Maya, measured 149 lunar cycles to establish that the length of the average month was 29.53020 days, only 33 seconds from the exact period. By the mid-eighth century, the Maya knew that lunar and solar eclipses occurred within plus or minus 18 days of the node, where the Moon's orbit crossed that of the Sun.

Venus is the only planet for which the Maya have been known to make astronomical calculations, although there are indications that similar calculations may have been made for Mars. In the Dresden Codex of the Postclassic period, five Venus years of 584 days each, (583.92 is the actual period), and eight solar of years of the Earth appear in a table. The 584-day period is divided into four intervals: a 236-day period when the planet appears as the morning star; a 90-day period when the planet disappears; a 250-day period when it reappears as the evening star, and an 8-day period when it again disappears. The Dresden Codex also has a table predicting possible solar eclipses.

It is worthy of note that neither the Greeks nor the Romans knew that Venus was both the morning star and the evening star. Nor did they have any notion of the mathematical concept of zero, which the Maya may have developed before it was discovered by the Hindus.

Yet the Maya failed to discover the wheel.

THE MAYA CALENDAR

The basic calendar of all Mesoamerican cultures was the Calendar Round, a combination of the 365-day Solar Year with the 260-day Ritual Year. The Solar Year consists of 18 months of 20 days, and five additional days at the end to bring it into agreement with the calendar year. (There was no intercalary day.) The days in each month are designated by numeral coefficients.

The 260 days of the Ritual Year, on the other hand, have 'months' of twenty days, each day of which is designated by one of thirteen numeral coefficients. There are no known astronomical or periodic solar phenomena associated with the Ritual Year, but the human gestation period has been suggested as its basis.

The two calendars are combined in such a way that a cycle of 73 Ritual Years and 52 Solar Years passes before both calendars return to the starting date. Without the Long Count, however, the Calendar Round was unable to fix a date in historical time.

The Long Count is a modified vigesimal system, in which, with one exception, multiples of 20 are the basic numeral coefficients. It contains five elements, starting with one day as its fundamental unit. Its schema is

1 kin =1 day
1 uinal = 20 days
1 tun = 360 days
1 katun = 7,000 days (approximately 20 years)
1 baktun = 144,000 days (approximately 400 years)

When these units are multiplied by numerical coefficients, a count of the years, months, and days from a fixed date in the past can be calculated. For the Maya, their world began in 3114 BC and will end in AD 2013. The significance of neither date is known. Their ability to measure time, however, stretches into the infinite past, perhaps millions of years.

To the Maya, however, the calendar was not a simple accounting of days and years. To them, each element of time was a god who brought a preordained cycle of events into the world. According to legend, the days of the ancient calendar were once men who walked the Earth, and the names of the days are those of the men. They are always referred to as *he*, never as *it*.

Four of these gods, 1 Lamat, 2 Ben, 3 Eznab, and 4 Akbal, are known as the Year Bearers, the days that mark the start of the New Year. The Akbal and Lamat years were good years, although Lamat was prone to drought. Ben was a mean year: fainting fits and eye troubles plagued the people, and there were hot suns, drought, famine, theft, slavery, locusts, and war. The most ominous of the years, however, was Eznab. With it came fiery suns, swarming ants, and birds that ate the new seeds.

Before the conquest, the coming of the Year Bearer was one of the most important ceremonies celebrated by the Maya. The Bishop Diego de Landa observed it once in the mid-sixteenth century in the Yucatán, then it disappeared until 1926, when the anthropologist Franz Blom discovered that it was still performed in Jacaltenago, a remote village deep in the Cuchumatane Mountains of Guatemala.

The Book of Chilam Balam, the prophet of Chumayel, describes how the *uinal* came into being even before the appearance of the sun.

> This is the song of how the *uinal* came into being before the dawn of the world. Then he began to march by his own effort alone. Then said his maternal grandmother, then said his maternal aunt, then said his parental grandmother, then said his sister-in-law, 'What shall we say when we see the man on the road?' These were their words as they marched along, when there was as yet no man. Then they arrived there in the east and began to speak. 'Who has passed here? Here are footprints. Measure it off with your foot.' So spake the mistress of the world. Then he measured the footsteps of our Lord God the Father. . . . Then he spoke its name when the day had no name, after he had marched along with his maternal grandmother, his maternal aunt, his parental grandmother, and his sister-in-law. The *uinal* was

created, the day, as it was called, was created, heaven and earth were created, the stairway of water, the earth, rocks and trees; the things of the sea and the things of the land were created.... The *unial* was created, there was the dawn of the world; sky, earth, trees, and rocks were set in order.

Warfare

Monumental glyphs, murals on the walls of temples, and carvings on lintels are a rich source of information about the history and culture of the Maya élite. Their stelae are engraved with the names of rulers, their genealogy, the day and year they were born, the date of their accession to power, their conquests, the names of their cities, and those of their

The Lord of Yaxchilán stands over his defeated enemy 'The Jewelled Skull'. Carved around AD 755.

enemies. From the murals, we learn that the Maya were a war-like people, given to trophy headhunting, and that warfare was an activity limited to the élite. Their choice of weapons was primarily spears, knives, and rocks, and hand-to-hand combat was common. The murals at Bonampak speak for the savagery of Maya warfare. In them we see prisoners being sacrificed while others plead for mercy with blood dripping from torn fingernails. A severed head lies at the feet of the conquering lord as he receives honours from his nobles.

Texts on the stelae give the name of the conqueror and that of the defeated, and prestige was often gained by taking captives rather than killing them. The illustration is from lintel 8 at Yaxchilán, carved in AD 755, which records 'Bird Jaguar', the lord of Yaxchilán, standing over a defeated enemy known as 'Jewelled Skull'. Their names are taken from the glyphs below each character.

THE TEOTIHUACÁN INTRUSION

With two exceptions, there is no indication that the Maya waged war at the state level with large armies. Along the northern approaches to Tikal, a moat six miles long, anchored at both ends by impassable swamps, would indicate that a foreign army was operating in the area. The only city capable of supporting a large military force 600 miles from home at that period was, of course, Teotihuacán. A stela at Tikal, dated AD 445, shows a Maya priest-ruler with Mexican warriors on either side bearing shields with the image of Tlaloc. It was at about this time that the moat was built, but there is no evidence of a full-scale occupation of Tikal; rather, the Mexican presence seems to be associated solely with élite-class activities.

The Becan moat, 40 feet deep and 65 feet wide at its widest point, surrounds the centre. Seven narrow stone causeways crossed the moat, and all show signs of having been deliberately cut. Again, a Mexican presence is indicated. A ritual deposit with distinctive Teotihuacán features was found in a cache from about the time the moat was built.

The fourth century was a period of imperialistic expansion for Teotihuacán, and the pressures brought about by this movement were clearly felt in the lowlands. The Mexicans were in residence for sixty years, and during this time, the Maya erected no stelae.

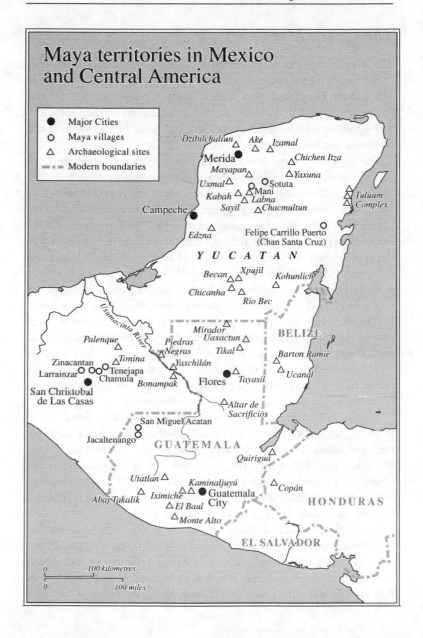

Maya territories in Mexico and Central America

- ●   Major Cities
- ○   Maya villages
- △   Archaeological sites
- ⋇ ⋇ ⋇   Modern boundaries

Dzibilchaltun △   *Ake*   *Izamal*

Merida ●   △ △ △ *Chichen Itza*

Mayapan △   △ *Yaxuna*

Uxmal △   ○ *Sotuta*

Kabah △ △ **Mani**   △ *Tuluum Complex*

Sayil   △ *Labna*

Campeche ●   *Sayil*   △ *Chacmultun*

△   *Felipe Carrillo Puerto* ○

Edzna   (Chan Santa Cruz)

Y U C A T A N

Becan △ △ *Xpujil*   *Kohunlich* △

Chicanha △ △

Rio Bec

Mirador △   **BELIZE**

Palenque △   *Piedras*   *Uaxactun* △

Negras △   *Tikal* △   *Barton Ramie*

Zinacantan   *Tonina* △   *Yaxchilán* △   △ *Ucanal*

Larrainzar ○ ○○○ *Tenejapa*   ● **Flores**   *Tayasil*

● *Chamula*   *Bonampak* △

San Christobal de Las Casas

△ *Altar de Sacrificios*

San Miguel Acatan ○

Jacaltenango ○○

G U A T E M A L A

Quirigua △

Utatlan △   *Kaminaljuyú* △ △ *Copán*

Abaj Takalik   *Iximiche* △△ ● **Guatemala**

△ *El Baul*   **City**

△ *Monte Alto*   **HONDURAS**

EL SALVADOR

Usumacinta River

| 0 | 100 kilometres |
| 0 | 100 miles |

The Classic Maya Collapse

The event, or series of events that triggered the collapse of Maya civilization at the pinnacle of its flowering is still a matter of speculation. The collapse swept from west to east. The first major centre to go was Palenque *circa* AD 810. Piedras Negras and Yaxchilán on the Usmacinta River were quick to follow, then Tikal and Altar de Sacrificios in the ninth and tenth centuries.

The people who remained in the lowlands after the collapse were pitiful shadows of the Classic Maya, possessing neither their technical skill nor any knowledge of their customs and traditions. Evidence of their character is shown by a dramatic shift in the occupation pattern of Tikal. After 830, all major construction ceased, and the entire population of Tikal lived in the palaces. Piles of garbage and refuse accumulated in the rooms, the stairways, and in the palace courtyards. As the palaces decayed, the roofs collapsed, and the occupants simply shifted to other sheltered areas and continued to live as before in the crumbling city. They made some attempts to restore the broken stelae, but glyphs were placed in upside-down positions and stelae were moved to locations inconsistent with the traditional rules of the priesthood, indicating a loss of ritual knowledge.

What caused the Maya to abandon the lowland sites in such a short period of time? A great deal of time and talent has been devoted to the problem, but as yet, no consensus has been reached.

Ecological factors such as soil exhaustion, water loss, erosion, and savanna grass encroachment into the tropical forest could account for the rapid depopulation of the countryside and the ceremonial centres, but exhaustive studies have yet to establish any as the principal cause. Other factors, such as earthquakes, hurricanes, social unrest, invasion, and disease have been studied to a lesser extent, but all are considered unlikely candidates at this time.

The sudden failure of élite-class culture at this time suggests that socio-political factors may also have contributed to the collapse. In this relatively short time, administrative buildings and palaces were abandoned, stelae were no longer erected, luxury items, such as jade carvings and polychrome pottery were no longer manufactured, and élite activities such as the ball game, processionals, rituals, and other characteristics of Maya aristocratic life came to a halt. In other words, the Maya élite class of the Classic period simply ceased to exist.

THE NORTHERN MAYA

The greatest concentration of Classic period Maya sites in Yucatan lies along a straight line in the Puuc hills, a low-lying range some fifty miles south of Merida.

The major sites – Uxmal, Kabah, Sayil, Xlappahk, and Labna – show intensive Maya occupation and development from about AD 700 to 1000. These places survived the lowland centres by nearly a century, and ceramic evidence shows that, like the lowland ones, they were abandoned at the peak of their development. At Uxmal, the last recorded date is 909, at Labna, 869, and at Kabah, 879.

Although the sites are readily accessible, little is known about the people that occupied them. The region has been, and remains to this day, an enigma to historians and archaeologists. For over a thousand years, the Puuc has been sparsely populated, and not a single known legend concerning the sites can be traced back to aboriginal times.

Uxmal is the largest and most spectacular of the Puuc sites, surpassing Tikal, Palenque, and perhaps Copan for the beauty and splendour of its architecture. Three restorations show the mastery of its builders.

The Governor's Palace dominates the entire complex from a massive platform that rises above a sea of swamp grass. For what was once three separate buildings, centuries of construction, burying, and rebuilding merged them into a single structure. Openings between the original buildings were filled in, but recessed and vaulted in such a way as to present a cohesive and artistic frontal elevation, and thousands of separate masonry elements were used to form a mosaic of elaborate latticework and *chacs* (rain gods) across the top of the structure.

In 1843, John Lloyd Stephens described the palace in these words:

> There is no rudeness or barbarity in the design or proportions; on the contrary, the whole wears an air of architectural symmetry and grandeur; and as the stranger ascends the steps and casts a bewildered eye along its open and desolate doors, it is hard to believe that he sees before him the work of a

race in whose epitaph, as written by the historians, they are called ignorant of art, and said to have perished in the rudeness of savage life.

In this same year, he described the quadrangle known as the Nunnery:

> We enter a noble courtyard, with four great façades looking down upon it, each ornamented from one end to the other with the richest and most intricate carving known in the buildings of Uxmal; presenting a scene of strange magnificence, surpassing any that is now to be seen among its ruins.

The Pyramid of the Adivino, the magician, is the tallest structure at Uxmal, rising 93 feet above the plaza. The structure is a series of five temples built one upon the other at various times during the Classic period. The façades of each temple face west, the most elaborate being that of Temple IV, which is designed to reflect the image of the rain god, whose mouth serves as the entrance to the temple.

The name of the temple is of Spanish origin, but it was based upon a myth whose origins are unclear, although elements of it are clearly aboriginal to the Maya. According to an ancient legend, a dwarf was hatched from an egg by an old woman, who lived in a hut where the pyramid now stands. The old woman, a powerful sorceress who wanted her son to be a great lord, sent him to challenge the king for the throne of Uxmal. They agreed upon a series of tests, and the dwarf, aided by his mother, defeated the king in every one. The king, now desperate for his throne, offered the dwarf the ultimate challenge – he ordered him to build a house higher than any other in Uxmal in a single night.

The sorceress told her son not to be discouraged, that he must accept the king's challenge. When the dwarf awoke the following morning, he found himself in a magnificent temple, the ruler of all Uxmal.

The dwarf has long since disappeared from the legend, but his mother, the sorceress, moved to Mani when Uxmal was abandoned, and she lives there today in the town *cenote* with a giant serpent.

Of the other sites in the Puuc-Kabah, Sayil, Labná and Xlappahk, Sayil is the largest. With the exception of a single palace, however, most of its structures are inaccessible in a dense forest of trees, bushes, and vines.

As in the Maya lowlands, the fate of the inhabitants who built these great structures is lost in history. What is known, however, is that the powerful Xiu family, a dynasty of Mexican lineage, lived in Uxmal *circa* AD 1200, suggesting a Toltec occupation after the Maya civilization collapsed.

CHAPTER FOUR

The Militaristic States

The Toltecs

After the fall of Teotihuacán, several tribes from the north migrated into the Valley of Mexico and the surrounding territories. One of these tribes, a powerful militaristic state, would dominate the lake region and project Mexican influence and that of their god Quetzalcoatl as far south as the Yucatán and Guatemala.

Native documents tell how Mixcoatl (Cloud Snake), the semi-legendary leader of the Toltecs, led his people through northern Jalisco and southern Zacatecas into the Valley of Mexico early in the tenth century. They settled first in Culhuacán, on the north shore of Lake Chalco, where, according to legend, Mixcoatl met Chimalma, who bore him a son he never saw. In a power struggle for leadership of the tribe, he lost his life to his brother Ilhuitimal.

His son, Topiltzin, was born in either AD 935 or 947 and raised by the priests of Quetzalcoatl. Upon reaching manhood, he killed Ilhuitimal and assumed leadership of the Toltecs.

Under pressure from the Olmeca Uixtotin at Cholula (not to be confused with the ancient Olmec on the Gulf coast), the Toltecs abandoned Culhuacán and moved north, settling at Tula about 960 in what is now the state of Hidalgo. Topiltzin was a priest of the Quetzalcoatl cult, and, according to legend, opposed human sacrifice. In a power struggle with Tezcatlipoca, a semi-deity who preferred the sacrifice of men, he lost control of the tribe and was forced to leave Tula sometime between AD 980 and 987.

Topiltzin took his people first to Cholula, then moved south to the

Gulf of Mexico. Here, according to a Nahuatl poem, dressed with the brilliant plumage of the quetzal bird and wearing a turquoise mask, he died in a rite of self-immolation. When the fire died out, his ashes rose into the darkening sky as the Evening Star dipped below the horizon. Eight days later, Quetzalcoatl rose from the dead and reappeared as the Morning Star, and took his place among the pantheon of Mexican gods.

A better-known version of the Quetzalcoatl legend, one that would strike fear into the heart of Moctezuma when Cortés arrived, tells of his departure to the east on a raft of serpents. This second version of the legend is perhaps more compatible with history, since Maya archival documents tell of the arrival of a man called Kukulcan, the Maya name for Quetzalcoatl, at Chichen Itza in the Yucatán in 987.

CHICHEN ITZA

Murals, frescos, and scenes on medallions describe the violence as the Toltecs descended upon the city. Murals in the Temple of the Warriors show the Toltecs reconnoitering the coast in war canoes while Maya warriors in rafts attempt to intercept them, and paintings in the Temple of the Jaguars show the Maya falling before the Toltec onslaught on land. Battle scenes showing the Toltecs throwing spears at the retreating Maya are engraved on gold discs found at the site, and Quetzalcoatl hovers over Maya leaders as they meet death on the sacrificial stone.

The Quetzalcoatl of Tula is said to have limited his sacrifices to butterflies and snakes. The Kulkulcán of Chichen Itza, however, more closely resembled his arch enemy Tezcatlipoca, for he introduced idol worship and human sacrifice in the Yucatán on a scale never before experienced by the Maya.

From the Motul Manuscript:

> . . . originally a god had been worshipped here who was the creator of all
> things, but that a great prince called Kukulcan . . . had come from a foreign
> country, and that he and his people were idolaters, and from that time the
> inhabitants of this land also began to practise idolatry, to perform bloody
> sacrifices, to burn copal, and the like.

The architecture of Toltec-Maya Chichen Itza is magnificent in conception and realization. Giant serpents, poised to strike with gaping mouths and enormous fangs, descend from imposing balustrades along the stairway of the Castillo, the temple of Kukulcán. Enigmatic Chac Mools recline on temple floors, clutching bowls to receive the still-beating hearts of sacrificial victims while they stare fixedly towards the distant horizon. And tier upon tier of grinning skulls, engraved on the massive stone platform called the Tzompantli, give evidence of sacrifice on a massive scale.

On the east side of the Kukulcán plaza, the Temple of the Warriors rests upon a platform flanked on both sides by two hundred columns engraved with Toltec warriors in relief. The temple is similar to the Pyramid of Quetzalcoatl at Tula, but far more impressive, due, perhaps to the craftsmanship of the Maya masons whose ancestors built Uxmal and Kabah. Inside, Quetzalcoatl faces Toltec warriors as they file past a mural of the feathered serpent, a theme that also appears in the ante-chamber of a palace at Tula.

The ball court, the longest in Mesoamerica at 492 feet, lies in the northwest corner of the site. At the entry, the Temple of the Jaguars stands on top of the 30-foot east wall, and two ornate serpentine rings mounted at near-impossible heights on opposing walls testify to the

A Chac Mool figure holding a bowl to receive the hearts of sacrificial victims

difficulty of the game. Little is known how the game was played, but hearsay has it that a player who managed to get the ball through the ring won the clothes and all the possessions of the spectators. As for the losing team, it may be their skulls that are engraved on the Tzompantli.

The Well of Sacrifice, a great circular *cenote* 190 feet in diameter, is a fearful sight as one approaches it from the causeway. Sheer vertical walls, pockmarked with recesses that house lizards, snakes, and iguanas, rise from the surface of the water 65 feet below the rim. The depth of the water is 36 feet, below which there is a layer of black mud 40 feet deep. The water is an impenetrable murky green mirror, reflecting images of the forest and the sky above from its quiet, motionless surface. For the victims, there was no hope of rescue from its waters. Years of dredging have yielded approximately fifty skulls, many of which are those of children. Nearly all the artifacts recovered were of Mexican design. Human sacrifice at the well evidently occurred as late as 1535, when a sacrificial party with male and female slaves was ambushed by a rival tribe.

The fall of Chichen Itza came about AD 1200, when Hunac Ceel, or Ah Nacxit Kukulcán, the chieftain of Mayapán, the capital of Yucatán until 1446, captured the city.

TULA

While there is some degree of consistency in the literature about the rise and fall of the Toltec capital at Tula, there is a near-complete lack of information regarding the middle period, when Toltec culture was at its pinnacle. What is known about those who remained at Tula with Tezcatlipoca comes primarily from archaeological records and native chronicles.

By AD 1000, Tula had a population of 40,000 to 50,000 people, and covered an area of 4.2 square miles. It occupied a position on a lime-stone promontory, and was surrounded on three sides by steep banks. The main buildings and temples lie in the acropolis group, which, like the Avenue of the Dead at Teotihuacán, is oriented 15½° east of north.

The most important structure is the Temple of Quetzalcoatl, where he is shown in his manifestation of the Morning Star. In its latest phase of construction, the entire platform was encased by sculptured jaguars, heart-devouring eagles, buzzards, and, of course, Quetzalcoatl. On top of the staircase, human figures and jaguars hold banners, and the ubiquitous chacmool reclines in the doorway with his bowl. The temple had two rooms: the roof of the outer room was supported by four Atlantean figures of Toltec warriors each carrying an *atlatl*★ in one hand and an incense bag in the other. In the rear chamber, square columns supported the roof. A serpentine wall, the *Coatepantli*, bars entry to the northern access to the temple, The same type of wall encloses the ceremonial centre in the heart of Aztec Tenochtitlán.

The tentative boundaries of the Toltec empire extended some 65 miles east of Tula, 15 miles west, 25 miles north, and 80 miles south, beyond Cuernavaca. Their influence, however, was felt far to the north. From trading posts in Chihuahua, Toltec *pochteca* (merchants) travelled to the Hohokan and Anasazi areas of Arizona and New Mexico, trading copper bells and other artifacts for turquoise, slaves, peyote, and salt. Wall paintings in the Hopi area show Tlaloc, the water god, and images of Quetzalcoatl appear in a number of places.

Tula ceased to exist as the Toltec capital about 1156, when Huemac, the last ruler, took his followers to Chapultepec and consequently hanged himself. The chronicles speak of dissensions among internal factions and wars with external forces, but whatever the cause, the city was destroyed. Huge trenches were dug across the major temples, the Atlantean pillars were overturned, Toltec symbols were defaced, and the serpent wall was overturned. But their memory lingered on for the Aztecs, who went to great effort to deny their Chichimec heritage and establish a claim of descent from the great Toltecs.

The Aztecs

ARRIVAL IN THE VALLEY OF MEXICO

The people who built the first Mexican empire called themselves the Mexica, or the Culhua Mexica, the latter term chosen to identify themselves as descendants and heirs of the Toltecs. The term 'Aztec'

★ A throwing stick for javelins

was derived from their traditional place of origin, Aztlán. It was first used by the eighteenth-century historian Clavijero, and brought into popular usage by the nineteenth-century historian William Hickling Prescott.

Aztlán itself is shrouded in mystery. Some authorities believe it to be located in a lagoon on the coast of the present state of Nayarit; others place it as far away as the American southwest; and some consider it to be in the realm of myth.

In any event, the Aztecs began their migration from Aztlán about 1111, some two hundred years before they brought their god Huit-zilopochtli to the Valley of Mexico. After a journey that can be best described as rich in allegory, they arrived at Chapultepec, the last of fourteen tribes to settle in the valley. The dominant groups at that time were the Acolhua, on the eastern shore of Lake Texcoco, and the Tepanecs, on the western shore.

In 1319, the Tepanecs, possibly coveting the strategic location of Chapultepec, drove the Aztecs into the lagoon, and the refugees threw themselves on the mercy of Achitometl, the ruler of Culhuacán. The Culhua lord, sympathetic to their plight, allowed them to settle in Tizapan, a wasteland of volcanic lava occupied by poisonous snakes.

In spite of their hostile surroundings, however, the Aztecs thrived, and eventually ingratiated themselves with the Culhua by supporting them in a successful war against Xochimilco. Encouraged by their newly gained prestige, they approached Achitometl and asked for one of his daughters to be honoured as the bride of their god Huitzilopochtli.

Achitometl loved his daughter very much, but flattered by her becoming a living goddess of the Aztecs, agreed. On the day of the ceremony, he gathered his nobles and they carried offerings of incense, feathers, and fine foods for Huitzilopochtli and the new goddess. When the Aztecs led him into the darkened temple, he sacrificed quail and scattered their blood upon the altar, then threw incense into a brazier, lighting up the room. There before him stood the dread figure of Huitzilopochtli, wearing the skin of his daughter. For a moment, his heart stopped, unable to comprehend the sight before him. Then he dropped the brazier and dashed from the temple, screaming for his people to take up their weapons.

A symbolic drawing of the founding of Tenochtitlan between 1135 and 1372 by Tenoch, in line with the prophecy by Huitzilopochtli

They drove the Aztecs back into the waters as far as Ixtapalapa, then to Acatzintitlán, where they managed to build rafts and move far out into the lake. Now, in their hour of greatest need, Huitzilo-pochtli appeared and told them to seek out a place where they would see a cactus with an eagle perched upon it. His prophecy was fulfilled upon a muddy island, where they would build their houses and temples, and call their city Tenochtitlán in honour of Tenoch, their first priest-ruler.

Tenoch was the leader of the Aztecs while they lived among the Culhua, and he served them after they founded Tenochtitlán, some-time between 1335 and 1345. Upon his death in 1372, however, they chose not to elect one of their own to succeed him, but to look towards Culhuacán for a descendant of the Toltecs to rule over them. Their choice was Acamapichtli, the son of a Mexican nobleman and a princess of Culhuacán, and in 1376 he was named the first *tlatoani* of Mexico. Acamapichtli was said to have twenty wives, all daughters of local rulers, to allow him to produce a generation of Mexican nobles of Toltec heritage.

The Aztec capital straddled two adjacent islands, and in about 1358, the islands became the independent principalities of Tenochtitlán and Tlatelolco. While Acamapichtli proclaimed his Toltec ancestry in Tenochtitlán, Cuacuapitzahuac, the eldest son of Tezozomoc, the great lord of Azcapotzalco, became the first of a line of Tepanecs to rule Tlatelolco.

At the time of the founding of Tenochtitlán and Tlatelolco, power in the Valley of Mexico was divided among Culhuacán, Acolhua, and Azcapotzalco. The latter city was connected to Tenochtitlán by a causeway some three miles long. The proximity of the Tepanec capital left the Mexicans no choice as to whom they would serve.

For more than fifty years, for the mere privilege of eking out a meagre existence on a swampy, pestilent island, they fought Tezozomoc's battles. They would pay his harsh levies, and suffer every humiliation possible from their Tepanec neighbours. The relationship improved, however, when Huitzilíhuitl, the second lord of Mexico, took a Tepanec princess for his wife. Their son, Chimalpopoca, Tezozomoc's favourite grandson, was in time elected lord of Mexico, and he all but eliminated their tribute.

Tezozomoc died in 1426, after a reign that spanned more than fifty years. The old emperor had chosen his son Tayauh to succeed him, but his succession to the Tepanec throne was challenged by Maxtla, the lord of Coyoacán. Chimalpopoca chose to support Tayauh, and together they plotted to assassinate Maxtla by strangling him with a rope disguised as a garland of flowers. Unfortunately, the plot was revealed, and Maxtla strangled Tayauh by his own device.

Maxtla persuaded the Tepanec nobles and the newly elected lord of Atzcapotzalco to reinstate the old, unsparing levies upon Mexico, and the outraged Mexicans were ready to fight. Chimalpopoca, however, chose to appease his Tepanec kinsmen, and his Mexican nobles assassinated him. Wisely, they hired Tepanec assassins to kill Chimalpopoca, knowing the blame would fall upon Maxtla. With the death of the

Mexican ruler, the Tepanecs blockaded the causeway, and war seemed inevitable.

REVOLUTION

Itzcoatl, the son of Acamapichtli by an Azcapotzalca slave girl was elected the fourth *tlatoani* of Mexico. Determined to resist Maxtla at all costs, he sought the support of Netzahualcóyotl, the lord of Texcoco, who had been driven from his country by Tezozomoc, and that of his nephews, Moctezuma Ilhuicamina and Tlacaelel.

Many of the Mexican nobles, however, feared the wrath of the powerful Tepanecs more than the shame of bondage. They removed Huitzilopochtli from his temple and set out for Atzcapotzalco, intending to present their god to the new lord as a symbol of Mexico's enduring vassalage. When they reached the causeway, they found Itzcoatl and Tlacaelel waiting for them.

From the *Cronica Mexicana*, by Hernando Alvarado Tezozomoc, a grandson of Moctezuma:

> 'Mexicans', Tlacaelel said, 'have you no shame? Have you become so craven as to throw yourselves at the feet of the Atzcapotzalaco? Have you given no thought to how this contemptible act will reflect upon the honour of Mexico for generations to come?' Turning to Itzcoatl, he said, 'Lord, reason with your people. If they want peace and security, prevail upon them to seek a more honourable course.'
>
> 'Kinsmen', Itzcoatl said, 'your fears are well founded, but do not deliver our god into the hands of the Atzcapotzalaco. Let me instead offer you a compromise, one that should prove honourable and satisfy all.'
>
> 'You are all celebrated lords; lords of unquestionable courage. Now I call upon one of you to go to the lord of Atzcapatzolco himself to remind him that we were once loyal servants of his father and ask him why he is so bent upon destroying us. Which of you can put his fears aside and go to their lord and petition him in my name for peace with honour between our people?'
>
> Only Tlacaelel stepped forward.
>
> 'Nephew', Itzcoatl replied, 'I am deeply moved by your courage. If you succeed, you will rank among our greatest lords. If, however, you are killed by the Atzcapotzalca, these same rewards and honours will be bestowed upon your sons and grandsons, and your sacrifice will live in our hearts forever.'

Wearing the time-honoured robes of an ambassador, Tlacaelel convinced the sentries to let him pass, and was granted an audience with the lord of Atzcapatzalco.

Tlacaelel told the lord of Atzcapatzolco that Itzcoatl saw no purpose in a war between Mexico and Atzcapotzalco, since he and people had no intent other than to serve him as they had served his father before him. This war that Maxtla and the Tepanec lords were determined to pursue, he said, would leave both cities devastated. It would bring about untold suffering among the common people, especially the elderly and the very young. and the people of one nation or the other would be slaves forever.

If he and his lords would accept Itzcoatl once again as their honoured servant, he offered his solemn pledge that Mexico would do nothing to provoke the Tepaneca.

Moved by Tlacaelel's sincerity, the lord of Atzcapoptzalco promised to present Itzcoatl's petition before the council of the lords, but he warned him that his powers were limited − if the council refused to yield, war was inevitable. Their decision would be waiting for his return in the morning.

Itzcoatl was pleased to hear that the lord of Atzcapotzalco would present his offer of peace before the Tepanec Council, but held out little hope that Maxtla and his followers would offer him any compromise or concession.

'Nephew', he said, 'if the lord of Atzcapotzalco fails to persuade his nobles to accept my offer, this is what you must do. Give him this shield and these golden arrows, and arm him with this *maquahuitl* so he may defend himself. Then place these feathers upon his head and anoint his body with bitumen and blue pitch, just as we do the dead, and tell him that we must do that which we must do.'

Once more before the lord of Atzcapotzalco, Tlacaelel said, 'Lord, your servant and vassal Itzcoatl, the lord of Mexico, awaits your decision. Will you, O Lord, raise your hand to protect your servants, will you favor us as your father did in the past, or have you forsaken us? Is it still the will of the Tepaneca to destroy our people.'

'Tlacaelel, my son,' the king responded, 'What am I to say? Though I am lord, it is the will of my people that we wage war upon you, and I am powerless to prevent them. They are angry with your people, and they are determined to kill them all. If I attempt to stop them, I will forfeit my life and the lives of all my children.'

'Then, O lord,' Tlacaelel said. 'your servant the lord of Mexico stands in defiance of you. He advises you to gather up your courage and prepare for war for now he is your mortal enemy. He sends you these arrows, this

shield, and this *maquahuitl* so that you can defend yourself, and he com-
mands me to anoint you with this pitch, this unction of the dead, so that you
may prepare yourself for death.'

The lord of Atzcapotzalco permitted Tlacaelel to arm him and anoint his
body, and when he was finished, he asked him to thank Itzcoatl for his offer
of peace.

Itzcoatl, however, was not alone in his war with the Tepanecs.
Tezozomoc's enemies had long memories, and had no intention of
allowing Maxtla to dominate the valley as had his father.

The siege of Atzcapotzalco lasted nearly four months. Itzcoatl
launched his assault against the eastern defences of the city, Moctezuma
attacked from the south, and Nezahualcóyotl, supported by the
powerful lord of Huexotzingo, struck from the north. Mexican losses
were heavy, but the Tepanecs were a house divided, with neither allies
nor mercenaries to fight alongside them, and when the granaries were
exhausted, they were forced to yield.

But Itzcoatl had little time to relish his victory. Maxtla set about
seeking allies among those nations who had cause to fear and hate
Mexico. Maxtla's first overtures were to Atzcapotzlaco, but he received
no encouragement from his kinsmen. They were still bitter for his
failure to aid them against Itzcoatl, and they had no desire to shed their
blood again to satisfy his ambitions.

Failing to find allies on either the western or eastern shores of the
great lake, Maxtla proposed that the lords of Xochimilco, Mixquic,
Culhuacán, and Cuitlahuac meet in Chalco and resolve the Mexican
problem for once and all.

There was a general agreement among the lords who gathered in
Chalco that Mexico should be destroyed before the Mexicans found
allies, but when it came to working out the details of the alliance, they
could find no common ground. Who among them would lead the
alliance? How would the spoils of war be shared? Which of them
would the Mexicans serve as vassals when they were defeated? In the
end, it was the lord of Amecameca, one of the Chalco rulers, who,
convinced that their differences were irreconcilable, suggested that if
Maxtla was determined to wage war on Mexico, better he do it alone.

With his newly found independence from the Tepanecs, Itzcoatl

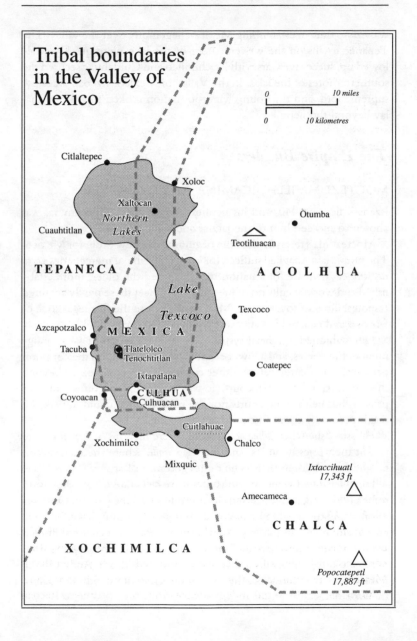

Tribal boundaries in the Valley of Mexico

0   10 miles

0   10 kilometres

Citlaltepec

Xoloc

Xaltocan

Northern Lakes

Ótumba

Teotihuacan

Cuauhtitlan

TEPANECA

ACOLHUA

Lake

Texcoco

Texcoco

Azcapotzalco

MEXICA

Tacuba

Tlatelolco
Tenochtitlan

Coatepec

Ixtapalapa

CULHUA

Coyoacan

Culhuacan

Cuitlahuac

Xochimilco

Chalco

Mixquic

Ixtaccihuatl 17,343 ft

Amecameca

CHALCA

XOCHIMILCA

Popocatepetl 17,887 ft

wasted no time in establishing Mexican hegemony over the valley. The Tepanec towns on the western shore of the lake were quickly swallowed up, successive wars with Xochimilco and Cuitlahuac secured the southern shores of the lake. In the Valley of Mexico, Itzcoatl was now supreme lord, and the young, vigorous nation looked to a future that lay beyond the sierra.

The Empire Builders

MOCTEZUMA ILLHUICAMINA. THE LAW-GIVER

Itzcoatl died in 1440, and his nephew, Moctezuma Ilhuicamina, was chosen to succeed him to the jaguar and eagle throne.

Moctezuma's reign marked the beginning of a new order for Mexico. The simple laws that had sufficed for a migrant tribe of mercenaries were no longer adequate for a nation that governed the older, more established and worldly cultures of the valley. To meet these newly acquired responsibilities of sovereignty, Moctezuma wrote the first legal code of Mexico and enacted the statutes required to enforce it.

He established a judicial system whereby a high court sat in judgment of the nobles, and a lower court passed judgment on the common people. If the matter before either court was too complex or beyond the jurisdiction of either court, it was referred to a council of four princes, but neither the courts nor the royal council could impose the death penalty without first notifying the king.

He established the *Calmecac*, a school where the sons of the élite were taught their priestly duties, and the *telpochcalli,* where the commoners taught their children their civic duties and martial arts.

He determined when religious rites were celebrated, how they were to be performed, and stipulated a dress code for all the people. Only the nobility and the great captains could wear gold, precious jewellery, and cotton clothing: commoners could wear no more than coarse shifts and sandals woven from maguey fibre. The penalty for violating the dress code, adultery, and breaking a vow of chastity was death. And of all the nobles, only the *Cihuacóatl*, the vice-emperor, could stand shod before the emperor.

Now Huitzilopochtli was supreme over all the gods of the valley, and Moctezuma felt obliged to build a fitting home to pay him homage. He set about the monumental task of laying the foundation of a temple that would not be completed for forty years, and bonded it with gold and precious jewels from his people and the blood of five hundred Chalca warriors he sacrificed for the occasion.

Moctezuma's ambitions and the fate of his budding empire, however, hung in the balance when a series of disasters struck the valley and the surrounding highlands. In 1449, heavy rains raised the level of Lake Texcoco until Tenochtitlán was inundated. Strong swells, driven by the winds that blow across the valley late in winter, destroyed so many houses and temples that it was feared the city would have to be abandoned. In desperation, Moctezuma turned to Nezahualcóyotl, who had built the viaducts, dykes, and canals that fed the parks and fountains of Texcoco.

It was obvious that the city could be protected from unseasonable floods if a levee were built across the strait between Tenochtitlán and the peninsula that separates Lake Texcoco from Lake Xochimilco. A permanent seawall, however, would have a disastrous effect upon the economy of the city, since it would isolate Tenochtitlán from the tens of thousands of canoes that supplied its markets every day.

Nezahualcóyotl's solution was to drive heavy wooden piles in parallel rows across the strait and fill the space between with rock and earth. To accommodate the lake traffic, he devised flood gates that could be opened to allow free passage of the canoes during seasons of normal rainfall, yet sturdy enough to hold back the flood waters when closed, and set them at intervals along the dyke. Using forced labour from the towns surrounding the lake, Nezahualcóyotl built a massive dyke 30 feet in width and eight miles long between Ixtapalapa and Atzacoalco, on the eastern shore of Tenochtitlán.

When the flood waters abated, famine came to the land. The rains disappeared, streams dried up, rivers ceased to flow, and the land became barren. Moctezuma opened the royal granaries, but within a year they were empty, and he was forced to acknowledge that he could do no more for his starving people. With a heavy heart, he advised them to leave the city and survive the best the could in regions that had been spared the drought. For no more than a single basket of maize, parents sold their sons and daughters to merchants who could feed them, and the Totonacs, whose fertile lands on the eastern seaboard never failed to provide them with abundant harvests, bought their children by the hundred.

After four years of drought, the rains returned, and harvests were so plentiful that many were able to ransom their children and re-establish their homes in the city and the surrounding valley.

Blessed once more with a bountiful land and sheltered from the floods by the great dyke, Mexico embarked upon an unprecedented era of prosperity and expansion. As Tenochtitlán flourished, so did the merchants of neighbouring Tlatelolco, who journeyed throughout Anahuac, extending Mexican commerce as far as distant Xicalango, the centre of the vast trade network of the Maya. This newly acquired affluence did not come cheap, however. As the Tlatelolca strived to reach the farthest markets, they were forced to enter hostile territories, where they were often tortured and put to death. In order to protect his profitable enterprise, Moctezuma was compelled to maintain a large standing army and mount campaigns as far as the eastern seacoast and into the southern sierra, the land of the Zapotecs.

If Mexican commerce was to flourish, Moctezuma knew that it was vital that he open a route to the rich eastern seaboard. The most direct route lay to the southeast, where a pass crossed the sierra beneath the Orizaba volcano. Tepeaca, a small town some 90 miles from Mexico, commanded the entry to the pass, and Moctezuma lost no time in overwhelming its defences and establishing a garrison to secure the western approaches to the seacoast. From Tepeaca, he launched an attack against the Totonacs, and with that their defeat.

Moctezuma's furthest-reaching campaign sent Mexican armies nearly 300 miles into Oaxaca, but there he found that he had reached the limit of his ability to project Mexican power into the southern sierra. Neither the Zapotecs nor the Totonacs were easily controlled, and other enemies, at home and abroad, demanded his full attention.

Although there were peaceful interludes between his campaigns, there was little time for his warriors to enjoy them. Moctezuma periodically arranged for ceremonial wars to be fought at mutually

An early map of Tenochtitlán-Tlatelolco

agreeable sites with Taxcala, Huexotzingo, and Cholula. These wars, called the flowery wars, would sustain the fighting edge of Mexico's warriors throughout the great era of expansion that followed his reign.

AXAYÁCATL

Moctezuma Ilhuicamina died in 1468, and Axayácatl, the 19-year-old grandson of Itzcoatl, fell heir to an empire greater than Tezozomoc and the Tepanecs ever imagined.

During his 13-year reign, Axayácatl pushed the frontiers of the budding empire beyond the Valley of Toluca to the west, and into the Valley of Oaxaca to the southwest. His greatest achievement was along the eastern seaboard, where he established Mexican control over more than eighty leagues of coastline, from the Tuxpan River in the north to the province of Tochtepec in the south.

But Axayácatl's military successes were overshadowed by his ill-advised expedition against the Tarascans. In a disastrous campaign into Michoacán, his outnumbered squadrons were massacred by the well-trained Tarascans, and for the first time in 50 years, Mexico witnessed an emperor returning from war in disgrace.

Axayácatl's reign was also marred by a bloody civil war that opened a breach in the kinship between Tenochtitlán and Tlatelolco that never fully healed, leaving a bitterness in the hearts of the proud Tlatelolca long after they reclaimed their rightful role in the affairs of Mexico. Moquihuix, who ruled Tlatelolco for twenty years, resented Tenochtitlán's predominance in affairs of state, and with the advent of the young and inexperienced Axayácatl to the jaguar and eagle throne, he sought to seize control of the empire. Believing that Axayácatl was unaware of his preparations for war, he attempted a night attack on the city, but the Tenochca lay in ambush, and his squadrons were driven back.

Axayácatl gathered his squadrons on the edge of the city and sent the insignia of the dead to Moquihuix. After a furious battle, he drove the Tlatelolca into the market place, where they milled about in confusion as they watched Axayácatl pursue their lord to the summit of the great temple. He found Moquihuix cowering at the foot of the altar of Huitzilopochtli, and struck him down with a single blow of his

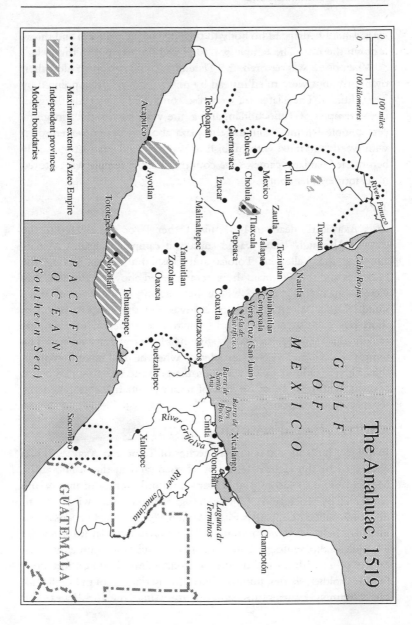

The Anahuac, 1519

- .... Maximum extent of Aztec Empire
- ▨ Independent provinces
- ═══ Modern boundaries

0 ___ 100 miles
0 ___ 100 kilometres

PACIFIC OCEAN (Southern Sea)

GULF OF MEXICO

GUATEMALA

River Panuco

Cabo Rojas

Acapulco
Ayotlan
Tototepec
Nopolan
Tehuantepec
Quetzaltepec
Xalotepec
Soconusco

Tetoloapan
Toluca
Guernavaca
Izucar
Mexico
Cholula
Tlaxcala
Jalapa
Malinaltepec
Tepeaca
Yanhuitlan
Zozolan
Oaxaca
Cotaxtla
Coatzacoalcos

Tula
Zautla
Teziutlan
Nautla
Quiahuitlan
Cempoala
Vera Cruz (San Juan)
Isla de Sacrificios

Tuxpan

Barra de Santa Ana
Barra de Dos Bocas
Cintla
Potonchan
Xicalango
Laguna de Terminos

River Grijalva
River Usumacinta

Champoton

maquahuitl. He dragged his body to the edge of the platform and threw it down the side. The temple was fired and the city put to the sack.

When peace was restored, the Tlatelolco could no longer elect their own lords, but were ruled instead by military governors appointed by Tenochtitlán. The Tlatelolca were also compelled to worship the gods in the temples of Tenochtitlán, and as the years passed, their magnificent temple fell into ruin and the plaza about it became overgrown with weeds and filled with rubbish. It was not until years later, shortly before the Spaniards came to the country, that the temple was restored to its former splendour.

TIZOC

After Axayácatl's death in 1481, his brother Tizoc was elected to the throne. Although Tizoc waged successful campaigns against Matlatzingo in the Valley of Toluca and crushed uprisings among the Huastecs and the Totonacs, he is remembered above all for his costly victory against Metztitlán, where he exchanged the lives of three hundred good warriors for forty captives. For the greater part of his short reign, he spent his energies on the construction of the great temple that Moctezuma had begun nearly forty years earlier. The temple was within a year of completion when he died unexpectedly in the fifth year of his reign. It was rumoured that he was poisoned by his council, who feared that his lack of military initiative threatened the security of the empire.

AHUITZOTL: THE WARRIOR KING

In 1486, Ahuitzotl, the younger brother of Tizoc and Axayácatl, was chosen to be the eighth *tlatoani* of Mexico, and in the young ruler, Mexico found an incomparable warrior, a lord worthy of the empire conceived by Moctezuma. Unlike the aging Moctezuma, who chose to direct his military campaigns from Mexico, Ahuitzotl led his squadrons into the field of battle, inspiring them on the one hand with his example, and discouraging his chieftains and warriors from faint heart on the other with his uncompromising discipline. First and foremost, he was a soldier, sharing the hardships and discomforts of the road with the common warrior instead of exercising the privileges and

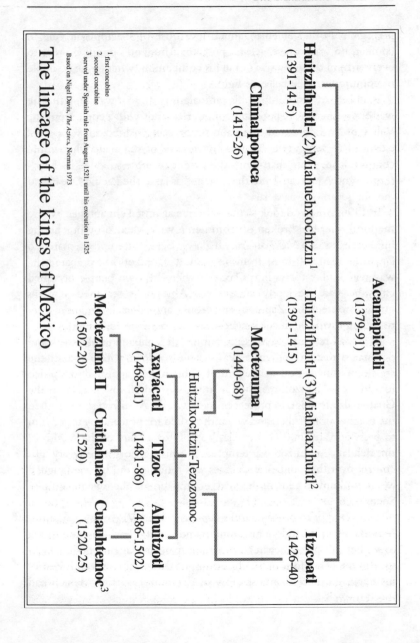

The lineage of the kings of Mexico

Acamapichtli
(1379-91)

Huitzilíhuitl-(2)Miahuehxochtzin[1]
(1391-1415)

Huitzilíhuitl-(3)Miahuaxíhuitl[2]
(1391-1415)

Itzcoatl
(1426-40)

Chimalpopoca
(1415-26)

Moctezuma I
(1440-68)

Huitzilxochtzin-Tezozomoc

Axayácatl
(1468-81)

Tizoc
(1481-86)

Ahuitzotl
(1486-1502)

Moctezuma II
(1502-20)

Cuitlahuac
(1520)

Cuauhtemoc[3]
(1520-25)

[1] first concubine
[2] second concubine
[3] served under Spanish rule from August, 1521, until his execution in 1525

Based on Nigel Davis, *The Aztecs*, Norman 1973

prerogatives of a nobleman, much less those of an emperor. And in combat, no warrior ever left his post, for Ahuitzotl's standing order to every man in the army was to kill his companion, whether he be noble or commoner, if he failed to fight.

Ruthless towards his foes, his campaigns were so devastating that he was often forced to repopulate conquered lands with people from the Valley of Mexico. Headstrong and unforgiving, Ahuitzotl was a difficult lord to serve, but this was the nature of the man who would conquer lands more than twice the extent of those subdued by Moctezuma and Axacayatl, lands that reached as far as the Pacific Ocean and the Kingdom of Guatemala.

In 1496, Ahuitzotl took to the offensive against Tehuantepec, where the local ruler had broken off commerce with Mexico by butchering his merchants. No Mexican army had ever before attempted a march so far, more than 360 miles from home, but Ahuitzotl had prepared the way with earlier forays into Oaxaca, where his own people occupied cities he had previously conquered. Ahuitzotl's seasoned veterans quickly routed the Zapotec squadrons, and after looting the surrounding towns, he incorporated the province into his empire.

Ahuitzotl returned to Mexico, but he left Tehuantepec so weak and devastated that the province was unable to defend itself against the attacks of its neighbours. The lord of Tehuantepec appealed to Mexico for aid, and Ahuitzotl marched nearly six hundred miles, as far as the Guatemalan frontier, to protect his new vassals. Ahuitzotl soon crushed the neighbouring tribes, and when they sued for peace, they urged him to press onwards into Guatemala, hoping for a share of the wealth of this rich land. Ahuitzotl was tempted, but his warriors were weary. His control over these distant provinces was tenuous, and he was fatigued by an unknown ailment he had contracted in the swamplands of Soconusco.

This war was to be Ahuitzotl's last campaign. When he returned to Mexico, he began to lose his strength and vitality. Each day he seemed to wither; his bones began to protrude from his sagging flesh, and in spite of the best efforts of his physicians, he died in the sixteenth year of his reign, no more than a shadow of the robust warrior Mexico had loved so well.

MOCTEZUMA XOCÓYOTL: THE PRIEST

In 1502, Moctezuma Xocoyotl, the son of Axayácatl was elected the ninth *tlatoani* of Mexico. He was 34 years old, a lord whose eloquence and courtly manners were befitting a noble prince, and respected by all as a wise and devout man who observed his priestly duties as well as his secular obligations.

In Mexico, power was passed on only by election. Acamapichtli, the first *tlatoani*, had not named his successor at the time of his death, but left it to the people to select the one most fit to rule. As the city and the empire grew larger, however, the privilege of election passed into the hands of a small élite group, and succession to the throne was more often to a brother than a son.

The day of Moctezuma's election to the throne found him at his devotions in the Temple of the Eagle Knights, where a major-domo informed him that the lords of Mexico, Texcoco, and Tlacopan awaited him in the council chamber. When he stood before them, priests removed his clothing and dressed him in the vestments of purification, then led him to the house of fasting, where he would do penance for four days. Each day he prayed and offered Huitzilopochtli blood drawn from his earlobes, and after prayers, he bathed.

On the fourth day, the priests led him back to the council chamber and into a circle of jaguar and eagle bones, where they invested him with the robes and royal devices of the emperor. He knelt before Nezahualpilli, who had succeeded to the throne of Texcoco when Nezahualcóyotl died, the *Cihuacoatl,* and the lord of Tlacopan, and each in turn recited the homilies that bound a newly elected emperor to his people.

They warned him of the great labours that lay ahead of him, of the self-restraint he must exercise if he was to rule wisely and capably, and of the demanding studies he must pursue if he was to recognize and interpret the signs and omens manifest in the motions of the stars. They spoke of the emperor's binding duty to their religion, his duty to honour the priesthood, and his obligation to satisfy the unending needs of the gods for the blood of men. When they were finished, Neza-haualpilli pierced the cartilage of Moctezuma's nose with a sharp bone and thrust a jade rod through the incision. He then set the turquoise diadem on his head and proclaimed him lord of Mexico and sovereign of all its provinces.

Unlike Ahuitzotl, Moctezuma believed that only those of noble birth were fit to govern. His first edict purged the army and the royal household of the commoners that Ahuitzotl, in recognition of honours earned in warfare, had elevated to high office, and in their stead, he appointed sons of the royal families of Mexico, Texcoco, and Tlacopan.

Under his guidance and tutelage, the young nobles learned the art of government and the ways of the royal court, the required protocol when they waited upon the emperor and his vassal lords, and were enlightened as to the courtesy and respect due to the wives and concubines of the emperor. He restored the titles of the Tlatelolcan nobility and allowed them to rebuild their temple, but he reinstated the heavy tribute levied upon them by Axayácatl, which had long since been forgiven by Ahuitzotl.

If Moctezuma was a severe man, he was also a just man. None, no matter what his station in life, was exempt from the harsh and unsparing punishments prescribed by the laws and statutes he had inherited from his ancestors. He demanded the same exacting interpretation of the laws from his judges as his own, and he often wore disguises in the courts to judge for himself the soundness of their verdicts. As insistent as Moctezuma was in enforcing the severe laws of Mexico in the community at large, however, he was even more intolerant of wrongdoing within the palace, for he considered the palace to be the house of god, and for offences no more than irreverence or a foolish oversight, the punishment was often death.

But if history would condemn Moctezuma Xocóyotl for his cruelty, let it also be recorded that compassion on the part of a Mexican ruler was unthinkable, for his enemies never failed to look upon clemency as a sign of weakness and lack of resolution, and by his nobles and chieftains as a threat to the security of the empire. And Moctezuma was all too well aware of the untimely deaths of Tizoc and Chimalpopoca.

Although Moctezuma exercised his command of the armies of Mexico in a manner different from Ahuitzotl, he was no less an able and skilled general in the field. The vast and rapid expansion of the empire under Ahuitzotl had stretched Mexico to its utmost ability to control its thirty-eight provinces. The difficult task of consolidating and maintaining Mexican authority over these troublesome regions, however, was left to his successor. Revolts throughout the province of Oaxaca forced Moctezuma to undertake one campaign after another in the southern sierra to protect his merchants and maintain his lines of communication to the southeast. Whether he led his warriors across the ramparts wearing his battle dress of red spoonbill feathers or sent them under the command of his generals, his armies never failed to return in triumph.

The Cosmos

As the year 1507 approached, the empire prospered as never before. Peace prevailed throughout the provinces, and the tribute that flowed into Mexico every eighty days exceeded that ever imagined by Moctezuma's predecessors. Yet there was little joy in Tenochtitlán. Instead, an atmosphere of dread and apprehension lay over the people, a sense of foreboding for their future, a fear that had existed since time immemorial, long before they left their ancestral home in Aztlán.

The Aztecs were the people of the Sun, who lived in a shifting, unstable world, a world that would endure only as long as the sun rose in the morning and the blood of their sacrifices fuelled its journey across the sky each day. But now the year 2 Reed was nearly upon them, and with it came the fateful night when the very existence of the Sun was threatened by a cataclysm that neither the gods nor all their sacrifices could forestall.

The passing of the year 1 Rabbit into the year 2 Reed marked the end of a fifty-two year cycle, and between the final moments of the old year and the first of the new, there was a gap in the flow of time. If the gap failed to close, the Sun would vanish, leaving the world in the void of everlasting night.

The sages told how the first sun had survived thirteen cycles before the years failed to bind, leaving it to be eaten by jaguars; how the second sun had been swept away by the wind after but six; of the fire that rained down from the heavens and consumed the third after seven; and of the flood that swallowed the fourth after thirteen. Only through the intervention of the gods would the fifth sun be born, but it would be the last sun of all.

When the fourth sun perished and the world lay shrouded in darkness, the gods gathered at Teotihuacán, seeking to bring light into the world once more. But who would cast himself into the eternal flames to be reborn as the Sun, who among them would follow him into the fire to be reborn as the Moon? Only the least of them stepped forward, however; Nanahuatzin, the scabby god of lesions, and Tecciztecatl, the god of snails.

Bravely, they cast themselves into the flames, and when the fire dwindled into glowing embers, the gods waited in the darkness for the sun to appear. Hour upon hour they waited, and when it seemed the lightless canopy above them would never be broken, a glowing disc rose in the east. Slowly the light climbed into the morning sky, but it faltered midway to the zenith. The gods drew their blood and offered it to the sun, and for a moment it halted, then fell back, but Ecatl, the Wind God, stepped forward and sent it into endless motion across the heavens.

The binding of the years last took place in 1455, during the reign of Moctezuma Ilhuicamina. The preceding year was one of promising auguries, and when 2 Reed came to pass, Moctezuma embarked upon the conquests that would one day make Mexico master of the world. But now, in the fifth year of the reign of Moctezuma Xocóyotl, there was an ominous shift in the omens as the crucial date approached.

When the *nemontemi*, the five unlucky days that marked the closing of the old year arrived, people throughout the city emptied out rubbish, scrubbed the walls and floors of their homes, and threw their hearthstones and figures of the household gods into the canals. On the eve of 2 Reed, every man, woman, and child gathered on the rooftops and looked to the south, toward *Uixachlan*, a hill about eight miles southeast of the city, waiting for the sign that would tell them the world had survived the junction of the years.

On the summit of the hill, priests watched anxiously as the Pleiades rose above the horizon and mounted toward the zenith. As the constellation grew nearer, a priest ordered a high-born captive to be stretched across the sacrificial stone, and placed a wooden block on his chest. When the stars reached their proper alignment, the priest spun his fire drill into the block, and with the first flicker of flame, he thrust it into a brazier and fed it until it blossomed into a beacon that could be seen from one end of the valley to the other. Then quickly, he thrust his knife into the captive's breast and cast his heart into the fire.

As soon as the people saw the burst of fire, they drew blood from their ears and sprinkled it towards the east to set the Sun in motion. Then runners brought the new fire into the city. The first to reach the temple of Huitzilopochtli carried his torch to the top and cast it into a pile of fagotts, and a towering blaze lit the plaza below. Drums, conch horns, and whistles sounded as priests relayed the new fire to every barrio in the city, and when Tenochtitlán was bathed in the light of a thousand fires, the people left the rooftops and rekindled their hearths with embers from the new fire.

For the people, the crisis had passed and was all but forgotten as they returned to the commonplace tasks of daily life. New mats were spread throughout each household, old clothing was replaced by new mantles, new shifts and blouses, and new clay figurines of the tutelary gods were returned to their customary places alongside the hearth.

For Moctezuma, his universe was once again secure, but the unfavourable omens and the sinister prophecies that threatened his future and that of the empire continued.

Possibly no emperor in the history of Mexico was as susceptible to divinations, dreams, and omens as Moctezuma, for he consulted his necromancers every day to seek good omens or to interpret those he deemed unlucky. There were many in his court to accommodate him, but few, if any, ever brought good news.

From the first day he assumed the throne, the diviners foretold that Moctezuma would be the last of his lineage to rule Mexico; that in the eighth year of his reign, a more powerful lord would take his place. This was his worst nightmare – Quetzalcoatl's promise to return to his native land was never far from his mind.

Then there were natural phenomena that could not be explained, such as a solar eclipse, and the sudden appearance of a great comet.

Both were interpreted as signs that the end of Mexico was near. Nezahualpilli, his only confidant, nearly drove him to suicide when he interpreted the comet as a sign that Mexico's days were numbered.

There was also the mysterious fire that destroyed the shrine of Huizilopochtli. To satisfy the god, Moctezuma proposed to refurbish it with golden walls and turquoise inlays, but when a wise and trusted friend tried to discourage him, he ordered him put to death at the hands of his own family.

Moctezuma, The Angry Lord, the emperor who created a court more noble than that of the great Toltecs, the warrior who led one army after another across the sierra to make war on the most distant provinces in the land, now spent his days and nights frantically searching for dreams and divinations that would prove the omens wrong, only to learn that the worst was yet to come.

Human Sacrifice

Human sacrifice for religious purposes was common among emerging civilizations, but few, if any, reached the level and frequency of that practised in Mexico during the late fifteenth and early sixteenth centuries. From the reports of Spanish eyewitnesses and early chroniclers, wholesale sacrifice took place in every major city in Mexico, and all of its various cultures participated. None, however, matched the massacres of the Aztecs in Tenochtitlán.

The principal victims were captives taken in war, slaves bought and stored for specific ceremonies, and children. The sacrifice of children, however, was a sacrifice of the tribe's very own, and children of the élite as well as those of the commoners were at risk. Child sacrifices were generally for ceremonies preceding the rainy season, and the chosen method was by drowning. Prisoners and slaves had their hearts torn out across a stone slab in the temple.

Spanish estimates of sacrifices in Mexico covering the last years before the conquest vary from 10,000 per year to 50,000 per year, but the disparity is perhaps due to the propensity of the early chroniclers to overestimate. Descriptions of festivals given by natives during this same period yield an average count of 18,000 per year. The numbers are not exaggerated. Bernal Diaz, a Spanish soldier, counted 100,000 skulls in the plaza of Xocotlan, and Andres de Tápia, one of Cortés's officers, counted another 100,000 mounted on a rack in the ceremonial plaza of Tenochtitlán.

The most detailed account of a major sacrificial ceremony is given in an aboriginal document written some time between AD 1536 and 1539. The occasion was the dedication of the great temple of Tenochtitlan to Huitzilopochtli in 1487, during the second year of the reign of Ahuitzotl.

> Ahuitzotl demanded that every vassal lord bring his court of nobles to the ceremony, and he assessed each, according to his resources, the number of sacrifices he must bring. He also invited the lords of the independent states that lay within the borders of the empire to attend, and though they were often at war with Mexico, all considered it prudent not to offend the young emperor. And he decreed, under penalty of death, that every man, woman, and child in the city witness the spectacle.
>
> On the week of the ceremony, the vassal lords arrived, and as they led their captives along the causeways, priests censed them and pressed nosegays of flowers into their hands, and they gave them bread that had been con- secrated in the temple. They comforted each in turn and encouraged them to take heart, for now they were the children of the Sun, soon to realize eternal fame and glory.
>
> They led them to the temple and served them *octli,* then led them up the steps to the summit, where they paid homage to Huitzilopochtli. They escorted them past the palace gates for the emperor's inspection, then took them to the marketplace, where they were clothed, given sandals, feathers, and flowers, and forced to perform the ritual dance of sacrifice. Afterwards, they gave them tobacco and took them to various barrios in the city, where they were treated as honoured guests.
>
> On the eve of the ceremony, Ahuitzotl's major-domos met the lords of the independent nations on the outskirts of the city and led them to the palace of the *Cihuacoatl* disguised as Mexicans. Ahuitzotl had no intention to let his people know how he entertained their enemies, against whom they had sacrificed so many husbands, lovers, and brothers.
>
> The following morning, long before first light, the captives were taken from the barrios and formed into four queues, each beginning at the foot of the temple and stretching out along the causeways and the street that led to the lakeshore.

There the priests prepared them for sacrifice. They painted their bodies red and set feathered plumes on their heads, while others covered the stairs leading to the shrine with leafy branches and flowers of every variety.

At sunrise, a priest on the summit of the temple sounded a conch horn, and the crowd fell silent as Ahuitzotl, Nezahualpilli, the Lord of Tlacopan, and the *Cihuacoatl* mounted the steps of the temple. At the summit they separated into four groups. Ahuitzotl took his accustomed place before the altar of Huitzilopochtli, and the others moved to altars of the lesser gods.

When the lords stood ready, the *Tlalpanhuehuetl*, the great temple drum, began its heart-stopping cadence, and with the first thunderous boom, conch horns, bone whistles, wooden drums, tambourines, tortoise-shell timbrels, and rattles sounded from every temple in the city.

Ahuitzotl stepped up to the altar, and at his nod, four priests whose bodies, hands, and feet were painted red and black, seized the first victim and dragged him to the altar. As they spread the captive across the arched surface of the sacrificial stone, Ahuitzotl squatted in front of Huitzilopochtli and touched the middle finger to the ground. Then he licked the dirt of the temple floor from the finger, and pointed to the god before him. He stood up and raised his knife to the north, then to the east, the south, and the west.

Suddenly he turned and drove the knife into the victim's breast and ripped it open from one side to the other, exposing the still-beating heart through a surge of blood. He slashed again at the gaping chest and the heart seemed to leap into his hands as he raised it on high, offering it in turn to each of the cardinal points. He handed the heart to a waiting priest, who took it to a brazier in the centre of the eagle stone, and others tumbled the body down the side of the temple.

The other lords performed their sacrifices in the same manner as Ahuitzotl performed his, and when they tired, they gave their knives to the priests.

Soon a steady stream of blood flowed down the sides of the temple, and as quickly as the wash of blood spilled over the rim of the lowest platform, waiting priests scooped it into buckets and set out to smear the doorways, lintels, and walls of the lesser temples. Whatever was left over was poured on the heads of the tutelary gods.

The carnage lasted for four days, and by the second day, the air was foul with the stench of blood, excrement, and flesh decaying in the afternoon sun. At night, fires glowed throughout the city as the bodies of the victims were dismembered. Their thighs and arms were boiled in steaming caul-drons for the feast that followed, and their heads were reduced to bare skulls

A human sacrifice as shown in an ancient manuscript

and mounted on the commemorative rack in the plaza to whiten in the sun. The torsos were thrown into the lake, and the entrails into a deep well that runs into the bowels of the Earth, where they also cast albinos, two-headed babies, and other deformed creatures during time of drought.

Only Ahuitzotl's guests and enemies were spared the ungodly stench of the city and the unsightly disposal of the remains of the captives. They saw only the spectacle taking place on the temple, hidden from sight on the roof of the *Cihuacoatl's* palace, in a retreat covered with leafy branches and fragrant flowers. When the ceremony was over, Ahuitzotl sent them home with precious jewels, gold shields, luxurious feathers, and elegant mantles as keepsakes of the wholesale slaughter of 4,000 men.★

Mass killing of innocent people was not limited to the Aztec, however. During Ahuitzotl's reign, Thomás de Torquemada burned 2,000 heretics at the stake in civilized Europe.

★ The number of sacrifices made by Ahuitzotl varies widely from one source to another. Of the two Spanish chroniclers known to have had access to the aboriginal document, known as the Chronica X, Fray Diego Duran states that 80,400 captives were killed, and Juan de Torquemada sets the number at 72,344. Tezozomoc, the nephew of Moctezuma, agrees with Duran. Many historians, however, accept 20,000 as the most likely number, since it is inscribed on a tablet commemorating the ceremony. Nigel Davis suggests that number may have been no more than 2,000 if the number of units on the tablets had been misread. If one considers how many minutes the priests needed for one sacrifice, and the logistics of disposing of the bodies, 4,000 appears to be the maximum number possible.

Aztec Culture

THE ARTS

Poetry was a highly esteemed art among the Mexicans, and usually combined with song and action when recited. Many noblemen were among Mexico's finest poets, the most notable of whom was Nezahualcóyotl, the great king of Texcoco. Some of his odes were translated into Castillian as early as the seventeenth century, and modern translations are available in Nahuatl, English, and French.

The themes of Mexico's leading poets deal with the deeds of heroes and the grandeur of Mexico, but more often with the vanities, delights, melancholy, and fickleness of life. Much of Mexican poetry associates flowers with death. The recital of their poetry often contains elements of the dramatic arts. Actors wore the clothing of national and mythical heroes, and combined verse and song with dialogue in their plays.

> Now I would sing, since time and place
>   Are mine,-and oh! with thee
> May this song obtain the grace
>   My purpose claims for me.
> I wake these notes on song intent,
> But call it rather a lament
> Do thou, beloved, now delight
> In these flowers pure and bright,
>   Rejoicing with thy friend;
> Now let us banish pain and fear,
> For, if our joys are measured here
>   Life's sadness hath its end.
> (Introduction to a ten-stanza poem by Nezahualcóyotl.)★

ARCHITECTURE AND SCULPTURE

The most powerful expression of Aztec architecture was its great temples, shrines, and palaces. In the central plaza of Tenochtitlán, the temple dedicated to Huitzilopochtli and Tlaloc rose 200 feet above the plaza floor, and a mile to the north, in what is now the Plaza of

★ William Hickling Prescott, The Conquest of Mexico n.d.

Three Cultures, the Tlatlolco temple once stood in the great market place of Tenochtitlán. One hundred and fourteen steps led to the summit, where a shrine held a grotesque representation of Huitzilopochli.

The ingenuity of the Mexican architects is found in the novel design of their temples. In pre-Columbian times, the Aztecs were aware that the city was settling into the lake bed, as it does today. To reduce the weight of their temples, the builders used *tezontle*, a light, porous volcanic rock, to construct the cores of the walls and the platforms, and used basalt and other hard stone for the stairways, the outer walls, and façades.

Moctezuma I, Axayácatl, Ahuitzotl, and Moctezuma II built their sumptuous palaces about the central plaza. Of these, the palace of Moctezuma II was the grandest. *Tezontli,* the red porous stone of the valley, was combined with a decorative touch of marble to form the outer walls, and a medallion above the entry bore an eagle holding an ocelot in its talons. The vast ceilings were inlaid with cedar and other decorative woods, and held together without nails.

The armoury, where Moctezuma's military costumes and weapons were exhibited, lay outside the gates. Next to the armoury, a spacious aviary displayed every species of bird in Anahuac. Parrots, golden pheasants, hummingbirds, and the rare and prized quetzal soared freely as if they were in their native habitat. Eagles, vultures, hawks and other birds of prey were isolated from them in a separate section. Adjoining the aviary was a menagerie of wild animals, and a building for every variety of serpent found in Mexico. Three hundred workers managed and maintained the facilities, and 500 turkeys a day were needed to feed the collection. On the outer perimeter of the palace grounds, ten large basins were stocked with every variety of fish, and by each, a pavilion was provided for spectators.

The most magnificent examples of residential architecture were designed and built by Nezahualcóyotl, the great lord of Texcoco. His complex of royal residences, public offices, and estates for his nobles, more than 400 buildings in all, covered more than 250 acres. Around the circumference, he built a brick wall six feet wide and nine feet high to enclose the market place, his council chambers, halls of justice, embassies, accommodation for scientists and artists, and the great library of Texcoco.*

Netzahualcóyotl's favourite residence lay on a hill about six miles from Texcoco. The palace was built upon terraces covered with hanging gardens, and a flight of 520 steps rose from the base of the hill to the summit. In the garden at the top of the hill, a large rock, carved with the years of Nezahualcóyotl's reign and his principal achievements, stood in the middle of a reservoir. On the lower terraces, three reservoirs contained statues of women, and at the ground level, a winged lion holding a picture of Nezahualcóyotl in its mouth stood in a fourth reservoir.

From these basins, water flowed into spacious gardens, where baths and pavilions were available for the household.

Much of Aztec sculpture illustrates their preoccupation with physical and carnal motifs rather than moral or spiritual forces. The theme is most evident in the statue of Coatlicue, the mother of Huitzilopochtli. The figure stands eight feet high, and the head is formed by two snake heads staring into each others eyes. A skull medallion hangs from a necklace of hands and hearts to a skirt of writhing snakes. There are claws on her feet, and she stands upon the Earth monster.

Gentler themes are seen in life-sized sculptures of the gods of nature, maize, agriculture, and common people. Exceptional examples of the gods of nature are those of Xochopilli, the god of flowers, and the Corn Goddess. Seated, Xochopilli looks skywards and sings as he holds a rattle in each hand. The Corn Goddess is a beautifully carved figure of a bare-breasted young girl, praying upon her knees.

The Monument of the Fifth Sun, a great stone disc 12 feet in diameter and weighing 24 metric tons, was once thought to be a calendar because of the ring of day signs carved about its centre. Its purpose, however, is to provide a permanent record of the Aztec cosmos. The

---

* Despite their high level of culture and political skills, however, the Mexicans possessed no alphabet or written language, relying instead upon oral tradition, songs, hymns, and poems to recall their history, and upon pictorial representations to portray their gods, religious ceremonies, social order, conquests, tribute lists, laws, events of note, daily life, and dates. Although they did develop a few phonetic signs, they were used primarily for the names of persons and places.

face of Tonatiuh, the god of the Fifth Sun, is carved in the centre of the stone. The god wears an elaborate head-dress, jade ear plugs, and a sacrificial knife hangs from his mouth. Concentric circles about the god contain hieroglyphs and the twenty name days of the Aztec calendar. The outer border is formed by the bodies of two great fire snakes. Reliefs around the central figure identify the dates when each of the previous suns perished; the first by jaguars, the second by wind, the third by rain and fire, and the fourth by water.

Painting was used more often to record commercial and legal proceedings rather than the pursuit of fine arts. The justice system used painted records for registering laws, filing the proceedings of trials, and for the recording of real property transactions. In the last case, the Spaniards found them sufficiently accurate to use in their legal system.

Hieroglyphic painting was also used to record tributes from the provinces, mythology, calendars, and rituals, but more often the Aztecs used direct representation of the subject. The mediums used for paintings were cotton cloth, skins, and the leaves of the agave cactus. Many of the hieroglyphs were grotesque caricatures of the human figure, such as monsters with overgrown heads on puny, misshapen bodies. All were hard and angular in outline, and bore little resemblance to the objects they represented. The colours were gaudy and bright, and contrasted sharply with each other. The figures had no perspective – the head appeared only in profile with an eye in the middle. Emblems were used for things the painter could not represent, such as years, months, days, seasons, elements, and heavens. A tongue, for instance signified speaking, a footprint travelling, and a man sitting on the ground an earthquake. They did develop a few phonetic signs, but they were used primarily for places and persons. None of the fine shadings of nature is seen in their paintings.

The walls of all the palaces were decorated with frescos, as were many of their monuments. They were not, however, comparable with the great murals of Teotihuacán, nor the codices of the Maya. The frescos of Tenochtitlan did not survive the conquest, but examples may still be found in places far from the city.

Accurate paintings were sent from the sea coast to Moctezuma describing the Spaniards, their ships, horses, cannon, and weapons long before they arrived in Tenochtitlan.

JURISPRUDENCE

Crime was relatively rare among the Aztecs, since punishment for what would be considered today as a minor infraction might demand the death penalty. The harshness of the law was applied to all classes of society, more so for the upper classes, and was applied more to enforce personal security than property disputes. Torture was unknown, and detention was never considered as a penalty for crime.

Death was the penalty for murder, even if the victim was only a slave. Adultery was punishable by death, and thievery, depending upon the degree, was punishable either by death or by slavery. Robbery and minor theft in the market place were summarily punished by stoning the thief to death. Public drunkenness, save for those over seventy, was considered a capital crime, but only for a second offence. Drinking *pulque* at festivals, however, was within the law.

Civil jurisprudence was both liberal and enlightened. The institution of marriage was recognized under the law, and no matter how many concubines were in the household, only the descendants of the legitimate wife could inherit the estate. Divorce was also recognized by the law, but would be granted only in cases of desertion by either party. If a wife was sterile or neglectful of her household duties these were grounds for divorce. A divorced wife, however, was entitled to half the assets of the couple and could remarry.

Women also had the right to sue in court, engage in commerce, and enter the priesthood, albeit on a limited basis.

DAILY LIFE

The moment a Mexican child was born, the parents consulted a priest to see if the day of birth was lucky or unlucky. If the date was found to be auspicious, a feast was held on the fourth day and the child was given its name. If the child was a boy, a shield and four arrows were placed in his hands; if it was a girl, a shuttle and a box. Should the day prove to be unfavourable, however, the priest would search the book of fate for a more propitious time for the baptism.

The name chosen for a boy was usually that of the day of his birth, such as 4 Reed, or one that could be represented in pictographs, such as Itzcoatl (Obsidian Serpent), Chimalpopoca (Smoking Mirror), or Moctezuma (Angry Lord). Girl's names were usually combined with *xochitl,* the word for flower.

During the early years, children received a practical education that consisted of little more than simple household tasks. In the pre-teen years and early teens, boys were taught fishing and handling water craft, and the girls spinning and weaving. For the first eight years, punishment was limited to scolding, but after that, discipline was enforced by pricking the hand with agave thorns, lying bound and naked in a mud-puddle, or being forced to breathe the fumes of red peppers cooking over an open fire.

Nevertheless, the Mexican people were devoted to their children, and all, regardless of their status in the community, were guaranteed an education.

Male children of the upper classes attended the *calmecac,* a preparatory school for the priesthood or high office in government, although children of the lower classes sometimes gained admission. The training was rigorous, and punishment severe for the least fault.

Life in the *telpochcalli,* the lower class school, could be quite pleasant. During the day, the masters taught military science, tradition, history, religious orthodoxy, and a variety of crafts. The hours after sunset, however, belonged to the students, which they devoted to pleasure in the *cuicacalco,* the 'House of Singing', dancing with each other and with their mistresses well into the night.

Young women were either trained to become priestesses in the temple, or taught weaving, featherwork, and other crafts in schools that were equivalent to the *telpochcalli.*

A young man might marry when he was twenty, but a girl was considered mature and ready for marriage by the time she was sixteen. Before the couple could marry, however, the boy must have completed his instructions at the *calmecac* or the *telpochcalli,* and have the consent of his masters.

Both were free to select the partner of their choice, but marriage within the same clan was forbidden. After the soothsayers consulted the book of fates to determine if the marriage signs were favourable, the families called upon two elderly women to negotiate the bride's dowry and the gifts of the bridegroom to her family.

On the eve of the wedding, the bridegroom received a lecture from his masters, calling for him to behave like a worthy servant of the gods, to work hard to feed and provide for his family, and to show courage in times of war. The father and mother of the bride-to-be each delivered a homily on how she was to conduct herself as a woman and a wife.

The mother's lecture:

O dove, little one, my child, thou hast grasped the spirit of thy father. Although thou art a woman, thou art his image. And of this, what more shall I say? What more shall I tell thee?

Nowhere reject the spirit, the works, of thy father, for they are as precious as green stones, as precious as turquoises. Take them, place them by thy heart, inscribe them on thy heart. If thou art to live by them, thou wilt instruct and indoctrinate thy children.

And behold a second word which I give thee. Look to me, for I am thy mother. I carried thee for so many months, and when they were ended, I lulled you to sleep, I lay thee in thy cradle, I placed thee on my lap, and certainly with my milk I gave thee strength.

In order that thou wilt live prudently, thou art not to clothe thyself ostentatiously. Thou art not to place on thyself finely worked clothing, replete with design, for it achieveth gaudiness.

And never long for, never desire the colour, the cosmetics, the darkening of the teeth, the colouring of the teeth, the colouring of the mouth; for they denote perverseness, they mean drunkenness. That is the property of the restless ones, the dissolute ones, the evil women; that is the domain of those who have become drunk, those who go eating jimson weed; that is the way of life of those who drink pulque. These are the ones called harlots.

And thy speech is not to come forth hurriedly. As thou art to speak, thou art not to be brutish, not to rush, nor to disquiet. Thy speech is to come forth in tranquillity and with gentleness. Thou art not to squeak, nor to murmur.

And when thou art to travel, do not travel in great haste, nor art thou to amble; for this achieveth pompousness. Thou art to go deliberately; but when thou findest it necessary, go swiftly, use discretion. Jump at thy jumping place in order that thou wilt not become a fat one, an inflated one.

As thou art to go, thou art not to look here and there, not to look from side to side not constantly to look upward, nor art thou to be a hypocrite. Nor art thou to put hatred in thine eyes; thou art not to put hatred in thy face. Look joyously at everyone.

Behold yet another thing with which I end my words. If thou art to live, if thou art to continue a little on earth, do not anywhere be friendly by means of your body, my little one. Do not anywhere give thyself wantonly to another.

If still thou hast not been good, if already thou art a woman, and thou hast been asked for, never will thou be at peace with another, for it will always be remembered, of thee; it will always cause thy misery, thy torment. Never wilt thou achieve peace, never tranquillity. Thy helpmate, thy husband, will always suspect.

Never at any time abuse thy helpmate, thy husband, never ever betray him; as the saying is said, do not commit adultery. If it becometh discovered of thee, if it becometh known of thee, thou wilt be cast upon the road, thou wilt be dragged on the road, thy head will be crushed with a stone, thy head will be fractured.

And this, my youngest one, my daughter, child, little one: live in calm, in peace on earth, if thou art to continue for a while. Do not with anything dishonor thyself. And do not with anything raise up the head of thy father, from whom thou art descended. And as for us, may we through thee gain glory; may we gain renown.

As related by the Mexicans to Bernardino de Sahagun, and documented in the Florentine Codex.

After marriage, the groom was entitled to a plot of land to feed and house his family. This was the inalienable right of every married man within the *calpulli*, the tribal unit that controlled the community lands. None could take the land from him save as punishment for serious crimes, refusal to work the land, or to leave the land uncultivated for three years. The system was not too different from the *ejido* of the modern Mexican Indian.

The register of land and its distribution was kept up to date by one of the elected officers of the *calpulli*, and as his family grew, his land allotment was increased to meet its needs, and when the children married and left, it was accordingly reduced. When he died, his son inherited the right to work his father's land, and for widows and people

too old or infirm to work the land, the *calpulli* arranged for its cultivation.

His children were entitled to attend the local *telpochcalli*, and his
family took part in the religious ceremonies and social life of the
community. His obligations included maintenance and upkeep of the
community, such as building roads and temples, and he was subject to
taxes. In time of war, he served his country in the military, which was
considered a privilege and a religious duty.

If he was diligent and contributed to the welfare of the gods, he
could rise to high office among the elders of the *calpulli*. If he lived in an
urban community, there was always the opportunity to move upward
in the priesthood, the military, or the government. And for an
opportunistic few, there was always the chance, though remote, that
one might enjoy the emperor's favour.

CHAPTER FIVE

Conquest

The Discovery of Mexico

Francisco Fernández de Córdoba, an entrepreneur seeking gold and slaves for service in the haciendas of Cuba, set sail for the coast of Honduras on 8 February 1517. A storm drove his ships far north of his course, and after seven days lost at sea, he reached the unknown coast of Yucatán. On shore, the crew saw large towns, temples built of stone, and natives wearing cotton clothing dyed in many colours.

Upon landing, he found a few gold medals, pendants, bits of jewellery, and some fine pottery. The gold in the artifacts was an alloy of low-grade ore and copper, but the workmanship was that of a culture far more advanced than any other in the New World. He captured two Indians to learn the language, and sailed down the Gulf Coast.

He received a warm welcome from the natives when he reached the site of the present city of Campeche, but met with disaster when he attempted to land at Champotón. Less than half the men survived to reach Cuba, and Córdoba died of his wounds shortly afterwards.

The evidence of wealth in the new land to the west was specious at best, but it was sufficient for Diego Velásquez, the governor of Cuba, to organize an expedition to lay claim to it. He chose Juan de Grijalva as his captain-general, and on 4 May 1518, his fleet of four ships reached the island of Cozumel, 12 miles off the Caribbean coast of the Yucatán Peninsula.

He explored the Yucatán coast as far south as the Bahia de Ascención, passing by a number of towns where people on the beaches waved banners at him. Convinced that Yucatán was an island, he sought a passage through the bay, hoping to reach the Gulf of Mexico. The effort proved fruitless, and he abandoned the search and sailed around the peninsula to the Gulf Coast.

On 5 June the fleet arrived at Potonchán, where the confluence of the Usmacinta and the Río Grijalva★ sends a current of fresh water six miles out into the sea. The Indians were friendly, and during his stay Grijalva received the first hints that Yucatán was not an island. An Indian captive told him that the natives gathered gold from a river three days inland, and that further in the interior, there were high sierras, broad savannas, great forests, and cities where the inhabitants made sacrifices to their gods. When he made preparations to depart, the crew begged him to establish a colony there, but he ordered them to keep to the ships.

On 14 June Grijalva reached a small island three miles off the shores of Veracruz. By now he had reached the conclusion that the land was an unknown continent. Two hundred and fifty miles of unbroken coastline and high sierra lay between Potonchán and their present position, and the volume of fresh water that flowed from the interior into the sea could come only from a vast land. He claimed the continent in the name of Diego Velásquez.

The following day the Spaniards set out to explore the island, and in a small temple, they came upon the first evidence of human sacrifice and cannibalism in Mexico. From an Indian, Grijalva learned that it was customary to sacrifice captives, then eat their legs and arms. He named it the *Isla de Sacrificios*.

The fleet moved to an anchorage close to shore, which Grijalva named *San Juan de Ulúa*, where the Spaniards found the Indians friendly and hospitable. They fed them, taught them the use of tobacco, and traded with them. When asked about gold, they told them that it could be found in the interior, a half-day's journey from the coast. In the sierra, an Indian could sift nuggets from the sand on the bottom of the rivers.

The fleet sailed northwards as far as Cape Rojo, but adverse winds and currents forced Grijalva to turn back. After a hazardous journey, he reached Cuba on 29 September 1518.

★ The crew named the river after their commander.

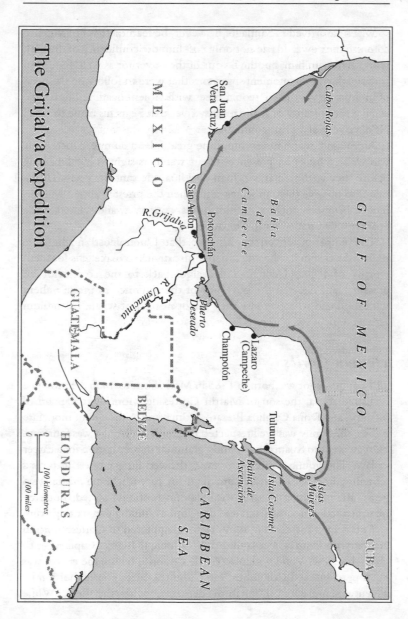

The Grijalva expedition

When he arrived in Santiago, however, he learned that his failure to colonize the new land had not only cost him the confidence of the men who sailed with him, but the favour of the governor as well. Instead of participating in the momentous events that were to follow on the heels of his historic voyage, he would meet with violent death in Nicaragua, leaving for posterity only the mighty river that bears his name to recall his discovery of a great continent.

Although Grijalva never found the great inland empire, Moctezuma was well aware of his presence. Coast watchers sighted his ships long before they anchored at San Juan de Ulúa. He sent the priest Tlilancalqui to observe them in secret, and when the priest returned with his report, he also brought with him beads, conserves, and wine that the Spaniards had traded with the natives.

The emperor, driven by his fear that Quetzalcoatl might have returned to claim his throne, ordered his artisans to make gifts for them worthy of a god. He sent Tlilancalqui back to the coast with his presents, and directed the governor of the province to provide them with food and whatever else they might need. But when Tlilancalqui arrived, Grijalva was gone.

Hernán Cortés

The conquistador was born in 1485 in Medellin, a town in the province of Estremadura, the son of Martin Cortés de Montroy, a captain of infantry, and Doña Catalina Pizzaro Altimarino. Although of moderate means, the family was well respected in Castile. When he was fourteen, Hernán went to Salamanca to study grammar in preparation for a career in law. The young Cortés, however, showed little interest in formal schooling and books, and returned to his parent's home within two years. But his time in Salamanca was not entirely wasted, since he managed to learn some Latin and developed considerable writing skills.

At the age of seventeen, two prospects appealed to Cortés: to go to Naples with Gonzálo Fernández de Córdoba, the Great Captain, or to go to the New World with Nicolas de Ovando, whom the crown was sending to succeed Columbus. He chose the latter course, but a misadventure prevented him from departing with the fleet. While

Hernán Cortés, the conqueror of Mexico

climbing a garden wall to keep a rendezvous with one of his lovers, the wall crumbled and gave way, tumbling him down on to the pavement and burying him under the stones. Cortés's injuries were severe enough to confine him to bed until well after Ovando sailed.

Cortés finally departed for the New World in 1504, the year Isabella died. In Santo Domingo, Cortés was given a *repartimiento*★ and an appointment as notary of the town of Azua, where he engaged in trade for the next five years. During this period, however, his philandering continued, and on occasion, resulted in affairs of honour that cost him life-long scars.

In 1509, Diego Columbus succeeded Ovando, and in 1511, the eldest son of the Great Admiral assigned Diego Velásquez the task of pacifying Cuba. Cortés accompanied him as clerk to the royal treasurer,

★ Lands given as a fief to the conquistadors.

whose duties were to keep account of the royal revenues and the king's fifth share.

In time, Velásquez granted him a generous *encomienda** of Indians and appointed him mayor of St Jago. He now devoted himself to agriculture, and raised sheep, cattle, and mares. He enjoyed some success in gold mining, and eventually gained sufficient wealth to invest 2,000 castellanos into a partnership with Andrés de Duero, Velásquez's secretary.

Life was comfortable and rewarding for the young Cortés when news of Grijalva's discovery reached Cuba.

Velásquez immediately set about organizing a major expedition to the new land, and there was no lack of prominent cavaliers who offered to serve as his commander. The governor, however, was more interested in a commander who could provide enough capital to finance the greater cost of the endeavour. Many were considered for the command, but Cortés had military experience, and more important, he had 2,000 castellanos in gold and a lucrative partnership with Andrés de Duero.

With his appointment as captain–general of the expedition, Cortés purchased three ships with 5,000 castellanos of his own money, assumed a note to buy enough salt pork to feed the company for five months, and, with the aid of his friends, secured loans to buy four more ships and to finance all volunteers who were short of funds. The contribution of Velásquez is not clear, but word had it that he provided three weatherworn ships and provisions which he sold to the company at outrageous profits.

Diego Velásquez's instructions to Cortés were to update the charts along the coast of New Spain, spread the Catholic faith among the Indians, encourage them to become vassals of the King of Spain, learn more about the presence of a cross that had been observed among the natives, search for six castaways that were reported lost in the area, determine the resources of the country, especially gold, and send news of his progress as soon as possible, along with all the gold, jewels, and other products of the land he obtained.

---

* A grant of Indians who paid tribute to his master in exchange for his welfare and religious instruction.

No instructions were given to Cortés to establish a colony in New Spain, inasmuch as Diego Velásquez had not yet received a warrant from the Crown, and the *Audienca* in Santo Domingo had granted him no more than the right to trade with the natives.

Velásquez, however, reminded by relatives of his past difficulties with Cortés, began to have second thoughts about his choice of a commander. He was further troubled when a court jester called out, 'Have a care, master Velásquez, or we shall have to go ahunting someday or other after this same captain of ours!'

The governor spoke of his concerns to Andrés de Duero and Amador de Lares, but Cortés was too heavily indebted to them, and they had no intention of jeopardizing their investment in the expedition. They urged Cortés to leave immediately if he was to retain his command.

Cortés had not yet a full complement of ships, men, and provisions, but he weighed anchor and sailed out of port that same day. Stopping only long enough to pick up rations and crew along the coast, he rounded Cape San Antonio on the western end of Cuba on 18 February 1519, and set sail for New Spain.★

THE EXPEDITION TO MEXICO

Cortés made his first landing on Cozumel, where he mustered eleven ships, 553 soldiers, 110 mariners, 200 Cuban porters, and a few women. His armament included 16 horse, 10 heavy guns, 4 falconets, 13 muskets, and 32 crossbows.

He sent a company into Yucatán to seek the Spaniards Córdoba reported as being held in captivity, but when no trace of them was found, he set sail for Yucatán. One of the ships began taking in water, however, forcing him to return to the island for repairs. Two days later, as Cortés was again preparing to set sail, a canoe with four Indians aboard was seen landing on the beach. Three fled when the Spaniards approached, but the fourth stepped forward and said, 'Gentlemen, are you Christians?'

While travelling from Darien to Hispaniola, Jerónimo de Aguilar,

★ The name given to Mexico by Grijalva.

had been shipwrecked off the coast of Yucatán in 1511. All the crew, save for Aguilar and Gonzálo Guerrero, perished from hunger or were sacrificed by the natives. Guerrero married a wealthy Indian woman, and eventually became a Maya chieftain. Aguilar fell into the hands of a powerful chief, to whom, in time, he became a valued servant. When word reached the interior eight years later that bearded men had again landed on Cozumel, the chieftain released Aguilar with his promise that the Spaniards would reward him with a rich treasure. Aguilar's knowledge of the Maya language would be crucial for Cortés's campaign.

Three weeks later, the Spaniards defeated a superior Maya force at Centla, a town near Potonchán. As a peace offering, the chieftain gave Cortés 20 women to cook for his men. Among them was a young woman who had been raised in a Nahuatl-speaking village and subsequently sold to the Chontal Maya, where she learned their language. Through Aguilar and the woman, whom the Spaniards called Marina, Cortés had access to the lingua franca of Mexico.

Nothing that Grijalva had seen or experienced prepared Cortés for the imperial reception he received when he reached San Juan de Ulúa. Grijalva, for want of an interpreter and over eager to return to Cuba with the profits of his enterprise, failed to learn that the petty chieftains he bartered with were no more than minor vassals of a supreme lord who controlled the immeasurable wealth of the land. By his failure, he presented Cortés with an opportunity seldom realized in the course of history.

Moctezuma's nobles welcomed them as if they were gods. When Teuhtliltl, the governor of the province, learned that the strangers planned to remain in Mexico, he sent 500 natives to set up shelters for them and 4,000 porters laden with roasted fowl, tamales, beans, and every variety of fruit in the province. The following day he arrived with an entourage of nobles, bearing gifts for the Spaniards and a message of welcome from Moctezuma.

Moctezuma was confused and upset when Teuhtliltl's message arrived, informing him that Cortés was determined to meet him. Cortés claimed to be the ambassador of a powerful lord across the sea, and spoke of bringing a new religion to Mexico. But if he was truly an ambassador, why had he come with an army and an arsenal of the most powerful weapons Mexico had ever seen? Choosing a course of discretion, Moctezuma decided to welcome him as a god, but keep him at a safe distance until his intentions became clear.

He sent the gifts he had prepared for Grijalva, but added a sun disc 30 inches in diameter cast from pure gold, a moon disc cast from silver, and the costumes of Quetzalcoatl. He also sent an apology for not being able to receive Cortés at this time, since he was ill. If, however, he insisted on coming to Mexico, he was welcome to come with a few companions, and the emperor would send an armed escort of Mexican warriors for his protection.

The terms were unacceptable to Cortés, and the following morning, Teuhtliltl withdrew his support and left the Spaniards stranded on the coast.

Cortés was now faced with an urgent problem. Fresh water was in critically short supply, the men were plagued with the oppressive heat of the dunes, and tortured constantly by sand flies and mosquitoes. He could not go forward, and retreat was unthinkable – the opportunity granted him by fate could not be squandered.

Luck was once again on his side. A Totonac chieftain, a reluctant tributary of Mexico, invited him to bring his company to Cempoala, a coastal town some 25 miles north of his position. Furthermore, the pilot-major had found a suitable anchorage in the lee of a rocky prominence just 15 miles north of the city.

Cortés's decision to move to Cempoala was not well received by many of the company, however. The fighting at Centla had cost the lives of 40 men, and Moctezuma, who could field an army as great as Spain, had proved hostile. Better to return to Cuba now, they argued, and allow Diego Velásquez to organize an army capable of mounting an effective campaign. Furthermore, the governor had as yet no warrant to colonize the country, and Cortés was obliged to return to Cuba now that he had satisfied his commission.

Cortés realized that once they returned to Cuba with Moctezuma's treasure, every fortune hunter in the New World as well as the Old would descend upon New Spain. He was determined to stay, and all the penniless adventurers and minor landholders who lacked the patronage of Diego Velásquez supported him. With him were also those who had sailed with Grijalva, still bitter about the lost opportunities that his failure had cost them. They had been promised a colony when they were recruited, and notices to this effect had been posted throughout Cuba. If Velásquez had no warrant to colonize the land, then they were no longer bound by his orders.

In the end, Cortés's supporters prevailed, and a charter for a crown colony was drawn up and prepared for submission to the King of Spain. Cortés submitted his resignation to the elected leaders of the colony, and left them to their deliberations. The colony was recorded as the Villa Rica de la Vera Cruz, and the council asked Cortés to serve as Chief Justice of New Spain and captain-general of the armed forces until they received instructions from the Crown. For his investment in the venture, they awarded him one-fifth of all future profits.

The Totonac chieftain of Cempoala, who was so fat that two men had to support him when he stood, proved to be a gracious host. Cortés found him to be shrewd and well informed, and spent every moment listening to his complaints about Moctezuma.

During his two-week stay in Cempoala, Cortés learned that 38 provinces recognized the imperial eagle of Mexico, but other than a select few, none profited from their alliance with the empire. Nothing more than tributaries, Moctezuma systematically stripped them of their resources, leaving behind only enough to sustain them until his tax collectors returned again. The military force that held this vast empire hostage was made up of three city states in the Valley of Mexico: Tacuba, Texcoco, and Tenochtitlán. There had been periodic revolts against Mexico, some as distant as the uncharted Southern Sea, but each time the alliance crushed them with a bloodletting that left the population weak and impotent into the following generation.

Oddly enough, while Moctezuma's control over his most distant provinces was absolute, he tolerated provinces within a few miles of Tenochtitlán that openly defied him. Three independent states, Tlaxcala, Huexotzingo, and Cholula, warred incessantly with him, but their alliances were too fragile to form a united front.

From Cempoala, the Spaniards moved a few miles north to

Quiahuitzlan, where there was a safe anchorage. There they laid the foundations for the first colony in New Spain.

It was now time for Cortés to justify his decision to colonize the land contrary to Velásquez's directives from the Spanish Crown. It would not be easy. Francisco de Saucedo, a cavalier who had followed Cortés's track from Cuba, brought word that the king had appointed Diego Velásquez governor-for-life of Yucatán and all the lands he discovered nearby.

If Cortés submitted his case through the normal channels of communication between the New World and the Crown, he would surely be denied and most likely tried for treason. There was, however, a legal instrument that would allow Cortés to circumvent the Crown's administrators and submit his case directly to the king. In the thirteenth century, Alfonso X created the *Siete Partidas,* a covenant between the king and his subjects that upheld the right of all men to act in the Crown's interest whenever self-serving private enterprise conflicted with the public interest.

To this end, Francisco de Montejo and Alonso de Puertocarrero, the *alcaldes* of the colony, wrote to the king asking him not to grant any concessions or judicial authority to Diego Velásquez, lest his corruption and favouritism despoil New Spain as it had Cuba. They requested that in his place, Cortés be named chief justice and captain-general of New Spain until a judge was appointed to investigate their charges against Velásquez. Their letter to the king was accompanied by every item of Moctezuma's treasure to ensure a favourable hearing before the capital-hungry court.

Montejo and Puertocarrero set sail for Spain on 16 July 1519, bound for the port of Palos. Alaminos, the pilot-major, was under orders to pass well north of Cuba, keeping to the hazardous Bahama Channel, where one of the governor's ships would be less likely to intercept him. Under no circumstances was he to stop at any port in Cuba.

Word of the king's grant to Diego Velásquez, however, had its effect upon his supporters. The priest Juan Díaz prevailed upon a few mariners to seize a ship and make sail for Cuba, and if they reached Santiago in good time, the governor could intercept the treasure ship north of Hispaniola, or failing that, send word to have it impounded when it

reached Palos. The plot would have succeeded had one of the conspirators not betrayed his companions. Cortés ordered two conspirators
hanged, the feet of the pilot cut off, and a hundred lashes for each of the
mariners. Díaz, as a priest, could not be tried in a civil court.

Cortés now realized that he could not leave a hundred and fifty men
in garrison at Vera Cruz while he marched off to Mexico, not while a
single ship remained in port to tempt others to reach the outside world.
The ships were stripped of rigging, chains, and everything useful, then
scuttled in ten fathoms of water.

THE MARCH TO THE INTERIOR

On 16 August 1519, the Spaniards left Vera Cruz and set out for
Mexico. The army numbered some 450 foot, 300 Cempoalan warriors,
15 horse, 6 cannon, 200 Indian porters, and 40 Cempoalan nobles,
taken as hostages to guarantee the lives of 150 men Cortés left behind in
the garrison.

Guided by three Totonac nobles, Cortés chose the difficult northern
route to the tableland rather than risk crossing the pass through Tepeaca
to the south, where a large Mexican army was in garrison.

The northern route climbs to a height of 10,000 feet before it reaches
the pass between Orizaba to the south, and Nauhcampatepetl, a massive granite block, to the north. The heavy layer of ash that covers the
slopes of Nauhcampatepetl provides a precarious footing at best, and
the raw winds that blow from its crest make the climb wearying to the
very soul. Beyond the pass lies a barren desert, a vast area of salt lakes
and marshes interrupted by desolate stretches of sand as far as the eye
can see. Water is scarce, but during the rainy season, the route is all but
impassable. Before the army reached the other side of the wasteland, all
the Cuban porters died of exposure.

On the thirteenth day of their journey, the Spaniards reached the
borders of Tlaxcala. Cortés sent two Cempoalan nobles to speak with
the leaders of the republic to request safe passage through their territory. In return, he offered an alliance with Tlaxcala to protect them
against Mexico. Maxixca, the spokesman of the republic, favoured
Cortés's proposal, but Xicotencatl, the captain-general of Tlaxcala,
considered the Spaniards a threat to the republic. Backed by the army,

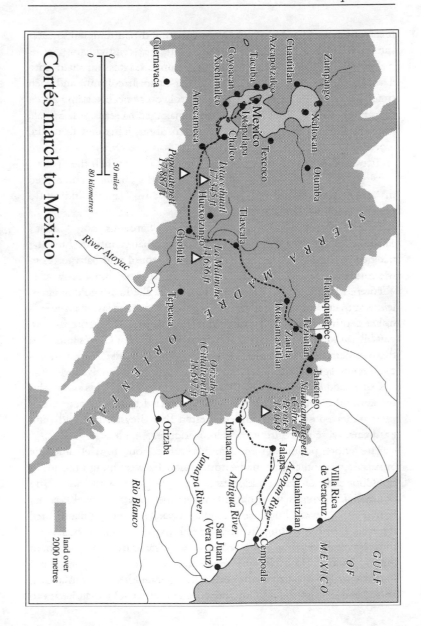

Cortés march to Mexico

the decision was made to attack the Spaniards if they attempted to enter the republic.

When the Cempoalans failed to return, Cortés marched into Tlaxcala. Twice Xicotencatl attacked the Spanish column, and each time the Spanish cavalry took a heavy toll on the Tlaxcalans. Xicotencatl regrouped his forces, but Cortés managed to reach a defensible position in Teocacingo, a fortified town about 35 miles from the capital.

The siege lasted less than a week. The end came when the Spanish cavalry caught Xicotencatl by surprise in a nearby cornfield and routed his army. Maxixca ordered Xicotencatl back to Tlaxcala and sent a peace mission to Cortés.

By now Moctezuma had grown increasingly anxious about Cortés's steady advance into the tableland. Rather than confront him, he decided to appease Cortés with an offer he would find hard to resist. Moctezuma's ambassadors reached Cortés in Tlaxcala shortly after Xicotencatl surrendered. They gave him quills filled with gold nuggets, jewellery, and cotton mantles, and when the last gift lay at his feet, a noble stepped forward and spoke. Moctezuma, he said, was prepared to pay tribute to his emperor each and every year, and for Cortés himself, a treasure worthy of a king was waiting for him. The offer, however, was contingent upon Cortés's leaving the country immediately.

Cortés said he kissed the hands of Moctezuma for his gifts and for his recognition of the King of Spain. He promised to take Moctezuma's offer under consideration, and suggested that they remain with him until they were rested from their long journey.

The entire population of Tlaxcala turned out to welcome the Spaniards when they marched into the city. Flowers hung from every house, arches of pine branches were interlaced with roses, and honeysuckle boughs were spread across the streets. Several days of festivities followed, but Cortés, always wary of a trap, maintained rigorous discipline among the troops. He imposed a 24-hour curfew on the army, and none was permitted outside the gates of the encampment unless accompanied by an armed squad.

It was in Tlaxcala that Cortés first demonstrated his evangelistic zeal. When the lords of the republic proposed to give 300 female slaves to the army, Cortés refused to accept them. His religion, he said, forbade them from consorting with women who had not been baptized as Christians. The men were naturally upset by his decision, and the Tlaxcalans were hurt and humiliated by his refusal to accept their gift of friendship. But Cortés, ever resourceful, satisfied both sides by placing the women in the service of Marina.

He failed, however, to persuade the Tlaxcalans to cast down their idols and accept the one true God for their salvation. They were perfectly willing to accept his god and place him alongside their idols, and they would worship and serve him as their own, but Cortés was insistent upon replacing them. A confrontation was avoided when father Bartolomé de Olmeda, the chaplain, cautioned Cortés that the Indians were not ready to forsake their gods. Cortés finally yielded, and as a concession to him, the Tlaxcalans allowed the Spaniards to convert the main temple into a Christian shrine.

At the end of twenty days, Cortés, despite the objections of Maxixca, prepared to march to Cholula accompanied by 5,000 Tlaxcalan warriors.

Like Tlaxcala, Cholula was a republic, governed by the lords of six districts. Cholula and Mexico, however, were currently allies, and Cortés was well aware that less than a day's march from the city, 20,000 Mexican warriors were in garrison.

Cortés suspected a plot from the moment he entered the city. Stones were piled high on the rooftops, barricades were set up along the streets, and pitfalls were dug and camouflaged at strategic points throughout the city. The Cholulans made matters worse by quartering the Spaniards in a run-down palace and neglecting to send them provisions. By the end of four days, neither women nor children could be seen in the streets.

Cortés chose not to wait for the Cholulans to attack. He seized a priest and a noble, and after an hour of intense and ruthless torture, they confessed that a plot was in the making. The ruling lords of the republic denied everything, and insisted that their lack of hospitality was by Moctezuma's order. They offered to provide the Spaniards with food and anything else they needed, but Cortés refused to spend another day in Cholula. He would leave for Mexico in the morning, and demanded porters to carry the army's baggage and an escort of 2,000 warriors to protect him from the Mexicans.

When the porters and warriors gathered in the plaza the following morning, the Spanish foot formed into ranks behind the cavalry, as if preparing to depart. At a signal, the Spanish horse charged into the crowd as crossbowmen fired into their midst. The people fled from the plaza, only to be driven back by swordsmen posted at the gates. When the carnage was over, the Spaniards dashed out into the streets, where they were joined by the Tlaxcalans, and together they swept through the city, firing temples and houses. Within two hours more than 3,000 Cholulans were dead, and at the end of five, all resistance ceased.

If the slaughter of the Cholulans was meant to terrorize Moctezuma, then Cortés had achieved his objective. The emperor withdrew to the temple with his priests and made sacrifices to the gods for eight days. When he left the temple, he sent word to Cortés that he would receive him in Tenochtitlán as soon as it was convenient for him to leave Cholula.

The Spaniards began the long and arduous climb to the Valley of Mexico, and when they reached the pass between Popocatepetl and Ixtaccíhuatl, Cortés caught first sight of the destination he had fought so hard to reach. It was more than he had hoped for. Even from this distance, he could make out massive towers that seemed to float on the mirrored surface of a great lake, and the long, slender strands of causeways that moored the city to the shore. Along the lakeshore, he could count city upon city, all larger than any he had seen before. The sight of this vastly populated valley, however, did not please all. It would not do to tempt God further, they argued, by entering a valley where there were a thousand Indians for every one of them.

On 8 November 1519, Cortés led his army up the great Ixtapalapa causeway to meet Moctezuma. Three miles up the causeway, they halted before a fortress that commanded a junction with a smaller causeway that lead to the western shore. It took them the better part of an hour to pass through the gates of the fortress, since a thousand nobles had to place their hands on the ground and kiss them in welcome before they could move forward.

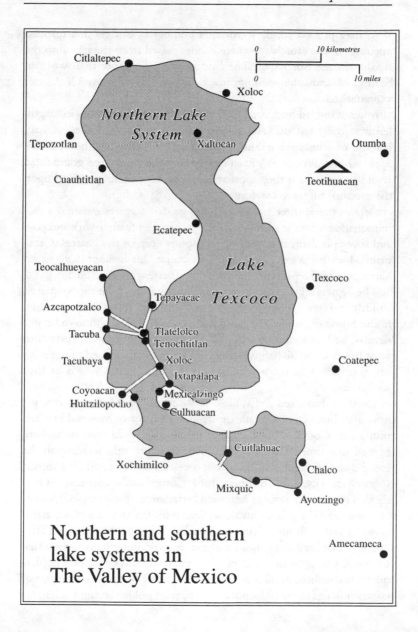

Northern and southern
lake systems in
The Valley of Mexico

As they proceeded, they crossed a number of bridges that spanned openings in the causeway, where canoes passed from the lake into the lagoon on the other side. The bridges were no more than wooden beams laid across the openings that could be easily removed if the city was attacked.

Beyond the last bridge, a broad avenue, nearly three miles in length, led into the heart of Tenochtitlán. Here Cortés was forced to halt, because two hundred nobles, wearing robes of the royal house, were approaching in single file. Each carried a brightly coloured gourd filled with flowers, and as they approached, they kept their eyes fixed upon the ground. All were barefoot.

Behind them, three nobles carrying golden sceptres escorted a pallium shaded from the sun with a canopy of green featherwork and gold and silver pendants that swayed with every step of the bearers. Cacamac, Moctezuma's nephew, and Cuitláhuac, his brother, walked on either side of the pallium, and like the others, were unshod.

The bearers set the litter down some thirty paces from the Spaniards, and Moctezuma stepped forth. The emperor was about forty years old, in the prime of his life. He was tall for an Indian, and although he was slender, he was well proportioned. His skin was somewhat fairer than most Indians, and his hair was short, no longer than needed to cover his ears. His long face was accentuated by a scanty beard, which he kept well trimmed.

Cortés dismounted and walked towards him, but when he reached out to embrace him, Cuitlahuac stepped in front of him and brushed him aside. Cortés stepped aside and bowed to him, and he in turn bowed to Cortés. Then Moctezuma placed his right hand upon the ground and brought it to his lips in a gesture of welcome. He turned towards the city, and Cuitlahuac took Cortés by the arm and led him up the avenue, a few steps behind Moctezuma.

They halted in an open area, and Cortés took a necklace of pearls and glass diamonds from his corselet and handed it to Moctezuma. The emperor hesitated for a moment, then bowed slightly, signifying that Cortés might approach and place it about his neck. At his signal, a major-domo handed him a small packet, and he took out a pair of collars made of rare translucent seashells, with golden shrimps as large as

a man's hand hanging from each. He placed them about Cortés's neck
and made a sign that he was to follow him into the city.

With the army close behind, he led Cortés to the palace of his father,
Axayácatl. Then he spoke for the first time.

'Now you are in your house,' he said, 'eat, drink, and rest from your
long journey, and when you are ready, I shall return.'

Cortés kept his men confined to the palace grounds for four days
before permitting any contact with the Mexicans. On the afternoon of
the fourth day, he asked Moctezuma's permission to visit the market
place in Tlatelolco. Moctezuma agreed, and when his nobles appeared
at the palace gates, the company, fully armed and accompanied by the
horse, followed them to the plaza of Tlatelolco, the great market place
of Mexico.

We marvelled at the number and variety of wares sold here, for they
equalled and perhaps surpassed those offered at the weekly fairs at Medino
del Campo, my home in Castile, and the Indian merchants displayed them
in the same systematic manner as the Spaniards

Along one avenue we saw dealers who sold feathers, mantles, precious
stones, and finely crafted artifacts of gold and silver. Others sold gold ore and
nuggets from the mines and streams of the sierra. The nuggets were tightly
packed inside goose-feather quills so transparent that the amount of gold
they contained was clearly visible to the buyer. The quills are the master
currency of the realm, against which the values of all commodities are
weighed. Accounts are calculated by the length and thickness of each quill –
what it is worth in terms of mantles, slaves, cacao beans, and whatever else
they barter and sell in Mexico.

In another quarter of the market, merchants sell ropes, sandals, robes, and
other items of clothing woven from henequen, a material more coarse than
cotton, along with the roots of this versatile plant. In this same quarter, they
sell tiger pelts, otter and beaver furs, and the hides of deer and jackal, some
tanned and others raw.

In the food markets there are heaps of beans, sage, herbs, fresh vegetables,
fruit, and cacao. Butchers sell chickens, turkey, rabbit, hare, deer, ducks, and
small dogs. Some are sold alive, and others dressed and ready for the table. In
another section women sell jars of honey, molasses, and prepared foods,
such as corn paste soaked in honey and sugar, cooked tripe, and a delicacy
made from a flour paste that tastes like honey-nut. Fisherwomen sell cakes

made from an ooze they skim from the surface of the great lake, which, when curdled, tastes like cheese.

In another quarter of the market they sell earthenware of every size and variety, from large jars to small jugs; cups made from gourds; and pitchers carved from wood. Everything is painted with bright colours.

Beneath the gates of the marketplace, merchants sell flint knives, copper hatchets, cradles, benches, firewood, lumber, beams, and pitch-pine for torches. Here we also found paper, which they call *amal,* and reeds scented with the sap of the sweet gum and filled with tobacco, salt, and grain.

There is also a slave market, where men and women with wooden yokes about their necks and tied to long poles are sold, and this market is every bit as large as the markets where the Portuguese sell slaves they bring from Guinea.

One cannot see all the merchandise sold in the market place in two days. Soldiers who have been to Constantinople, to Rome, and to other parts of the world swore that they had never before seen a marketplace of this size, nor one so well administered.

That great and evil temple dominates the city and its surroundings as far as the eye can see. To the south, we could see the full length of the Ixtapalapa causeway, by which we had crossed the lake to reach the city. To the west, we saw the causeway that leads to Tacuba and the aqueduct that brings fresh

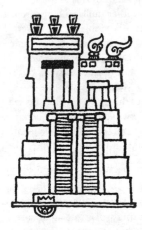

The temple of Huitizilopochtli and Tlaloc in Tenochtitlán, from an ancient manuscript

water to the city from Chapultepec, and to the north, the causeway that crosses the lake to Tepeyacac. At intervals along the causeways we could make out bridges where the waters of the lake pass from one side to the other, and on the surface, we could see canoes by the hundreds, bringing provisions, merchandise, and other goods into the city.

Directly below us a network of canals gives canoes access to every part of the city, and where the canals intersect with city streets, wooden bridges allow traffic to cross from one side to the other. And the city itself, with every house freshly whitewashed and every cue, adoratorio, and palace faced with gypsum, is a wonderland in white.

[In our tour of the city] . . . we stopped to examine a small temple not far from the great temple. This house of idols was a veritable hell. The entry passed through a gaping mouth that the native painters portray in pictures of hell, frightful mouths with vicious fangs to devour the souls of the condemned. Images of devils and serpents stood beside the entry, and close by was a sacrificial platform bloodstained and blackened with encrusted blood. Like any slaughterhouse in Spain, chopping blocks and knives were conveniently arranged alongside it. Firewood was piled in heaps some distance behind the temple, and beyond the stacks of firewood stood a large reservoir filled with water. Inside the temple there were vats and jugs and pitchers of water for the priests to cook the flesh of the poor Indians they sacrificed. I have always called that charnel house the *Inferno.*

Tenochtitlan, as seen by Bernal Díaz, a young soldier, from the top of the great temple of Tlatelolco.

THE OCCUPATION

On the fifth day, Indian runners brought word to Cortés that seven Spaniards, including the commander at Vera Cruz, had been killed in a battle with Mexican warriors. Worse, the Totonacs, sensing the colony was in trouble, withdrew and refused to bring food to the Spaniards. If word of the attack reached Tenochtitlán, the army, isolated and vulnerable in a city surrounded by water, could expect the worst.

The following day, with four captains and a few foot, Cortés marched into Moctezuma's palace and accused him of instigating the attack on his garrison. The only guarantee of their safety now, he said, was for Moctezuma to accompany him to the Spanish quarters. Once there, they would treat him as an honoured guest, but if he refused, his captains stood ready to kill him.

Moctezuma denied everything. He was not, he told Cortés, a person to whom such an order could be given. They argued for nearly an hour, but Juan Velásquez settled the situation by demanding that they seize him or kill him. It was too late to do anything else. Either way, the fat was in the fire.

Moctezuma offered his son and two legitimate daughters as hostages, but Cortés would not be budged. In the end, Moctezuma yielded, and a guard of honour led him to the Spanish quarters.

Once there he was free to hold court with his chieftains, to hear and judge civil suits, to enjoy his wives and concubines, and even make his sacrifices at the temple.

In the days that followed, Moctezuma and Cortés often passed the time playing *totoloque*, a game played by tossing gold balls and gold discs across the floor to a marker. Pedro de Alvarado measured Cortés's counters, and a nephew measured Moctezuma's. Alvarado always gave Cortés one more toss than he was entitled to, but Moctezuma only smiled and said that he did not like *Tonatio* (Alvarado), because he used too much *yxoxol,* meaning he cheated.

> I was a young man at the time, and whenever I was assigned to guard him, I never failed to remove my helmet when he passed by. He knew my name and my rank, and he learned from the page Orteguilla that I had come to New Spain twice before on expeditions. When I asked Orteguilla to speak to Moctezuma for a pretty woman, he summoned me to his quarters and said, 'Bernal Díaz del Castillo, they tell me that you have very little gold and clothing. Today I have ordered my major domos to give you gold and mantles, and a pretty girl. Treat her well, for she is the daughter of an important noble.'
>
> Thus Moctezuma passed the days of his confinement, at times cheerful and laughing, but more often lost in thought.
>
> *Bernal Díaz*

At Cortés's direction, Moctezuma ordered every provincial governor in the empire to appear before him. Once there, the emperor informed them that he had sworn allegiance to the King of Spain, and ordered them to do the same. Cortés now ruled the empire. Armed with no more than Moctezuma's safe conduct, the Spaniards moved freely about the nation to lay claim to its wealth. And as the Spaniards entered the provinces, the empire disintegrated as one vassal after another paid tribute to Cortés rather than to Moctezuma.

Within months, Mexico lost control of the Oaxaca highlands and the strategic route across the southern sierra. Cortés formed alliances with Cholula, Huexotzingo, and Tlaxcala, and controlled the pass at Tepeaca. Cempoala and the Totonacs were firmly under Spanish control, and Cortés was in a position to establish a second colony at Coatzacoalcos, on the Gulf Coast.

The Expedition against Cortés

More than six months had passed since Cortés left Cuba, and in all that time, Diego Velásquez had not received a single dispatch from him. The first word to reach the governor of the fate of the company came from an *encomendero* who lived on the western shore of the island, and his letter sent Velásquez into a colossal rage.

Montejo and Puertocarrero, despite Cortés's orders to the contrary, landed near the *encomendero's* hacienda to bargain for bread, cassava, wild hogs, and sufficient fresh water for the crossing to Spain. The *encomendero*, a friend of Montejo's, was invited aboard ship and shown the treasure. There, according to his letter, he saw a cargo of gold, silver, jewels, and other artifacts worth at least 300,000 castellanos. The ship carried so much gold that he swore the pilot-major was using it for ballast.

Diego Velásquez lost no time in assembling a company to chase down Cortés and bring him to justice. He chose Pánfilo de Narváez as his captain-general, a well-respected hidalgo noted for courage and prudence, but considered by many to be inordinately arrogant.

Narváez's forces numbered 19 ships, a crew of 200 mariners, a company of 400 foot, 80 horse, 150 crossbowmen, and 90 musketeers. His heavy weapons were 20 cannon.

On 23 April 1520, the fleet anchored off the shore of New Spain at San Juan de Ulúa. Once ashore, Narváez was fortunate enough to meet

three Spaniards from Cortés's company. From them, he learned that
Cortés was in Tenochtitlán with the greater part of his army, 70 more
men were in garrison at Vera Cruz, and 150 men were on their way to
establish a colony at Coatzacoalcos. He also learned that Moctezuma
was Cortés's prisoner, and that no Indian lord or chieftain dared
challenge him or his men as they travelled from one end of the country
to the other.

Moctezuma was the first to hear of the new arrivals, and he lost no
time in sending emissaries to the coast to offer them food, shelter, and
anything else they needed. Narváez thanked him for his hospitality, and
informed him that he, not Cortés, was the king's captain-general. Under
orders from the king, he had come to arrest him as a common criminal.
When Moctezuma was restored to his rightful throne, he would make
restitution for all the wrongs done by Cortés and depart for his country.

Moctezuma received Narváez's message with mixed emotions.
Should he accept Narvaez's word that he and not Cortés spoke for the
King of Spain? Could he depend upon his promise to release him and
leave the country after he arrested Cortés? Narváez's troops outnumbered those of Cortés, but a victory over Cortés was far from
certain. His was a veteran army firmly entrenched in an invulnerable
city. A clash was inevitable, but if Mexico remained neutral, it seemed
certain that both armies would be left crippled and vulnerable. After
three days of reflection, Moctezuma decided it was politic to inform
Cortés of Narváez's arrival before word reached him by other means.

Cortés warned Narváez against stirring up rebellion among the
Spaniards. If the Indians suspected that there was any discord between
them, everything he had accomplished would be lost. Narváez's only
response was that the Crown had appointed Diego Velázquez governor
of New Spain, and he was now captain-general of the armed forces. He
had created a municipality and named civil officers, and since Cortés's
authorization from the governor was now invalid, he ordered him to
come to Cempoala at once and submit to his authority.

Cortés warned him that New Spain was now a Crown possession
with proper tribunals and municipal bodies, but if he held any valid
warrants from the king, he would honour them.

Leaving 150 soldiers and several hundred Tlaxcalan allies in

Tenochtitlán under the command of Pedro de Alvarado, Cortés set out for Cempoala on 15 May with 70 Spanish foot and 2,000 warriors from Chinantla, a militant tribe from the highlands of Oaxaca. At Cholula he joined forces with Juan Velásquez de Leon, whom he had recalled from Coatzacoalcos with his force of 120 soldiers. Taking the same route he had used to reach the tableland, he entered Totonac territory, where Gonzalo de Sandoval joined him with 60 more men from the Vera Cruz garrison.

Meanwhile, Narváez assembled his foot, cavalry, and artillery in the fields of Cempoala and waited for Cortés. As the rains came and night began to fall, however, he was convinced that Cortés would not attempt to cross the Rio de Canoas, now in a flood stage, after dark, and withdrew to Cempoala. He posted sentries on the outskirts of the city, sent a mounted patrol along the roads, staged his artillery in the plaza, and retired with the rest of the company, who were quartered in the largest temples.

The rain was still falling, and the hour was approaching midnight when shouts from below shook the men from a fitful sleep. 'To arms! To arms! Cortés is coming! The enemy is upon us!' It was Hurtado, a sentry who had been posted on the river road. He told Narváez that he heard the sound of men moving quietly along the road, and fled for Cempoala to warn him.

Narváez asked how many men he had seen, but Hurtado was unsure. From the noise they made, it might have been as many as eight.

Narváez smiled. 'Hurtado, my son, go to bed. I think you let your imagination run away with you in the dark, or else you had a bad dream. Cortés will not come this night, not in this rain.'

Back in his quarters, Hurtado said, 'Cortés is coming, even though the captain does not believe me. When I heard Cortés's men, I was as wide awake as I am at this moment. Unless there are phantoms in this country, the voices I heard were speaking Spanish. I swear to god I was not asleep or drunk, for it has been far too many days since I tasted a drop of wine. If Cortés does not fall upon us before daylight, then I will be the ass you say I am.'*

---

* Dialogues from Cervantes de Salazar, *Crónica de la Nueva España*.

The men had hardly settled down again and the sentries back at their posts when Cortés struck. In the darkness, points of light flickered on and off, and it seemed that hundreds of musketeers were priming their matchlocks.

The artillerymen rushed to clear their touchholes, but succeeded in firing only four rounds before their attackers were upon them. Narvaez's cavalry charged, but Cortés's foot, armed with long pikes, struck at their flanks, unhorsing riders and scattering their mounts.

Narváez's men rushed down the sides of the temples, but Cortes's men drove them back inside and fired the roof. Smoke drove them back out, and Narváez began to rally his men, but as chance would have it, a lance was thrust in Narváez's eye.

The battle was over. Gonzalo de Sandoval arrested Narváez and led him away. Narváez's only casualties were Diego de Rojas, Fuentes the standard bearer, two foot, and one of Cortés's renegades. Cortés lost four men in the battle, and two more who drowned when he crossed the river by the ford that Narváez could not find.

Dawn saw Narváez's proud army herded into the plaza, and one by one, they laid down their arms. They looked upon their captors in shame, for they were little more than a ragged band of vagabonds, less than half their number. They had no horses, their swords were rusted, and their filthy cotton armour was a humiliating contrast to the shiny steel corselets of the invaders.

Cortés invited every man of Narváez's army to join his company, and promised them they would share and share alike with his men. About half the company and several captains joined Cortés, but many chose to remain loyal to Narváez and return to Cuba. Unfortunately, there were no ships available, since Cortés had seized the fleet and sent it north to Quiahuitzlán.

But their troubles were just beginning. A Negro in Narváez's company brought smallpox to Cempoala, and the Indians began to die faster than they could be buried. Soon a putrid stench spread over the city as bodies rotted in the streets. Before the plague ran its course, some five million Mexicans would die in the epidemics of 1520, 1531, and 1545.

They were still burying the dead when an urgent message arrived from Alvarado. The Mexicans had risen against the garrison in Tenochtitlan, and his entire company was under siege. Moctezuma could not, or would not control his people. Several Spaniards were dead, and unless help arrived soon, they would all be massacred.

Cortés appealed to Narváez's loyalists to march to Mexico with him, and offered them the same shares as the others.

They were reluctant, but what else could they do? Without ships, without provisions, and left to themselves in a plague-ridden city, where could they go?

ALVARADO'S FOLLY

Eight cheerless months had passed since the arrest of Moctezuma, and during that time, not a single public ceremony had been celebrated to lift the spirits of his people. Now the time had come to celebrate Toxcatl, the agrarian ceremony that marked the end of the dry season, and Moctezuma was determined that his people would sing and dance again. He sought Alvarado's permission to observe the feast, explained the significance of the ritual to him, and described how it was to be conducted. It would take place in the great plaza, where the people would gather to sing and offer their gifts to the gods, and young nobles from the finest families of Mexico would perform the ritual dance for a bountiful harvest. He promised Alvarado that there would be no uprising and no human sacrifices. Alvarado was suspicious, but grudgingly gave his permission.

The Tlaxcalans, however, eager for the spoils of Tenochtitlán, warned Alvarado that the Mexicans were using the ritual as a cover for an uprising. Alvarado inspected the preparations in the plaza, where he saw three idols set upon litters, and beside each sat a Mexican with shorn hair. Although the idols were made up of nothing more than a heavy dough of wild amaranth seeds and syrup, he was suspicious.

He seized the Indians and tortured them to reveal the plot. The interpreters, however, were with Cortés, leaving Alvarado with only Francisco, a Maya Indian who had little knowledge of Nahuatl. The Spaniards kept asking Francisco if the Indians were planning an attack, and each time he responded 'Si señor'.

That was enough for Alvarado. He took half the company with him and left the others in the palace with orders to kill the hostages when he attacked the Indians in the plaza.

When he arrived, six hundred young nobles, wearing nothing more than a ceremonial breechcloth and a panache of feathers, were holding hands and dancing. Their bodies were adorned with gold necklaces that hung to the waist, gold and silver breastplates, and gold bracelets on their arms and ankles. More than three thousand spectators gathered about them, caught up in the sinuous movements of the dance.

Alvarado posted ten men at the gates and surrounded the dancers with the others. At his signal, the Spaniards drew their swords and charged into the dancers. The spectators panicked and rushed for the gates, only to be driven back by the soldiers guarding them. The massacre continued for three hours, and when it was over, the Spaniards moved among the bodies, systematically stripping them of gold and jewellery. When they finished, the Spaniards withdrew in order, weapons at the ready, watching for any sign of attack.

The following day a leaderless mob of warriors surrounded the palace, showering the Spaniards with arrows and javelins.

On the twenty-third day of the siege, Cortés arrived with 1,000 Spanish foot, 90 horse, and 2,000 Tlaxcalan warriors. He met no resistance as he entered the city, and reached the palace without trouble. He demanded that Moctezuma open the markets and provision his men, but Moctezuma refused, and suggested that Cortés send his brother Cuitláhuac instead.

Allowing Cuitlahuac to leave the palace proved to be a mistake. Instead of opening the markets, Cuitlahuac organized his squadrons and resumed the attack on the palace.

Cortés knew he had to abandon the city, but eight canal crossings stood between him and the causeway to the western shore, and the Mexicans had removed every bridge. He called for a truce, and led Moctezuma to the roof of the palace to urge his people to put down their arms. But Cuitláhuac was now lord, and the people stoned Moctezuma before he had a chance to speak. A stone struck him in the temple and he collapsed.

Four days later, Moctezuma was dead. According to Cortés, he refused to take food and water or allow the Spaniards to care for his wound. Cortés called for another truce, and the Spaniards took his body and laid it before the gates.

The nobles wept at the sight of Moctezuma's body, and the people cried out when they heard the emperor was dead, but none stepped forward to claim his body. Finally one of Moctezuma's major-domos picked it up and carried it into the city to seek a resting place. One barrio after another turned him away, but he eventually found one who was willing to cremate the emperor. When nothing but ashes remained of the great prince, the major-domo put them in an urn and buried them in a rubbish heap.

THE NIGHT OF SORROWS

Cortés had no choice now but to leave the city at once. He ordered the treasure they had accumulated to be heaped in the great hall of the palace, and he summoned the royal treasurer to count out the king's fifth. When this was done, he assigned him seven wounded horses and 80 Tlaxcalan warriors to carry it out of the city. The remainder of the treasure he gave to the soldiers, and told them to take whatever they wished of it.

Cortés was now faced with the problem of what to do with the lords and nobles whom he had imprisoned with the emperor. He could not leave them behind when he withdrew, and he could not take them out of the city, since they would hinder the retreat. Only the royal hostages, out of necessity, would be taken along. One by one the Spaniards garrotted the nobles, and when they were finished, they cast their bodies outside the gates, hoping they would cause the Mexicans enough grief to distract them long enough to escape.

At ten o'clock that night, as Francisco de Aguilar stood watch on the palace roof, more than a score of women emerged from the darkness, seeking the bodies of their husbands, brothers, and sons. His blood ran cold as he heard the screams of the women when they found a loved one, and he turned to his companion and said, 'If you have never seen hell, my friend, look upon it now in the misery and despair below us.'*

That night the moon was bright, and fires that blazed from every

* Francisco de Aguilar, *Relación breve de la conquista de Nueva España*.

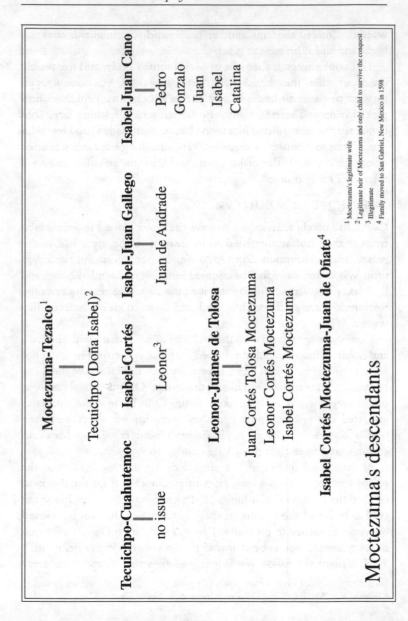

Moctezuma-Tezalco[1]

Tecuichpo (Doña Isabel)[2]

Tecuichpo-Cuahutemoc   Isabel-Cortés   Isabel-Juan Gallego   Isabel-Juan Cano

no issue   Leonor[3]   Juan de Andrade   Pedro
                                             Gonzalo
                                             Juan
                                             Isabel
                                             Catalina

Leonor-Juanes de Tolosa

Juan Cortés Tolosa Moctezuma
Leonor Cortés Moctezuma
Isabel Cortés Moctezuma

Isabel Cortés Moctezuma-Juan de Oñate[4]

Moctezuma's descendants

[1] Moctezuma's legitimate wife
[2] Legitimate heir of Moctezuma and only child to survive the conquest
[3] Illegitimate
[4] Family moved to San Gabriel, New Mexico in 1598

rooftop flooded the city with light. Towards midnight, however, a light drizzle began to fall, obscuring the moon, then a thunderstorm passed over the city, followed by a pelting hailstorm that drove the Mexicans indoors. The Spaniards, to their dying day, believed that the storm was a miracle wrought by the hand of God to spare them from the Mexicans. A portable bridge was set across the first canal, but it soon collapsed under a steady procession of men, horses, and baggage. Now there was no way across the remaining canals save for what fate had provided them – their baggage and the Indian porters who carried it. The press of men behind them thrust them into the canals, and as they drowned, their bodies formed a bridge for those who followed.

The city was now alert, and as they reached the sixth canal, the Mexicans fell upon them in force. Canoes closed in on them from both sides of the causeway, and as warriors swarmed up from the canals to attack them, the army panicked and pushed Indians, Spaniards, and anything else in its path into the breaches before them.

Forty Spaniards charged with transporting the heavy equipment were forced to turn back before they reached the sixth canal, and they

An Aztec jaguar knight ready for battle with an obsidian-edged weapon and wearing a pelt

retreated to the palace with a horde of Mexicans screaming for their blood.

Those who crossed the sixth canal found their progress easier as the enemy attacks slackened. The Spaniards who were forced back had drawn off many Indians, and others broke off the attack to ransack the baggage lost in the canals, cutting off each other's hands in their frenzy.

At nine o'clock in the morning the army reached a clearing where the Spaniards treated their wounded and Cortés took muster. More than 700 foot had perished at the breaches and along the causeway, and only 23 of his 80 horse had survived, most of which were wounded or crippled. The cannon, the muskets, and all the powder had been lost. The losses suffered by the Tlaxcalans were well over a thousand, and all the royal hostages, save for two sons of the house of Texcoco, were dead. Cortés's pregnant concubine was dead, and of the Tlaxcalan women, only Doña Luisa, Alvarado's woman, survived.

The army moved north around the less-populated shores of Lake Zumpango and Lake Xaltocan. Once around the lakes, Cortés planned to travel southeast until he reached Tlaxcala, where he hoped the lords of the republic would grant them asylum. Whether his army could survive a 90-mile journey through hostile territory without provisions and a Mexican army close at his heels, was another matter.

Once clear of the lakes, provisions were scarce. There was nothing to eat but herbs, Indian sorrel, and stalks of maize. Food not close to the road was done without, since the enemy was all about them.

One soldier, half crazed with hunger, cut open a dead comrade and dined on his liver. Cortés would have hanged him on the spot save for the pleas of his comrades, who understood his temptation all too well. In one battle a horse was killed, and that night the men roasted it, and knife fights broke out as they fought each other for a share of it. When they were finished, nothing remained of the horse – even the entrails and the hoofs had been eaten.

At Otumba, a Mexican army so large that it covered the entire plain confronted them. Cortés drove his cavalry into the heart of the enemy to open a gap for the foot. Before the enemy could close in on the column, the cavalry returned to drive them back, then charged back into the crowd to open up another gap. But the Mexicans were too many – the gap closed, and the cavalry was forced to fall back to defend the foot.

The Spaniards were surrounded, they could neither advance nor retreat. The end seemed inevitable. At this precise moment, however, Cortés spied the litter of the Mexican general. Cortés and four of his captains fought their way to his litter, and a lance thrust tumbled him to the ground. Juan de Salamanca dismounted quickly and cut off the general's head. He held it high for all to see, and the Spaniards began to shout 'Victory! Victory!' At the sight of their fallen chieftain, the Indians faded away and vanished into the hills.

On the eighth day after their flight from Mexico, the Spaniards entered the province of Tlaxcala. Only 440 men and 20 horse had survived the flight from Mexico, and all had suffered one or more serious wounds. To their relief, the lords of the republic received them like lost brothers. Although they grieved for their lost kinsmen, they placed no blame on Cortés.

Cuitláhuac sent the heads of the dead Spaniards and their horses throughout the provinces, and proclaimed a year's exemption from tribute for any who refused sanctuary to Cortés. He sealed off their retreat to the sea by closing the passes, and reinforced his garrisons to the southeast to prevent them from seeking refuge in Oaxaca.

Spaniards travelling the trade routes, unaware of the defeat at Tenochtitlan, were now at the mercy of every warrior in the land. Provinces that had once befriended the Spaniards now turned against them and attacked every party passing through their territory. The chieftain of Coatzacoalcos, once Cortés's staunchest supporter, killed the entire population of the new colony, massacring 80 men and 5 women.

Cortés knew he could not depend upon the continuing good will of the Tlaxcalans if he remained there too long. Twenty days after their arrival in Tlaxcala, the Spaniards, many still nursing their wounds, were again on the march.

Three days later, he recaptured the garrison at Tepeaca and reopened the route to the seacoast. He established his headquarters there, and sent punitive expeditions against the cities where Spaniards had been killed.

During this period, ships arrived from Cuba bringing men, horses, and ammunition. By winter, he had enough men, arms, and provisions to launch an attack on Tenochtitlán.

Cuitláhuac, however, would not be waiting for him. Three months after he drove the Spaniards from the city, smallpox struck, and for sixty days, death reigned over the city. When the plague passed, Cuitláhuac lay dead, and Cuauhtémoc, son of the mighty Ahuitzotl, now in his twentieth year, sat upon the jaguar and eagle throne.

THE SIEGE

On 28 December 1520, Cortés left Tlaxcala with an army of 550 foot, 40 horse, an arsenal of 80 crossbows and muskets, and nine field guns. When he reached the Valley of Mexico, he established his headquarters on the eastern shore of the lake at Texcoco.

Control of the lake and the causeways was vital if the siege was to succeed. To this end, Cortés sent the shipwright Martin López into the mountains of Tlaxcala to cut timber for a fleet of brigantines. Thirteen ships were to be built with sufficient speed and manoeuvrability under sail to overcome the numerical superiority of the Tlatelolcan war canoes on the open lake. The ships would be armed with a falconet and a reinforced prow for ramming. The beams were to be narrow enough to enter the canals of Tenochtitlán, and propelled with six oars on each side of the vessel.

Cortés's plan was to have his commanders take up positions at the ends of the causeways, cut the Chapultepec pipeline that supplied Tenochtitlán with water, then, with support of the brigantines, move the troops up the causeways into the city. First, however, he had to sweep the lake clean of the enemy's war canoes.

On 13 May 1521, Cortés ordered the brigantines into the lake and Cuauhtémoc sent more than 500 war canoes out to meet them. As they closed on each other, the wind died, and the sails of the brigantines sagged and fell. Dead in the water, they were at the mercy of Cuauhtémoc's canoes, but the Mexicans hesitated, just beyond the range of the crossbows and muskets.

Mexico paid dearly for that lost opportunity, that brief moment when the brigantines, heavier and slower without sail, were vulnerable to Tlatelolco's lighter and faster craft.

A strong offshore breeze from the northeast rose and swept across the lake, and one by one, their sails billowed out. The brigantines were underway again, headed directly for the densely packed canoes in their path. The fragile craft shattered and disappeared beneath the heavy prows of the brigantines, and in their wake, broad trails of debris and mangled bodies rose to the surface. Some managed to reach the safety of the canals, but most fled to the north and the east, with the brigantines in close pursuit.

After six days of skirmishing for control of the causeways, Cortés managed to cut off all approaches to the city by land and by water. On the seventh day, Cortés sent his gunships into the canals and launched an attack along the causeways. Filling in open breaches across the canals as he proceeded, he managed to reach the central plaza of Tenochtitlán. The Mexicans, however, rallied and drove them back, and at each step of the way, they pelted the attackers with stones from the rooftops.

Cortés's second attack on the city followed the first by three days. The Spaniards found the going more difficult than before, since the breaches were wider and deeper, the barricades stronger and better defended, and every rooftop along the way stockpiled with weapons, rocks, and warriors.

The Spaniards forced their way into the plaza, and while the cavalry skirmished in the streets, the gunships penetrated deeper into the canals. When they withdrew in the evening, they fired the palaces of Moctezuma Ilhuicamina, Axayácatl, and Moctezuma Xocóyotl. When the flames reached the cages of the royal aviary, the screams of egrets, hawks, and songbirds filled the evening air long after they were gone.

Cuauhtémoc sent pleas for support to the cities around the lake, but one by one they abandoned him. Xochimilco promised help, but looted their homes and temples, and carried off their women while the Mexicans were fighting. With the defection of Xochimilco, the Culhua lords of Mexicalzingo, Culhuácan, Ixtapalapa and Huitzilopochtlo denounced Cuauhtémoc. They ordered their people to build shelters to protect the Spaniards from the rain, and they provisioned them with fish and fresh fruit, provisions Mexico so desperately needed.

Cuauhtémoc could no longer defend the perimeter of the city, and ordered Tenochtitlán abandoned. He moved the women and children to Amaxacac, a barrio on the northeast sector of the city, and set up his headquarters at Yacacolco, near the market-place.

The point of attack now shifted to the market-place of Tlatelolco, and Cortés sent Alvarado in from the west while he moved up from the south. Alvarado, however, grown careless with easy victories, fell into a trap at a canal, and the offensive was delayed until he could fill in the breach.

The second attack fared even worse than the first. A foolish commander failed to fill the breach properly when he crossed a canal, and when it collapsed, the Indians fell upon the Spaniards threshing about in the water. Those who were not killed were carried away. That evening, as the Spaniards withdrew, they witnessed 50 of their comrades climbing the stairs of the temple to be sacrificed.

Fifteen days later, Cortés resumed the offensive, but chose to advance only after the breaches had been filled and packed with adobe. As he advanced, an army of labourers, armed with copper pickaxes, followed, tearing down every building in his wake.

On the fiftieth day of the siege, he launched a major offensive against Yacacolco. Cuauhtémoc was forced to withdraw to Amaxacac, and the marketplace fell to Alvarado. The war was clearly over. During the 27 days that followed the Mexican victory over the Spaniards, hard fighting, meagre rations, and sleepless nights opening breaches and building barricades had taken their toll on Cuauhtémoc's warriors.

When Cortés entered the market-place, warriors gathered above the gateway arches looked down upon him in silence, and none had the heart to cast a stone or throw a javelin. Cortés dismounted at the foot of the great temple and climbed to the summit, where he knelt in prayer before the heads of his comrades mounted on the skull rack. He set his banner above them, then descended the stairs.

Cortés sent an offer of amnesty to Cuauhtémoc, but the emperor replied that there could be no peace between his people and the Spaniards. All, he said, were determined to see this war to the very end, to fight until the last Mexican warrior fell in battle. Mexico had lost so much in the war that there was little left to live for. Mexico had lost its tributaries, its vassal states, and its great city – what more was there to lose?

Other overtures were sent to Cuauhtémoc, and the emperor finally agreed to meet Cortés in the market-place. An elegant table was set for the emperor in the shade of Cortés's pavilion, but midday came and passed without his appearing. Instead, five nobles arrived with gifts and apologies. The emperor was ill and could not come.

Cortés gave the nobles food and drink, and they departed, only to return in a few hours with more gifts and word that Cuauhtémoc had changed his mind. There would be no meeting, for he was more resolved than ever to fight.

Cortés lost patience and marched into Amaxacac with the Tlax-calans. The Mexicans could offer little resistance, and the Tlaxcalans rampaged through the streets, killing and looting as they pleased. Even the Spaniards were sickened by their atrocities, but outnumbered by their allies ten to one, they could not control them.

The next morning the *Cihuacóatl*, who spoke for the emperor himself, met Cortés on a rooftop and informed him that Cuauhtémoc preferred to die with his people rather than yield. They spoke for a few moments, then embraced, and the *Cihuacóatl* returned to the royal barge.

The people panicked when they saw the Spaniards preparing to attack and rushed out into the street, trying to force their way out of the barrio through streets choked with the enemy. In the crush, nearly all were pushed into the canals and drowned beneath bodies floating on the surface.

Cortés ordered the artillery to open fire, and when the first salvo failed to dislodge the Mexicans, he sent in his foot and the Tlaxcalans. Those still able to fight were either killed or driven into the lake to drown.

But Cuauhtémoc was not among them. He had fled for the opposite shore in his barge, only to find Gonzalo Sandoval and his gunships waiting for him.

A Paper Lion

The fundamental flaw of the Aztec Empire was that, of its thirty-eight provinces, not one had any political ties to a central authority, nor any goals in common. In several provinces, Nahuatl was not the native language. It was an empire created to gather wealth and enforce its collection by force of arms.

Other than fortified towns on the frontiers, there were no Mexican garrisons or provincial governors appointed by the emperor to enforce the law. The principal towns of Anahuac were governed by a variety of political systems. Some were ruled by native chieftains, others by natives appointed by Mexico, but in every case, the cities retained their political and administrative autonomy. The only restraint placed on the chieftains was that they paid Moctezuma's tribute every 80 days, provide conscripts to his army, and send slaves to be sacrificed on Mexico's altars. The only representative of the central government in the provincial towns was a civil servant, whose only duty was to oversee the collection of taxes. Inability to meet the tribute on time resulted in heavy penalties, some so harsh that they left the natives with little more than what was needed to sustain life. Refusal to pay tribute was intolerable and considered a threat to the empire, and the townspeople could expect no mercy from Moctezuma's army.

Within the borders of the empire, and closer to home, were five independent nations hostile to Mexico. The most powerful, Michoacan, bordered Mexico to the west. Metztitlán, a minor province lay to the northeast, and to the southeast, Tlaxcala, Huexotzingo, and Cholula lay across the strategic route from Tenochtitlán to the seacoast. Tlaxcala, the traditional enemy of Mexico, maintained an army of 8,000 veteran warriors, all spoiling for a fight with Mexico.

Within the Valley of Mexico, the Triple Alliance, made up of the city states of Mexico, Texcoco, and Tlacopan, was the dominant political force. All shared in the tribute from the provinces, but not to the same extent. Mexico and Texcoco received four-fifths of the tribute, and Tlacopan one-fifth.

Mexico, however, had enemies as well as allies within the valley. Along the southern approaches, Mexican troops were forced to keep an uneasy peace by occupying the territories of the Chalca confederacy. On the western shore of the lake, the powerful Acolhuaque tribe was divided. The southern group subject to Texcoco supported Moctezuma, and the northern group at Otumba was determined to over-throw him.

Moctezuma was too powerful for a revolution within Anahuac to unseat him, but his empire was a house of cards, waiting for a catalyst beyond its borders to bring it to its knees.

On 8 November 1519, Hernán Cortés arrived at the gates of Tenochtitlán with 439 heavily armed Spaniards and as many as 2,000 Tlaxcalan warriors, Moctezuma's avowed enemies. Their only entry into the city of 200,000 people was by invitation: any attempt to take the city by force would leave the Spaniards and their Indian allies dead on the causeways. Yet this feared warrior king who ruled with an iron hand the empire created by Ahuitzotl, welcomed this threatening force into the heart of his city as he would a friend and ally.

The only explanation for Moctezuma's strange behaviour lies in a severe shift of personality he suffered before the coming of the Spaniards. Native literature written in the early post-conquest years speaks of his obsession with a continuous series of omens that his diviners interpreted as foretelling his death and the end of his kingdom. These omens caused Moctezuma to begin a frantic search among diviners for a more favourable forecast, and brought on an increasing paranoia when one failed to materialize.

The bases of many of these tales lie in his fear of natural phenomena, such as earthquakes, volcanic eruptions, and eclipses of the sun and the moon. Many of the stories lie in myth, in allegorical tales found in pre-conquest native literature, and in oral traditions passed down from one generation to the next. Some were pure invention, but the sheer volume of stories dealing with his depression cannot be ignored. In an early chronicle, it was reported that Moctezuma's fear of a comet drove him to attempt suicide.

The most compelling factor for Moctezuma's strange behaviour, however, may have been his fear that Quetzalcoatl Topiltzin, the Toltec king exiled in AD 987, would one day return to claim his throne. Cortés was aware of Moctezuma's fear of Quetzalcoatl before he arrived in Tenochtitlan in 1519, and used it to his advantage. According to Cortés's second letter to Charles V, Moctezuma told him of the legend in his welcoming speech, and implied that the Spaniards might

Quetzalcoatl, as depicted by the Aztecs, said to be tall, with a white skin, long, dark hair and a beard

even be the sons of Quetzalcoatl, returned to claim his throne. In his response, Cortés told him that Charles V was indeed Quetzalcoatl, and that he had sent him to bring the word of God to Moctezuma and his people.

Without a doubt, Cortés's version of Moctezuma's welcoming speech was a fabrication, but the important point is that Cortés was aware of the legend and used it to intimidate Moctezuma.

Moctezuma's submissive behaviour towards the Spaniards after Cortés took him hostage is more difficult to explain. Time after time he refused to listen to his nobles and generals when they begged him to allow them to set him free. When Cacama, the lord of Texcoco, raised an army to attack the Spaniards, Moctezuma ordered him to lay aside his arms. Cacama refused, and Moctezuma promptly betrayed him to the Spaniards.

Moctezuma was afforded another opportunity to rid the country of the Spaniards when Cortés marched against Narváez at Cempoala, leaving Alvarado with no more than 289 men to hold Tenochtitlan. When the Mexicans besieged the Spaniards after the Toxcatl slaughter, Moctezuma allowed Cortés to bring reinforcements to Alvarado without lifting a hand. His inaction cost him his kingdom and his life.

CHAPTER SIX

The Colonial Period

The conquistadors did not find their fortune in gold, as they had hoped, but in the more durable form of land and cheap labour. Their right to exploit native labour in Mexico after the conquest was, however, not without limit.

The papal bull of Alexander VI in 1493 assigned responsibility for the protection and conversion to Christianity of the native population to the Spanish Crown, but the Crown was also obliged to reward those who had conquered and invested their fortunes in the New World. Without firm control and strict supervision of the Indian workforce, the colonists faced bankruptcy and the Crown loss of much-needed revenue. The Church in the New World was genuinely concerned for the souls of the Indians, but like the colonists, it had needs for cheap labour to build its cathedrals, schools, and churches to carry out its religious programmes.

The Dominican Fray Antonio de Montesinos, the first cleric to preach against Indian abuses in the Indies, convinced Ferdinand that reform was needed, and the king appointed a council of theologians and learned men to examine the problem. The result of their deliberations was the Laws of Burgos, enacted in 1512.

The Laws recognized that the Indians were entitled to freedom and humane treatment, but, convinced that Indians were inclined to idleness and vice, advocated that they be compelled to work and live in close proximity to Spaniards to effect their conversion. In essence, the Laws justified and upheld the *encomienda* system in common practice throughout Spanish America.

Encomienda was a system whereby a trustee, the *encomendero*, was granted native villages in which he was responsible for the welfare of the inhabitants and their religious instruction. In turn, he was entitled to tribute and unrestricted personal services from the inhabitants.

The system was not popular with the Crown, however, since it was wary of powerful landlords who controlled economic, military, and judicial power so far from Spain. In 1509, to break up large estates, the Crown decreed that ownership of the *encomienda* must revert to the Crown after the death of the *encomendero*. The law was seldom enforced, however, and in 1526, the Crown, aware of the hardships suffered by widows and children, authorized Ponce de Leon to dispose of titles to the *encomiendas* in Mexico at his discretion. In 1530, the *Audiencia* of New Spain affirmed the right of inheritance of the *encomienda* to widows and children when the *encomendero* died.

In 1542, however, the Council of the Indies created chaos in Spanish America when it issued the New Laws, which abolished Indian slavery, prohibited the clergy and public servants from holding *encomiendas,* forbade granting new *encomiendas,* and once again decreed that all *encomiendas* would revert to the Crown upon the death of the *encomendero*.

If the Viceroy Mendoza had chosen to enforce the New Laws in New Spain, the country would without question have faced the devastating civil wars they brought about in Panama and Peru. Under pressure, Charles V was forced to retreat, and the laws were modified. The Indians still paid tribute to their masters, but now the Crown controlled the labour that fuelled industry and commerce.

The New Laws also abolished Indian slavery. Spanish law permitted enslaving Indians captured in warfare and rebellion, and it was common practice to provoke the Indians for the sole purpose of obtaining slaves. By 1550, there were two or three hundred thousand slaves in the New World, and possibly as many as 65,000 in New Spain, who were used primarily in the mines and the pearl-diving industry.

Exploration and Expansion

The years following the conquest saw New Spain invest heavily to expand the borders of the new nation as far north and south as resources and manpower would permit.

Pedro de Alvarado, Cortés's lieutenant and the conqueror of Guatemala

In 1523, Cortés, prompted by reports of rich lands in Guatemala, sent Pedro de Alvarado into the mountainous terrain of the country with 300 foot, 170 horse, four cannon, and a host of Mexican allies.

At the time of the conquest, four independent states: Quiché, Cakchiquel, Tzutujil, and Uspantic controlled the Guatemalan highlands. Of these states, Quiché was the most powerful, dominating the others by its political astuteness and superior military capability. Tecum Uman, the lord of the Quichés, who claimed direct descent from Quetzalcoatl, was recognized as King of Guatemala by Moctezuma himself.

Utatlán, the Quiché capital, was at the height of its power and influence when the Spaniards invaded Guatemala. Moctezuma had warned Tecum Uman of the powers of the Spaniards, but the Quiché king elected to attack Alvarado, who was laying siege to Xelaluh, near the modern city of Quetzaltanango. After a series of bloody battles, the

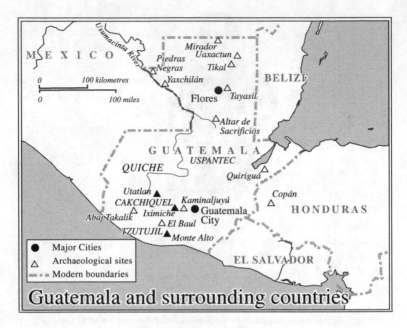

Guatemala and surrounding countries

Spaniards routed the Quiché army, and Tecum Uman lay dead on the battlefield, possibly by the hand of Alvarado himself. Chinanvalut, the son of Tecum Uman, sued for peace and invited the Spaniards to Utatlán. Alvarado accepted and moved the main body of his army to a plain outside the city.

Alvarado, experienced in the ways of treachery, was quick to note that the streets of Utatlán were narrow, and that the city had but two exits. One passed down a flight of thirty steps, and the other crossed a causeway that had been cut in several places. His suspicions were further increased by the absence of women and the large quantities of wood stored alongside the principal buildings. Fearing a plot against the Spaniards quartered in the city, he quietly moved them to the safety of the open field.

Alvarado then sent gifts to the king and the principal lords of the Quiché, and invited them to come to his camp as honoured guests. Chinanvalut was seized upon his arrival in the Spanish camp, and promptly hanged with other prominent leaders. With the execution of their king, the Quiché rose again and fought one more battle, but their cause was futile. Alvarado now ruled Guatemala as captain-general.

Guatemala, however, would not be subject to New Spain. Cortés, as a reward for Alvarado's contribution to the conquest, petitioned the Crown to recognize Guatemala as a new state, subject only to the king.

That year Cortés also sent Luis Marin up the Chiapas Plateau, then part of Guatemala, to subdue the war-like highland Maya and establish a colony. The colony lasted only as long as Marin occupied the plateau. When he left, the Chamula, as fiercely independent then as they are today, revolted. The region was finally pacified in 1527 by Diego de Mazariegos, one of the more humane conquerors. After their defeat, Mazariegos resettled the Chamula in the present city of Chiapa de Corzo, and, contrary to Spanish practice with rebel Indians, refused to brand them as slaves.

Pacification of the southeast against the lowland Maya was more difficult than either Guatemala or Chiapas. Francisco de Montejo undertook the conquest of Yucatán 1527, but found himself not up to the task. The deep forests of the peninsula limited the effectiveness of his horse, constant guerrilla attacks by the Maya resulted in heavy casualties, and his supply lines were difficult, if not impossible, to maintain. After suffering the loss of 93 of his original force of 165 men, Montejo abandoned the enterprise and sailed for Spain. The conquest of Yucatán was shelved for a later time.

The second phase of the conquest of Yucatán began in 1531, when Montejo returned from Spain and appointed his son, Don Francisco, as lieutenant governor of Yucatán. Don Francisco's campaign was long, and the lack of logistical support in the interior constantly threatened the enterprise, but Maya resistance in the north was finally overcome in 1535, and colonization of the upper region of the peninsula began.

In the early 1530s, the northernmost outpost of the Spanish conquest lay at the frontier of New Galicia, near Culiacán. Beyond this outpost lay the Sonora Desert, a desolate and unexplored land. Nevertheless, the region was a rich source of speculation for a nation hungry for another Mexico, another Peru. To the Spaniards hungry for conquest, this was the land where they would find the Seven Cities of Cibola, which, according to legend, had been discovered by seven fugitive bishops in the eighth century.

Unfortunately, there were no hard facts or evidence to convince the Crown that an expedition into the region was worth the risk. Furthermore, Cortés had explored the coast of the Sonora as far as the narrows at the head of the Sea of Cortez (Golfo de California), and found nothing but barren wastes in either the Baja or the mainland.

In March of 1536, however, a Spanish patrol encountered a naked Spaniard in the desert. He had travelled 6,000 miles on foot to reach New Spain, and the tale he told convinced the Crown that a great civilization lay to the north.

Álvar Núñez Cabeza de Vaca was second in command to Panfilo de Narváez when he set out to pacify the territories that lay between Florida and the Gulf Coast of Mexico.

Narváez reached Tampa Bay in April of 1528, and sent his ships ahead to the Rio Grande while he led a company of 300 foot and 40 horse into the interior of Florida. The task did not seem difficult – his pilots informed him that the Rio Grande lay no more than ten or fifteen leagues from his present position. Narváez never saw his ships again.

By June Narváez reached an Indian village on the Florida Panhandle, some 250 miles from Tampa Bay. Finding the land swampy and heavily wooded, and his company under constant attacks by primitive tribes, he moved south to the sea. By the time he reached the coast, more than half the company was sick with malaria and dysentery. The sea offered their only escape from this hostile land.

With little food and no tools, the company undertook the formidable task of building rafts to continue their journey to the west. Using stirrups, spurs, crossbows, and other equipment containing iron, and with pitch made from pine resin, they constructed five rafts 30 feet long with sails and oars, each capable of holding 50 men.

Forty-nine days later, they reached the mouth of the Mississippi, but they were swept back out to sea by the current and scattered by a storm before they could make land.

On 6 November after six more days at sea, the storm drove Cabeza de Vaca's craft ashore on Galveston Island. The crew stripped and stowed their clothes in the raft and tried to pull it back into the sea, but a huge wave inundated them and capsized the raft. Three men were lost, and the survivors were left naked in the bitter November winds. The Indians took them into their huts and fed them, but without clothing and a raft, they had no choice but to spend the winter on the island.

From Cabeza de Vaca's journal:

> ... the weather turned so cold and stormy that the Indians could not pull up roots, their cane contraptions for catching fish yielded nothing, and the huts being very open, our men began to die. Five Christians on the coast came to the extremity of eating each other. Only the body of the last one, whom nobody was left to eat, was found unconsumed. Then half the natives died from a disease of the bowels and blamed us.
>
> We named this place *Malhado* – the Island of Doom.

During their stay, the Indians prevailed upon them to cure their various illnesses, and withheld food until they complied. The only thing the Spaniards could offer was a *Pater Nostra*, an *Ave Maria*, and the sign of the cross, but it was effective, and word of their powers reached the mainland.

Some continued their journey to the west on foot, but Cabeza de Vaca, being too ill to travel, was forced to stay another year with the Indians. It was a year of hardship and suffering; a year of hard work and harsh treatment from his hosts.

> My life had become unbearable. In addition to much other work, I had to grub roots in the water or from underground in the canebreaks. My fingers got so raw that if a straw touched them they would bleed. The broken cranes often slashed my flesh; I had to work amidst them without benefit of clothes.

In February of 1530, Cabeza de Vaca escaped, and made good use of what he had learned from his captivity. He became a trader, a neutral merchant who could cross lines with enemy tribes with his goods. For nearly six years, naked and alone, he ranged as far north as Oklahoma and as far south as Matagorda Bay, trading cones, sea snails, conchs,

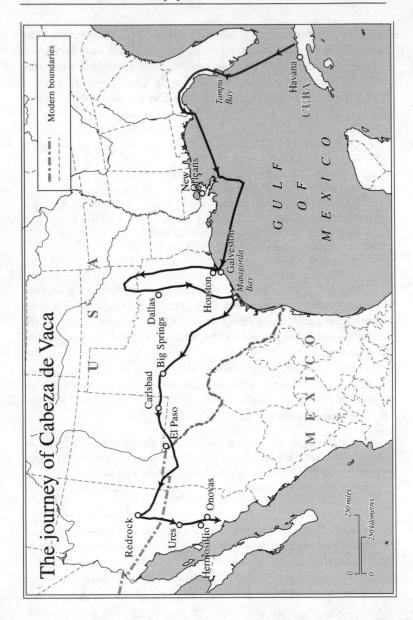

The journey of Cabeza de Vaca

beads, and fruit in exchange for skins, canes for arrowshafts, flint for arrow heads, sinews, cement, tassels of deer hair, and red ochre.

In November of 1532, he took Oviedo, one of three survivors of the Island of Doom, to Matagordo Bay. There he met Alonso de Castillo, Andrés Dorantes, and Estavánico, a black slave, all captives of the Indians.

On 22 September 1534, the Spaniards made their break and found their way to a friendly tribe on the shores of the Colorado River. They spent eight months with the tribe before moving on, during which time they improved their skills as medicine men. Castillo blessed the sick at sunset and commended them to God, and by the following morning, each had recovered. Cabeza de Vaca took his turn as medicine man when the Indians asked him to attend a kinsman near death. When he arrived, he saw the man was already dead. He could do no more than say a prayer for him, then went on to treat others who had fallen into a stupor. But before he had finished, the 'dead' man was up and eating his dinner. Word of the miracle spread up and down the Colorado, and before long, the Spaniards had a thriving business curing the sick and blessing their children.

The Spaniards left the tribe and undertook the difficult journey up the Colorado to where it crossed the Concho river, some hundred miles northwest of Austin, Texas.

> I have already said that we went naked through all this country; not being accustomed to going so, we shed our skins twice a year like snakes. The sun and the air raised great and painful sores on our chests and shoulders, and our heavy loads caused the cords to cut our arms. The region is so broken and so overgrown that often, when we gathered wood, blood flowed from us in many places where the thorns and shrubs tore our chests.

From the junction of the Colorado and Conchos, the Spaniards moved northwest 180 miles to Big Spring, Texas. Here rabbit and deer were plentiful, but before each meal, 3,000 Indians had to be blessed. From Big Spring, they travelled 180 miles west to Carlsbad, New Mexico, then across the Sacramento Mountains, where they received gifts of copper rattles, silver (mica), pearls, and buffalo hides.

It was here that Cabeza de Vaca was to gain fame throughout the southwest as a medicine man. Indians brought a man with an arrow-head lodged above his heart, and asked if he could save him.

> I probed the wound and discovered the arrowhead had passed through the cartilage. With a flint knife I opened the fellow's chest until I could see that the point was sideways and would be difficult to extract. But I cut on and, at last, inserting my knife-point deep, was able to work the arrowhead out with great effort. It was huge. With a deer bone, I further demonstrated my surgical skill with two stitches while blood drenched me, and stanched the flow with a hide.

On October of 1535, the Spaniards reached the Rio Grande at a point just south of El Paso. From here they travelled to Redrock, Arizona, then across the Chiricahua Mountains into the Sonora Desert of northern Mexico.

On the Sonora river near Ures, 40 miles northeast of Hermosillo, the natives gave Cabeza de Vaca coral beads from the Gulf of Mexico, turquoises from the north, and five emerald arrowheads they used in their rituals. (The last may have been malachite.)

> These looked quite valuable. I asked where they came from. They said from lofty mountains to the north, where there were towns of great population and great houses, and that the arrowheads had been purchased with feather bushes and parrot plumes.

Eighty miles to the south, at Ónovas, the Spaniards saw an Indian wearing a belt buckle about his neck, and learned that bearded men with horses, lances, and swords came seeking slaves, but they had left by sea.

Beyond Ónovas the Spaniards found a once fertile land now abandoned and burned, and the natives that had not fled from the Christians thin and weak, reduced to eating bark and roots. As they travelled south, they saw the tracks of the Christians and their abandoned camps. On the day they reached what seemed to be a fresh campsite, Cabeza de Vaca took Estavánico and eleven Indians in search of the Spaniards, and the following day, he overtook four mounted men thirty miles to the south. The date was March, 1536.

Cabeza de Vaca had no trouble convincing a nation aroused by the riches of Mexico and Peru of his belief that a fabulous aboriginal nation existed in the north, and that the land would prove rich in gold, silver, turquoise, and emeralds. The fact that he had lost the emerald arrowheads made no difference to men who wanted to believe. Many prominent men contended for the privilege of leading the expedition, but the Viceroy Mendoza, jealous of Cortés's achievements, took the mission upon himself.

Mendoza sent a Franciscan friar, Marcos de Niza, with Estavánico as an advance guide and interpreter, north to reconnoitre the territory and locate the Seven Cities of Cibola, Unfortunately, the Indians killed Estavánico, but a survivor of the advance party led him to the vicinity of what may have been the Zuñi pueblos in New Mexico.

Fray Marcos was evidently endowed with an overactive imagination. In his report to the Viceroy, he claimed to have seen a city larger and more splendid than Tenochtitlán, which was the smallest of the Seven Cities of Cibola.

Mendoza never doubted the Friar. He chose his close friend, Francisco Vásquez de Coronado to lead the way to the Seven Cities.

Coronado left Compostela in 1540 with 336 Spaniards, 1,000 Indian allies, and thousands of cattle and swine to serve as provisions for his army. After an arduous journey of more than a thousand miles, he reached the disappointing conclusion that the Seven Cities of Cibola were no more than the adobe dwellings of the Zuñi and the Hopi. Nevertheless reports of another 'fabulous' city, Quivira, encouraged him to move on. Coronado spent the next two years travelling through Arizona, New Mexico, Texas, and Oklahoma, and ventured as far north as Great Bend, Kansas. Quivira turned out to be nothing more than the grass huts of a Wichita village, but his expedition would establish the Crown's claim to a territory as large as France and Germany.

The loss of lives and money on the expedition was so excessive that the Crown ordered strict limits on funding for all future expeditions, but New Spain suffered an even greater loss. Coronado had drawn off so much manpower from New Galacia that the province could no longer defend itself from the semi-barbarous Caxcanes, who raided settlements throughout the region from fortified positions on mountain tops.

Juan de Oñate, the governor of New Galicia, led a Spanish force against the Indians, but heavy casualties forced him to retreat. He appealed to Pedro de Alvarado for help, who was readying a fleet at Colima for an expedition to the Spice Islands. Alvarado, with no more than a hundred men could do no better, and he was killed in the retreat when his horse rolled over him.

Mendoza took to the field himself to wage a costly campaign against the Caxcanes, and when the rebels surrendered, he branded them as slaves and distributed them among his men.

In 1542, Mendoza sent Juan Rodriguez Cabrillo to explore the coastline of California. In ten months he sailed as far north as the California–Oregon Border, but other than San Diego Bay, he discovered no settlements of any consequence nor any promising straits, and further exploration of the west coast was shelved for a later time.

Perhaps the most ambitious undertaking was to the west, when Spain sought to break the Portuguese monopoly in the Spice Islands. In 1542 Ruy Lopéz de Villalobos set out from Acapulco with six ships, and in a voyage lasting three months he reached the islands by way of the Philippines. He failed, however, to establish a viable trade route from New Spain to the Philippines. The return journey to Acapulco required tacking back and forth against adverse winds, and no ship of that era was large enough to carry sufficient provisions for the voyage. Villalobos eventually made his way back to New Spain via the Cape of Good Hope.

Twenty-two years later Miguel López de Legazpi sent Felipe de Saucedo from Manila in search of the eastward passage. Among his crew was an aging friar who spent eleven years sailing and trading in the East Indies in his youth, and was familiar with the Western Pacific. Fray Andrés de Urdaneta once held a command in Villalobos's fleet, but after ten years at sea, he took the habit of Saint Augustine.

During the journey back to New Spain the pilot and ship's master died, and Urdaneta assumed their duties. He was under the impression that the westerly winds in the Atlantic might also prevail in the Pacific, and persuaded Saucedo to sail northwards in search of them. They beat their way northwards for 2,000 miles, and reached the westerlies at a latitude of 32° north. Along the way, however, scurvy swept through the crew, leaving fourteen crew members dead, and only Saucedo and Fray Andrés were able to stand watch.

Urdaneta sailed before the wind to the coast of California, then down the coast to Acapulco, arriving on 13 October 1565. As the ship entered the port, the old friar was at the helm, still wearing his tattered habit. The eastward passage had been found – New Spain was now in a position to challenge the Portuguese monopoly in the East Indies.

Meanwhile, expansion northwards progressed at a steady pace. By 1560, New Spain laid claim to a territory that encompassed the present states of Sinaloa, Durango, Sonora, and Chihuahua, and by 1579, the territory encompassed the states of Coahuila and Nueva León. By the end of the century, the nation's borders reached as far as New Mexico.

The Silver Mines

In 1546, Juanes de Tolosa led a small party of Spaniards and Indian allies to the foot of a high promontory some 150 miles northwest of Guadalajara. In exchange for a few trinkets, the natives gave Tolosa several specimens of silver ore promising enough for him to locate the deposits and send a few wagonloads south to be assayed. The report that came back convinced Tolosa to found a city at the foot of the promontory. Within four years, 34 mining companies built foundries and stamping mills in Zacatecas, and in their wake, churches, missions, stores, a government house, and mansions for the wealthy followed.

Encouraged by Tolosa's good fortune, prospectors found other rich deposits at the present sites of Guanajuato, San Luis Potosí, Durango, and Santa Barbara. In 1557 the mercury amalgam process of extracting silver from ore was developed, reducing the cost of separation and profitable exploration of low-grade ores. Soon a steady stream of silver flowed into Mexico City and across the Atlantic to Spain. But mining was risky business, dependent upon credit, machinery, and transport. And, needless to say, upon cheap native and slave labour, many of whom died in the mineshafts from overwork and disease.

At the end of the sixteenth century, the annual return from the mines was 3 million pesos a year, and by 1750 the yield was 13 million a year. By the end of the eighteenth century, Zacatecas produced a fifth of the world's silver. Two billion dollars were coined in the mints, and two billion more exported in ingots. New Spain now exported two-thirds of the world supply of silver from Vera Cruz.

The mines were also the driving force for the northward expansion of the ranching industry. As mining towns spread rapidly throughout ore-bearing regions, the growing demand for food and transport brought herdsmen and breeders up from the south. Once the haciendas were established, the ranchers looked northwards into the vast open spaces to claim open rangeland in Indian territories.

The Church

Three Franciscan missionaries were the first clergy to reach New Spain, arriving in 1523. The most notable was Pedro de Gante, who founded the first school for the education of Indian boys in Texcoco. The following year, twelve Franciscan friars arrived in Vera Cruz and walked barefoot to Mexico City, where, to the amazement of the Indians, Cortés knelt before them and kissed their tattered robes. The Dominicans, noted for their intellectual achievements, arrived in 1525, bringing with them Bartolomé de Las Casas, the firebrand protector of the Indians who would later become the Bishop of Chiapas. The Augustinians arrived in 1533, and the Jesuits not until 1571, long after the other orders were well established.

A special relationship existed between the Spanish Crown and Rome in the New World. By accepting the obligation of Chris-tianizing natives and building churches, the Crown was granted a wide range of concessions usually reserved for Rome. In effect, the Crown was the Church in the New World. It had the right to nominate candidates for all church offices, including cardinals, bishops, and canons. It could allocate tithes and revenues for religious purposes, choose locations for the various orders, determine the boundaries of sees, approve papal bulls for the Indies, and censor all religious com-munications from the colonies. Only dogma, doctrine, and *fuero*, the right of clergy to be tried only in Church courts, were withheld from the Crown.

Service in the Church offered an attractive career for men from all

Mexico Cathedral

classes of society, even those with a poor education and questionable qualifications. The upper echelons were generally the sons of nobles, whose political function was to preach obedience, punish liberals, and support the Crown's position on all matters.

The secular priests were supported by special taxes, tithes, ten per cent of Indian crops, marriage and burial fees, and bequests. The secular was also privileged to engage in commerce and entrepeneurship. Because of its enormous revenues, the Church controlled most of the liquid capital in Mexico by the end of the colonial period, and became the nation's principal lending agency. After 300 years of colonization, half the wealth of New Spain was in the hands of the clergy.

The regulars, or friars, on the other hand, reported only to Rome until the reign of Isabella the Catholic. Their relative freedom from censorship attracted some of the finest intellects in New Spain. During the early post-conquest years, scholars such as Bernardino de Sahagún, Andres de Olmos, and Toribio de Benevente perfected Nahuatl, the native tongue, into a written language, and established colleges to instruct sons of the Mexican élite in Latin, logic, and philosophy. From their works, and those of their native students, comes much of what is known of pre-conquest Mexico. Besides maintaining schools and colleges, the friars were responsible for establishing monasteries, hospitals, and frontier missions. When the Indians were Christianized, baptized, and civilized, their churches were turned over to the parishes of the secular clergy.

As the colonial period progressed, however, the relationship between Crown and Church cooled as the latter assumed more and more control over the economy of New Spain while continuing to enjoy its special legal privileges. The threat to royal authority created an increasing anti-clerical sentiment in Spain, which burst into open conflict in New Spain when the Viceroy Marqués de Gelves issued reforms in 1624 that struck down the privileges enjoyed by wealthy *criollos*.* To add insult to injury, he forbade the Archbishop Don Juan Pérez de la Serna from operating an illegal slaughter house in his palace. The order set off a sequence of events that pitted the *criollos*, with Serna at their head, against the Viceroy, who enjoyed little popular support. The upshot of the conflict resulted in the Archbishop excommunicating the Viceroy and the *Audiencia*. More excommunications were issued, and Serna suspended the Mass and all sacraments. Church bells tolled night and day throughout the city as the anathema was read from the pulpit of the cathedral.

The apostolic judge reversed the excommunications, ordered the archbishop arrested and fined 4,000 ducats, and sent him into exile. He was placed under guard at Teotihuacan, and immediately excommunicated the entire government of New Spain. The outcry in the capital caused the *Audiencia* to reverse the decree of exile, whereupon Gelves arrested the *Audiencia*. A riot broke out in the city as priests and *criollos* showered the windows of the palace with stones, then broke down the palace doors with heavy beams. Gelves saw that further resistance was futile when they opened the jail and set fires throughout the plaza, and fled to a Franciscan convent.

When the rioting was over and order restored, Serna was recalled to Spain, where he met a cold reception from the Crown. In New Spain, four leaders of the mob were executed, and five priests sentenced to the galleys. Gelves was exonerated and resumed his career in Spain.

* A *criollo* was a Spaniard born in New Spain.

THE CHURCH AND THE INDIAN

The acceptance of European Catholicism by the Indians is eloquently summarized by Octavio Paz in his essay, 'The Conquest and Colonialism'. He states that

> ... the fate of the Indians would have been very different if it had not been for the church. I am not thinking only of its struggle to improve their living conditions and to organize them in a more just and Christian manner, but also of the opportunity that baptism offered them to form a part of one social order and one religion. The possibility of belonging to a living order, even if it was at the bottom of the social pyramid, was cruelly denied to the Indians by the Protestants of New England. It is often forgotten that to belong to the Catholic faith meant that one found a place in the cosmos. The flight of their gods and the death of their leaders had left the natives in a solitude so complete that it is difficult for a modern man to imagine it. Catholicism re-established their ties with the world and the other world. It gave them back a sense of their place on earth; it nurtured their hopes and justified their lives and death.
>
> It is unnecessary to add that the religion of the Indians was a mixture of new and ancient beliefs ... the important thing was that their social, human, and religious relationships with the surrounding world and with the divine had been re-established.

But while the Indian readily accepted the Catholic religion and its rituals, his relationship with the Church was that of an inferior, not on the same level as the *criollo* and the *mestizo*.

The Church was responsible for the education of the Indians, and in every village a parish priest taught Catholic doctrine, reading, writing, and the Spanish language. The principal beneficiaries of a Spanish education, however, were only a select number of young men who were groomed as town scribes. For the remainder of the population, the influence of Spanish education and Catholic ideology was minimal at best. Even in the twenty-first century, 80 per cent of the Indians in highland villages speak no Spanish, and the education of the remaining 20 per cent, who may have had one to four years of schooling, included reading and some Spanish taught from simple primers.

In the seventeenth and eighteenth centuries, the gap between the peasant and the Church widened when exorbitant taxes, levied solely for the benefit of the clergy, were imposed upon the Indians. All the basic elements of Catholic ritual–baptism, confession, mass, marriage, and the holy sacrament for the dying, were priced out of reach for most. Even the village hierarchy were forced to sell lands and stock to meet the high cost of religious functions.

As the Indians became more and more adamant in their refusal to carry the increasing burden of sanctioned ritual, the Church retaliated by withdrawing priests from the villages and denying all forms of orthodox religious celebrations. As a result, the Indian *alcaldes* began to take over many of the priestly offices, performing the rites of baptism, marriage, and burial. Thus Spanish control of Indian religion, never very secure, was weakened by making it impossible, from a purely economic standpoint, to participate in Catholicism, even on the elemental level granted at the time of the conquest.

After the Caste War of Chiapas in 1869, the Church was never again able to control Indian religious life in the highlands with the same authority it had in colonial days. Ownership of village churches passed into the hands of the Indian community, the resident priest was no longer a fixture in the local churches, and formal relations with the church were limited to periodic visits by the priest for specific cere-monies within the financial means of the community.

Administration and Government

After the conquest of Mexico, Charles V established the Council of the Indies in Seville to administer the affairs of the Indies. The body was composed of lawyers, clerics, and high-ranking officials returning to Spain. They drafted royal laws and ordinances, reviewed legislation enacted in the colonies, exercised judicial powers, approved expedi-tions, oversaw Indian welfare, authorized inspections of colonial offi-cials, and nominated appointees for high office in the military, clerical, and civil hierarchy.

Earlier, in 1511, an *Audiencia* in Santo Domingo acted upon all judicial matters in the New World not referred to Spain, and assumed executive and legislative functions for the colonies. In 1527, the first *Audiencia* of New Spain was established, and in 1529, the notorious

Beltran Niño de Guzmán assumed the presidency. Guzmán's administration was arguably the most corrupt administration in the history of
Mexico. Prior to his appointment in the capital, he served as governor
of Panuco, where his slaving raids nearly depopulated the province of
Huasteca. In the capital, he continued to profit from the misery and
suffering of the natives as well as from Spaniards incurring his disfavour.
Word of his excesses eventually reached Spain through the efforts of
the Bishop-elect Juan de Zumárraga, and Guzmán departed for New
Galicia leaving his deputies to be sent to Spain for trial.

In 1530, the second *Audiencia*, a caretaker of the coming vice-regal
government of New Spain, arrived. Headed by the capable Bishop
Sebastián Ramírez Funleal, the *Audiencia* was able to restore law and
order in the provinces by the time the Viceroy Antonio de Mendoza,
the first of 62 viceroys to serve in Mexico, arrived in 1530.

The viceroy's authority was broad and comprehensive, encompass-
ing, with few exceptions, that of the Crown, the captain-general of the
armed forces, and President of the *Audiencia*. Although the viceroy was
the central authority, the *Audiencias* of Mexico City and Guadalajara
enjoyed broad latitude in administration, politics, and judicial authority
for their jurisdictions.

As the provinces grew, they were divided into districts governed by
corregidores and minor officials with a variety of titles. The *corregidores*
were responsible for maintaining law and order in their jurisdictions,
but were considerably limited in judicial and administrative authority.
These offices were by law reserved for the Spanish-born. At this level of
government, the quality of administration took a sharp drop.

The *corregidores* were usually the sons of *conquistadores* or settlers, the
office granted in lieu of a pension or *encomienda*. Most had little education and seldom any training for administration, and the pay was so
low that incomes were usually supplemented by graft or other illegal
means. Gradually they were replaced by more qualified appointees, but
the office passed through the entire colonial period with the same
reputation of corruption and greed.

Government of Spanish municipalities was invested in the *cabildo*, a
body of councilmen responsible for local matters, such as land divisions,
municipal facilities, and peace keeping. These were the only offices

open to the native-born. The offices were created in the reign of Philip II to provide for the democratic process in the towns and villages, but seats on the council were sold to the highest bidder in perpetuity, offering future generations of councilmen an unparalleled opportunity for corruption.

Government of Indian towns in the Valley of Mexico differed little from native rule of pre-conquest days. Major towns, called *cabaceras* by the Spaniards, were governed by Indian rulers who bore the title of *tlatoani*, which was a hereditary position. The town was further subdivided into *calpullis*, a group of families living in a single location who assigned arable lands within the community. In the late Aztec period, there were some fifty *cabeceras* in the Valley of Mexico supported by tributes from lesser towns under their jurisdiction, and in turn, the *tlatoanis* were tributaries to the *ueytlatoani* in Tenochtitlan. Thus by replacing the *ueytlatoani* with a central government, the Crown and its colonial administrators became the beneficiaries of Moctezuma's tribute system.

Colonial Economy

Mining yielded rich returns, but agriculture and ranching drove the economy of New Spain in the colonial period. The introduction of the metal plough and draught animals opened new lands for cultivation to meet the demands of a burgeoning population. In central Mexico, wheat, maize, and pulque, a fermented drink extracted from the agave plant, were grown for internal consumption. In the south, large plantations were established to produce export products for Europe such as henequen, cotton, sugar, beans, vanilla, tobacco, and cacao. Cochineal, a brilliant red dye extracted from tiny insects that thrived in the nopalli cactus, and indigo were much in demand for dyes in Europe's rapidly growing textile industry. Other than bullion, cochineal yielded more export income than any other commodity.

New Spain also served as a trading post for goods from the East Indies and the Philippines. Merchant vessels from the Far East unloaded their cargoes at Acapulco, and pack mules carried them across the country to Vera Cruz for trans-shipment to Europe.

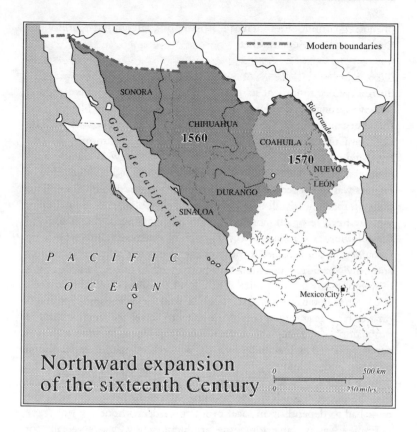

SONORA

CHIHUAHUA
1560

COAHUILA

1570

NUEVO
LEÓN

DURANGO

SINALOA

Golfo de California

Rio Grande

Modern boundaries

P A C I F I C

O C E A N

Mexico City

Northward expansion
of the sixteenth Century

0   500 km

0   250 miles

To the north, breeders drove cattle, sheep, goats, and pigs into the mining regions of Zacatecas, Guanajuato, and Durango to feed the growing population, and raised donkeys, horses, and mules for the mines to transport ore to the capital. Beef was cheap, but mutton was the preferred meat for the settlers, and flocks of two million sheep were common in Zacatecas. From the mining regions, the ranchers moved their growing herds into readily available land further north, which, for the greater part, was fit only for grazing. By the end of the colonial period, there were more than a thousand cattle ranches extending as far north as New Mexico, Texas, and California, and 3,749 *haciendas* producing commodities such as leather goods, tallow, hides, and wool for local and overseas' markets.

COLONIAL COMMERCE

Spanish protectionism of its home industries and merchants imposed such unreasonable restraints on commercial growth in the New World that it became a major factor leading to the War of Independence. The Casa de Contratación, established in Seville in 1503, monitored and regulated all commerce between Spain and the New World. Spain's economic policy during the colonial period demanded that the value of exports was to exceed that of imports by a factor of two or more. This policy forbade nearly all manufacturing in the colonies. Raw materials were shipped to Spain, converted into merchandise, and sent back to the colonies at exorbitant prices. Foreign merchants and investors were forbidden in the colonies to protect merchants in the mother country and only Spanish ships could transport merchandise and other goods between Spain and the Indies. The cost of transport across the Atlantic also contributed to the price the colonist paid for goods, since privateers on the high seas forced merchant ships to travel in fleets under the protection of warships. Growers were forbidden to produce such commodities as wine and olive oil to protect Spanish agricultural interests, and all luxury goods had to be imported from Spain, even though their origin was in other European countries. The result was that the price of goods in Mexico limited the market to the rich; the poor had to depend upon local products or do without.

Capital was available for home production, however, especially for wool and cotton textiles. For their investment, the merchants controlled raw materials, production, and distribution of finished goods. By 1604, twenty-five textile mills, called *obrajes*, were producing dry goods in Mexico City, and numbers of other mills were producing textiles in Cuernavaca, Puebla, Tlaxcala, and Querétaro. Water-driven machinery, the horizontal loom, and the spinning wheel were, however, still primitive.

In time, the *obrajes* became the commercial hub of the major cities. Puebla, for instance, had thirty mills at the start of the seventeenth century, and developed a profitable trade with Havana, Caracas, and

Lima. The downside of the *obrajes* was the unconscionable use of native workers. The Indians were forced to work long hours and often incurred respiratory problems from breathing in lint in the close confinement of the mill.

Race and Status

By the end of the seventeenth century, a highly stratified, multicultural society had developed in New Spain. At the top of the pyramid were 15,000 Spanish-born *peninsulares*, or *gauchupines*, as they were commonly called, a minority population who controlled the economy, the army, the Church, and the government. Of the sixty-two viceroys, fifty-eight were Spaniards, and all but one of the archbishops was from Spain. The *criollos* were next with a population of more than a million. The lower classes were made up of some 700,000 *mestizos*, people of Spanish-Indian mixed blood, 600,000 *mulattos* (Spanish-black), and *zambos* (black-Indian), and 10,000 Negros. At the bottom of the pyramid were, of course, the Indians, with a population of nearly four million.

A colonial cavalryman with his lance and pistol

The *peninsulares* looked down upon the *criollos* as mentally and morally inferior. While restricted from occupying positions reserved for Spaniards, they could, however, rise in the upper echelons of the Church and to middle levels of the bureaucracy. Many became lawyers, physicians, teachers, and priests in the regular and secular hierarchy, although their less prestigious education limited their opportunities. Many turned to commerce, considered below the dignity of Spaniards, and acquired status and wealth in ranching, agriculture, textiles, and the mines. They wore silk, velvet, linen, and lace clothing, which, as in Moctezuma's time, were forbidden to Indians, and scorned manual labour. In time, they came to regard Spain and its royal representatives in New Spain a hindrance to progression and their taxes as a drain on badly needed capital for commerce.

The *mestizos* were the lower middle class. They generally held minor government positions, or were foremen on plantations, ranches, mines, and textile mills. In urban areas, many were artisans and shopkeepers. During the early colonial period most were illegitimate, unrecognized by their fathers and raised by their Indian mothers, and adopted Indian ways and culture.

Blacks made their appearance in the colonies as slaves. Some 200,000 were imported into the New World over three hundred years, and put to work in mines, plantations, sugar mills, and ranches. With them they brought their culture, their oral traditions, and their music, which in time had a significant influence upon the music of Mexico. They also brought skills in animal husbandry, agriculture, folk arts, and ceramics.

For the greater part, slaves, whether black or Indian, received better treatment than Indians held in *encomienda*. The period of ownership of the *encomienda* was at best uncertain, given the Crown's vacillating position on hereditary rights, and the *encomendero* had an incentive to overwork them as much as possible while they were in his possession. Slaves, on the other hand, were expensive, a capital expenditure that could be justified only by realizing long-term benefits from their labour. The slave in New Spain, however, enjoyed privileges denied slaves in America. He had the right to take a wife of his own choosing, to seek employment in his free time, and to accumulate enough capital to buy his freedom and that of his family.

In populated areas, in *haciendas*, mines, ranches, and other functions that required heavy manual labour, the Indian was the major source of supply. In time, he was assimilated into urban society, albeit at the lowest level. In areas sparsely inhabited by whites and *mestizos*, however, the Indian peasant led a life relatively independent of government supervision, but it was a communal rather than an individual life. Each community was allocated 6.5 acres of land, which could not be sold without the consent of the viceroy. Indian authorities collected tribute from the community, a portion of which went to the Crown, and the remainder to the community treasury to finance community projects. They also administered justice according to their traditional ways whenever it did not conflict with the state or the Church. In the highlands of Mexico and Guatemala, Indian communities still preserve the customs, traditions, and Indian dress of their ancestors.

The dynamics of the Indian community depend as much upon its religious system as its municipal government. Every adult male has a moral and civic duty to assume, to the limit of his financial ability, one or more posts in the religious cargo system of the village. A cargo is an obligation to service one of the village saints for a full year, during which time the holder is responsible for the care of the saint, the costumes, jewellery, and other accoutrements. For each ritual, the cargo-holder and his assistants must select the appropriate dress and jewellery, and on the name day of the saint, parade him or her through the village on their shoulders.

The importance and prestige of any cargo is always directly related to its cost. For the most prestigious cargoes, it is common for the appointee to pay the equivalent of a year's income, and to forego income for the following year of his service. Furthermore, if he hopes to rise in the political as well as the religious hierarchy, he is obliged to serve more than one cargo; in some cases as many as four if he has ambitions to rise to high office in the community.

At the other extreme, Spaniards recognized and accepted Indian nobility into the élite society of New Spain. The most prominent of the Mexican nobility were Doña Isabel, Moctezuma's daughter by his first wife and his only surviving heir; three daughters by his second wife; two sons, Don Pedro and Don Martin, by a princess of Tula; and Don

Rodrigo, whose mother has not been identified. Other noted Indian nobles accepted into Spanish society were Fernando Alvarado Tezozomoc, a grandson of Moctezuma; Diego Munoz Camargo, a grandson of Maxixca, the ruling lord of Tlaxcala during the conquest; Domingo Francisco de San Muñon, a direct descendant of the ruling family of Amecameca during the conquest; and Fernando de Alva Ixtlilxochitl, a direct descendant of Nezahualpilli, the great Texcocan ruler of the pre-conquest era.

The bitter hatred the *criollo* held for the Spaniard was in evidence from the beginning of the colonial era, when descendants of the *conquistadores*, tired of seeing their *encomiendas* threatened by servants of the Crown who had contributed nothing towards the subjection of the country won by their fathers, began to speak of sedition. The leaders of the group were Alonzo and Gil Gonzáles de Avila, sons of one of Cortés's commanders, who had a following of some 120 sympathizers. For leadership to rally the masses about them, they turned to Martín Cortés, recently arrived in New Spain to manage his father's vast estates.

The young Marqués was raised in the court of Charles V, and was a favourite of Prince Philip. When he petitioned the court to return to the land of his birth, Philip, feeling he was no danger to the Crown, granted him the rights and privileges held by his father. Accompanying him were his two bastard brothers, Martin, who bore the same name as the Marqués, and Luis Cortés.

The Indians, they were certain, would stand with them, as they gave the Marqués the same adoration and devotion as they had given his father. More important, The Franciscans, who were always partial to Hernán, were in a bitter fight with the Council of the Indies to save their parishes from secularization. Further, Jerónimo de Valderrama, the Licenciado sent by the Crown to investigate a conflict between the Marqués and the Viceroy, sided with the Marqués. Spain was so weakened by the everlasting wars of Charles V and Philip II that they felt the Crown could not mount a campaign strong enough to put down a well-organized rebellion so far from home.

The Avila brothers and their followers met in the palace of the Marqués, where they developed a plot that was sound and feasible, and once it was executed, they would proclaim the Marqués King of New Spain. It might have succeeded had the Marqués had the strength of his convictions and the fortitude of his father, but he vacillated, and the plot began to wither on the vine. In 1566, the *Audiencia* acted. The Marqués was placed under house arrest, the Avila brothers tried for treason and beheaded, and their heads displayed on pikes as a warning to any would-be conspirators. The Marqués was sent back to Spain to stand trial, but the evidence was weak. He spent several years under house arrest, and was released after paying a fine of 50,000 pesos.

In the first three hundred years of the colonial period, riots and rebellion shook the cities constantly, and the *mestizos, mulattos, zambos*, and blacks were quick to join the struggle. In 1611, 1,500 blacks rioted in Mexico City when a black woman was flogged to death. In 1612, the authorities tortured and killed black leaders, lynched thirty-five men and women in the central plaza and displayed their heads on pikes. In 1665 there was a number of outbreaks of violence by blacks and mulattos, which were finally suppressed with the aid of the Inquisition. In 1692, two years of crop failures brought about a crisis in the Valley of Mexico, forcing the people in Mexico City to depend upon the public granary. Faulty distribution, rumours of corruption, and the treatment of women by the central government led to riots by Indians, *mestizos*, and the rest of the lower classes.

Two soldiers were killed by Indians showering the palace with rocks, the mint was sacked, the market-place fired, the gibbet and the stocks torn down, and the chambers of the *Audiencia*, the jail, and the town hall were fired. The riot eventually ran its course when the *pulquerias* were looted and the mob, reduced to a drunken stupour, left the plaza. Only the lack of a leader, a cause, and a plan saved the city from destruction.

The Late Colonial Period

SPAIN IN THE EIGHTEENTH CENTURY

Foreign wars and internal revolts found Spain in a state of economic ruin at the turn of the century, and the reign of Charles II (1665–1700) had left the nation in administrative chaos. Charles, the epileptic son of Philip IV, succeeded to the throne at the age of four, and his mother, Mariana de Austria, served as regent during his minority. But Charles was never competent to rule, a helpless tool dominated by conflicting interests in the Spanish court. Charles, the last of the Spanish Habsburgs, would leave no heir, and after his death the throne passed to Philippe d'Anjou, a grandson of Louis XIV, who, as Philip V (1700–46), was the first of the Bourbon dynasty to rule Spain.

Philip inherited a demoralized and undermanned military, a weak economy, his trade with the colonies in the hands of foreign merchants, and heavy debts to foreign interests.

The first steps of Philip's economic recovery programme were stimulation of trade at home by reducing high tariffs, and lowering prohibitive taxes on commerce that were strangling Spain's economy. Looking to the colonies for added income, Philip upgraded overseas' commerce by replacing Seville with Cadiz as the official port for New Spain, where better facilities were available, and, with the decline of piracy, eliminated the costly fleets that accompanied his merchant ships.

The reforms of Philip V had relatively little impact on New Spain, but a significant change was in store when Charles III (1759–88) assumed the throne and looked to the colonies for increased revenues. To accomplish this, a significant improvement in trade was vital. English, French, and Dutch contrabanders were penetrating Spain's colonial network, consuming more and more of New Spain's discretionary resources, and British smugglers were handling more than half of the commerce of the Indies. In 1762, the British seized Manila and Havana, and were threatening Vera Cruz. The British occupation of Havana lasted 11 months, during which time Havana received fifty times more ships than before, bringing English manufactured goods and slaves into the colonies. To meet the competition, Charles eliminated the Cadiz monopoly by authorizing more ports in Spain to trade with the colonies, and abolishing the monopolies held by Acapulco and Vera Cruz in New Spain by adding competitive ports at Campeche and the Yucatán. Over the next two decades, he liberalized trade by reducing and equalizing duties for ports in the colonies, opened channels whereby foreign traders could legitimately operate, and authorized Mexican merchants to trade with other ports of Latin America.

In 1765 Charles sent José de Gálvez as *visitador general* to determine the economic and political reforms needed in New Spain, and to evaluate the weak defences of the northern frontier.

In 1769, Gálvez led a militia of Indian and *mestizo* conscripts commanded by Spanish and *criollo* officers to settle and protect the exposed northwestern border of New Spain. Threatened by rumours of Russian occupation of Upper California, he sent military expeditions headed by Gaspar de Portolá and Juan Bautista de Anza into California, and commissioned Fray Junípero Sierra to establish missions from the borders of New Spain to San Francisco Bay.

The king also assigned Gálvez a more covert mission. The Bourbons did not share the Habsburg's partiality for the Church, and Charles set out to reduce the influence of the clergy in New Spain. He chose the Society of Jesus for his point of attack. The order's allegiance to the pope rivalled and reached beyond their allegiance to the king, and suspicion of political intrigue amid the Jesuits was never far from the mind of the Spanish Court.

The order had grown powerful and wealthy in New Spain. The Jesuits maintained more than a hundred missions, 23 colleges, and a number of seminaries. Jesuit holdings consisted of valuable urban real estate and some eighty estates with an estimated value of ten million pesos. Furthermore, their accomplishments in agriculture and manufacturing based on Indian crafts were models of early capitalism.

Gálvez and the viceroy Marquis de Croix were assigned the task of expelling the Jesuits from New Spain. In February 1767, Charles ordered the deportation of the Jesuits and confiscation of their properties and sent sealed orders to the military. On 25 June the orders were executed and officers entered the convents, schools and missions, and arrested all 678 members of the order, 400 of whom were born in New Spain.

Confined to miserable quarters in Vera Cruz and other ports until October, they were finally sent to Spain, arriving in Cadiz on 30 March 1768. Before they found refuge in the Papal States, 150 died of starvation and disease.

Their expulsion caused riots in a number of cities, particularly in the volatile Bajio region of Guanajuato, San Luis Potosí, Patzacuaro, and Vallodolid. Gálvez crushed the uprising and hanged 85 rebels, lashed 73 to bloody ribbons, jailed 674, and exiled 117.

Through the influence of the pope, the Jesuits were permitted to return to New Spain in 1772, but the Crown continued to confiscate their assets. In 1804, Charles IV put the Act of Consolidation into force and appropriated the charitable funds of the Church, a total of some 44.5 million pesos, to finance Spain's wars in Europe. The effect on the economy of New Spain was disastrous. The Church, a major source of credit, was forced to call in notes and mortgages, ruining many land-owners and substantially reducing the Church's social programmes.

COLONIAL ECONOMY AT THE END OF THE EIGHTEENTH CENTURY

Despite the Bourbon demands for revenue from New Spain, the economy of the nation improved as its political reforms and trade liberalization policies took effect. With improvements in technology and the discovery of new mines, silver production rose to 27 million pesos by 1804, manufacturing production was now 72 million pesos a year, and the value of exports increased by 50 per cent from 1770 to 1780. Indian economy was also on the upswing, with more than 30,000 now employed in the cochineal industry. Sugar production was up, the textile industry in Puebla sent more than a million pounds of cloth a year to Mexico City, and by 1803, New Spain exported more cotton to Europe than the United States.

Agriculture led both manufacturing and mining, accounting for 62 per cent of the gross national product compared with 25 per cent for manufacturing, and 13 per cent for mining. Of the three, mining accounted for 84 per cent of the export market. As a gross measure of the nation's productivity, the Crown's income from New Spain quadrupled in the last quarter of the century. By 1803, its income from the colony was nearly 19 million pesos, with the greater part, 4.5 million, coming from its tobacco monopoly in Orizaba, Tezuitlán, and Córdoba.

The growth in the nation's economy, however, was not shared by the greater population of New Spain. By the late eighteenth century, more than four-fifths of the population was non-white, mostly in the lower classes. Wages were barely sufficient to meet basic needs, and debt peonage was common. Peasants were forced to surrender their lands to an expanding *hacienda* system, and without their lands, many joined an ever-increasing labour force crowding into the cities seeking work. For most, begging on the streets was their only option. The level of poverty was such that in 1784, more than 3,000 died of under-nourishment. Those remaining in the rural areas eked out an existence as sharecroppers or by tilling subsistence parcels granted by *hacendados*. In spite of their destitution, the Indians still paid tribute to the Crown and the Church, and they were forbidden to wear the clothes of the white man under penalty of a hundred lashes and a month in jail.

In the mines wages were good, but working conditions were little improved from the early days. The Prussian scientist Alexander von Humboldt, who visited the mining areas of New Spain in 1803–04, wrote of the working conditions in the Valencia mine.

> The Indian *tenateros*, who may be considered as the beasts of burden in the mines of Mexico, remain loaded with a weight of from 225 to 350 pounds for a space of six hours. In the galleries of Valencia and Rayas, they are exposed ... to a temperature of from 22° to 25° [72°–77°F], and during this time they ascend and descend several thousands of steps in pits of an inclination of 45°.... We meet in the mines with files of fifty or sixty of these porters, among whom there are men above sixty, and boys of ten or twelve years of age.

Revolution, however, would not arise from the lower classes – their culture was too heterogeneous for organized revolt. It would come not from the *mestizos*, *mulattos*, Negroes, and especially not from the Indians, but from the *criollos*, in their search for equality with the *gauchupines*.

CHAPTER SEVEN

The Wars of Independence

Instability in Spain and New Spain

The death of Charles III brought about a disastrous decline in Spanish power at the end of the eighteenth century, creating chaos in the mother country as well as in New Spain. Charles IV was now king, and quickly proved himself incompetent to rule the nation. The real powers behind the throne were the queen, María Luisa, and her lover, Manuel de Godoy, a twenty-five-year-old guardsman she appointed prime minister.

In 1793, Godoy formed an alliance against Revolutionary France to avenge the execution of Louis XIV, which resulted in a series of disastrous defeats for Spain. In 1795, he further alienated the people when he allowed French troops to cross Spain and attack Portugal. This concession opened the door for Napoleon to march on Madrid in 1808 and take Charles IV and his heir, Ferdinand, as his prisoners. Charles abdicated in favour of Ferdinand, but Ferdinand VII was king in name only – Napoleon placed his brother Joseph on the throne of Spain.

With Charles and Ferdinand prisoners in France, Spain established a resistance government, the Central Junta, in the fortified city of Cádiz. The news caused an immediate power vacuum in New Spain. The Mexico City council, with its *criollo* majority, refused to recognize the Junta, opting instead for the formation of an independent junta in New Spain to rule in the name of Ferdinand VII. The *Audiencia*, however, demanded that the nation recognize the Central Junta in Spain as the rightful governing body. The Viceroy, José de Iturrigary, an appointee of Godoy, was convinced that the *criollos* would prevail, and, perceiving that this could be his opportunity to rule New Spain as king, allowed the *criollos* to form a junta of municipalities.

It soon became evident to the royalists that the junta was more interested in independence than in accepting a monarchy, and they decided to take action.

On the night of 15 September 1808, vigilantes broke into the palace and seized Iturrigary. They sent him to Vera Cruz for transportation to Spain, and then arrested several prominent *criollos*. They chose Pedro de Garibay, an eighty-year-old general, as viceroy, and the *Audiencia* recognized him, despite its lack of authority to do so.

Garibay was too old and senile to contend with the various militant factions in the new government, and his incompetence did not escape the attention of the Central Junta. The Junta replaced him by appointing Archbishop Francisco Xavier de Lizana as acting viceroy, and the archbishop was in turn replaced the following year by Francisco Javier Venegas. The new government was not yet stable when a severe downturn in the economy occurred, resulting in a nationwide shortage of food that fell hard upon the lower classes, and there was talk of revolution.

Meanwhile, *criollos* in the provinces formed social and literary clubs, ostensibly to discuss novels, plays, and the political scene, but in reality they were a breeding ground for conspiracy. The conspirators had no interest in social revolution for the masses – their motivation was directed solely at assuming the power in government and society that was traditionally reserved for the Spaniard.

Among their number they counted many of the secular and regular clerics, who resented their second-class status in the religious hierarchy. They had not forgotten the expulsion of the Jesuits and the Act of Consolidation, which had sequestered their charitable funds to finance Spain's wars. The lower clergy in particular was well aware of the disparity in income between the upper echelon of the Church and priests serving in Indian communities. While an archbishop's annual income could be as high as 130,000 pesos, they might earn as little as 100 pesos a year.

Perhaps the most active of the groups was the Literary and Social Club of Querétaro headed by Ignacio Allende, the commanding officer of the local militia. The firebrand of the group, however, was Father Miguel Hidalgo y Costilla, a fifty-seven-year-old priest who served the parish of Dolores in the state of Guanajuato.

Miguel Hidalgo y Costilla

Born of *criollo* parents of moderate means, the young Hidalgo matriculated first at the College of San Francisco Javier, then at the College of San Nicolás Obispo in the Mexican Valladolid (now Morelia, in Michoacán). In 1774 he received his Bachelor of Theology degree at the University of Mexico, and in 1778, he was ordained to the priesthood. His first posting was at Valladolid, where he taught Latin, theology, and philosophy at his Alma Mater, San Nicolás Obispo.

His views, however, were too liberal and his conduct unbecoming for a priest, and he was soon relieved of his post. In the years that followed, he served at three pastorates before his appointment to the parish of Dolores.

From the viewpoint of the Church, Hidalgo was a renegade priest, a candidate for investigation by the Holy Office of the Inquisition. He

Miguel Hidalgo y Costilla who provided the first impetus for the move towards independence

was known to question the infallibility of the pope, the virgin birth of Mary, and the doctrine of celibacy among the clergy. He advocated that fornication out of wedlock was not a sin, indulged in gambling, read forbidden literature, and supported the French Revolution. Furthermore, he kept a mistress, Josepha Quintana, who bore him two daughters. Hidalgo also defied secular law by pressing wine and fabricating silk, illegal industries that infringed upon the Crown monopoly, which brought down the local authorities upon him. In 1800 he was ordered to appear before the Inquisition, but charges were dismissed for lack of evidence.

His parishioners, on the other hand, were devoted to him. He mastered Otomi, their native language, and promoted the economy of the parish by introducing ceramics, tanning, saddlery, carpentry, wool weaving, blacksmithing, and bee keeping, which provided them with a source of income other than their meagre returns from community agriculture.

Politically he was a conservative, favouring retaining sovereignty of a new order in the name of Ferdinand VII instead of an independent government in New Spain.

Early in 1810, the Querétaro Literary and Social Society conceived a plan to overthrow the Spaniard-controlled government of New Spain. The plan was simple: Hidalgo would head the movement, and Allende would initiate it by leading an armed force to the annual fair in San Juan de Lagos, where he would pronounce a new government in the name of Ferdinand VII. It was presumed that the people would pick up their weapons and join the movement, and that the war would be financed by seizing the properties of Spaniards. The Indians could be counted upon for support – not for a place alongside the new ruling class, but simply for a promise that the new government would abolish their enforced tribute to the government and the Church.

The plot did not remain secret for long. A postal clerk leaked it to his supervisor, and word of the impending revolt reached the ears of the local government of Querétaro and the *Audiencia*. On 13 September the authorities moved in on the conspirators and arrested several principals of the plot, including Miguel Dominguez, a former *corregidor* of Querétaro. His wife, Doña Josepha, sent word of the arrest to

Allende, but when he could not be reached, the news was relayed to Hidalgo in Dolores. Allende was with Hidalgo when the messenger arrived, and they knew that they could wait no longer – the revolution had to be launched at once if it were to succeed.

THE CALL TO ARMS

Early in the morning of 16 September Hidalgo assembled the *mestizos* and Indians at the church and delivered the immortal *Grito de Dolores*. The exact words of the speech are not known, but the context of his message was clear – 'Death to the *gauchupine*!* Long live independence! Long live our Lady of Guadalupe!'

Hidalgo's rag-tag army left Dolores at mid-morning, armed with machetes, clubs, axes, knives, swords, a few rifles, and headed for San Miguel to join forces with Allende. Hidalgo took the banner of the Virgin of Guadalupe, the icon of Indian religion, from the local church and declared it the standard of the revolution.

By the time Hidalgo reached San Miguel, his army of 700 was an uncontrolled mob, ransacking and pillaging homes of Spaniards and wealthy *criollos* throughout the city. Allende's militia finally managed to contain them in the small hours of the morning and form them into a semblance of an army.

By the time they reached Guanajuato, a town nearly as large as Mexico City, Hidalgo's army had grown to 20,000 men. They found the militia and the entire Spanish population of the city barricaded in the Alhóndiga de Granaditas, the public granary, a massive expanse of solid stone with only one entrance through two wooden gates. The insurgents wasted no time in firing the gates and butchering the militia.

Within a month after the fall of Guanajuato, Zacatecas, San Luis Potosí, Saltillo, and Valladolid fell to the rebels.

The day of 30 October 1810 found Hidalgo and Allende with 60,000 men on a hill between Toluca and Mexico City, facing a force of 7,000 royalist troops commanded by General Torcuato Trujillo. After a long and bloody battle, the royalists withdrew, and the capital was there for the taking.

---

* *Gauchupine* was the coloquial name for the Spanish-born.

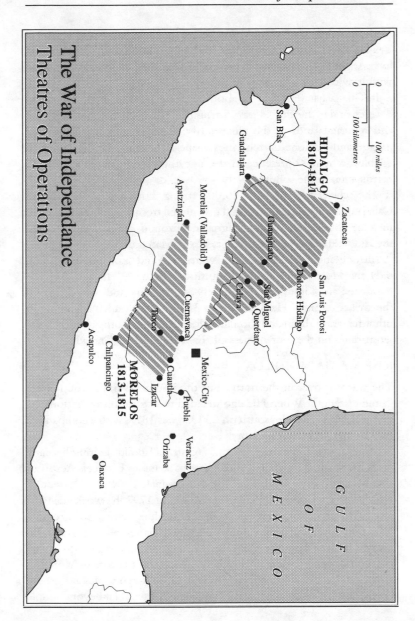

The War of Independence
Theatres of Operations

HIDALGO
1810-1811

MORELOS
1813-1815

San Blas

Guadalajara

Apatzingán

Morelia (Valladolid)

Guanajuato

Zacatecas

San Luis Potosi

Dolores Hidalgo

San Miguel

Celaya

Querétaro

Cuernavaca

Taxco

Mexico City

Acapulco

Chilpancingo

Cuautla

Izúcar

Puebla

Orizaba

Veracruz

Oaxaca

GULF
OF
MEXICO

0
0
100 kilometres
100 miles

Hidalgo hesitated. The army had suffered high casualties against Trujillo's well-disciplined forces, and ammunition and supplies were low. Allende pleaded with him to follow up their victory, but Hidalgo withdrew to Guadalajara.

In Guadalajara Hidalgo set about forming a government. He issued decrees under the title *Alteza Serenísima*, His Most Serene Highness, and returned lands to the villages, issued rebel currency, appointed judges, and published a rebel newspaper. He sent Mario Jiménez to establish a military presence in the north, and José María Morelos to recruit men in the south.

The rebel army was now 80,000 strong, but General Félix María Calleja, with no more than 6,000 disciplined troops, scattered the rebels into the countryside. Colonel Ignacio Elizondo, an ex-rebel, crushed the last of Hidalgo's army near Saltillo in March of 1811.

Allende and other non-clerics were tried and shot, but as a priest, only the Holy Office of the Inquisition could try Hidalgo. He was defrocked and found guilty of heresy and treason, and turned over to the civil authorities. He was shot on 31 July 1811, and as a warning to other rebels, his head and those of Allende and two other leaders were set in cages on the four corners of the Alhóndiga de Granaditas.

JOSÉ MARÍA MORELOS

The war was over in the north, but the insurgents in the south were gaining strength. When Hidalgo decided to expand his operations, he sent José María Morelos south on 25 October 1810, with a company of twenty men to recruit an army.

Morelos was a *mestizo*, born in 1765 in Valladolid. During his early years, he worked on a farm and drove pack mules between Acapulco and Mexico City. At the age of twenty-five, he was a student of Hidalgo at the College of San Nicolas, and in 1797, he was ordained a priest. He served for twelve years in the parish of Carácuaro, a remote village in southern Michoacán, and raised cattle to supplement his meagre income from the Church.

Guerrilla bands headed by local chieftains were the core of Morelos's army, and he used them effectively with hit-and-run tactics against the enemy. But Morelos visualized a campaign that went far beyond simple strikes from the back country, and he formulated a plan to do what Hidalgo failed to accomplish when he had the opportunity – seize the capital. His plan was to cut off Mexico City from both oceans by severing the city's line of supply from Acapulco and Vera Cruz. When this was done, he would then isolate the city from support from the provinces by deploying a ring of troops about it.

By November of 1811, Morelos's forces occupied Chilpancingo, Tixtla, and Chilapa in Guerrero, and by 1813, Taxco, Cuernavaca and Cuauhtla and Izucar, lying in an arc south of the capital, fell to the rebels.

Having achieved his military goals, Morelos convened the Congress of Chilpancingo to formulate the principles for an independent nation. The ten articles he set forth were:

1. Mexico was to be independent of any foreign power.
2. Catholicism was to be the only religion tolerated, the seculars were to be the sole interpreters of dogma, and the Church was to be supported by tithes only.
3. Sovereignty was to reside with the people (the fiction of Ferdinand VII as head of state had long been abandoned), whose voice would be heard in government by their elected representatives.
4. All government employees were to be citizens of Mexico, regardless of their social status.
5. Foreigners with needed skills would be tolerated.
6. Slavery and caste distinctions were abolished, and all peoples were to be known as Mexicans.
7. Laws were to be the same for all people, regardless of position.
8. The right to possess property and the sanctity of a man's house was to be the law.
9. Judicial torture was abolished.
10. Government was to be financed only by an income tax of 5 per cent, and an import tax of 10 per cent.

Morelos's strategy of isolating Mexico City from the sea and the surrounding countryside was sound, but his forces were too meagre to hold and defend cities separated by such great distances. General Félix María Calleja, now the viceroy, was on the move with the royalist

army. In December, 1813, he broke the siege of the capital by occupying Cuernavaca, Cauahtla, and Taxco, then moved south and drove
the rebels out of Oaxaca and Chilpancingo.

Morelos and his congress were forced to move frequently, but they
managed to issue a formal declaration of independence on 6 November
1813. A year later the congress published a constitution of 24 articles at
Apatzingán, reflecting the principles set forth by Morelos at Chilpancingo.

Late in 1815, Apatzingán was surrounded by Calleja, and Morelos
decided to move his base to Tehuacán in the province of Puebla. He set
out across Michoacán and Guerrero with his congress, but Calleja's
forces intercepted them en route. Morelos, in charge of the rear guard,
knew the cause was lost, but stayed behind until the congress escaped,
then surrendered to Calleja. The Inquisition defrocked him and
charged him with the usual crimes, then turned him over to the civil
authorities to be shot. Fearing trouble from Morelos's sympathizers in
the city, they took him to San Cristóbal Ecatepec, where he was
executed on 22 December 1815.

Ferdinand VII and the Constitution of 1812

With the death of Morelos, the independence movement all but collapsed. Only two of Morelos's lieutenants were able to conduct
effective guerrilla operations – Guadelupe Victoria in the hills of Vera
Cruz, and Vincente Guerrero from the mountains about Acapulco.
Bands of 300 to 400 men continued to harass the villages, but their
numbers were gradually reduced as Calleja shot some and granted
amnesty to others.

The second move for independence in New Spain came not from
liberal *criollos*, *mestizos*, or Indians, but from *criollo* conservatives and the
clergy. As the movement under Morelos was rapidly declining in New
Spain, the Central Junta of Seville was calling for a more liberal state. A
Cortes with representatives from Spain and the colonies was convened
at Cadiz to draft the Constitution of 1812. The document called for a
constitutional monarchy with sovereignty in the hands of the people, a
representative government, and an independent press. The Inquisition

was abolished, and although the Catholic Church was to be the State religion, there were limits on the rights of the Church to acquire property, and various privileges of the clerics and the military were abolished.

Laws were enacted in the New World to protect the Indians and their lands from the *haciendas*, and the Acts of Consolidation of 1804, sequestering Church funds for Spain's military adventures, were revoked.

In 1814, however, Napoleon was defeated, and Ferdinand VII was restored to the throne of Spain. He revoked the Constitution, dissolved the *Cortes*, imprisoned and exiled the liberals, and restored the Inquisition. The Constitution of 1812 would not be reinstated for six years, not until Colonel Rafael Riego, preparing to embark with his troops for Buenos Aires in 1820, marched on Madrid instead and forced Ferdinand to comply with it.

On 3 May 1820, the Constitution of 1812 was restored in New Spain, and conservatives, clergy, Spaniards, and even the *Audiencia* reacted with alarm. Now, ironically, they found that the only way to protect their position and privileges from Spanish liberals was to reverse their position and form another independence movement against the government.

Various conspiracies were formulated, and though the conspirators could not support any single plan, they agreed that military support would be vital for any plan they selected. They persuaded the viceroy to appoint a proven commander to lead the effort for the coming struggle, and he chose Colonel Augustín de Iturbide, a conservative *criollo* who had defeated Morelos at Valladolid.

Augustín I, Emperor of Mexico

Iturbide set out with a force of 2,500 men to contain Guerrero, the only rebel leader still active. After a few skirmishes against the rebels near Acapulco, Iturbide called for a truce at Iguala, a village on the Acapulco road. Instead of offering a peace proposal, Iturbide invited Guerrero to join forces with him in the struggle for independence. After some haggling about terms and principles to be observed, Guerrero agreed, and on 24 February 1821, they issued the *Plan de Iguala*.

The *Plan* guaranteed independence from Spain, Catholicism as the State religion, equality for all men, independent of race or position, and privileges for the clergy and the military reinstated. The form of government was to be a constitutional monarchy, and the crown would be offered to Ferdinand VII. If he refused, the ruling junta would choose a European prince.

Iturbide found no difficulty in finding support among the military, who were to guarantee the principles set forth in the *Plan*, and among the clergy, whose rights and properties were restored.

When Guanajuato, Puebla, Durango, Oaxaca, Querétaro, and Zacatecas fell to Iturbide, the Viceroy Juan Ruiz de Apodaca tendered his resignation to the Crown. The last viceroy, General Juan O'Donojú arrived in July, 1821, only to find every city in the nation, other than Mexico City, Vera Cruz, and Acapulco, flying the red, green, and white flag of Mexico. The red symbolized the blood lost for the union, green for independence, and white for religion. O'Donojú never assumed office. Instead, he called for a conference with Iturbide at Córdoba, a village on the Mexico City–Vera Cruz road, and on

The first emperor of Mexico, Augustín de Iturbide

24 August they issued the Treaty of Córdoba, declaring the independence of Mexico from Spain and confirming the terms set forth in the
Plan de Iguala. Looking to the future, however, Iturbide insisted upon a
provision that if no suitable European royal would accept the crown,
the Mexican congress was free to elect an emperor of its own choosing.

Iturbide and his army met no resistance when they marched upon
the capital on 21 September 1821. Instead, he received a hero's welcome, the keys to the city, and a *Te Deum* in the cathedral in his
honour.

In accordance with the Treaty of Córdoba, Iturbide appointed a
provisional junta made up of twenty-eight delegates to act as an interim
congress. The junta invested executive authority in a regency of five
conservatives, headed, of course, by Iturbide. In recognition as head of
both governing bodies, he was awarded the title of *Generalissimo de
Tierra y Mar* and a stipend of 120,000 pesos a year. The junta organized
the election of delegates to Congress from the provinces, but with the
caveat that each Congressional contingent contain a clergyman, a
military representative, and a lawyer.

The Congress set out to determine the form of government for the
new nation, but it was split by contesting factions. Some favoured a
republic, others a monarchy headed by a European prince, but Iturbide's adherents were determined to see the monarchy offered to their
leader.

A *coup d'état* in the city streets decided the issue. On the evening of
18 May 1822, troops from the local barracks gathered in the business
district and began firing rockets and muskets into the air while shouting
'Viva Augustín I, Emperor of Mexico'. Thousands of civilians joined
the demonstration, and together they marched upon Iturbide's residence, demanding that he assume the throne of Mexico.

Iturbide declined to accept, but he met Congress the following
morning, where the assembly, intimidated by his clamouring partisans
in the galleries, named him Augustín I, Emperor of Mexico.

Iturbide's empire lasted no more than ten months. Eleven years of
civil war had practically destroyed the economy. The mining industry
was in shambles, many of the operators and managers had been killed or

fled the country, miners had abandoned their jobs by the thousands to join the insurgents, machinery and other critical equipment were destroyed or damaged, and many mines were flooded while others lacked mercury for processing ore. Silver and gold production, a driving force in Mexico's economy, fell from 26 million pesos in 1808 to 6 million pesos in 1821. And matters were not helped by the flight of an estimated 100 to 300 million pesos back to Spain.

Agriculture fared no better. Crops had been destroyed by both sides, *hacendados* had been killed or forced to leave their estates, sheep and cattle had been slaughtered to prevent provisions from reaching the enemy, and a good portion of rural labour had been lost to the revolutionary forces. Unemployment was at epidemic proportions throughout the country.

The budget was beyond repair. In 1822, income was no more than 8 million pesos, while expenses were more than 13 million. In 1823, the situation took a turn for the worse as expenses rose to more than 20 million pesos, 1.5 million of which supported the royal household of Augustín I. The major expense was the Ministry of War and Navy, which amounted to nearly 10 million pesos. In vain, the Congress sought to finance the government with a series of loans, but those with capital were unwilling to invest in the 'cactus throne', and money lenders were asking outrageous interest rates.

In an effort to bolster the economy, Congress tried several means to balance the budget and pay the army, the latter mandatory if Iturbide hoped to stay in power. Duties across the board were lowered from 16 to 6 per cent to stimulate world trade, taxes were lowered on tobacco and pulque, import duties were lifted on mercury and machinery for the mines, and farm produce and manufactured goods could now be exported duty free. But trade with new countries was slow to take up the slack left by the loss of trade with Spain. In desperation, the Congress resorted to forced loans, including one on church properties, and issued worthless currency.

The voice of the republicans grew louder as newspapers began to attack the regime, complaining about the extravagant expenses of the monarchy while revenue diminished and inflation increased month by month. Iturbide responded by suppressing several liberal newspapers and arresting 19 deputies accused of conspiring against him. The legislators protested, and as positions hardened against the monarchy, Iturbide dissolved the Congress.

The impact was felt throughout the nation as the republican movement grew. Liberals again met in secret, and even senior military officers, disgruntled by delays in receiving pay and lack of promotions, joined the conspiracy to overthrow the emperor.

The core of the revolution began in Vera Cruz, where the young *criollo* commander of the garrison, Antonio López de Santa Anna, proclaimed Mexico a republic on 1 December 1822. Within the month, old-guard insurgents such as Vincente Guerrero, Nicolás Bravo, and Guadalupe Victoria joined his movement. On 1 February 1823, with the support of José Antonio Echáverri, the captain-general of Vera Cruz, they wrote the *Plan de Casa Mata*. It abolished the empire, instituted a federal republic and a constitution, and exiled Augustín I under penalty of death. As support for Santa Anna and his plan gained momentum throughout the provinces and among the military, Iturbide, in desperation, reconvened the Congress, but it was too late – Santa Anna was marching upon Mexico.

Iturbide resigned and accepted a pension that would allow him to live comfortably in Europe, but foolishly, he returned to Mexico a few months later. He was arrested and faced a firing squad in July of 1824.

Although Iturbide's reign had been a disaster from the beginning, he could point to one significant accomplishment – the recognition of Mexico as an independent nation by the United States. President James Monroe had hoped for a democratic nation rather than a monarchy, but reluctantly recommended that Congress recognize the sovereignty of the Mexican nation.

The Early Republic

With the demise of the empire, a provisional junta governed the nation until elections were held for delegates to a constitutional congress. The members were Nicolás Bravo, Guadalupe Victoria, and Pedro Celestino Negrete; all, unfortunately, were military men, unqualified to fill the void in government left by the departure of the Spaniards. Their first orders of business were to negotiate a loan of 16 million pesos from England to bail out the bankrupt nation, and call for the election of delegates to draft a constitution for the new republic.

The delegates convened on 27 November 1823, and within the week, a line was drawn in the sand between liberals and conservatives. The issue that divided them was whether the new government should be centrist or federalist, and whether governmental authority was to be concentrated in the capital or delegated to the states.

The conservatives were primarily the clergy, the military, *hacendados*, mine owners, the landed élite, and prosperous merchants. All favoured a strong central government controlled, of course, by the élite, censorship of the press, Roman Catholicism as the national religion, Church control of education, titles of nobility reinstated, and *fueros,* exemptions of the clergy and military from civil law, restored. The leading advocates of centrism were Lucas Alamán, Nicolás Bravo, Fray Servando Teresa de Mier, and Carlos Maria Bustamante. For the greater part, the Indians, surprisingly, supported the conservatives.

The federalists were primarily liberal *criollos*, educated *mestizos*, intellectuals, teachers, journalists, and lawyers. Their platform was an egalitarian society free from privileges and titles, a free press, religious freedom, and public education. Prominent leaders in the movement were Miguel Ramos Arizpe and Valentín Gómez Farías.

The Constitution of the United States of Mexico was drafted in 1824, modelled to some degree on the United States' Constitution of 1787. It established a federal republic of nineteen states and four territories with an executive branch, a judiciary, a Senate, and a Chamber of Deputies. Each state was represented by two senators, and each deputy represented a constituency of 80,000 people. The federalists had clearly gained the constitution they sought, but the conservatives won the ideological high ground. The Catholic church still held its monopoly on religion, the clergy and the military retained their *fueros*, and extraordinary powers were granted to the president in times of emergency.

Compromises between liberals and conservatives, however, resulted in two fatal flaws in the Constitution of 1824. The first was that the office of the vice-president was not elected by popular vote, but assigned to the losing candidate for the presidency, clearly a recipe for revolt in a nation where both parties were so widely separated by ideology.

The second flaw was that the powers granted to the states that allowed them to accept or ignore the Constitution. This crippled the authority of the central government in regions where local *caudillos* (political bosses or military commanders) commanded armies and controlled a political process that reached down to every peasant through a chain of *caciques*, priests, mayors, *hacendados*, and block captains.

In the autumn of 1824, the state legislators chose Guadalupe Victoria as the first president of the Mexican republic and Nicolás Bravo as his vice-president. Both were prominent generals who had distinguished themselves during the insurgency. Victoria was fair minded but indecisive, unable to cope with the intense political rivalry between the centrists and the federalists during his term of office.

Notwithstanding the compromises reached in framing the Constitution of 1824, the rivalry between the two parties soon developed into acrimonious ideological differences, and the differences were manifested as much in Freemasonry as in organized politics.

Freemasonry took hold early in the history of Mexico, and has thrived through the ages. By 1981, the order numbered 1.7 million members, and its strength in the government was indicated by 26 of 31 state governors and 8 cabinet ministers who were Masons. In the early years of the republic, Masonic lodge meetings, which were by charter secret, served both conservatives and liberals for their cabals and plots. Many ranking officers belonged to the lodges, where they mingled with civilians and even priests with similar politics to air their grievances against whatever party was in power. The liberals were generally York Rite (*yorkinos*) Masons, and the conservatives Scottish Rite (*escoceses*) Masons, but the orders were not divided along strict ideological lines. Both were more or less political action groups to support candidates of their choice.

Though Victoria lasted out his term as president, the intense political atmosphere drove his vice-president, Nicolás Bravo, to armed revolt against the liberals. Bravo's plan demanded an end to Masonic secret societies, a centrist government, and the expulsion of Joel Poinsett, the

American ambassador, who was a *yorkino* aiding and abetting the federalist cause. General Vincente Guerrero, the grandmaster of the *yorkinos,* put down the uprising and ordered Bravo tried and exiled.

POLITICAL CHAOS

The period from 1828 to 1834 were years of endless conflict between liberals and conservatives, and the Constitution was forever in a state of flux with reforms and counter-reforms from both sides.

The election of 1828 saw the presidency change hands three times. The candidates were the far-left Vincente Guerrero, an uneducated soldier, and the moderate Manuel Gómez Pedraza, an intellectual *escocino* who enjoyed support from his conservative friends his moderate politics. Although Guerrero was more popular with the people, the conservative candidate, Pedraza won 10 out of 19 states, but the margin was close enough for Guererro's supporters to contest the election. Santa Anna and General José Lobato quickly 'pronounced' for Guerrero, and Joel Poinsett, the American minister to Mexico and an eternal meddler in Mexican politics, threw his support behind them. Troops and civilians demonstrated in the plaza, and soon a riotous mob, that was beyond the control of the army, swept through the city, demolishing everything in its path, including the Parían market-place.

Pedraza had no choice but to vacate the presidency and leave the country. Vincent Guerrero accepted the office in April 1829, and the centrist General Anastasio Bustamante became his vice-president. For his support of Guerrero, Santa Anna was promoted to the rank of major-general.

Guerrero's tenure in office was brief, lasting slightly more than eight months. His primary reforms were to expel all the Spaniards remaining in Mexico and abolish slavery in every state but Texas, where American colonists were dependent upon slave labour.

In Spain, where the independence of Mexico was not recognized, the political unrest in its former colony did not go unobserved. Believing the time was ripe to retake the country, a Spanish expeditionary force of 3,000 troops under the command of General Isidrio Barradas landed in Tampico. The landing was unopposed, since the Mexicans, expecting a larger force, had abandoned the city.

But the invasion was short-lived. Bottled up in the city by Mexican forces, the Spaniards weakened under the summer heat with yellow fever, malaria, and a shortage of potable water. When his line of supply with Cuba was cut, Barradas surrendered to the Mexican commander, none other than the ever-opportunistic Antonio López de Santa Anna. For his victory, he was hailed throughout the country as the 'Victor of Tampico' and 'Benefactor of the Homeland'.

By the end of 1829, Anastasio Bustamante denounced Guerrero as a dictator and revolted against him. The Congress, concerned that Guerrero's refusal to yield the extraordinary powers granted him in the war would lead to a dictatorship, disqualified him and recognized Bustamante as president.

The pendulum now swung to conservatism, centrism, and despotism. Freedom of the press was abolished, liberal governors were removed from office, vengeance was taken on the *yorkinos*, liberal leaders were exiled, and Guerrero was executed. In ordering Guerrero shot, Bustamante showed poor judgement.

After his government was overthrown, Guerrero withdrew to Acapulco, where he planned to leave the country on the *Colombo,* an Italian vessel commanded by an old friend, Francisco Picaluga. Instead, his 'friend' promptly sold him to the government for 50,000 gold pesos. The revered and respected old warrior of the War of Independence was executed in Michoacán on 14 February 1831.

The country was grief-stricken and furious with Bustamante, and the mood of the nation did not escape the attention of Santa Anna. He immediately 'pronounced' in favour of Gómez Pedraza, and the ensuing revolt forced Bustamante into exile. On 3 January 1833, Pedraza returned as provisional president and serve out the last three months of his original term. Congress rewarded Santa Anna by granting him the title of 'Liberator of the Republic'.

Santa Anna, the Rise of a Mexican Hero

Antonio López de Santa Anna Pérez de Lebrón was born on 21 February 1794, and he began his illustrious career in the army at the age of sixteen. While still young, he fought against Hidalgo's insurgents and won several commendations for valour. His growing reputation in the military and his charisma did not go unnoticed in the capital, and in time, he won a choice position as an aide to the Viceroy Apodoca. His flair for politics served him well, and eventually earned him the post of commandant of the Mexican forces in Vera Cruz. His assignment was to drive the last remaining Spaniards out of the harbour fortress of San Juan Ulúa.

He was one of the first to give his complete support to the *Plan de Iguala*, but Iturbide had reason to suspect Santa Anna's loyalty, and ordered him to return to Mexico. Santa Anna refused, and on 1 December 1822, he 'proclaimed' for a republic, and with the support of 400 troops, seized control of Vera Cruz. Rebel groups from other regions were eager to join the revolt, and soon his army grew large enough to threaten the fading empire. Santa Anna prepared to march

The dashing General Santa Anna

upon Mexico City, but Iturbide, facing certain defeat, abdicated and went into exile. For Santa Anna, it was the beginning of a 23-year career that would see him serve Mexico eleven times as the nation's chief executive.

On 30 March 1833, Antonio López de Santa Anna was elected the third president of Mexico by the greatest majority in the history of the nation. His vice-president was Valentín Gómez Farías, and since both were liberals, the government now seemed safe from revolt from within through differences of ideology.

This proved to be an illusion. Santa Anna had little interest in the daily routine of government, and retired to Manga de Clava, his estate in Vera Cruz, leaving Farías to administer the nation.

Farías wasted no time in persuading Congress to enact draconian reforms. He reduced the size of the army, abolished military *fueros*, and ordered the clergy to limit their sermons to religious subjects. He proclaimed the right of *patronato*, the power to name bishops and other church leaders, allowed priests and nuns to retract their vows, made tithes voluntary, secularized the California missions and sequestered their funds, closed the University of Mexico, where the faculty was predominately clergy, and established a system of education from the primary level to the college level.

'*Religión y fueros!*' The conservatives closed ranks as the army, the Church, and the clergy revolted. Puebla fell to the insurgents, and Santa Anna returned from Manga de Clava to deal with the threat. The general was once again in his milieu. His first love was warfare, for which there were ample opportunities in Mexico. When the action in the field was over and done, he reluctantly returned to the capital to exercise his prerogative as chief executive.

The conservatives, meanwhile, searched for a leader to rally around, but found no one with sufficient stature to unify the country against the liberals. They remedied the problem by offering Santa Anna a deal he couldn't refuse. For his acceptance of the command, they offered him the *Poder Conservador*, the post of a supreme executive answerable to none, not even to those who created the post. In the spring of 1824, after due consideration, the Great Liberal accepted command of the conservative army.

He joined the insurgents at Puebla and led an assault on the capital. The liberals, struck by an epidemic of cholera, were unable to defend the city, and Santa Anna marched in to a hero's welcome.

For eight months, Santa Anna enjoyed absolute power. He dissolved the liberal Congress, revoked the reforms of Farías, replaced liberal governors with his own men, exiled Farías and the liberal leadership, fired all liberal government employees, and appointed a new Congress.

The Constitution of 1824 was replaced by the *Siete Leys,* designed to strengthen the central government by reducing the states to military departments governed by political bosses, and extending the presidential term from four years to eight. To insure that all public office would be limited to the élite, all candidates were obliged to furnish evidence of a high annual income. Election to the Chamber of Deputies called for 1,500 pesos, the Senate 2,500, and the presidency 4,000. In time, the *Siete Leys* would replace the Constitution of 1824 and be incorporated into the Constitution of 1836.

The new centrist state created by Santa Anna would precipitate events that would haunt Mexico for the next twelve years. The abrogation of the Constitution of 1824 led to the Texas revolt, which was followed by wars with France and the United States. These wars contributed more to Mexico's impoverishment than any other event of the nineteenth century.

CHAPTER EIGHT

The Texas Rebellion

> They were the aggressors and we the attacked, they the ingrates, we the benefactors. When they were in want we had given them sustenance, yet as soon as they gained strength they used it to destroy us.
>
> *Lieutenant-Colonel José Enrique de la Peña, Mexican Army*

During the colonial period, population growth had been slow in the province of Texas. At the beginning of the eighteenth century, some 3,000 settlers lived in the territory, and by 1800, at the end of the colonial period, the population had grown to no more than 7,000. Mexico was eager to populate the region and establish a provincial capital, and in the late 1820s, encouraged colonists from the United States to emigrate to Texas.

The response was overwhelming. Prime land was cheap, ten cents an acre, and exceptionally suitable for cotton. Each settler would receive a grant of 640 acres, his wife another 320, each child 120, and Americans married to Mexicans would receive extra land as an inducement to integrate the population. Furthermore, there would be a general exemption from taxes and customs duties for seven years. To encourage settlers from the southern states, Mexico granted a special dispensation to allow them to bring their slaves, even though emancipation was the law of the land.

To qualify for immigration, Americans would have to convert to the Roman Catholic religion, become Mexican citizens, and speak Spanish which was mandatory for all official transactions.

By 1827, 12,000 Americans migrated to Texas, and by 1835, their population grew to 30,000, while in the same period the Mexican

population of the province grew to no more than 7,800. The hoped–
for integration of the Americans into the Mexican population did not
occur.

The immigrants settled in remote areas, while the Mexicans con–
tinued to live in or near the populated centres, where they subsisted
primarily by small-scale farming. Their economic disadvantage with
the new settlers was substantial.

The Americans exported cotton grown with slave labour to the US
and England, while the Mexicans neither owned slaves nor exported
their surpluses abroad. Although the Americans professed Catholicism
when they entered the country, they continued to adhere to the
Protestant Church once inside, which led to an enduring religious
conflict.

The Americans in turn found themselves at political and legal dis–
advantage, inasmuch as the seat of government for the state of Texas
and the appellate courts were located in Coahuila, 300 miles southwest
of San Antonio, where the population was nine times that of Texas.
The situation grew worse when Santa Anna declared the Constitution
of 1824 null and void, and the Americans viewed his centrist
government a threat to their autonomy. What little voice they had in
local affairs was now further reduced, and the *de facto* capital was now
even more distant than Coahuila.

The Settlers' Revolt

The settlers began to talk of revolt, and Mexico's fear of an American
takeover of Texas increased. These fears were reinforced when Hayden
Edwards fortified his settlement in eastern Texas and declared inde–
pendence as the Republic of Fredonia. Stephen Austin and the
majority of settlers opposed his unilateral action, and fortunately it
collapsed before Mexican troops arrived. Another crisis followed
quickly when James Long invaded Texas with a small army and cap–
tured Nacogdoches, then declared Texas independent and a territory of
the United States under his jurisdiction. Mexican forces easily defeated
Long's army, but these incidents clearly reflected the sentiments of the
settlers and that of their countrymen across the United States' border.

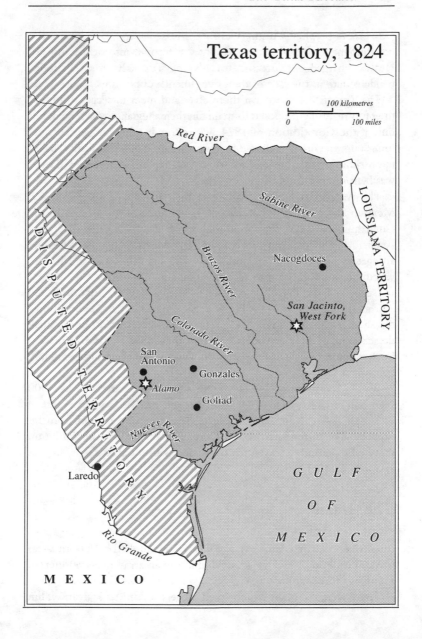

Texas territory, 1824

In 1833 Stephen Austin went to Mexico City to petition the government for Texas statehood, but was thrown into prison instead. He was charged with treason for advising Texans to form an independent state in the face of the government's opposition.

The Texans began to arm themselves and meet in secret to decide their future. Some proposed to maintain their allegiance to Mexico, but only if the Constitution of 1824 was restored; others suggested pursuing a union with the United States or Britain, but the majority, based upon rumours that a Mexican army was preparing to occupy Texas, was bent upon outright independence.

The Americans were not alone in their pursuit of independence. Mexican liberals, led by Lorenzo de Zavala, one of the framers of the Constitution of 1824, supported their cause. Zavala claimed that Santa Anna forfeited his right to represent the Mexican people when he abrogated the Constitution, and Texas, like any other state in Mexico, was under no obligation to recognize his administration.

General Martín Perfecto de Cos, a brother-in-law of Santa Anna, led a peace-keeping force into Texas in September of 1835, and immediately met armed resistance. Colonists at Gonzales fired upon a small detachment of Mexican soldiers when they tried to commandeer a small cannon, and a week later the colonists captured the military garrison at Goliad.

Within the month Stephen Austin assembled a force of some 300 men, half of which were of Mexican descent, and laid siege to a force of 700 men at San Antonio. Unable to break out and cut off from his supplies, Cos surrendered on 10 December 1835, with the condition that he be permitted to return to Mexico with his army.

The Alamo

It was time for Santa Anna to go to war. He established his headquarters in San Luis Potosí, and set about mobilizing an army of 6,000 men to join Cos's forces at Laredo.

There were still many experienced officers in the Mexican army, but the civil war had taken a heavy toll on veteran soldiers. To bring the army up to strength, Santa Anna filled the ranks with green recruits from the cities and the provinces, married men, who were usually poor soldiers, and conscripts from the jails of Mexico. Many were too young, some too old, and some too soft and feeble to withstand the long march to Texas. Had the navy been properly maintained, much of the army could have been transported to the theatre of war, and arrived rested and better prepared to fight.

In his anxiety to reach Texas, Santa Anna allowed little time to consider the logistics of supply for a march of 500 miles, and none for proper military training of his recruits. He decreed that the horses would need no grain – they could feed on forage along the way, and his supply lines were often so unreliable that the men had to depend on what they could carry on their backs for days. Military training was unnecessary, since the commander-in-chief felt that the men would become accustomed to gunfire in battle soon enough.

On 23 February 1836, the First Division, under the command of General Ramírez y Sesma, entered San Antonio and sent word back that the enemy, 150 strong, had withdrawn to the Alamo fortress, armed with rifles, bayonets, and 15 artillery pieces.

Santa Anna immediately marched for San Antonio with three companies of light infantry and three companies of grenadiers. As he entered the plaza, an artillery round was fired from the Alamo, but it did no damage. The Mexicans replied with four grenades from a howitzer, and the enemy immediately raised a white flag. James Bowie, second in command to William Travis, sent a message to Santa Anna that they wanted to negotiate an agreement. Santa Anna sent an officer forward with a message that he did not deal with bandits; unconditional surrender was the only terms he would accept.

For the next 10 days, the siege continued without much of note happening. On 3 March, however, it was evident that an assault was in preparation when some 900 sappers marched into San Antonio wearing full dress uniforms.

Had Travis obeyed his orders from Sam Houston, he might have withdrawn from the Alamo before the siege began, but now he was committed. The reinforcements he was expecting never arrived,

The Alamo: its 13-day siege in 1836 has gone down in history

although 32 volunteers from Gonzales managed to enter under the cover of night. Infuriated by Santa Anna's demand for unconditional surrender, he gathered his company and spoke to them of his decision.

> Fellow citizens and compatriots, I am besieged by a thousand or more of the Mexicans under Santa Anna. I have sustained bombardment and cannonade for twenty-four hours and have not lost a man. The enemy has demanded a surrender at [his] discretion, otherwise the garrison are [*sic*] to be put to the sword if the fort is taken. I have answered the demand with a cannon shot, and our flag still waves proudly over the walls. *I shall never surrender or retreat.* Then, I call on you in the name of Liberty, of patriotism, and everything dear to the American character, to come to our aid. If this call is neglected, I am determined to sustain myself as long as possible and die as a soldier who never forgets what is due to his own honor and that of his country. Victory or Death!

> *José Enrique de la Peña's translation of the Travis letter*

An assault on the Alamo would not have been necessary if Santa Anna had waited for his main artillery force to arrive. With few cannon, the Texans could not have held out for very long. Furthermore, he needed no more than a small force to bottle up the Alamo and its defenders while the army moved on to more important objectives. According to Peña, however, the fame and honour of the army were now at stake. The enemy had held back a superior Mexican force for 12 days, and Santa Anna considered it a point of honour that the siege should not last another day.

In the Alamo, Travis was beginning to yield to his company's urging him to surrender, since lack of food and ammunition made it unlikely that they could hold out much longer. He finally accepted the inevitable, and if no reinforcements arrived by the fifth, he promised to surrender or attempt an escape under the cover of night.

On 6 March at one o'clock in the morning, four columns began to take up positions about the Alamo. At first light, the bugler sounded the attack, but Travis was ready. Each defender had three or four loaded rifles by his side, and the first salvo left a swathe of wounded and dead along each column. The second salvo was from Travis's heavy artillery, blowing away half a company of light infantry, and the steady cannonade that followed killed Mexicans by the score, but still they advanced.

The attackers reached the walls, and scaling ladders were brought forward, but they were poorly constructed and most were too short. A parapet on one side of the Alamo, however, was no more than nine feet in height, and the Mexicans concentrated their attack at this point. The first wave was driven back by bayonets, and the second was all but annihilated by rifle fire from the roofs of the barracks, yet they came, climbing over the bodies of their comrades. Their losses were such that Santa Anna ordered in his reserves, but they only added to the confusion.

When the walls were breached, the defenders took cover inside the rooms facing the plaza and bolted the doors. A few, including Travis, refused to retreat. He fought coolly and with discipline, and in the end, he traded his life dearly.

The Mexicans turned the Alamo's cannons on the rooms, and the carnage began. The poorly trained Mexicans began firing in all directions, killing as many of their men as Texans. The firing did not cease until 50,000 rounds of ammunition had been spent and there were no Texans left to kill.

Shortly after six in the morning, it was finished – only seven men in the Alamo had survived the fighting. One was David Crockett, an ex-congressman from Tennessee. With the loss of his land bill to the Polk political machine, Crockett set out for Texas and found himself in San Antonio when Santa Anna arrived. Fearing his neutrality as an American citizen would not be respected, he chose to take refuge in the Alamo.

Without a moment's hesitation, Santa Anna ordered all seven executed. The officer corps hesitated to support the order, hoping that time would moderate the decision, but to no avail. Several officers, favourites of Santa Anna, fell upon the defenceless men with swords in hand and butchered all seven.

The only survivors of the massacre were an elderly woman and a Negro slave. Of the defenders, 202 were killed, but the Mexicans fared worse: eight officers and 252 soldiers were dead, and 33 suffered serious wounds.

In retrospect:

> The responsibility of the victims sacrificed at the Alamo must rest on General Ramírez y Sesma rather on the commander in chief.... When General Ramírez y Sesma sighted the town, the enemy was still engaged in the pleasures of a dance given the night before; he therefore could have and should have prevented them from taking refuge in the Alamo.... At the very moment that General Ramírez y Sesma was advised to enter Béjar (San Antonio), there were only ten men at the Alamo, and it would have required an equal number to take it. Had he just placed himself at the bridge over the San Antonio that connects the fort to the city, as he was advised, he would have prevented the enemy from taking refuge there, thus avoiding the painful catastrophe that we witnessed.
>
> *José Enrique de la Peña*

SANTA ANNA'S BLUNDER

'Remember the Alamo.' The cry would unite and galvanize the Texans to avenge their comrades. But a brutal incident a few weeks later would arouse even stronger feelings and bring about increased support from the United States.

On 20 March the Mexicans scored a major victory at Goliad.

General José Urrea engaged a force commanded by Colonel James W. Fannin as he was attempting to abandon the fortress. Fannin was hopelessly outnumbered, and he chose to surrender his force of 365 men rather than sacrifice them to no avail. Urrea demanded unconditional surrender, and Fannin, under the assumption that Urrea would treat his company as prisoners of war, conceded.

Urrea did not dally in Goliad. Instead he marched immediately on Guadalupe Victoria, leaving Colonel Morales with instructions on how to deal with the prisoners. Urrea kept his word and interceded for the prisoners with Santa Anna, but the commander-in-chief cited his earlier communication stating that any foreigners invading the Republic be tried as pirates whenever found armed.

Santa Anna gave the order in triplicate that the prisoners at Goliad be executed, and sent an aide, Colonel Miñon, to witness the execution. The officer responsible for the execution, Lieutenant-Colonel Nicolás de la Portilla, was not the man to deny his commander-in-chief.

On the dawn of 26 March he ordered the prisoners to be awakened. The wounded were taken from the hospital, and those unable to stand were killed in their beds. The remainder of the company was divided into three parties and led outside, under the impression that they were being taken to Matamoros. They were given their knapsacks and led away from Goliad singing. When they reached a clearing, they were lined up in rows with their backs to the troops, and the Mexicans opened fire.

Fannin received the order for his execution calmly, asking only enough time to write a farewell letter to his wife and one to Santa Anna, declaring he was opposed to independence and would die for his love of the Constitution of 1824. They took him from his room to the place of execution, and he asked that they call Lieutenant-Colonel Portillo so he could ask him to send his watch with the letter to his wife. Don Carlino Huerta, the captain of the guard, however denied his request. After the execution, Huerta kept the watch and the ten pesos Fannin gave the squad to aim at his head and heart. The only survivors of Goliad were a few bedridden rebels that some compassionate Mexicans had hidden beneath their bodies.

In view of Santa Anna's edict to execute armed foreigners, it would seem that Travis and the men at the Alamo had no course open to them other than to die fighting.

The Texans were, without question, in full retreat, and a well-ordered march would have ended the war without firing another shot. Santa Anna, however, chose this moment to make the mistake that would cost Mexico the war. Eager to press forward, he crossed to the east side of the Brazos River with only 700 men. Self-confident and assured of an early victory, he chose to move forward rather than wait for Ramírez y Sesma's division of 1,400 men to join him.

At three o'clock on the afternoon of 21 April a Negro slave appeared before Sam Houston, informing him that General Santa Anna was asleep in his camp at San Jacinto, and that the company was relaxed and standing down. Houston mobilized his forces immediately and he found the situation just as the slave had described it.

In fifteen minutes, it was all over. With the cry *Remember the Alamo!*, the attackers carried out the raid with a vengeance. None of the the officers, not even Houston, could control the carnage that followed. When the time came to assess the damage, 400 Mexicans were dead,

Sam Houston

200 wounded, and 730 taken prisoner,* while Houston's casualties were two dead and 23 wounded. Santa Anna, however, was not to be found among the captives. He had disguised himself in a soldier's uniform and escaped on horseback, but two days later he was captured by one of Houston's patrols.

On 14 May 1836, Santa Anna, as president of Mexico and commander-in-chief of the armed forces, signed the Treaty of Velasco with David Burnet. It specified that all Mexican troops would be withdrawn from Texas, that Mexico would not take up arms against the Republic of Texas, and it provided for an exchange of prisoners of war.

In a private agreement, in exchange for transportation to Vera Cruz, Santa Anna agreed to work for a formal recognition of the Republic of Texas in Mexico.

Back in Mexico, Santa Anna found himself in disgrace. In April of 1837, the Congress named the centrist Anastasio Bustamante to the presidency and left Santa Anna in limbo in the army. The first act of the new government was to throw out Santa Anna's treaty, then to refuse recognition of the independence of Texas. There was talk of sending another army to Texas, but more urgent affairs at home prevented that.

Non-payment of loans to France precipitated a war in 1838–39, known familiarly as the 'Pastry War'. Mexico owed Louis Philippe 600,000 pesos, the smallest claim of which was for 800 pesos by the owner of a French pastry shop in Tacuba. The claim stemmed from the night Mexican soldiers raided the shop, locked the proprietor in the back room, and ate all his pastries.

The French minister demanded full payment of the 600,000 pesos, and when the money was not forthcoming, a French fleet appeared off the coast of Mexico and blockaded the port of Vera Cruz. In October, the Mexican government agreed to retire the loan, but the French added an additional 200,000 pesos for the cost of the blockade. The Mexicans refused, and the French admiral bombarded the fortress of San Juan Ulúa and occupied the garrison at Vera Cruz.

The Mexican Congress responded by declaring war on France, and,

---

* At some point before the attack, Santa Anna received enough reinforcements to give him a force of some 1,200 men.

conveniently forgetting his fiasco at San Jacinto, put Santa Anna in command of the army again.

The general arrived at Vera Cruz on 4 December just in time to meet a French landing force of 3,000 men. He drove the French from Vera Cruz in short order, and rather than commit more men and money to the venture, the French agreed to settle for 600,000 pesos. At the height of the action, a cannon ball took off Santa Anna's left leg, and the general, wounded and victorious, was again the darling of Mexico. The leg was buried with full military honours in the Santa Paula cemetery.

CHAPTER NINE

The Mexican-American War

James K. Polk and the Manifest Destiny

During the colonial period, the western boundary of the Texas territory lay at the Nueces River. In 1836, however, the Republic of Texas claimed the Rio Grande as its western border, some 150 miles south of the Nueces. The claim was specious, based upon the fact that settlers from the United States had settled in the territory, and that Santa Anna had withdrawn his army south of the Rio Grande after his defeat at San Jacinto. Furthermore, Texas claimed the Rio Grande as far as its source, incorporating thousands of square miles of Colorado and New Mexico into the Republic. Mexico found this bold-faced land grab of their territory difficult to swallow.

The annexation of Texas had been the great issue of the presidential campaign of 1844, and James K. Polk, running on a ticket advocating annexation of Texas, California, and Oregon, won the election by a narrow margin. In March 1845, Texas became the 28th state of the Union. The Mexican Congress reacted by declaring that a state of war would be in force if the United States laid claim to any other territories belonging to Mexico.

Nevertheless, the Mexican president, José Joaquín Herrera, agreed to receive Polk's special envoy, John Slidell, to negotiate the boundary dispute and to settle some two million dollars of claims against Mexico by American citizens. Slidell also carried Polk's confidential offer to Herrera of twenty-five million dollars for California and five million for New Mexico.

Slidell, however, never met Hererra. Word of his mission was leaked to the press, and the president, faced with a rebellion, refused to receive him. Instead, he sent General Mariano Paredes north with an army, but this proved to be a costly error. Instead, Paredes returned to the capital and used his forces to overthrow Herrera and assume the presidency.

Polk now tested the waters for war in the United States. Congress was hesitant, and neither the Secretary of the Navy nor the Secretary of State would support him unless the United States was first attacked by Mexico. It was not long before Polk was granted his opportunity.

In February of 1846, he ordered General Zachary Taylor to move his army from the Nueces and take up a position on the Rio Grande. General Pedro Ampudia immediately moved his forces north and took up a position facing him across the river in Matamoros.

Conflict was inevitable, and in April, Mexican cavalry ambushed an American patrol. Eleven Americans were killed, six wounded, and sixty-three taken prisoner. Polk now had his justification for war – American soldiers had been attacked by Mexican forces on 'United States' soil'.

James Knox Polk, US President, who won on his policy for annexing Texas

Polk had drawn up articles of war as early as January of 1846, and with the incident on the Rio Grande, he received Congressional approval in May. The vote, however, was not unanimous. Abraham Lincoln challenged the government to provide details of the exact site where the incident occurred, and called Polk's declaration of war 'the insane rumours of a feverish dream'. Later, when he emerged as presidential hopeful, he was asked if his opposition to the war had damaged his candidacy. His reply was 'would you have voted up what you knew to be a lie?'

As both sides gathered their forces, the American military numbered 104,000 men under arms and a navy of 70 warships. The Mexican army, on the other hand, numbered 20,000 men, 24,000 officers, a navy of six warships, and a war chest empty but for 1,839 pesos.

In Mexico, it was politics as usual. Paredes was overthrown, and the nation was beset by Maya uprisings in Yucatán and Yaqui uprisings in the north. In desperation, Santa Anna, the only commander with the stature to unite the country, was recalled from exile in Cuba in July 1846.

THE AMERICAN OFFENSIVE

In June, 1846, Polk launched a massive offensive against Mexico. The Army of the West, under the command of General Stephen Kearny, left Fort Leavenworth with 1,500 troops bound for New Mexico and California. In August, the Army of the Center, 6,600 strong, under the command of General Zachary Taylor, crossed the Rio Grande and marched upon Monterrey. The Army of Occupation, led by General Winfield Scott, would wait until the following year to strike at the heart of Mexico.

Taylor reached the outskirts of Monterrey on 19 September and launched his first attack two days later. After four days of combat, the outcome of the battle was beyond doubt, and General Ampudia signalled for a truce.

Terms were reached with Taylor whereby Ampudia would withdraw to Saltillo, keeping all his weapons save the artillery, and Taylor would remain in Monterrey for eight weeks, or until the truce was abrogated by higher authority.

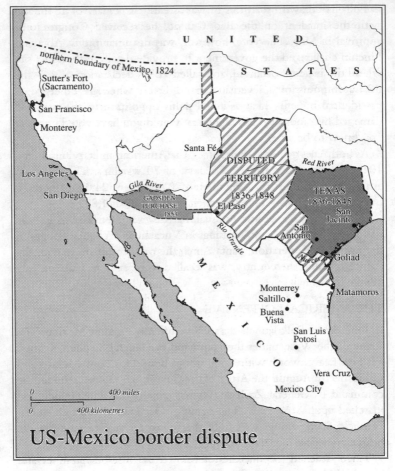

US-Mexico border dispute

Polk was furious with Taylor for failing to destroy or capture the Mexican army.

In San Luis Potosí, Santa Anna raised a new army of 20,000 green troops and marched north to meet Taylor at Saltillo.

The weather of February 1847 was particularly harsh, and the hard march over rough terrain and the lack of water and food took its toll on the Mexicans. By the time they reached the outskirts of the city, desertions and illness left Santa Anna with a force of 15,000 men to face the Americans. But with an army still three times larger than Taylor's, Santa Anna remained confident.

The battle for Saltillo took place near the *hacienda* of Buena Vista on 22 and 23 February. The road to Saltillo passed through the steep walls of a narrow canyon, and Taylor had deployed his artillery on the overlooking heights. Santa Anna, overconfident with his superior forces, took the offensive and marched into the face of the American artillery. After two days of heavy fighting, with many casualties on both sides, Santa Anna withdrew to Año Nuevo, leaving a trail of dead and wounded in his path of retreat. His troops, who had neither eaten nor taken any water during the fighting, were exhausted and unable to continue. The Mexicans suffered more than 1,600 killed or wounded, but they had inflicted more than 600 casualties on the Americans.

Word of a Mexican victory at Saltillo was quick to reach San Luis Potosí, but when the army straggled home, the truth was evident – more than a half of the men who left for Saltillo were dead, wounded, or missing. Santa Anna, as usual, walked away from the disaster unscathed, and returned to the capital to assume the presidency.

In the west, Kearny reached Santa Fe in August and found that Governor Manuel Arjimo had ordered his 3,000 troops to evacuate the town before the Americans arrived. Without firing a single shot, Kearny claimed all of New Mexico for the United States, then set out for California with a hundred dragoons.

By 1845, about seven thousand Mexicans had migrated to California, but distance, the mountains, and the deserts had all but isolated them from the mother country. As with Texas, Mexico encouraged foreign settlers to populate and develop the rich resources of the state, and the United States was quick to respond. In time, a thriving community of Americans arose at Sutter's Fort.

In the spring of 1845, Captain John Charles Frémont, ostensibly on a mapping mission, passed through Sutter's Fort with sixty-five heavily armed men. Before moving on to Oregon, he raised the American flag on a nearby mountain.

The implication of his act was not lost on the Californios. Mexico could not defend them, and they began to consider an alliance with either the United States or Britain to protect their interests from another Texas-style takeover.

General Mariano Guadelupe Vallejo, the Mexican commander in Northern California, knew there was little he could do to prevent annexation by the Americans. Mexico provided his troops with no rifles, no horses, and no cannon. Even the food they ate, the uniforms they wore, and the barracks they lived in were furnished by Vallejo.

In June of 1846, Frémont returned to California and listened to the complaints of his countrymen, who were troubled with their deteriorating relations with the Californios. Frémont wasted no time negotiating with Vallejo. Instead, he and his thugs broke into Vallejo's home, arrested the general, and declared California an independent republic. The flag of Mexico was torn down and replaced with the Bear Flag of the new republic.

In the summer of that year, Commodore John Sloat, commanding a fleet of seven frigates, sailed into Monterey bay with orders to seize Mexican ports in case of war. He met no resistance, and raised the American flag on the *presidio*. Word of the occupation of Monterey was quick to reach Frémont, and he yielded the Bear Flag Republic to the United States.

Kearny's troops, meanwhile, weary and nursing wounds suffered at the hands of Californio lancers, managed to struggle into San Diego by December of 1846. The only military offensive of any consequence in California took place in Los Angeles, where Kearny defeated a unit of Californio lancers at San Pascual.

On 13 January 1847, General Andrés Pico surrendered the entire territory of California to Major John Frémont.

On 9 March 1847, General Winfield Scott made an unopposed landing on the beaches of Vera Cruz with 10,000 men. He bypassed San Juan Ulúa, the island fortress in the harbour, and marched directly to Vera Cruz. Four thousand troops defended the walled city, but Scott cut off all supplies to the city and issued an ultimatum for unconditional surrender to the military commander. The ultimatum was rejected, and Scott launched his attack on the city.

Ignoring the pleas of foreign consuls to permit women and children

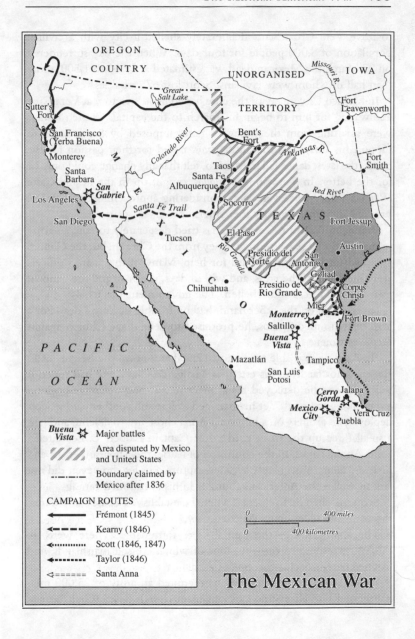

OREGON
COUNTRY

UNORGANISED   IOWA

Missouri R.

Great Salt Lake

TERRITORY

Fort Leavenworth

Sutter's Fort

San Francisco
(Yerba Buena)

Monterey

Santa Barbara

San Gabriel

Los Angeles

San Diego

Colorado River

Bent's Fort

Arkansas R.

Fort Smith

Taos

Santa Fe

Albuquerque

Socorro

Santa Fe Trail

Red River

T E X A S

Fort Jessup

Tucson

El Paso

Rio Grande

Presidio del Norte

Austin

San Antonio

Goliad

Corpus Christi

Chihuahua

Presidio de
Rio Grande

Nueces R.

Mier

Monterrey

Fort Brown

Saltillo

Buena Vista

PACIFIC

OCEAN

Mazatlán

San Luis Potosi

Tampico

Cerro Gorda

Jalapa

Mexico City

Vera Cruz

Puebla

Buena Vista ☆ Major battles

Area disputed by Mexico and United States

Boundary claimed by Mexico after 1836

CAMPAIGN ROUTES

⬅ Frémont (1845)

⬅--- Kearny (1846)

⬅······· Scott (1846, 1847)

⬅------ Taylor (1846)

⬅====== Santa Anna

0 _____ 400 miles
0 _____ 400 kilometres

The Mexican War

to leave Vera Cruz, Scott deliberately shelled a city with a civilian population of 8,000 people for four days. When the city surrendered on 27 March the Mexican dead was estimated at 1,000 to 1,500, more than half of whom were civilians. Scott lost 67 casualties.

In Mexico City, many of the élite hailed Scott's victory at Vera Cruz and waited for him to begin his march to the capital. Church leaders were smarting from the excessive taxes imposed by Santa Anna to support his army, and the élitist *pocos*, noted for their passion for the polka, the latest dance fad in Mexico, felt that any change could only be for the better. In Yucatán, the *criollos*, caught up in the deadly Caste War with the Maya, were even considering approaching Scott to feel him out for annexation by the Americans.

Presidente Valantín Gómez Farías tried desperately to raise an army to meet Scott by sequestering money from the Church, but the Church appealed to the national guard for help. Many of the guard's officers were members of the *pocos*, and within days, the *pocos* and the national guard joined forces and rebelled. The government was paralysed.

Santa Anna, on the other hand, had no trouble making a deal. For a loan of two million pesos, he promised to defend the Church against the government.

By April he was able to deploy 12,500 troops on the heights of El Encerro, not far from his estate at Manga de Clava. He had superior numbers, and he deployed his artillery in a strong defensive position overlooking the road. Yet he managed to lose still another battle. Scott deployed his artillery on a hill Santa Anna chose not to defend, and sent a small force up the main road while Captain Robert E. Lee circled Santa Anna's flanks. In the confusion of battle, the Mexicans broke and fled, and Santa Anna barely avoided capture. His leg, however, did not fare so well – the Americans found it in his abandoned carriage.

Scott marched on to Puebla, where he established a base camp to rest the army and reconnoitre Mexico City.

The approaches to the capital were formidable. There were six causeways leading to the city, four of which crossed marshlands, and fortified gates stood at the end of each.

While Scott waited, Santa Anna recruited an army of 25,000 men and busied himself casting cannons from church bells. When he was

The victorious US General Winfield Scott

ready, he sent 7,000 national guardsmen to El Peñon, a hill that overlooked the southern causeway, the principal artery leading to the capital.

Scott chose not to force his way past El Peñon. Instead, he circled the southern shores of Lake Chalco and Lake Xochimilco and took up a position at San Augustin, ten miles south of the capital. Santa Anna responded by deploying 2,000 men along Scott's route, which would squeeze him between Lake Xochimilco on the right, and the pedregal, a vast extense of broken lava considered impassable, on the left.

Santa Anna's plan was good, but General Gabriel Valencia, a presidential hopeful, broke ranks with Santa Anna and moved his troops south to Contreras instead, counting upon the pedregal to protect his left flank as he struck Scott from the west. It was not a wise move.

On 20 August disaster struck. Robert E. Lee led 3,500 troops across the impassable pedregal and routed Valencia's forces in seventeen minutes, killing 700 Mexicans and capturing 813.

That same day American forces attacked Churubusco along the route left undefended by Valencia, taking a fortified convent defended by 1,500 National Guardsmen and seventy-two American deserters, forty of whom were Irish Catholics, fighting for the faith against Protestants.

On the morning of 7 September the bloodiest encounter of the war took place at a flour mill rumoured to be a cannon works. Mexican artillery and ten thousand infantry engaged 3,500 Americans, and in two hours, Scott suffered 800 casualties. Ironically, the flour mill proved to be just that.

The war ended on 13 September 1847, when the Americans breached the walls of Chapultepec Castle. Among the Mexican casualties were six cadets from the military academy, one of whom, it is told, wrapped himself in the Mexican flag and jumped to his death. A monument to the memory of *Los Niños Héroes* now stands on Cha-pultepec Hill. Less memorable than the defenders of Chapultepec were the Irishmen who fought alongside the Mexicans to defend Catholi-cism. The moment the American flag was raised above the ramparts of Chapaltepec Castle, Scott hanged 50 facing the flag.

On 14 September Santa Anna withdrew his troops from the capital and renounced the presidency. He avoided a court-martial by retiring to Jamaica.

The Treaty of Guadelupe Hidalgo was signed on 2 February 1848. Under its terms, Mexico lost all claim to an area larger than Spain, Italy, and France combined. In return, the United States paid $15 million and assumed all claims of American citizens against Mexico.

Yet the Americans wanted more. In 1853, James Gadsden, a railway tycoon representing President Franklin Pierce, offered the Mexican government 50 million dollars for Baja California, Sonora, Sinalola, Durango, and Chihuahua. The negotiations, however, ended with the United States purchasing the Mesilla Valley of lower New Mexico for 10 million dollars. This purchase secured the strategic travel routes south of the Gila river, giving the United States access to the California ports.

In his memoirs, Ulysses S. Grant would write '. . . the war was most unjust, waged by a stronger against a weaker nation'.

One hundred years after the fall of Mexico, Harry S. Truman became the first United States president to visit Mexico. Upon that occasion, he honoured the cadets who gave up their lives at Chapultepec.

CHAPTER TEN

The Caste War of Yucatán

Christianity and the Maya

Distance, the rain forest, and the mountainous terrain of the Chiapas Plateau isolated the Maya Indians from mainstream Mexican history in the nineteenth century, and, to a significant extent, do so today. The two primary groups in this region are the lowland Maya of Yucatán and Campeche, and the highland Maya of Chiapas. Each has their own language, or to be more precise, group of languages: Yucatec and Chontal is spoken in the lowlands, and Tzotzil, Tzeltal, and Chol in the highlands.

Before the coming of the Spaniards and Christianity, the Maya concept of the cosmos encompassed the gods of the heavens and the underworld, the rain gods, and the spirits of the forest. Fundamental to Maya religion was, and is today, the First Tree of the World, a great ceiba tree with roots fixed firmly in the centre of the Earth and its branches spread upwards through each of the seven layers of the heavens.

In nearly every village in Yucatán, a ceiba tree once grew in the middle of the plaza, a living symbol of the primordial tree that marked the centre of the Universe. In villages where there was no tree, a cross stood in its place. The corners of the village were in turn marked by lesser crosses that represented four guardian spirits, whose function was to prevent evil spirits from passing across the village boundaries.

In the Books of Chilam Balam of Chumayel, written before the arrival of the Spaniards, the prophet of Mani wrote, 'And he had that sign of the cross and others made of cut stone and placed in the courtyards of the temples where it could be seen by all, and he said that it was the green tree of the world.'

Evidence that the cross was the primary religious icon of the ancient Maya is found at a number of sites, the most prominent perhaps in the Temple of the Cross at Palenque, where two priests face an ornate cross carved on a tablet, and in the Temple of the Inscriptions, where a cross is carved on the slab covering the tomb of Pacal, the seventh-century ruler of Palenque.

The first European to comment on the crosses of the Yucatán was Bernal Diaz del Castillo, who wrote, 'On the other side of the idols were symbols like crosses'. Other Spanish chroniclers noted that the walls of the temples were painted with trees that resembled crosses.

The ready acceptance of Christianity by the Maya after the conquest is not surprising, since both worshipped the cross, burned incense in their shrines, practised baptism, fasting, celibacy, and the ceremonial consumption of alcohol in their rites.

After the coming of the missionaries, the Maya had no difficulty incorporating the cross into the religion of their ancestors. They made an effigy cult of the saints, and converted the abstract Christian faith into a family and nature form of worship that preserved the beliefs that had endured for more than a thousand years. After all, the new god had no effect on Ah Kinchil, the Sun God, who climbed the seven layers of heaven each day, nor did He alter the ways in which the old deities nourished the crops. The chacs, the rain gods, were as unpredictable as ever, and the ancestral gods still convened at wayside crosses to hear their prayers and requests, provide guidance to the faithful, and cure the sick and ailing through the medium of the h-men, the shamans. The desire for a direct and individualistic ritual where the supernatural could be addressed personally did not abate after the Christianity arrived. During times of great stress, the cross and the saints still came to them and spoke directly to them through the medium of an interpreter.

Post-conquest life

Before the coming of the *dzul* (Spaniards, *criollos*, and *mestizos*), the Maya peasant raised his crops on communal lands, and in a good year, six months of labour was sufficient to feed his family and provide a surplus for trade. After the country was pacified, however, the Spaniards needed more and more land to raise sugar cane and henequen or sisal hemp, and more extensive range lands for grazing cattle. Towns were built, and land became privatized as the sale of communal lands, originally prohibited by law, became a commodity that could be bought and sold between the *criollos* and the Indians.

Without land, the Indian peasant was forced to work for his living on *haciendas*, either herding cattle, cutting sugar cane, or raising henequen. The wages were low, about thirty-five centavos a day, with no annual adjustment for the steady rise in the price of maize and beans. More often than not, his wages were paid in vouchers which could be redeemed only at the *tienda de raya,* the company store, where prices were inflated. Soon he found himself bound to the *hacienda* by a debt that could never be paid in his lifetime, and often not in that of his heirs, who were forced to assume it upon his death. And the worst labour abuses in all of Mexico were found on the henequen *haciendas* of Yucatán. Many of the *peones* were rebellious Mayas or Yaquis from Sonora, who were often forced to work in chains.

The other oppressive burden the peasant bore was the yearly tribute to the Church. Since the Indian had greater need of the Church than the Spaniard or the *criollo* for the salvation of his soul, it was reasoned, he must absorb the greater share of the cost for building and maintaining it with fees for rites such as baptism, marriage, and funerals much in excess of those charged to the whites.

THE WAR AGAINST MEXICO

When Santa Anna abrogated the Constitution of 1824, Mexican troops occupied Yucatán and conscripted Indians and *mestizos* to fight in the war against Texas. The Yucatecans, however, had no appetite to fight in what they considered Mexico's foreign wars, and in 1838 they rebelled and drove the Mexicans from the peninsula. In doing so, they were forced to recruit Maya Indians. The Maya had no love for the Yucatec *criollos*, but agreed to serve for relief from the heavy burden of taxes the Church levied upon them. When the rebellion was over, however, the *criollos* conveniently forgot the deal.

The renegade state formed a government and wrote the Constitution of 1841, which guaranteed religious freedom, abolished the *fueros*, the special privileges of the clergy and the military, and, for the first time, granted the Indians full citizenship.

After his defeat in Texas, Santa Anna sent a force of 5,000 Mexican troops by sea and by land to Mérida, but a Yucatán force of 6,000 men, among which were many Indians who again enlisted for promises of land and relief from Church taxes, turned the invasion into a rout.

Independence from Mexico did not last long, however. Yucatán could not survive economically with Mexican markets closed to its exports, and a peace commission was sent to Mexico to form a pact with Santa Anna. The commission agreed to acknowledge the Mexican government in exchange for control of state affairs, an exemption of the state militia from foreign wars, and Mexico markets reopened to Yucatán goods.

Civil War

The news of reunification with Mexico, however, was not well received in Campeche. Mexico was still at war, and although American gunships had not yet appeared in the waters off Campeche, the reunion with Mexico could bring them down upon the city with disastrous results. Campeche declared Yucatán neutral, and in January 1847, marched upon Mérida with four battalions of militia and Maya Indians to persuade the Mérida government to renounce Mexico. The governor of Mérida sent his troops south, but they were no match for Campeche's forces, and they drove them back to the security of the Mérida garrison.

Encouraged by their success, the Campeche insurgents took up arms and swept into the interior, and after taking Tekax and Peto, they moved on to Valladolid, the cultural centre of Yucatán. The city offered little resistance to the rebels, but the Indians, fired up with rum stolen from the cantinas, could not be controlled by their officers, and they brought down their wrath upon the whites with a fury.

The commandant of the local militia was dragged from his house and hacked to death, a priest was slashed to death in his hammock, and women from aristocratic families were raped and murdered, then staked to the grill work on the windows and mutilated. Before it was finished, the Indians had torn out the hearts of the dead and eaten them. After six days of rioting, the Maya withdrew, leaving eighty-five dead behind them.

Colonel José Dolores Cetina, a Mérida loyalist, raised money and weapons in Cuba, organized a cadre of 300 *mestizos*, and began recruiting troops among the southern Maya to support the Mérida forces.

He chose Manuel Antonio Ay and Cecilio Chi, both local chieftains, to lead the Maya forces, and set up his headquarters at the *hacienda* of Jacinto Pat, an influential rancher.

In July, reports reached Valladolid that the Maya were preparing to march on the city, and the commandante of the garrison, Colonel Eulogio Rosada, issued arrest warrants for Cecilio Chi and Jacinto Pat. Chi and Pat could not be found, but Antonio Ay was seized with papers naming both conspirators in a plot to overthrow the Campeche junta. After a brief trial, Ay was executed by a firing squad on 26 July 1847.

Maya from the surrounding villages poured into the city to watch his execution, the first revolutionary to face death rather than exile, the usual punishment given to whites. The message was not lost upon them.

Cetina, aware that the plot had been discovered, lost no time in reaching Valladolid with a demand that the city surrender. Colonel Rosada responded by informing him of Ay's execution and the possibility of a racial war, and suggested that it was time for whites to stand together. After due consideration, Cetina abandoned his Indian allies.

The Caste War

The whites threw up barricades about their towns and armed themselves as skirmishes between government troops and the Maya began in the south. There were needless killings on both sides, prisoners were executed, and rape was routine.

When word of the atrocities reached Mérida, the whites joined forces against the common threat and mustered the militia. All white or half-white men between the ages of sixteen and sixty were ordered to report for military duty.

On 6 August the Constitution of 1841 was amended to revoke citizenship for all Indians and strip them of their legal rights. They were now wards of the State under the supervision of white administrators. Prominent Indian leaders, even those defended by influential white friends, were placed before firing squads, while lesser Indian officials were shipped off to detention facilities in Campeche and Vera Cruz. Their duties and responsibilities were delegated to whites and trusted *mestizos.*

While the government was readying its forces, Cecilio Chi, Jacinto Pat, and other Maya chieftains began raiding *haciendas* for cash and jewellery to finance the coming war. The proceeds were given to Bonifacio Novelo, who went off to buy pack-horses, guns and ammunition in Belize. While they waited for their arms, the Maya

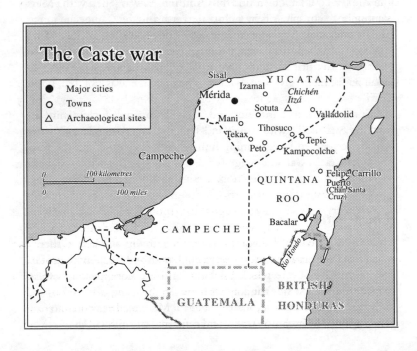

The Caste war

- ● Major cities
- ○ Towns
- △ Archaeological sites

limited themselves to minor skirmishes, then melted away into the forest before the enemy could react.

A coup in Mérida forced the whites to withdraw troops from the interior, and the Maya were quick to seize the advantage. With a few quick strikes, they took control of the territory between Peto and Valladolid, a distance of fifty miles, and their success drew scores of recruits from the Maya, including the powerful Cocoms from Sotuta in the northeast.

When order was restored in Mérida, the generals moved regulars and militia back to the south, driving the Maya from key positions as they advanced. The generals established a fortified base deep in the forest, then gathered their forces for a decisive offensive against the Maya.

But on 5 December 1847, the Maya attacked the base, and after six days of heavy fighting, the army was forced to abandon its position. Fighting their way through enemy lines, the soldiers managed to escort the women, children, and wounded to Peto. But by January, the Maya surrounded the city, and by February, Peto fell.

The Maya were now strong enough to split their forces into two divisions. The southern army, headed by Jacinto Pat, moved to the west, and Cecilio Chi took command of the offensive against Valladolid in the east.

The siege of Valladolid began on 19 January 1848, when 15,000 Maya warriors breached the defences and moved into the barrios of the city. Within two days, the Maya secured the roads around three quarters of the city and controlled the *cenote*, the only source of water for Valladolid.

On 19 March the whites abandoned Valladolid. With troops and artillery clearing a line of retreat, a column of ten thousand civilians began a forty-mile journey through the surrounding forest. People were still crowded in the city when the Maya struck, and the departing column was attacked along its entire length by machete-wielding warriors. The rear guard mustered enough men and weapons to protect the column until it reached Espita, where the commanding officer hoped to make a stand, but conflict between the Campeche troops and those of Mérida broke out, and the column was forced back on the road. The safety of Mérida was not reached for another three days.

A hurried peace initiative was opened with Jacinto Pat, and without inviting or consulting Cecilio Chi, he agreed to the following terms.

1. Baptism and marriage fees were to be reduced and made equitable for whites and Indians.
2. The Maya were to have free use of the *ejido* and uncultivated lands.
3. All indebted servants were to be freed from debt.
4. Barabachano was to be made governor-for-life.
5. Jacinto Pat was to be made governor of the Maya.
6. Rifles confiscated from the Maya were to be returned to Jacinto Pat.
7. Taxes on rum distillation were to be abolished.

Articles five and six of the pact split the Maya leadership. Neither Chi nor the Cocoms would accept Jacinto Pat as the supreme leader of the Maya, and the enemy sending him their confiscated rifles and ammunition was unthinkable.

With the prospect of peace now unlikely, the whites prepared to defend Mérida. The government fortified the garrison and deployed its forces to hold the eastern and southern approaches to the city, then waited for an estimated force of 24,000 Maya warriors to attack.

Ticul fell to the Maya on 26 March. As the whites fled from the city, the rearguard of the retreating column panicked and fled for the woods, leaving women, children and the aged to the mercy of the Indians.

On 28 May Izamal fell, and three Maya columns converged upon Mérida from the east and the south.

The noose was tightening. A hundred thousand residents and refugees crowded into the city, living in the college, the churches, the convents, and government buildings. Those who could not find shelter were forced to camp out in the plaza. Prices of food and clothing were now less than a tenth of their value, and shopkeepers offered their entire inventory to the refugees at a fraction of cost.

A defended corridor was established to evacuate the population to Sisal, where an assortment of canoes and other light craft waited to take them to foreign ships anchored offshore.

The exodus began, and scouts were sent out to locate the enemy

The central plaza of Mérida, Yucatán about 1850

forces, but surprisingly, they failed to make contact with Maya forces of any consequence. A day passed, then two. They found Izamal deserted, the surrounding villages abandoned, and wherever they met the enemy, his troops retreated before them with little resistance.

Time had run out on the Maya offensive. Clouds of winged ants, harbingers of the first rain of the planting season, swept down upon them from the north. The war would have to wait: the time had come to plant maize.

In the meantime, aid from abroad poured into Mérida. On 17 August 1848, Yucatán was reunited with Mexico, and the newly elected president was quick to send money, weapons, and ammunition.

Government troops reached Peto on 1 October and took the city without resistance, and when Bacalar fell in the spring of 1849, there was no village of any consequence left in Maya hands. The only refuge safe from government forces was the deep forest. The rebels and the greater part of the population, carrying sacks of dried corn to sustain them until the planting season, retreated into the forest.

In September leadership of the Maya forces changed hands. Venancio Pec denounced Jacinto Pat for excessive taxes to sustain the war, appropriating the spoils of war, and excessive use of the whip to enforce discipline. On 8 September Pec intercepted the general on the Bacalar road and murdered him. Pec now assumed control of the northern forces, and Florentino Chan, one of Cecilio Chi's lieutenants, took command of the south.

Bonifacio Novello continued to make sporadic raids in the neighbourhood of Valladolid, and José María Barrera distinguished himself by capturing a government column of 535 men and officers on the Bacalar road with all their supplies and weapons. But the momentum of the war had shifted – time, weapons, and manpower were on the side of the government.

THE DICTATORSHIP OF THE CROSS

Barrera led his weary company into the forest to Chan Santa Cruz, where a small *cenote* lay at the bottom of a cave. The depth of the water was only a few feet, but the level never changed, no matter how much water was drawn from it. A mahogany tree with a small cross carved into its bark stood on the brink of the *cenote*. According to legend, the cross was said to possess the miraculous power of speech, but whether it possessed the power before Barrera occupied the site or whether it gained it during his residence there has never been quite clear. He erected a wooden cross on a platform made of poles on the east side of the *cenote* for prayers, and it was not long before God answered them. The voice of God may have resembled the voice of Manual Nahuat, a ventriloquist, but it spoke with sufficient authority to launch Barrera on an ill-fated attack on Kampocolche, where, contrary to the promise of the Cross, the Maya did not find themselves immune to the bullets of the enemy.

Government forces swept down upon Chan Santa Cruz, now a village of more than a thousand people, and drove the rebels back into the forest. Barrera escaped, but Nahuat was killed in the battle, and the voice of the Cross was once again silent.

Neither the cult of the talking cross nor the practice of God speaking to man through an interpreter originated at Chan Santa Cruz. The Books of Chilam Balam, the prophet of Mani, written before the Spaniards reached Mexico, tell of diviners among the Yucatec Maya known as Chilans, who were the interpreters of the gods.

The Chilan generated his prophecies by first retiring to the inner room of his house, where he would lie in a self-induced trance as a supernatural being perched in the rafters communicated the will of the gods to him. Other priests, assembled outside the room, could hear the words but were unable to understand them. They waited, faces bowed to the ground, until the Chilan emerged and delivered the prophecy of the gods to them.

Archaeological indications of talking gods are also found in the religious practices of the Classic Maya of the eighth and ninth centuries. On the island of Cozumel, in the temple of Ix Chel, a large pottery image of the Moon Goddess was attached to the wall of the shrine with mortar. Behind the wall, a sacristy with a small hidden door opened into the back of the idol. Presumably, the secret passage allowed the priest to enter the temple covertly and speak to the people as if he himself were the deity.

With the death of Nahuat, God no longer spoke directly to the Maya, but the holy instructions continued, now transmitted by letter to the rank and file through Barrera. The letter bore the sign of three crosses, and was countersigned by Juan de la Cruz Puc, Barrera's secretary and interpreter.

The war dragged on, with both sides seeking an end. Truces and peace treaties were proposed and rejected, and in time the government, in spite of its superior weapons and manpower, tired of the whole affair. The economy of Yucatán was devastated, the army and the civilian population were apathetic and disinterested, and losses continued to mount. By 1850, 250,000 soldiers and civilians, almost half the population of the country, had been killed in the war, and rough estimates of Maya losses were as many as 275,000. Failing to reach a decisive victory, with support from the people dwindling, and the cost of pursuing the war draining the meagre resources of the State, the government declared the war was ended.

To the Maya, however, the war was an ongoing conflict against white domination and culture. The pause in hostilities was only temporary, a time to reorganize their forces and stockpile munitions. At Chan Santa Cruz, the old order was gone – Jacinto Pat, Cecilio Chi, Florentino Chan, Venancio Pec, and José María Barrera were all dead, but the Cross survived, a theocratic entity with absolute power over the Maya religious, political, and military State.

The cult of the cross now took on a more formal structure. The *Patrón* of the Cross, the *Nohoch Tata*, or Great Father, stood at the head of the cult. Beneath him were the *Tata Polin*, the Interpreter of the Cross, who summoned God with his whistle, the Organ of the Divine Word, from whom God's words echoed through a hollow barrel; and the Secretary to the Cross, who issued all policy directives. The chief military officers were the *Tata Chikuic,* the commandant of the army, and the *Tata Nohoch Zul*, the chief of intelligence, whose job was to

Barrera, the *Nohoch Tata*, or Great Father of the Mayan cult, of Chan Santa Cruz on the left

gather information from plantation workers and servants throughout the country.

The first to hold the office of the *Nohoch Tata* is in doubt, but the first Interpreter of the Cross was certainly Juan de la Cruz Puc, who was writing letters and signing them in the name of the Cross.

From his writings and Indian legends, the influence of Christianity is more in evidence than aboriginal religious beliefs. From sermons he delivered in Chan Santa Cruz on 15 October 1850, Puc clearly identifies himself with Christ, and by the style of the sermon, acts as an interpreter of Christ. To the average Maya peasant listening to the sermon, it would be easy for him to believe that Puc was indeed the second coming of Christ. Descendants of the Maya rebels believed him to be the son of God who was crucified and returned from the dead to lead them, and they looked upon the crucifixion as his persecution by government troops, whom they referred to as Jews.

By 1857, now well supplied with guns, powder, and ammunition from Belize and with frontier garrisons lightly manned by government troops, Crescencio Poot launched a major offensive against the city of Tekax. The Maya column, wearing uniforms and marching smartly, and their leaders proclaiming to be Campeche troops, entered the city with little resistance. Before the massacre had run its course, more than a thousand civilians and soldiers were dead.

By 20 February Bacalar fell to the Maya in less than twenty minutes, and the strategic route to Belize for supplies and arms was again open.

By now, it was clear that the generals no longer spoke for the Maya. At Bacalar, the magistrate of Corozal offered Venancio Puc 2,500 pesos to ransom the survivors, but the offer was presented to the Cross rather than to Puc. The Maya gathered before the Cross and prayed, and late in the evening, a whistling noise announced that the Cross had spoken. A non-negotiable price of 4,000 pesos was demanded for the prisoners.

With the strategic supply route from Belize to Chan Santa Cruz securely under Maya control, the Cross was now master of the south, and the Maya, secure in the forests of Quintana Roo, set about building their city and a suitable church to house their master.

The Balam Na, the first native church to be built in Mexico, is utterly devoid of Christian influence in its architecture. The grim,

The grim structure of the Balam Na, Felipe Carrillo Puerto, Quintana Roo

enigmatic structure was a massive front of stone blocks more than 100 feet long, 60 feet wide, and about 75 feet high. Five huge buttresses supported an arched roof and the walls on either side of the church. There was but one door and one window on the bleak façade.

Schools and barracks were built along each side of the church and in the rear. The residence of the *Tatich*, a building some 100 feet long, with living quarters and reception rooms, stood on the opposite side of the plaza from the Balam Na. Surrounding the plaza were the military barracks, a council house, and a prison.★

The rites performed in the Balam Na were much like those of the Catholic Church. The mass began with a priest chanting in whatever Latin words he could recall, which, although foreign to the congregation, were interpreted as the word of God. The host was a tortilla of corn and honey, and Mass was said in the standard Catholic form as recalled by former acolytes.

In January 1860, the government sent a force of 2,200 soldiers and a supporting labour force to solve the Chan Santa Cruz problem once and for all. In eight days, the column, finding little resistance along the

---

★ The Balam Na still functions in Felipe Carrillo (Chan Santa Cruz). Since the War of the Castes, it has served as store, a movie theatre, and even a Masonic temple before it was bequeathed to the Maryknoll Fathers in 1942.

way, reached Chan Santa Cruz only to find the city deserted. The occupation was short-lived. Crescencio Poot gathered forces from every village between Bacalar and Peto, and struck Chan Santa Cruz from every quarter. Overpowered, the enemy pulled out, loosing 1,500 men, all of its artillery, 300 mules, and even the military band before reaching the security of Tihosuco. The Cross now maintained absolute control of the interior, and would do so up to the turn of the twentieth century.

The loss was a financial disaster to Governor Augustin Acereto, who had borrowed money from Cuba to pay for the enterprise. His only resource was to pay off the Cubans by selling into slavery the peaceful Maya of the northern villages.

The practice of selling Maya prisoners into slavery had been a continuing one in Yucatán for some time, but Acereto's shipment was to be the last. In 1861, Benito Juárez, a Zapotec Indian, was elected President of Mexico and stopped the trade.

With the government troops disorganized and demoralized, Crescencio Poot began a series of raids in the north, reaching as far as the Mérida road and the ruins of Chichen Itza. Some northern villages were abandoned, and a pall of fear spread from Sotuta in the east to Valladolid in the west. The Cross had now consolidated a strong position in civilized Yucatán, and it would be a formidable force for the government to deal with in the years to come.

The next thrust into Maya territory began in the spring of 1865, during the reign of the Emperor Maximilian. By now, however, the leadership of the Maya had changed. Bonifacio Novelo was the *Nohoch Tata*, and Crescencio Poot the *Tata Chikuic*, or ranking general.

Maximilian poured troops and money into an effort to build a road into the interior, but when it reached Kampocolche, the government forces came under heavy attack. Maximilian's army was forced to pull back, and the Maya routed the rear guard, inflicting heavy casualties on the column. Nearly all the weapons and baggage were lost in the retreat.

The autumn of 1867 found Bonifacio Novelo, the old gunrunner, exercising complete control over an army of 11,000 men and resources sufficient to wage war indefinitely. According to Novelo, the Cross spoke no more. The ventriloquist was a thing of the past, and as in the best tradition of Christianity, God was worshipped through the Cross. The Cross, however, continued to write letters.

In 1884 there was a lull in military operations, and Crescencio Poot decided the time was ripe to open peace negotiations with Yucatán. Terms were agreed, and the pact was signed by the Vice-governor of Yucatán in Belize.

On 22 August 1885, however, the treaty was again broken when Aniceto Dzul killed Poot and fighting broke out along the frontier.

The war that had endured for fifty-three years finally came to a close in 1900. The Maya were now trapped between Mexican naval forces to the south and the railway that was aimed at the heart of the Maya capital.

On 3 May 1900, the Maya celebrated the last Ceremony of the Cross in Chan Santa Cruz, giving praise to La Santísima, partaking of blessed food, then filing into the Temple of the Speaking Cross to kneel and pray.

CHAPTER ELEVEN

Juárez and Maximilian

Benito Juárez: The Early Years

The firebrand of the early liberal movement was Melchor Ocampo, a scholar and a lawyer, who served as Governor of Michoacán and later as a Member of Congress in the national legislature. While in Michoacán, he gained acclaim among the liberals by protesting against excessive Church fees for the sacraments. A classic example he frequently cited was the case of a peasant who asked the local priest to give his son a free burial because he had no money to pay for the sacrament. The priest refused, and when the peasant asked what now could he do with his dead son, the priest answered, 'Salt him and eat him'.

Beyond his protests against oppressive Church fees, which in many cases resulted in debt peonage, Ocampo further alienated the Church with his views of freedom of religion and the discrimination of the clergy against the poor. The problem that concerned the Church was not so much his views, however, but that he aired them in public rather than before Church authorities. When the conservative establishment grew concerned about his audience among the masses, they exiled him to New Orleans.

If Ocampo was the spirit of the neo-liberal movement, its executor was Benito Juárez, a Zapotec Indian from Oaxaca, one of the most conservative provinces of the nation.

Juárez was born in 1806 in Guelatao, a village of no more than twenty families or extended families. Orphaned at an early age, he spent his childhood working as a shepherd for his uncle. Before he was twelve, with encouragement from an older sister working as a servant

in the city of Oaxaca, he left the village to join her. Knowing little
Spanish, he walked 25 miles across rugged mountain terrain to reach
the city.

His sister found him a position working for Antonio Salanueva, a
Franciscan lay brother who was a part-time bookbinder. Two years later,
Salanueva enrolled him in the Council Seminary, where he studied
Latin, philosophy, and moral theology. He seemed headed for a career in
the clergy, but when he was twenty-two, he had a change of heart and
worked his way through law school, receiving his degree in 1831.

Choosing politics as a career, he was elected to the Oaxaca City
Council, and as he gained a reputation among the legal community, his
career rose with positions in the judiciary, the legislature, and an
appointment as Minister of Government. Although he was a devout
Catholic, he consistently provoked the Church by defending the

Benito Juárez, one of Mexico's foremost politicians in the mid-nineteenth
century

peasantry against its exorbitant charges for the sacraments. For these services, he never charged a fee.

The conservatives were in power at that time, and in 1836, he was arrested on charges of aiding and abetting a liberal revolt. In time, the charges were dropped, and he moved to Mexico City, where he was elected a delegate to the liberal Congress of 1846. When the Mexican-American war broke out, Santa Anna dissolved the Congress, and he returned to Oaxaca, where he was chosen by the legislature as governor *pro tem*. In 1848 he was elected to a full term as governor of Oaxaca, the first Indian to hold high office in Mexico.

His tenure was characterized by fiscal conservatism and efficient management. He reduced the state debt, cut back the state bureaucracy, met the state payroll punctually, and created an atmosphere of conciliation between conflicting interests. Unlike his predecessors, he wore a simple black frock coat instead of a uniform festooned with oversized medals and gold braid, and he lived at home, where he was accessible to the public.

A conservative coup returned Santa Anna to power in 1853, and one of his first acts was to banish Juárez from the country. He had not forgotten 1848, when, exiled by his débâcle in the Mexican-American war, Juárez refused him sanctuary in Oaxaca.

A Peaceful Transfer of Power

The excesses of Santa Anna and those of his allies, the military and the Church, finally motivated competing liberal factions in Mexico to form a united political front. They included writers, intellectuals, farmers, teachers, lawyers, entrepreneurs, journalists, civilians, army officers, ranchers, traders, smugglers from the north, and even governors and political chieftains who distrusted the Church and despised the military. For the first time in history, the leaders of a liberal front were *mestizos*, not *criollos*.

Juárez met regularly with Ocampo and other liberal notables in New Orleans, and, aware of the brewing revolt in Mexico, they came up with a co-ordinated plan to overthrow the government. They chose Juan Alvarez, who was waging guerrilla warfare in Guerrero, to lead the revolution, and they sent him a statement of principles for the government they visualized. Alvarez incorporated them into the *Plan de Ayutla*, and the plan gained strong support among rebels in Nueva León, Guadalajara, and Jalisco. By August of 1855, popular support for the revolution had grown to the extent that Santa Anna resigned the presidency and went into exile for the last time.

A new government was formed with Alvarez as provisional president, Melchor Ocampo Secretary of the Treasury, Benito Juárez as Minister of Justice, and Ignacio Comonfort, the most moderate of the liberals, as Minister of War.

The new government's first reform was the *Ley Juárez*, which restricted the power of Church and military courts to trying only those cases involving Church or military law. Violations of civil laws by clergy or military were now subject to the secular courts.

The violent reaction to the law of the conservatives was sufficient to split the liberals into two factions – the moderates and the radicals. The moderates favoured backing down, but the radicals stood fast. A compromise was reached by inducing Alvarez to resign and place the presidency in the hands of the moderate Comonfort.

In June of 1856, Miguel Lerdo de Tejada, the Secretary of the Treasury, drafted the *Ley Lerdo,* a law prohibiting all institutions from owning real estate that was not needed for their day-to-day operations. The Church could keep its buildings, monasteries, and convents, and the towns their halls, jails, and schools, but they were forced to divest themselves of all urban and rural property.

The government did not confiscate the properties they seized, but put them up for public auction. The proceeds of the sale went to the former owner, and the government profited from transfer taxes. The primary objective of the law, however, was to create a new class of landowners by selling off Church estates, estimated to be one-quarter of the land value of Mexico, to the public. Only the wealthy, however, could afford to bid on the new lands – the *peon* could hardly afford them. For the Indian villages, the law was a disaster. Like the Church and the town, the villages were classed as institutions, and their *ejidos*, the community lands, were gobbled up by speculators and *hacendados*.

The third law, the *Ley Iglesias*, struck at the heart of the Catholic

Church. Henceforth, civil authorities were responsible for recording births, marriages, and deaths, and cemeteries were transferred to the Department of Hygiene. Furthermore, sacramental fees depended solely upon the ability of the supplicant to pay, and for those who could not pay, the priest could claim no fee.

The Constitution of 1857 contained most of the features of the three laws, but most importantly, it enacted a comprehensive bill of rights. Its guiding principles were equality before the law, freedom of the press, freedom of education, the right of assembly, the right to bear arms, bail, and habeas corpus. Slavery and compulsory service were abolished, and all titles of the nobility were cancelled.

There was no mention of freedom of religion, but in its place, the Constitution legislated the broader principle of freedom of conscience. Roman Catholicism was no longer the state religion.

The reaction of the Church was predictable. Education had always been its province, and freedom of speech would be a death blow to Church censorship. Furthermore, the abolishment of compulsory service, they claimed, would permit priests and nuns to retract their vows. The bishops immediately issued a proclamation threatening everyone who upheld the Constitution with excommunication, and Pius IX 'condemned, reproved, and declared null and void' the Constitution of 1857. In short, the Church would accept no laws that threatened its historical domination of the state.

THE WAR OF REFORM

The nation split into two factions with irreconcilable differences. The establishment reacted by denouncing the Constitution and sending troops under the command of General Félix Zuloaga into the capital. Zuloaga dissolved the Congress, arrested Juárez, and when Comonfort fled the country, a junta named Zuloaga president.

Juárez managed to escape to Querétaro, and as second in line for the presidency, he inherited the office and established a constitutional government in exile. Eleven states supported the liberal cause. To finance the coming war and buy arms, Juárez shifted the seat of the government to Vera Cruz, where he could seize custom receipts from overseas.

While in Vera Cruz, the government issued the Laws of Reform, which changed the social, economic, and political position of the Church for all time. Church property was nationalized without compensation, monasteries and convents were closed, civil servants were prohibited from taking part in religious rites, and freedom of worship was now the law of the land.

The War of Reform lasted from 1858 to 1861, and was characterized by excessive atrocities on both sides. The first two years of the war saw the conservative army holding the advantage. In the spring of 1860, however, the momentum shifted when the liberals defeated General Miguel Miramón at Vera Cruz. Shortly afterward, Guadalajara and Oaxaca fell. The war came to a close in late December of 1860, when General Jesús Gonzáles Ortega defeated the conservative army at Calpulálpan. The war had cost Mexico 50,000 lives, mostly those of poor *mestizos* and Indians.

The French Invasion

In January 1861, Juárez returned to Mexico City in triumph, and in March, he won the presidential election. But he inherited a bankrupt nation. The treasury deficit was 400,000 pesos a month, and the army, civil servants, and police had not been paid for months. Nationalized property worth 16 million pesos was sold to finance the new government, but only one million reached the treasury – the remainder went to pay off bonds, promissory notes, and other credits. Customs receipts generated the greater part of Mexico's income, but ninety per cent went just to pay the interest on a foreign debt of 80 million pesos.

In July Congress voted to freeze payments on all foreign debts, the majority of which were owed to Britain, France, and Spain. The European powers convened in London and agreed to a joint occupation of Vera Cruz, where they could garnishee all of Mexico's custom receipts. They further agreed to collect only their legitimate claims, and foreswore any effort to acquire territory in Mexico or to interfere with Mexico's chosen form of government.

The expeditionary forces from the three nations occupied Vera Cruz early in 1862, but a confrontation was avoided when an agreement on the debt was reached through diplomatic channels. All three parties were satisfied, and Britain and Spain withdrew.

Napoleon III, however, had ambitions to expand French influence in Latin America, and Mexico was his best opportunity. He chose his time well. Confederate victories in the United States left Lincoln in a poor if not impossible position to enforce the Monroe Doctrine.

A month after the British and Spanish forces departed, the French expeditionary forces, reinforced with an additional 2,500 troops, marched inland. They met a rag-tag Mexican army under the command of General Ignacio Zaragoza at Puebla on 5 May 1862, and suffered an embarrassing defeat. the Second Brigade, under the command of Brigadier General Porfirio Díaz, carried the day. The victory became a *cause célèbre* throughout the nation, and the date, *Cinco de Mayo*, is now a national holiday in Mexico.

Not all in Mexico, however, were pleased with the French defeat. Many conservatives and priests, still smarting from the War of Reform, lent comfort and aid to the enemy.

In April of 1863, the French, reinforced with 30,000 fresh troops, returned to Puebla, and the city fell after a 61-day siege. The defeat was a disaster for Juárez's army. Casualties were heavy, and 11,000 men and 300 officers, among them General Porfirio Díaz, were taken prisoner. Mexico City could no longer be defended, and Juárez withdrew to San Luis Potosí with his cabinet and what was left of his army.

The French forces entered Mexico City unopposed, and a *Te Deum* was offered in the cathedral to celebrate their victory.

The French commander established a Regency Council of two conservative generals and the archbishop Pelagio Antonio Labastida. The junta appointed 215 prominent Mexican citizens to form an Assembly of Notables who would decide upon the form of government to be adopted. Their decision was for a hereditary monarchy with a European prince as emperor, and they offered the post to Ferdinand Maximilian von Habsburg, Archduke of Austria.

MAXIMILIAN AND CARLOTA

Maximilian, the younger brother of Franz Joseph I, the Emperor of Austria-Hungary, was born in Vienna on 6 July 1832. Without duties of any significance, he wandered about Europe, touring Greece, Italy, Madeira, Tangiers, Spain, and Algiers. Later, as commander-in-chief of the Austrian Navy, he would pay state visits to Palestine, France, Belgium, Holland, and to his cousin, Queen Victoria. In 1857–59 he served as governor-general of Lombardy-Venetia, where he built Miramar, his palatial palace overlooking the Adriatic Sea.

In 1857 he married Charlotte Amélie, (better known as Carlota), the daughter of Leopold I of Belgium, and the couple took up residence at Miramar.

Even before the Assembly of Notables made their decision, Napoleon III had decided that Mexico would be ruled by a monarchy, and he had discussed the possibility with Maximilian as early as 1861, before the invasion. With Napoleon's endorsement, a delegation of Mexican conservatives met Maximilian at Miramar to offer him the monarchy. Maximilian accepted, but only upon the condition that he be acceptable to the Mexican people.

His stipulation proved no problem for the conservatives. A plebiscite was quickly engineered in Mexico City, and it came as no surprise that

The Empress Carlota and Emperor Maximilian

Maximilian received an overwhelming vote of approval from the Mexican people.

The conditions set by Napoleon for French support of the new monarchy was that Maximilian pay the costs of the French expeditionary forces and the army of occupation in Mexico until July 1864, which amounted to two hundred and seventy million francs. After that date, he was obliged to pay for 20,000 French troops that would occupy Mexico until the end of 1867. In addition, he would assume responsibility for all claims against Mexico. In return, Maximilian's salary was to be 1.5 million pesos, and Carlota's 200,000 pesos. Before he ever set foot in Mexico, Maximilian had tripled the national debt.

Maximilian was thirty-two years old and Carlota only twenty-four when they arrived in Vera Cruz in May 1864. Their welcome was the first taste of the reality they were soon to face. Vera Cruz was dirty, depressing, and unbearably hot. The official who was to meet them was late, and only a handful of people turned out to greet them. Maximilian, ignoring his icy reception, stood before them and said, 'Mexicans, you have wished for me; your noble nation, by a spontaneous majority, has chosen me, from today on, to oversee your destinies. I gladly surrender myself to this calling.' Carlota wept beside him as he spoke.

When they reached the tableland, however, they found their reception in the provincial cities considerably warmer. When they left Puebla, their carriage passed under seven hundred and seventy arches of branches and flowers, and when they reached Mexico City, they entered to cheering crowds and a triumphal welcome. The Archbishop Labastida had left nothing to chance.

The royal couple took up residence in Chapultepec Castle, which had been erected as a palace for Spain's viceroys in the eighteenth century, and it soon became the social hub of Mexico. The centre of attraction was always the Empress Carlota, seated on her throne on the eastern side of the great ballroom and attended by her ladies-in-waiting. For State functions such as balls, it was the Empress's prerogative to select her partner for the first dance, and when it was finished, the band struck up a lively tune as more than a thousand Mexican élite and foreign dignitaries selected partners for round dances, waltzes, *schottische*, and other dances in fashion.

The couple wrote a book of etiquette for the royal court, spoke Spanish whenever possible, occasionally wore Mexican costumes, and served Mexican food. To further their relationships with the people and create a line of succession to the throne, the couple adopted Augustín Iturbide, the grandson of the first emperor of Mexico.

The royal court, however, as gracious and charming as it was perceived on the outside, was not above scandal and reproach on the inside. The Mexican's lack of punctuality continually irritated the Austrians, Mexicans were not allowed to use toilets reserved for Europeans, and intolerance often led to nasty racial epithets during social functions. Nor were Maximilian and Carlota the devoted couple they appeared to be. Within months, Carlota moved into separate quarters and took an Austrian officer as her lover, and Maximilian soon followed by taking the gardener's daughter to his bed.

Maximilian made himself accessible to the people by opening the palace to his subjects once a week, and frequently toured the provinces better to acquaint himself with the people and their concerns.

For the conservatives who had put him in the seat of power, however, Maximilian was a political disaster. Expecting him to suspend the Reform Laws, they were sadly disappointed. He refused to return the Church lands despite pressure from Labastida and the Pope, and refused to declare education as the sole province of the Church. He advocated freedom of religion, established a free press, granted amnesty to political prisoners, and eventually committed the cardinal sin – he levied forced loans upon the Church.

He further shocked the establishment when he commemorated the independence of Mexico by visiting Dolores and delivering a speech from a window in Hidalgo's house. He ended his speech to a cheering crowd by shouting '*el grito!*', the cry of the independence movement.

Maximilian, a Mason and a self-styled liberal, was a contradiction to friend and enemy alike. How long could he remain on the throne of Mexico if he championed the cause of Juárez, his enemy, instead of the conservative principles he had sworn to uphold?

Maximilian's empire reached its zenith in early 1865. Marshal Achille Bazaine commanded 60,000 troops, half of which were French, the remainder Mexican and a few units from Belgium and Austria. He had defeated Porfirio Díaz in Oaxaca and now held the province, albeit temporarily. His armies were pushing northwards into Nueva León and Tamaulipas, but the French soon found that they could not hold the territories they captured. When they pulled out, the guerrillas returned from the back country and resuming their attacks.

JUÁREZ AND THE LIBERAL OFFENSIVE

In April 1865, the Civil War in the United States ended, and Juárez's fortunes improved substantially. Although Washington recognized the Juárez government, Lincoln was powerless to enforce the Monroe Doctrine during the French occupation. Within months of the defeat of the Confederacy, however, the Union sent thirty-thousand muskets to Juárez, and some three thousand Union veterans, lured by the promise of good pay and free land, joined Juárez's army.

The liberals opened offensives in Michoacan, Jalisco, Sinaloa, and Nueva León, steadily pushing back French forces as they moved south. Frustrated by his inability to deter the guerrillas, Bazaine persuaded Maximilian to sign the infamous 'Black Flag' decree, making the death penalty mandatory for any Juárista caught bearing arms. There could be no appeal, and the order was to be carried out within twenty-four hours. By this decree, Maximilian wrote his own death warrant.

On 15 January 1866, Napoleon III, facing a rising Prussian threat in Europe, an unpaid army in Mexico, and pressure from the United States, made the decision to pull the French army out of Mexico. The withdrawal would begin in November, and by early 1867, the last of the troops would leave Mexico.

Maximilian's letters to Napoleon accomplished nothing. He considered abdication, but Carlota refused to accept it. She travelled to Europe to plead their case in person with Napoleon, but when the emperor refused to receive her, she took her case to the Empress Eugénie, who chose not to interfere. In desperation, Carlota took her case to Pope Pius IX, hoping he would use his influence with the French court, but Maximilian's refusal to return Church lands in Mexico closed that avenue of appeal. While in Rome, the first symptoms of mental illness appeared, and Carlota returned to Belgium, where, hopelessly insane, she lived until 1927.

Maximilian, long a supporter of the Confederacy, now did an about-turn and petitioned the United States for help, but President Johnson chose to send General Sheridan with 50,000 troops to the Mexican border to enforce the Monroe Doctrine.

By March of 1867, the last French unit pulled out of Mexico, and Maximilian, no longer able to hold the capital, fled to Querétaro and took command of what was left of his Mexican troops.

On 15 May 1867, Querétaro fell to the liberal army, and Juárez ordered Maximilian court-martialled. Thirteen charges were brought against him, the most damning of which was the 'Black Flag' decree. Found guilty, Juárez ordered him executed.

Pleas to spare Maximilian's life came from Europe, the United States, the Vatican, and even from Garibaldi in Italy, but Juárez remained adamant. On 19 June 1867, Maximilian was executed on the Hill of the Bells in Querétaro. He was thirty-five-years-old.

On the morning of 15 July 1867, Juárez returned to the capital to a rousing welcome organized by Porfirio Díaz.

Juárez realized the most important task now was to stabilize the new government, and this, he felt, could best be accomplished by running for a third term as president. For the greater part of his first two terms, his most pressing task was to hold the government-in-exile together until the French were driven from Mexico. His only rival for the presidency was Porfirio Díaz, but Juárez won easily with 72 per cent of the vote.

Post-war Recovery

For Mexico, the Juárez administration was a period of reconstruction. If commerce was to be revitalized, major improvements in transport facilities would be necessary. The only transport link between Guadalajara, in the critical Bajio region, and Mexico City, was by stage, and often required a week to travel 300 miles.

A more vital transport task, however, was to bridge the gap between Mexico City and Vera Cruz by rail. It was no easy task. As the crow flies, the distance was no more than 200 miles, but there was more than an 8,000-foot difference in altitude between the two cities. For most of the distance, the right of way had to cross rugged mountain terrain and precipitous canyons.

Construction on the project started in 1837, but by 1860, only 150 miles of track had been laid. During Maximilian's reign, the British had made considerable progress, but work stopped in 1866 when the contractor ran into financial trouble. Through creative financing and subsidy, Juárez reactivated the project, and the Ferrocarril Mexicano was dedicated on 20 December 1872.

Juárez's other great dream was to make primary education mandatory and free for the entire population. His grand plan was to have one school for boys and another for girls in every town with a population of 5,000. Although Juárez never realized the full scope of his plan, he fulfilled a national need by substantially increasing the curriculum in science, engineering, and mathematics in the secondary schools.

Overall, the Juárez administration succeeded in most of its objectives. It made a substantial dent in the financial chaos Juárez inherited, reduced the national debt to one-fifth of that left by Maximilian,

The railway bridge across the Metlac Ravine was a superb piece of engineering

revitalized the mining and agricultural industries, and opened the door for foreign capital investment.

In 1871, Juárez again stood for re-election. His opponents for the presidency were Sebastián Lerdo de Tejada, one of his most loyal friends, and Porfirio Díaz, whose constituents were the young and the military. None of the three candidates received the required majority, and the decision, as required by the Constitution, fell upon the Congress, where the Juáristas were strong. Again the office fell to Juárez, but there was widespread criticism for the way he had manoeuvred the Congress.

In November 1871, Porfirio Díaz revolted in Oaxaca, claiming the election violated the principles of the *Plan de Ayutla*, and he refused to accept the decision of the Congress. Unable to gain enough support from provincial chieftains, federal troops soon cornered Díaz in the northwestern mountains. Before they could take him prisoner, however, word came from Mexico City that shocked the nation. Benito Juárez was dead. He suffered a heart attack on 18 July 1872.

CHAPTER TWELVE

The Porfiriato

Don Porfirio

In February 1908, Porfirio Díaz, after serving twenty-seven years as President of Mexico, granted an interview with James Creelman, a reporter for *Pearson's Magazine*. The purpose of the interview was to determine the stability and political future of Mexico. Would Díaz choose to run for re-election in 1910 at the age of eighty, support a successor from his immediate circle, or would he tolerate opposition parties? His answer was of vital importance to those American interests that were heavily invested in Mexico.

Creelman was obviously impressed with this giant among world leaders. In his article, he would write,

> There is no figure in the whole world who is more romantic or heroic than that soldier-statesman whose adventurous youth outshines the pages of Dumas and whose iron hand has transformed the warlike, ignorant, superstitious, and impoverished Mexican masses, after centuries of cruel oppression by the greedy Spaniards, into a strong, pacifist and prosperous nation that honors its debts.

Díaz told Creelman that he felt that Mexico was not yet ready for democracy as practised in America and Europe, but he believed that democracy had taken root in Mexico, and that the future was assured owing to the order, peace, and progress that had taken place under his long tenure. He then made a statement that stunned and electrified the nation.

> I welcome an opposition party in the Mexican Republic.... If it appears, I will regard it as a blessing, not as an evil. And if it can develop power, not to

exploit but to govern, I will stand by it, support it, advise it, and forget myself in the successful inauguration of complete democratic government in the country.... This nation is ready for her ultimate life of freedom.

No matter what my friends and supporters say, I retire when my term of office ends, and I shall not serve again. I shall be eighty years old then. I have waited patiently for the day when the people of the Mexican Republic should be prepared to choose and change their government at every election without danger of armed revolution and without injury to the national credit or interference with the national progress. I believe that day has come. I welcome an opposition party in the Mexican Republic.

Porfirio Díaz was born in the city of Oaxaca in 1830. His mother, Petrona Mori, was a pure-blooded Mixtec Indian, and his father, José Faustino Díaz, worked as a blacksmith, mule driver, and tanner.

His father died of cholera in 1853, leaving Petrona a widow with five children. When he was old enough to work, he made chairs and desks for the local school, carved out rifle butts, and repaired pistols. Between his earnings and those of his mother, who waited at table at the local inn and supervised a primary school, the family managed to make ends meet.

Díaz first studied for the priesthood at the Council Seminary, but his ambitions ran more to the military than the cloth, and he transferred to the State Institute of Arts and Sciences. At the Institute he registered to study law, but opted instead for a career in the military when Benito Juárez, at that time Director of the Institute, authorized courses in military theory and tactics.

In 1856 he joined the Oaxaca National Guard, and fought in nearly every battle during the War of Reform, earning him the rank of brigadier-general. After the war, Juárez appointed Díaz military commander of the Isthmus of Tehuantepec. The post received little direction and so few orders from Mexico City that Díaz was forced to take on the responsibilities of governor of the state in addition to his military duties. In Tehuantepec he managed to accomplish that which Juárez had failed to do during the war – form a loyal and effective fighting force from the war-like tribes of Santiago Cueva and Juchitán.

It was in Tehuantepec that Díaz met the woman who would become his lifelong friend and mistress, perhaps the only woman he would truly love.

The Porfiriato – Porfiro Díaz

Juana Catalina Romero, known familiarly as Juana Cata, was twenty-two years old when Díaz met her. During the day, she rolled cigarettes and sold various products in the market-place, and in the evening, she could be found playing billiards with Díaz and other leading citizens of the town. He built a chalet for Juana, and changed the route of the Transisthmanian Railroad to pass within six feet of the entry. Each morning the engineer would reduce speed to allow him to step into the train from his doorstep.

Juana could neither read nor write until she was thirty, but in her time, she became a leading political figure in Tehuantepec. She owned factories and sugar mills, founded a Marist college, and travelled through Europe and the Holy Land. When she grew old, she often visited Chapultepec Castle and dined with Díaz and his wife Carmelita.

In 1867 Díaz's ambitions led him to stand against Juárez for the presidency, which Juárez won by an overwhelming majority. In 1870, he was elected to Congress, and in 1871, he again waged a campaign for the presidency, this time running against Juárez and Sebastián Lerdo de Tejada. None of the candidates received the required majority, and the decision was passed to the Congress, which chose Juárez.

The unexpected death of Juárez a year into his term left Lerdo, the chief justice, as acting president. Lerdo scheduled elections for November, and easily defeated Díaz with 93 per cent of the vote.

The Lerdo Administration

Lerdo followed the policies set forth by his predecessor, and retained many of Juárez's appointees. He believed in firm executive control, and did not hesitate to use federal troops against revolts when deemed necessary.

During his tenure he proposed that the unicameral system be changed to add another house to Congress, and in 1874, a Senate was added to the Chamber of Deputies. Lerdo believed that the upper house would aid him in his efforts to establish a stronger central government. In that same year, he incorporated the Reform Laws into the Constitution, which established the separation of Church and State as a matter of law.

On the educational front, he made significant progress. By 1874, the number of schools in Mexico doubled, but the school enrolment of 349,000 students represented only one in nineteen school-aged children. Of these, only 77,000 were female. There was a shortage of qualified teachers, and in the rural areas and in the urban barrios, children were needed to work to supplement the family income rather than attend school.

During his tenure, contracts were let out to build several new railway lines. A group of British and Mexican investors won the contract for the Mexican Central Railroad line, which would connect the capital with the United States' border, and an American firm was promised a subsidy of 12,500 pesos for every mile of track laid across the Isthmus of Tehuantepec. In the area of communications, he succeeded in stringing 1,600 miles of telegraph wires in a project that would in time connect all the state capitals with Mexico City.

The Lerdo administration was capable and efficient. It had advanced the programmes begun by Juárez, and even succeeded in appeasing the *caudillos** that had pronounced for Díaz. But Lerdo seemed to have a talent for making enemies. He was hard and inflexible, and the press roasted him mercilessly. Nevertheless, Lerdo announced that he would seek re-election in 1876, but history will never know who might have won that election.

Díaz saw his opportunity. Rallying dissident officers to his side, he issued the *Plan de Tuxtepec*, which specified a number of charges against Lerdo, and called for the president to serve no more than one term. On 16 November Díaz defeated the government forces at Tecocac, and on 21 November 1876, he occupied Mexico City and assumed control of the nation.

1876: State of the Nation

Mexico in 1876 was still a backward country. Sixty years of near-continuous warfare and political instability had left Mexico hopelessly behind most of the civilized world in technology and science. In an era of steam power and telegraphic communication, Mexico still relied more upon mule trains and stage coaches for transporting goods and mail.

In the country, the *rurales*† were unable to cope with bandits and private armies of the *caudillos*, and the borderlands were an arena of lawlessness as cattle rustlers from the King Ranch operated with impunity. Díaz also had to contend with supporters of Lerdo, who launched a number of revolts along the border, where Lerdo had taken asylum.

The mining industry was in a shambles, and productivity of the few in operation was low because of outdated extraction and smelting techniques. In the farmlands, most of the equipment dated from the early colonial period, and modern methods of improving stock breeding were unknown.

The treasury was near-empty, foreign debts to a number of European countries were still outstanding, the salaries of most government

* Local strongmen.
† A rural police force authorized by Benito Juárez.

employees were in arrears, and investors, even native Mexicans, were
reluctant to infuse capital into a much-needed restoration programme.

THE PAX PORFIRIANA

Díaz knew he could accomplish little or nothing without first establishing law and order throughout the nation. To curb banditry and
revolt, he added a complement of 800 men to the *rurales*, pressed the
federal army into law enforcement, and enlisted the private armies of
local *caudillos* to round up bandits, put down rebellions, and keep the
peace.

Penal colonies were established in remote areas, such as the malaria-
infested Valle Nacional of Oaxaca, where his political enemies laboured
in tobacco plantations. Rebellious Maya Indians were sentenced to
hard labour in the mahogany logging camps, and jails throughout the
country were overcrowded. Rebels who were not killed in combat
were lined up against a wall and shot. If a commander asked what to do
about captured rebels, the reply was always '*Matalos en caliente*' [shoot
them on the spot!]

Failure to collect import duties along the United States border was
costing the government thousands of pesos each year, but Díaz was
quick to put a stop to the practice. He ordered government employees
caught taking bribes to be sentenced to ten years in prison, private
individuals five years, and commercial firms caught smuggling were
banned from receiving government contracts.

No mention of civil disturbances ever reached the ears of the people,
or crossed beyond the border of Mexico, since Díaz held the press on a
tight rein. He did, however, provide news to the outside world by
granting a monopoly to the Associated Press, but only with the proviso
that he approved all copy.

ECONOMY AND RECONSTRUCTION

To jump-start the economy, Díaz established a brains trust of *científicos*,
who believed that everything in politics and economics to promote
development of the nation should be done according to the rules of
science, statistics, and sound administration. The *científicos* comprised a
group of intellectuals, professionals, and entrepreneurs who had become

wealthy from the liberal measures taken against the Church and the appropriation of the *ejidos*, the community lands of the Indians. They were fascinated by French culture, and many had links with French capitalists. Advocates of opening up Mexico to massive foreign investment, they put everything in the nation on the bargaining table. Matías Romero, Diaz's ambassador to the United States, was said to keep a 'blue book' in his desk, listing available concessions with a price tag attached to each.

The leader of the *científicos* was José Ives Limantour, a financial genius who rose to be Secretary of the Treasury in a later Díaz administration. At the National Science Conference of 1901, he told the delegates, 'The weak, the unprepared, those who lack the necessary tools to triumph in the evolutionary process, must perish and leave the field to the strongest'.

Limantour, the son of a French *émigré*, was a scholar, a distinguished jurist, and an accomplished linguist. During his tenure, he lowered or eliminated the duties on many imports, negotiated loans abroad at favourable interest rates, and shifted Mexico from the silver to the gold standard. He enforced tariff laws, cleaned up the bureaucracy, and by 1890, paid off the debt to the United States. Due to his reforms, by the time Díaz left office, the treasury would hold 70 million pesos of cash reserves, the GNP would grow by 390 per cent, foreign debt would be paid off, and for the first time since the conquest, Mexico would enjoy a trade surplus.

One of the highest priorities of the reconstruction programme was the development of a railway system that would connect Mexico City to the state capitals. In 1876, no more than 400 miles of track had been laid, but by 1911, this had been increased to 15,000 miles. The new lines connected the mines of north and central Mexico with the gulf ports, with Texas border towns, and ultimately to the industrial centres of Chicago and Pittsburgh.

In 1880, three months before the end of Díaz's first term, the concession for the Mexican Central Railroad company, a 1,224 mile project, was awarded to a consortium of Boston investors that included the rail baron Hiram Nickerson, E. H. Harriman, and the Brown Brothers. In 1888, The Mexican National Company, owned by French and British investors, completed a narrow-gauge line between Mexico City and Laredo, Texas. After two abortive efforts to complete a line across the Isthmus of Tehuantepec failed, Díaz awarded the contract to the British magnate Weetman Pearson. When it was finished, goods from Pacific ports could be shipped across the Isthmus to Coatzacoalcos on the Gulf coast.

Mining was revived in 1884, and again in 1898 when the Mexican legislature changed the mining laws to give investors profitable subsoil rights. Later, the mining laws were again revised, granting rights to extract other minerals and lowering tax rates. With the introduction of the cyanide process, gold production rose from 1.5 million pesos in 1887 to 40 million pesos in 1908, and Mexico again was one of the world's leaders in silver production.

For an investment of 48,000 pesos, Colonel William Greene bought an option on a Sonoma copper mine. He sold stock in the venture on Wall Street, and within a few years, his Cananea Copper mine was one of the largest in the world. By 1910, more than 3,000 silver, copper, lead, and iron mines were in full production, and of the 1,030 mining companies in Mexico, 840 were American-owned, 148 Mexican, and the rest British and French.

Oil exploration began on the Gulf Coast in the 1860s, but met with little success until 1901, when Edward Doheny, a successful California oilman, brought in a gusher on 600,000 acres he purchased between Tampico and Tuxpan. Weetman Pearson entered the oil exploration field when the Petroleum Law of 1901 – which allowed tax-free entry for machinery – was passed. By 1906, his Águila Petroleum Company was the second largest producer of crude oil, and within a few years, Doheny and Pearson made Mexico one of the largest petroleum producers in the world.

Between 1882 and 1895, foreigners owned 70 million acres, and by 1910, foreign ownership had grown to 134 million acres. A firm jointly held by a Michigan investor and a German entrepreneur bought up 14.6 million acres in Sonora and the Baja, and 340,000 acres in Chiapas. Edward Doheny bought 620,000 acres in the Poza Rica region, Weetman Pearson received 800,000 acres in the Tampico-Tuxpan corridor for his Águila oil company, and a joint venture between J. P. Morgan and several investors in the British House of Lords bought 3 million acres in Chiapas and the Baja.

In southern Mexico, Pearson held a 300,000-acre plantation to grow chicle, hardwood, henequen, and coffee; and in the north, Randolph Hearst owned an immense ranch in Chihuahua.

During the Porfiriato, thousands of new factories were established, and more than two-thirds of new investments came from Mexican capital. The new ventures included, among other commodities, sugar, flour, textiles, paper, and chemicals. In 1890, José Schneider, a Mexican of German ancestry, opened the first brewery in Mexico, the Cervecería Cuauhtémoc, producing 10,000 barrels and 5,000 bottles of Carta Blanca, a world-class beer, every day. The eighty largest commercial and industrial establishments, however, were foreign owned. Twenty-one were held by Americans, twenty-three by the British, six by Mexicans, and the remainder by French, German, and Spanish, sixteen of which included Mexican parnerships.

Education during the Porfiriato, unfortunately, was limited to children of the élite. The curriculum included the teaching of English, because the educator, Ezequiel Chávez, believed it necessary in view of the growing relationship between Mexicans and Anglo-American people. Justo Sierra, the minister of public education, held the same view if Mexico was to develop the nation's culture as well as the economy.

A national normal school was created in 1887. The Appleton Publishing Company of New York was granted a monopoly on nearly all Mexican textbooks until 1919, written, of course, by American authors.

In 1878 there were some 5,000 primary schools in the entire nation, with an enrolment of about 50,000 students. By 1910, there were 12,000 schools with an enrolment of a million students. Only one in three children aged six to twelve were enrolled, however, and attendance was erratic. Eighty per cent of the population was illiterate.

The Francophiles

Wealth brought major changes in the architecture of urban areas as Mexican motifs were displaced by European styles in homes, churches, and public buildings. Even the Paseo Reforma was redecorated to look like the Champs Élysées, and foreign architects designed the Post Office, the Legislative Palace, and the Palace of Fine Arts. Elegant patios, marble staircases, carved doors, crystal chandeliers, gold candelabras, imported pianos and carpets, and private baths decorated with French fixtures were *de rigeuer* for the wealthy.

Lesley Byrd Simpson, a leading historian of Mexico, was escorted through one of these mansions in the 1940s. He described it as a 'museum piece of velvet draperies, pier glasses, marble tables, gilt, dazzling chandeliers, spindly chairs, artificial flowers, and stuffed birds. "Isn't it beautiful!," his hostess exclaimed. "They don't build houses like this anymore – there is not a thing Mexican in it!" '

The ladies replaced the graceful Spanish mantilla with the *dernier cri* of Paris, and their children were brought up by French governesses and sent abroad for a French education. Gustavo E. Campa's opera based on the life of Nezahualcóyotl, the great philosopher king of Texcoco, was entitled *Le Roi Póete*, and the libretto was prepared in French. Bastille Day was celebrated with the same enthusiasm as *Cinco de Mayo*, and the can-can was all the rage in the capital.

The social centre of the city was Plateros Street, where women shopped in boutiques for the latest French styles, and men in tailored suits sipped cordials and imported wine in the Casa de Plaisant. In less formal surroundings, one could drink coffee and eat pastries at the Café El Fenix, and purchase edible toys for their children and bonbons for their wives.

The exclusive Jockey Club stood at the end of Plateros Street, where the city's wealthiest men gathered in frock coats and top hats, and their wives in tight-waisted skirts, puffy blouses, and elegant hats. Membership was by invitation only, and for fees of 700 pesos a month, one could dine in elegant surroundings or play at the baccarat table with governors, ministers, and perhaps even Don Porfirio and Doña Carmen.

The city's theatres were located a block from Plateros. The Principal was built in 1753, the Nacional *circa* 1850, and the Arbeu in 1875. In these theatres, the élite enjoyed the plays of Racine and Shakespeare, and opera sung by international stars. The highlight of the opera season came to the Nacional in 1887, when Adelina Patti, the great Italian soprano, appeared in *La Traviata*, and after a stunning performance, she brought the audience to its feet by shouting 'Viva Mexico!' After Patti's final appearance, Don Porfirio presented her with a gold crown, earrings set with diamonds and rubies, and a golden locket,

In some areas, such as certain fields of medicine, civil engineering, and visual arts, Mexico was the equal of the European nations. The élite were knowledgeable in philosophy, theatre, and literature. They read Nietzsche, Bergson, William James, and attended the plays of Shaw and Ibsen.

Upper-class women, however, did not share the cultural level of their husbands. Their reading was, for the most part, limited to the Bible, and their social life to the Church. They had no concept of geography or history; their knowledge of Europe extended no further than Spain, Rome, and Paris.

A MONARCHY IN A REPUBLICAN DISGUISE

When Díaz's first term was nearing its end, a number of states, eager to keep the president in office, proposed an amendment to the no-re-election law. Díaz instead promoted a modification of the election laws that prohibited immediate re-election, but allowed ex-presidents and state governors to run for office after one term had lapsed. Consequently, his close ally, General Manuel Gonzáles, was elected president in 1880.

Díaz served briefly in the Gonzales cabinet, and another short period as Governor of Oaxaca during his sabbatical. Delfina Ortega, his first wife, died in 1880; and the following year, he married Carmen Romero Rubio. He was fifty-one-years-old, she eighteen.

In 1884 Díaz was re-elected, and three years later, sponsored a law that permitted immediate re-election. In 1890, a constitutional amendment removed all restrictions on re-election, and in 1904, another amendment increased the presidential term to six years.

Not since the time of Moctezuma had a Mexican leader enjoyed such absolute power. Through his political apparatus, highly selective appointments to key government posts, and control of the police and the *rurales,* he could force his will on Congress, state governors, and the judiciary. His power was so absolute that he often referred to the

Congress as '*mi caballada*' [my herd of tame horses]. Elections became such a farce that hardly anyone took the trouble to vote. And Díaz kept a wary eye on potential competition. Ambitious generals were periodically reassigned to other units to prevent them from developing a power base in the military, popular governors were encouraged to seek positions in the cabinet, run for congress, or accept assignments overseas as ambassadors.

Don Porfirio's administrative policy was simple – *pan o palo,* bread or the club. His punishment for non-conformists and critics was harsh. Exile was common, prison not unusual, and the *ley fuga* justified shooting prisoners while 'escaping'.

Editors who defended his policies were subsidized, those who opposed the administration were suppressed and often jailed. Filomena Mata, the editor of the *Diario de Hogar,* was imprisoned thirty times for his anti-re-electionist articles.

Surprisingly though, Díaz, unlike most dictators, amassed no personal fortune during his thirty-four years in office. On the other hand, however, those in high office and ranking military officers, with their access to information of new government projects in the planning stage, had ample opportunity for graft.

The Church

Despite the severe restrictions placed on the Church by the Constitution of 1857, the Church experienced a period of extraordinary growth during the Porfirato. Between 1876 and 1910, the priesthood increased from 1,700 to 4,405 to serve a rapidly growing population. Most of the increase in the priesthood, however, was due to an unprecedented immigration of Spanish, French, and Italian clerics. Five new archbishoprics and eight new dioceses were created, Church-owned property doubled, churches tripled, and the number of Catholic schools enjoyed a six-fold increase. Convents and monasteries were reactivated, and two new orders were established.

Díaz looked upon the Church as a potential political asset, and he had no mind to follow the example of Lerdo, who triggered a rebellion of Catholics in the west when he expelled the nuns of Saint Vincent de

Paul. Instead, he chose to ignore the Laws of the Reform as they applied to the Church. Don Porfirio, however, granted no concessions without receiving something in return. At the Fifth Provincial Council of Mexico in 1895, the bishops repaid him by ordering all parishes to obey the civil authorities.

In his private dealings with the Church, he wrote a letter renouncing the Laws of the Reform to allow his first wife, Delfina Ortega, to receive the last rites of the Church when she died. The letter was buried in the archives of the Cathedral of Mexico. When he married Carmelita Romero Rubio in 1881, he persuaded Father Eulogio Gillow to bless the union, and in 1887, he gave his blessing in return when Gillow was appointed archbishop of Oaxaco. As a private citizen, he declared himself a Catholic, but he still presided over Masonic ceremonies and maintained his friendship with his Protestant minister. When pressed for a formal commitment to the Church, however, he refused to sign a concordat with Rome.

But clouds were gathering in the north. A new generation of liberals, many of whom were former seminary students, was opposed to the tolerance towards the Church in the south. Díaz, they felt, had conceded to the Church that which rightfully belonged to the State, and the Church, as a result, was far too active in politics.

THE COST OF MODERNIZATION

The prosperity of the Porfiriato, unfortunately, was shared with neither the urban poor nor 80 per cent of the rural population, where seven million Indians and *mestizos* were bound to 834 *hacendados* and land-development corporations.

In 1883, the government enacted a new land law to encourage foreign colonization. Land companies were awarded contracts to survey public lands for subdivision and settlement, which granted them one-third of the land surveyed and the right of purchasing the remaining two-thirds at ridiculous prices. The impact on the peasantry and rural communities was devastating. If individual owners of the surveyed lands or the *ejidos* had no legal title, the lands were confiscated for public ownership. Not surprisingly, few rural Mexicans or villages held what the government considered a proper title. Their lands had been handed down from one generation to the next, and boundaries were indefinite; marked by trees, streams, and rock outcrops. Worse, if the *ejidos* held any form of title, the Laws of Reform were cited to permit seizure of their lands.

In nine years, nearly 100 million acres were surveyed, and most were bought up by the land companies and wealthy individuals. By 1910, there were between nine and ten million landless peasants in rural Mexico, and fewer than 10 per cent of the Indian communities owned any land whatsoever. Some eight thousand *haciendas* owned 90 per cent of the land, and *haciendas* of 50,000 acres were not uncommon. Some of the ultra-wealthy families controlled ten or more *haciendas*.

Some *haciendas* were productive enterprises. These were run on a business-like basis, where the *hacendado* was aware that productivity and efficiency depended upon the welfare of his labour force, and treated the peons fairly. Most of the larger ones, however, were unproductive, with much of the land lying fallow from one year to the next. Absentee ownership was common as the *hacendado* divided his time among his holdings and travel abroad, leaving the management of the work force to his major-domo. Most agricultural equipment was obsolete and generally in poor repair, and marketing techniques were little understood by the *hacendados*.

For the greater part, the peon was worse off than his ancestors of a century before. The average daily wage had remained constant at 35 centavos a day, but the price of staples such as corn, chilli, and beans had risen two to six times the price in 1800. In terms of purchasing power, the Mexican peon was twelve times poorer than a farm labourer in the United States. Furthermore, his wages were not paid in cash, but in chits that were redeemable only at the *tienda de raya,* the company store, where prices were considerably higher than those in the neighbouring villages. Credit was available with interest, and sometimes there was even a fee for the privilege of trading at the company store. It was only a matter of time before the peon found himself bound to the *hacienda* by a debt that could never be paid, and improving his position in life was a near impossibility, since the rarity of schools on the *haciendas* prevented him from ever becoming literate.

Treatment of the peon was arbitrary, and left to the discretion of the major-domo. Flogging was common for petty theft, rape was not unheard of, and living conditions could be intolerable. At the extreme, people might share quarters with donkeys, horses, and mules, living in the unbearable stench of animals mixed with that of fermenting pulque.

The urban poor were, in many cases, worse off than the rural peon. Factory workers were paid six to eight pesos a week, but the working day was as long as twelve or fifteen hours, and in times of high production, the work week was often seven days. There was no worker's compensation for job-related accidents or hazardous work. In many cases, the workers had no protection in law, since many foreign-owned businesses had a private police force and a jurisprudence system that superseded Mexican law.

A deficient diet of corn, beans, and chilli, and unsanitary living conditions led to a variety of diseases, and medical treatment was rarely available. Life expectancy for adults was about thirty years, and infant mortality 30 per cent. Indoor plumbing was unheard of; and in some districts, there was one public bathhouse for fifteen thousand people.

Alcoholism was endemic throughout the barrios, and temperance societies, fearing it would lead to an increase in crime and put more beggars on the streets, led a crusade against the *pulquerías*. To discourage patronage, the *pulquerías* were restricted in the hours they could stay open, and windows, chairs, and music were prohibited. Women, of course, were not allowed on the premises. But the effect was minimal – there was little if any change in alcoholism throughout the nation, despite the best efforts of the temperance groups and the Catholic Church.

LABOUR UNREST, UNIONS, AND REVOLT

From 1906 to 1908, growing numbers of rail, mining, and industrial strikes were incited by the Partido Liberal Mexicano (PLM), now in exile in St Louis, Missouri. Each was crushed by federal troops or the *rurales*, and in one case, by rangers from Arizona. The loss of life was frightful, but the strikes continued, and with each, the instability of the Díaz administration became increasingly evident.

The leaders of the early liberal movement in Mexico were three brothers, Ricardo, Jesús, and Enrique Flores Magón. In August of

1900, they began publishing *Regeneración,* a weekly newspaper opposed to the policies of the government, and in 1901, they were arrested and spent a year in prison for attacking a prominent *político.* When they were released, they continued their attack on the government in the columns of *El Hijo de Ahuizote,* a periodical that ridiculed leading members of the administration, and six months later, they were in jail again. Future arrests convinced them their only recourse was to leave Mexico and continue their campaign from exile in the United States.

With funds from liberal clubs and former subscribers, one of whom, surprisingly, was Francisco Madero, a wealthy *hacendado,* they were able to continue publishing *Regeneración,* and by 1904, were capable of distributing some 30,000 copies throughout Mexico.

Díaz retaliated by sending assassins to San Antonio, but the attempt failed, and the Magón brothers decided to move further from the border. They settled in St Louis, where they formed the PLM, and by 1905, were publishing *Regeneración* again.

In 1906 the PLM became a politico-military organization supporting the demands of workers and peasants. Their programme, which would eventually be incorporated into the Constitution of 1917, called for an eight-hour working day and a six-day week, a minimum wage, a ban on child labour, abolition of the *tienda de raya,* protection of Mexican immigrants in the United States, an end to United States' interference in Mexican affairs, and one term for the president. All uncultivated lands were to be taken over by the State and given to those who would work them, and illegally seized *ejido* lands were to be returned to the Indians.

In 1906, the PLM infiltrated the work-force at the Cananea copper mine in Sonora, and on 1 June the workers went on strike. Their grievances were wages and the unequal treatment existing between Mexicans and the American work-force. American workers were paid in dollars, and Mexicans were paid in pesos, but in 1905, the peso was devalued and the company made no effort to compensate for the loss of their earning power. They also protested at the company's discrimination against qualified Mexicans for positions of responsibility in engineering and management.

When Colonel Greene refused to arbitrate, the strikers forced their way on to company property. The manager ordered hoses to be turned on them, and when the workers were driven into the timber yard, soldiers fired on them. Within the hour, twenty-three miners and two American managers were dead. The strikers left the timberyard in flames and marched into Cananea, robbing pawn shops of guns and ammunition and began firing on American residents.

Colonel Greene telephoned the Governor of Sonora to send in the *rurales*, but when he was informed they could not arrive until the next day, the governor allowed 275 Arizona Rangers to cross the border. Small arms fire was exchanged between the Rangers and the strikers, and both sides suffered casualties. Later in the day, the *rurales* arrived, and the ringleaders of the strike were rounded up and hanged. The strikers were given a choice of induction into the army or returning to the mine.

The use of American soldiers to fire upon Mexicans on Mexican soil to protect American interests led to more than one eyebrow being raised in the capital about Díaz's policies.

One of the *rurales*

In January 1907, casualties were even greater when federal troops fired on strikers and their families at the European-owned Rio Blanco Textile Mills near Orizaba. Unfortunately, the tragedy could have been avoided had Porfirio Díaz any sense of compassion for the strikers.

Conditions at the mill could well have been the worst in the country. The working day was twelve hours long, wages were low, and the workers were forced to pay for the depreciation of the equipment they used. Children, some as young as eight or nine years old, were performing demanding work all day long. Strikes were illegal, and workers suspected of affiliation with the union were summarily dismissed.

Unwilling to risk a strike, the workers took their complaints directly to the President for arbitration. Díaz heard them out, but ruled for the owners on nearly every count, and on Sunday, 6 January the workers voted to strike.

Violence broke out when wives of the striking workers were refused credit at the *tienda de raya*. Pushing and shoving soon led to violence and gunfire, and when the strikers set fire to the *tienda de raya*, the *rurales* and federal troops were ordered in. They opened fire on the strikers with no regard for the women and children among them, and that night the *rurales* even shot down the few survivors who returned to collect the bodies of the dead. There are no reliable data of the number killed that day, but an American observer estimated the dead between 200 and 800, and reported that the bodies were stacked on flat cars and hauled away to Vera Cruz to be fed to the sharks.

The Elections of 1910

When James Creelman reported Díaz's statement that he would not run for president in the 1910 elections, political activity in Mexico took a quantum leap as potential candidates jockeyed for position. The most likely candidate to succeed Díaz was General Bernardo Reyes, the popular governor of Nuevo Leon. Reyes was a loyal supporter of Díaz, and even though he had his disagreements with the administration, he did not openly declare himself a candidate.

The *científicos*, however, pressed Díaz to run for another term and retain Ramón Corral as vice-president, and without a moment's hesitation, Díaz accepted their mandate. To insure that there would be no opposition from Reyes, the general was asked to undertake a military mission in Europe, and his acceptance forestalled any challenge to Díaz from within the party.

Prior to Díaz's acceptance of the candidacy, Francisco I. Madero, a *hacendado* from Coahuila, gained national attention by writing *La sucesión presidencial en 1910*. The book launched the anti-re-electionist movement throughout the nation and established Madero as a potential candidate for the presidency. In the latter part of 1909, Madero carried the message of anti-re-electionism to liberal clubs throughout the country. Despite arrests of his supporters, denial of hotel rooms and other forms of harassment by the authorities, thousands gathered to greet him at every stop. In April 1910, the first national convention of his party met in Mexico City, and Madero easily won the nomination for the presidency.

The campaign trail took Madero to twenty-two states, where he expanded upon the ideas in his book. In Puebla he was acclaimed by 30,000 people, in Jalapa 10,000, and in Orizaba, where the strikers at Rio Blanco had been butchered by Díaz's army, 20,000 people listened to the defining speech of his campaign:

> You desire freedom, you desire that your rights be respected, that you be allowed to form strong organizations, so that united you can defend your rights ... you do not want bread, you want only freedom, because freedom will allow you to win that bread.

In June he was arrested in Monterrey, and 5,000 of his supporters were jailed throughout the country. The election was held on 21 June and when Díaz was re-elected, he was released on parole with the provision that he remain in San Luis Potosí.

In September of that year, Mexico celebrated the centenary of its independence. September was also the month of Porfirio Díaz's eightieth birthday, and distinguished guests were invited from abroad, all expenses paid, to attend the extravaganza. There were parades, pageants, fireworks displays, banquets, and balls, and imported French champagne flowed like water for a month. The cost of the celebration was more than twenty million pesos, greater than the country's annual appropriation for education.

In early October, Madero escaped to San Antonio, Texas, where he drafted a manifesto for revolution, known as the *Plan de San Luis Potosí*. The *Plan* called for the election of Díaz to be declared null and void, and until the people could choose their own government, Madero would be the provisional president. Madero then called for a national uprising on 20 November 1910.

The *Plan* made few references to Mexico's social problems. There were no provisions to improve conditions for the labourer, and only a vague plan to return lands to property owners who had lost them to Diaz's land laws. There was no mention of the nation's opposition to the political influence of foreign capital or to that of the Church during the Díaz regime.

Madero crossed over into Mexico on 19 November with ten men, hoping to seize Piedras Negras. He expected his uncle Catarino to be waiting for him with 400 men, but was forced to withdraw and return to the United States when Catarino appeared with only ten. It seemed that the revolution would fizzle before it could get off the ground, but the PLM had been advocating revolution for the past four years, and the PLM had the only experienced political–military organization on the scene. Madero's call for revolution was evidently the catalyst that set it into motion. The response throughout Mexico for armed uprising was instantaneous.

The most significant forces in the north came from the ranks of the PLM and the armed groups of Pascual Orozco and Pancho Villa, while those in the south came from a peasant army led by Emiliano Zapata in Morelos. The major arena of action was Chihuahua, where town after town responded to the call to arms. PLM troops won major battles at Casas Grandes and Guadalupe, and captured Mexicali in Baja California. On 2 January 1911, Orozco ambushed and destroyed a large Federal force in Chihuahua, and in an act of defiance, he stripped the dead bodies of their uniforms and sent them to Díaz with the message, 'Here are the wrappers, send me some more tamales'.

In February, Madero crossed over into Mexico with 130 troops under the command of Lázaro Gutíerrez de Lara. Madero marched upon Casas Grandes, but without the support of Orozco, he suffered the worst defeat of the northern campaign.

In the late spring of 1911, Orozco and Villa persuaded Madero to attack Ciudad Juárez on the United States border. By May, seasoned rebel troops surrounded the city, but Madero changed his mind. Fearing artillery fire would fall on El Paso and cause United States intervention, he ordered a retreat. Neither Orozco nor Villa, however, would withdraw after accomplishing so much, and against orders, they attacked the city. On 10 May General Navarro, low on ammunition and supplies, surrendered the city to the rebels.

With the fall of Ciudad Juárez, the insurrection spread to eighteen states, including Morelos, Vera Cruz, Puebla, and Guerrero. Díaz realized that the end had come, and sent a team of negotiators to meet with Madero. The Treaty of Ciudad Juárez called for fourteen points that included pay for the revolutionary forces; the release of political prisoners; and the Revolutionary Party's right to name the Secretaries of War, Education, Interior, and Justice. Díaz' resignation and exile from Mexico were not mentioned, but were implicitly understood. Francisco León de la Barra, the Secretary of Foreign Relations in the Díaz Administration, would be interim president until elections could be held.

In June, 1911, Díaz sailed for Paris, and on 2 July 1915, he would cry out for Juana Cata as he lay dying.

CHAPTER THIRTEEN

The Mexican Revolution

Madero and Zapata

The trouble began when Madero accepted León de la Barra as interim president and allowed him to retain Porfirio Díaz's appointees in the cabinet. Even before Madero arrived in Mexico City, the Porfiristas were pressing for disarmament of the rebel forces before land reform could be considered. In particular, they demanded that Madero send troops into Morelos to pull the teeth of Emiliano Zapata, whom the press had labelled 'the Attila of the South'.

Emiliano Zapata was born on 8 August 1879, in Anenecuilco, a village of some 500 people in the state of Morelos. At the age of fifteen he was orphaned, inheriting a small plot of land and an adobe house from his father. He had no more education than elementary bookkeeping, and supplemented the family income from growing produce, running a pack train of mules, raising livestock, and share-cropping the lands of a nearby *hacienda*. By the time he was twenty, he was an expert horseman, competing in rodeos throughout Morelos and fighting bulls from horseback. In time, he was elected speaker of the village, an office that dates back to the *tlatoani*, 'he who speaks', of the ancient Aztecs.

In 1908 he left the village, a circumstance dictated, no doubt, by his kidnapping Inés Alfaro, who bore him a son and two daughters. Inés's father filed a complaint against him with the authorities, and Emiliano was enjoined to enlist in the militia. Later, he married Josepha Espejo, who brought him a small dowry.

Zapata concerned himself more with land reform than with politics and national movements. He took a dim view of Madero's *Plan de Potosí*. In a few months, however, he became convinced that Madero's movement could succeed, and the lands sequestered by the *haciendas*, including his own, would be returned to the peasants.

On 11 June 1911, Zapata and Madero met to discuss disarmament of the rebel forces. Zapata's terms were simple, but inflexible. He insisted that there would be no talk of disarmament until General Victoriano Huerta withdrew his forces to Cuernavaca, and the lands appropriated from the villages were restored in full.

Madero requested special powers from de la Barra to negotiate with Zapata, but landowners and the Governor of Morelos wanted Zapata's teeth pulled, and they had de la Barra's ear. The President's reply to Madero was that unless the rebels voluntarily disarmed within twenty-four hours, General Huerta had orders to take their arms by force. The deadline passed with no response, and federal

The fiery revolutionary: Emiliano Zapata in 1912

troops attacked Yautepec without offering the villagers the opportunity of surrendering.

Madero was furious when he heard of the attack, and pleaded with de la Barra to withdraw the troops, but it was too late. The peace had been broken, and with it, Zapata's faith in Madero.

On 11 November 1911, Madero was elected president, and a few days after he was sworn in, Zapata pronounced the *Plan de Ayala*, which called for a continuation of the rebellion until all peasant and community lands were returned, expropriation of one-third of the lands of the most powerful property owners with compensation, and the overthrow of Madero as president.

Without waiting for support from the north, Zapata took to the offensive. He struck at major centres of commerce, disrupted rail and telegraph services, and sent his guerrilla units south to attack the *haciendas*.

THE PRESIDENT STANDS ALONE

The Madero Administration was doomed from the very beginning. In the spirit of reconciliation, he retained the Porfiristas in his cabinet, and supported by a Senate held over from the Díaz administration, they constantly overrode his attempts at reform.

His plan for land restoration foundered from underfunding by the government and the high prices demanded by the *hacendados* for compensation. Labour reform suffered even worse. Congress authorized the formation of the Department of Labour, but allocated a budget of a paltry 46,000 pesos to carry out its programmes. On the positive side, however, Madero managed to legalize unions and give workers the right to strike. Education reform fared slightly better than land and labour reform. Madero built fifty new schools and initiated a programme of free lunches for the underprivileged, but there was no money for upgrading the curriculum.

Within months, counter-revolutionary forces rose from the right as reactionaries, sensing Madero's weakness, took up arms against him. General Bernardo Reyes, who had campaigned against Madero, began recruiting an army in the north, but failing to muster enough men, he was convicted of treason and sent to the Santiago Tlatelolco prison in Mexico City.

Before the year was over, Francisco Vásquez Gómez and his followers recruited another army in the north and formed a junta in Ciudad Juárez to oust Madero. Vásquez Gómez had been chosen as Madero's running mate in the 1910 elections, but in the 1911 presidential election, Madero dumped him in favour of José María Pino Suárez, a journalist from Yucatán. Madero ordered Pascual Orozco, a Chihuahua *caudillo,* to take action against the Vásquez Gómez faction, but it never came to armed conflict. Vázquez Gómez's recruits looked upon Orozco as a hero of the revolution and refused to take up arms against him.

A more serious threat to Madero came in March 1912, when Orozco, tired of Madero's inability to execute the reforms of the revolution, recruited an army of 8,000 men and marched upon the capital. Federal forces under the command of General José Gonzáles Salas intercepted Orozco at Rellano, and Salas was defeated so soundly that he committed suicide. Madero replaced Sala with General Victoriano Huerta, who was a better field commander than Pascual Orozco. With the help of Pancho Villa, a Chihuahua *caudillo* committed to Madero, Huerta drove the rebel forces north and forced Orozco to flee to the United States.

The beginning of the end came for Madero on 12 October 1912, when Félix Díaz, Don Porfirio's nephew, persuaded the Vera Cruz garrison to rebel against the government. The revolution, however, died almost as soon as it was born when Díaz failed to gain sufficient support from army units in the south. Díaz was captured and sentenced to death, but the ever-lenient Madero intervened and spared his life. Instead, Díaz was sent to the Santiago Tlatelolco prison, where General Bernardo Reyes was confined, and together, they formed the plot that would overthrow Madero.

On 9 February 1913, General Manuel Mondragón, supported by artillery units and cadets from the military school, freed Díaz and Reyes and marched upon the National Palace. Reyes was killed in the first exchange of fire with government troops, and Díaz was forced to retreat to the Ciudadela, an old arsenal fifteen blocks from the National Palace.

For the next ten days, now known as the *la Decena Trágica*, both sides shelled each other mercilessly, destroying government and commercial buildings, setting fires, and killing hundreds of civilians. Madero, desperate for an experienced officer to end the stand-off, summoned Huerta to take command of the federal forces.

Enter Henry Lane Wilson, the United States Ambassador to Mexico, who had a personal agenda to see Madero removed from office for his failure to protect American interests from Zapata's raids. Seeking support from other foreign powers, he constantly lobbied the embassies to support Díaz, and on one occasion, was so brazen as to demand Madero's resignation. He sent a letter to the German ambassador informing him that Huerta and Díaz were conducting negotiations for the overthrow of Madero, but were afraid to move for fear that foreign nations would refuse to recognize the new government. Wilson assured the German ambassador that he would recommend that Washington recognize any government that could restore peace and order in Mexico, and hoped that Germany would follow suit.

On 18 February Wilson summoned Huerta and Díaz to the American embassy, and together they drew up the 'Pact of the Embassy'. Huerta would be named provisional president when Madero was removed from power.

That day Huerta dispatched General Aureliano Blanquet to the National Palace, and within the hour, Vice-president Pino Suárez and most of the cabinet were arrested. Madero was forced to resign, and Congress appointed Pedro Lascuráin, Minister of Foreign Relations, as president. Lascuráin named Huerta as Minister of the Interior, then resigned the presidency. As Minister of the Interior, Huerta was entitled by the Constitution to succeed to the presidency.

On the night of 22 February a major in the *rurales* took Madero and Pino Suárez to the penitentiary, and when they stepped out of the car, both were shot down 'trying to escape'. No action was taken against the assassins, who had acted in accordance with the *ley fuga*.

On the afternoon of that day, Madero's mother had pleaded with Wilson to telegraph President Taft with a request that he intervene to forestall any attempt at assassination. Wilson refused to transmit her message, replying that he had no right to interfere in the affairs of the government of Mexico.

HUERTA UNDER SIEGE

Born of a Huichol mother and *mestizo* father in Jalisco, Huerta learned to read and write in the local parish school, where he showed a talent for science and mathematics. In his late teens, he became an aide to General Donato Guerra, who sponsored him for the National Military Academy. During the Díaz administration, he fought against the Yaqui in the north, and the Maya in the south, and by the turn of the century, he was promoted to the rank of brigadier-general.

The first warning of trouble to the new regime came from the north when Venustiano Carranza, the Governor of Coahuila, refused to recognize Huerta. Shortly afterwards, Álvaro Obregón, a rancher with a private army in Sonora, General Pablo Gonzalez, the commander in northeastern Mexico, and Pancho Villa followed suit. In the south, Huerta sent emissaries to Zapata inviting him to support the government, but Zapata had little reason to trust him, and let his opinion be known by executing Huerta's agents.

On 26 March 1913, Carranza announced the Plan of Guadelupe, a political tract, which demanded the re-establishment of the Constitution of 1857 and called for a national uprising against the government. The plan contained no social reforms. The coalition called themselves the Constitutionalists, and Carranza was named First Chief.

Venustiano Carranza was more a political opportunist than a zealous revolutionary. Born on 29 December 1859, the son of a wealthy *hacendado* in Coahuila, Venustiano studied at Fuente Athenium, the famous liberal school in Saltillo, and later at the Nacional Preparatoria in Mexico City.

In 1893, Carranza participated in an armed revolution against José María Garza Galán, who had been anointed Governor of Coahuila by Porfirio Díaz. Díaz turned the problem over to Bernardo Reyes for resolution, and through the offices of Reyes, Carranza was chosen to represent the cause of the rebels before Díaz. His success before Díaz launched a promising political career, first a municipal presidency in Coahuila, and later a number of legislative positions in the Díaz regime.

In the 1909 elections, Carranza's candidacy for Governor of Coahuila was approved by Díaz. With Díaz's endorsement and broad support throughout the political community, including Reyes, Governor Miguel Cárdenas, and Francisco Madero, Carranza had no reason to fear a threat to his candidacy. The Madero endorsement, however, caused Díaz to have a change of heart at the last moment, and he endorsed the opposing candidate instead. With the loss of the 'election', Carranza re-evaluated his political career and approached Madero.

On the international front, Huerta's government was recognized by fifty foreign governments, including that of Great Britain. Huerta turned to Britain for financial aid, and Weetman Pearson, the chairman of El Águila Petroleum, arranged for a loan sufficient to keep him in power. Woodrow Wilson, the new United States president, however, motivated on the one hand by his desire to see a democratic Mexico and on the other to protect American oil interests from British intrusion, refused to recognize Huerta and threw his support behind Carranza.

Wilson recalled Ambassador Henry Lane Wilson, who advocated recognition of the new regime, and sent John Lind, a special emissary, to Mexico. Lind was authorized to offer Huerta an immediate loan in exchange for new elections, provided he would not be a candidate, but the offer came too late. Huerta was heavily dependent upon the British for financing his administration, and had no alternative but to reject the offer. Having offered the olive branch and been refused, Wilson now felt justified in ordering an arms embargo against Mexico, and enforced it with a naval blockade of Vera Cruz.

Isolated from overseas, allies for arms, squeezed by Zapata to the south, the Constitutionalists to the north, and American forces to the east, Huerta mobilized his army for all-out warfare. From 50,000 men, the army grew to 100,000, then to 200,000, and finally to 250,000 men. But his army was a paper army, made up of conscripts seized from the streets, the cantinas, the bullfights, and the jails. Military training was rudimentary, discipline was marginal, morale was low, and desertion rates were increasing every day.

Between 1913 and 1914, the war took a heavy toll on both sides. Federalist generals hanged Zapatistas from trees and telegraph poles, took civilians hostage, and looted and burned rebel villages throughout Morelos. But the campaign of terror only stiffened the resolve of Zapata, and by 1914, the tide turned. Zapata took the key city of Chilpancingo, hanged a federalist general from a telegraph pole, and advanced upon Mexico City. In the north, the federalists were losing ground before the advance of Obregón and Villa, and a steady stream of deserters fleeing for the United States border was taking a heavy toll on Huerta's army.

The final blow came in April 1914, when a landing party from an American ship off the coast of Tampico came ashore to obtain fuel from a warehouse owned by an American citizen. The city was under siege by the Carranzistas, and government forces took the sailors into custody the moment they came ashore.

Within the hour, the crew was released with an apology, but Rear Admiral Henry Mayo considered the incident an affront to American sovereignty, and issued an ultimatum to the Mexicans – fire a 21-gun salute to the American flag or face the consequences. Huerta agreed on the condition that the Americans reciprocate by firing a 21-gun salute to the Mexican flag in return.

President Wilson was incensed by Huerta's request, and the incident escalated when Wilson was informed that a German ship, the *Ypiranga*, was due to arrive at Vera Cruz with a shipment of arms for Huerta. Without hesitation, Wilson sought permission to send troops ashore, which an indignant Congress was all too ready to grant.

Wilson's invasion of Vera Cruz was no less a disaster to the civilian population of the city than that of Winfield Scott in 1847. Seventeen Americans lost their lives in the assault of the Customs House, and 123 Mexican soldiers lay dead. Civilian casualties were estimated to be in the hundreds, but no count was ever made – their bodies were piled in the public square and burned to prevent the spread of disease.

The indignation that followed the invasion was shared by federalists and Constitutionalists alike. Carranza threatened to declare war on the United States, and Zapata swore to fight the Americans if they invaded Mexico, no matter how many troops they sent. Pancho Villa made no public statement, but reached an agreement with Carranza to attack the Americans only if Wilson invaded Mexico.

Huerta was forced to withdraw federal troops from the north and the south to contain the Americans, leaving both fronts undermanned. Zacatecas fell to Villa in June of 1914, and shortly afterward, Obregón took Guadalajara, leaving the route to Mexico City open. Huerta resigned the presidency on 18 July 1914, blaming his defeat on the Wilson administration, and went into exile in Spain.

In the seventeen months of Huerta's tenure, despite the difficulties he faced on the military front, he made more progress on the social problems of Mexico than his predecessor. His land reform programme restored 78 *ejidos* to the Indians, and he encouraged land redistribution by raising taxes on large estates, making land less desirable to hold for investment.

Huerto increased the education budget from the 7.8 per cent of the Madero administration to 9.9 per cent, and built 131 rural schools to accommodate 10,000 new students. Furthermore, he created a better balance between the humanities and the sciences by expanding the curriculum at the National Preparatory School in the areas of philosophy, literature, and history.

The Aguascalientes Convention

With the fall of Huerta, First Chief Carranza set about reaching a consensus among the Revolutionary leadership for a new government, a formidable task considering the gap in ideological differences among the principals.

Zapata, he knew, would be the most difficult of the leaders to bring to the table, and he sent emissaries south to feel him out on a platform he would support. Zapata and his generals, however, considered Carranza no more than a reformed Porfirista, and opposed putting power into his hands. Zapata refused to budge from the *Plan de Ayala*, and demanded that Carranza not offer himself as a candidate for the presidency. Furthermore, he proposed a more radical plan for agrarian reform and incorporated reforms into it for the urban work-force. Carranza refused to accept Zapata's terms, and broke off talks with him in September, 1914.

Pancho Villa's objectives, on the other hand, were much more flexible than Zapata's. The leadership of his forces was made up of *vaqueros* (cowboys), *rancheros,* and shopkeepers rather than peasant farmers, and his soldiers were generally miners, railway workers, and migrant farmworkers. Consequently, lands seized by Villa were given to the State, not to the peasantry. And Villa, unlike Zapata, was never forced to live off the land. The Centaur of the North financed his campaigns by extorting 'protection money' from American properties in the north, and rustling cattle to trade for arms across the United States border.

The combined forces of Carranza and Obregón were more élitist than commoner, made up of professionals, prosperous farmers, ranchers, and even landlords that shared the goals of the First Chief. Obregón was more to the left than Carranza, with a leadership made up of intellectuals and nationalists. His goals of labour and agrarian reform were adopted by Carranza primarily to keep him as an ally, even though the First Chief had no desire to align himself with the working class.

In October 1914, Carranza called for a convention in Aguascalientes, a neutral area, to select a provisional president, and sent invitations to all principal participants in the Revolution. The number of delegates was to be proportional to the number of troops committed to combat.

Neither Zapata nor his generals attended the convention. Instead, he sent the intellectuals of his staff to promote the *Plan de Ayala*. They arrived a few days late, and immediately threw the convention into pandemonium. When Paulino Martinez spoke to the delegates, he denounced Carranza and Obregón, and declared that Zapata and Pancho Villa were the real leaders of the Revolution. The Revolution, he said, had been fought not against re-election and suffrage, but for, and only for, land and liberty.

Antonio Díaz Soto y Gama, a radical lawyer, created even more chaos among the delegates when he crumpled up the Mexican flag and declared it a symbol of *criollo* independence, not a standard worthy of the Revolution. The charge brought the delegates to their feet, some with pistols in Soto y Gama's face.

The convention was thus polarized, and forced to choose between the *Plan de Guadelupe* and the *Plan de Ayala*. The latter was adopted, and the delegates chose Eulalio Gutiérrez as provisional president. Carranza and Obregón immediately withdrew their forces to Vera Cruz, leaving Mexico on the brink of civil war.

AN HISTORIC MEETING

On 4 December, Emiliano Zapata and Pancho Villa met for the first time in Xochimilco, a small town on the outskirts of Mexico City. The physical contrast between the two could not have been greater. Villa was tall and robust, and his carriage was that of a Douglas MacArthur or a Viscount Montgomery. He wore a pith helmet, a heavy brown sweater rolled at the collar, tight-fitting leather leggings, and heavy boots. Zapata, on the other hand, was small, a dark, brooding figure dressed in his customary *charro* outfit, and wore a huge sombrero that nearly hid his face. Everything about him spoke of the peasant, not the general.

The meeting, ostensibly to form a pact between the northern and southern forces, accomplished little. The only common bond the *caudillos* found was their intense hatred of Carranza and Obregón.

VILLA: 'They are men who have always slept on soft pillows.'

ZAPATA: 'Those *cabrones* [cuckolds]! As soon as they see a little chance, well, they want to take advantage of it to line their own pockets! Well, to hell with them!'

Two days later, the revolutionaries moved their forces into Mexico City. The citizenry was apprehensive and frightened by the bloody reputation of the Zapatistas, but instead of brutes and butchers, they found an army of bewildered peasants in their midst. Dressed in white cotton clothing, wearing sandals and enormous straw hats, with cartridge belts slung across their chests and machetes in their belts, they wandered aimlessly about the streets, begging for food.

By 15 January the Revolutionary forces from the north and the south had abandoned the city and returned home. Neither Villa nor Zapata were able to establish a stable government nor agree on a reform programme, and departed with nothing more than a vague promise to support each other.

Mexico City was now open to the Constitutionalists, and Gutiérrez, finding his position untenable, abandoned the city and fled for the United States.

Civil War

Meanwhile, Carranza and Obregón were mobilizing their forces for war with Villa and Zapata. If they were to succeed, it would be necessary to cull the army of peasants whose sympathies might be with Zapata and replace them with labourers from the cities. To carry out his plan, Obregón approached the 50,000 strong Casa de Obrero Mundial, Mexico's largest union. Obregón offered the Casa food, money, printing presses, and supplies it desperately needed to stay in operation in exchange for their mobilizing a fighting force from the membership. The union reluctantly accepted Obregón's offer, and organized 7,000 men into six battalions.

The turning point of the war occurred when Villa and Obregón met at Celaya in April 1915. Obregón's forces numbered 11,000 men, and Villa had at least twice than number. Obregón, a student of military tactics, established a strong defensive position surrounded by barbed wire and waited for Villa to attack. He did not have long to wait. Villa stormed Obregón's position with 25,000 men, but when they reached the wire, artillery and machine guns cut them to pieces. Villa pulled his men back and sent in his cavalry, but the horse fared no better than the foot. When it was over, 4,000 Villistas were dead, 5,000 wounded, and 6,000 taken prisoner. Obregón suffered only 138 dead and 227 wounded. Villa withdrew what was left of his army to Chihuahua, where he resorted to guerrilla tactics.

In August 1915, General Pablo González moved against Zapata. With an army of 30,000 men, he waged a scorched-earth policy of looting, burning, and mass execution of prisoners and civilians alike. At Joncatepec he stood 225 civilians against a wall and shot them all, and by June 1916, he overran Zapata's headquarters and executed 283 non-combatants.

Zapata responded by carrying out attacks on water pumps, trams, and other civilian targets in Mexico City. González was forced to pull back to protect the capital, and by early 1917, Morelos was once again secure. But the Zapatistas were contained within the state, and their army was no longer a force to be reckoned with outside of its borders.

Without a war to unite them against a common cause, the Zapatista leadership began to quarrel among themselves, and soon resorted to killing each other in a series of turf wars. Even Otilio Montaño, a co-author of the *Plan de Ayala* and Zapata's closest friend, was executed for conspiring against him. Meanwhile, Pablo Gonzáles was drawing the noose tighter about the Zapatistas, whose force now numbered no more than a few thousand, and Zapata was forced to move his head-quarters to Tochimilco, a small town at the foot of Popocatepetl.

When rumours of a falling out between Pablo Gonzáles and Colonel Jesús Guajardo reached Zapata's ears some months later, he invited Guajardo to meet with him and discuss the possibility of an alliance. The meeting was to take place on 10 April 1919, at a *hacienda* near Anenecuilco, his birthplace. On the day of the meeting, Zapata and his men surrounded the *hacienda*, and a deputy went inside to meet Guajardo. By early afternoon, Zapata decided that Guajardo was sin-cere, and rode towards the gate with ten men. As he approached the gate, a guard of honour presented arms, but before Zapata could pass through, they lowered their rifles and shot him at point-blank range. The Attila of the South was dead, four months short of his fortieth birthday.

The Rise of Pancho Villa

In October 1915, President Woodrow Wilson granted American recognition to the Carranza regime, and provided the First Chief with arms, ammunition, and most important, funds. Without help from the United States, the stand-off with Villa might have gone on indefinitely. Carranza had no credit – Mexico had been in default of its bonds since 1913 – his paper money was worthless, and his soldiers unpaid. At the same time, the United States cut off arms shipments to Villa and Zapata.

Villa's last stand took place on 1 November 1915, at Agua Prieto, a small town on the Sonora-Arizona border, where he was defeated by General Plutarco Elías Calles. The outcome of the battle, however, might have been different had the United States remained neutral.

General Frederick Funston, on orders from Washington, granted safe passage to Calles through Arizona to Douglas, a border town opposite Agua Preito, allowing Calles to attack Villa on three sides. On a battlefield illuminated by arc lamps, reputedly provided by Funston, Villa's army was cut down in a brutal crossfire from heavy salvos of artillery and Gatling guns. The defeat was the last hurrah for Villa's hopes of sharing power with the Constitutionalists, and on 3 November he rejected Funston's offer of asylum in the United States and took the remnants of his army south.

Doroteo Aranga, better known as Francisco Villa and more familiarly as Pancho, was born on 4 October 1877, the eldest of five children, in the village of San Juan del Rio in the state of Durango. After the premature death of his father, he supported the family by working as a field hand at a nearby *hacienda*. His employment, however, was cut short when he caught the son of the *hacendado* trying to rape his sister, and he defended her honour by shooting her attacker. He was captured and sent to jail, but managed to escape and fled to safety in the deep canyons of Durango.

From 1891 until 1910, Villa was undoubtedly the most notorious bandit in northern Mexico. Between 1901 and 1910, he is known to have murdered at least four people, and terrorized the north with arson, robbery, kidnapping, and cattle rustling. Villa and his gang made a practice of attacking remote ranches and looting them, and in one incident, he butchered the owner and his young son. When one of his closest henchmen betrayed him to the authorities, he waited in an ice cream parlour for him to stroll by with his girlfriend. He raised his pistol and shot him, then casually walked away.

Villa met Francisco Madero in Chihuahua in 1910, where Madero persuaded him to join the Revolutionary cause. Early in the war, Villa distinguished himself with several victories against superior forces. His rise to prominence in the Revolution came when he and Pasqual Orozco stormed the federal garrison at Ciudad Juárez and took the city. As they readied their forces to strike, Madero, fearing an attack so close to the United States border would cause an incident, ordered them to pull back their forces. Villa thrust a pistol into his face. But when Madero calmly dared him to shoot, Villa lowered his pistol and wept,

Pancho Villa in 1912. A notorious bandit or 'the greatest Mexican of his generation'?

begging his chief's forgiveness. After the fall of Ciudad Juárez, Madero rewarded Villa with 15,000 pesos, and he went into business as a butcher.★

In March 1912, Pasqual Orozco urged Villa to join him in the revolt against Madero, but Villa was a committed Maderista, and fought against Orozco with General Victoriana Huerta. Under the tutelage of Huerta, Villa proved to be an adept student of military strategy and tactics, and in combat, his leadership and courage were unmatched. Huerta, however, had reason to suspect his loyalty, and on trumped-up charges of insubordination, ordered him shot. Upon review of the court-martial proceedings, however, Madero, who had little stomach

★ The author is indebted to Enrique Krauze, *Mexico, Biography of Power*, New York, 1997, for the details of Pancho Villa's early years.

for capital punishment, commuted his sentence and sent him to the penitentiary in Mexico City.

In the penitentiary, Villa learned to read and write, and became converted to the Zapatista movement. Later, he was transferred to the Santiago Tlatelolco prison, where Bernardo Reyes taught him the elements of civics and history. In December 1912, Villa made his escape from prison and fled to El Paso, Texas.

In April 1913, Villa re-entered Mexico with seven men and began to recruit an army in Chihuahua. Within a few months, Villa formed the famous División del Norte, a force of more than 8,000 men, which he financed from a train robbery in northern Mexico. The robbery yielded 122 silver bars worth about $160,000, the equivalent of $2.6 million today. Villa's problem was to convert the numbered bars into arms, which was no easy task with authorities searching for the bullion and an embargo on arms in force with the United States.

The owners of the silver-mining firms in Mexico were willing to pay Villa to get the silver back, but had no way of making contact with him. Documents recently obtained by the University of California's Bancroft Library revealed how Villa's problem was solved.

The Wells Fargo Bank of San Francisco and its Mexican subsidiary, which handled the shipment, arranged a meeting with Villa whereby a Wells Fargo employee was held hostage until the mining firms came up with the money to buy back the bars. Villa received either $50,000 or 50,000 pesos from the mining companies in exchange for 93 bars. Villa said that his men had taken the rest of the bars.

In addition, the documents reveal that a Wells Fargo agent in Mexico apparently tipped off Villa about the shipment and then joined forces with him.

His first military campaign was against Torreón, the rail centre of northern Mexico. With rail transport at his disposal, Villa and his army rode north, stopping at each station on the route to Ciudad Juárez, where he seized the telegraph operator and telegraphed the garrison in the city, asking for instructions as if he were the officer in charge. He reached the city on 15 November and the garrison, expecting a shipment of coal, allowed the train to enter. Within hours, Villa's troops took the barracks, the armoury, and the bridges at the border. With this brilliantly executed victory, he became the darling of the American press.

On 3 January 1914. Villa signed a contract with Hollywood to film the exploits of the División del Norte. He agreed to schedule all his battles during the day, simulate combat if necessary, and postpone executions from 5 a.m. to after sunrise to provide daylight for the cameras. The film, *The Life of General Villa*, opened in New York on 9 May 1914, with Villa himself appearing in several scenes.

In March 1914, Villa moved south with 16,000 men and a hospital train capable of handling 1,400 casualties. In succession, he took Torreón once more, captured San Pedro de las Colonias, and defeated a large federal army at Paredón.

At the battle of Zacatecas, however, Carranza and Villa came to a parting of the ways. Carranza directed Villa to attack the garrison, but Villa refused to obey the order. The position was too strong, he protested, and his men would be cut down before they ever reached the garrison.

Villa resigned, and a letter of mass resignation, co-signed by eleven generals, was sent to Carranza. Villa laid siege to Zacatecas, and on 23 June the city fell.

Villa now found himself in favour with President Wilson, who called him the 'the greatest Mexican of his generation'. He stayed clear of American interests and established a working relationship with General Hugh Scott, the American commander across the border, and George Carothers, the consul in Chihuahua. Wilson, however, made no move to offer him American recognition, preferring to await future developments.

After his disastrous loss to Obregón at Celaya in April 1915, however, the tide turned against Villa. Soon he had no money to pay his men, and one by one, the leadership of the División del Norte deserted him to join Carranza. The final blow came on 19 October 1915, when the American government recognized the Carranza regime. After his defeat at Agua Prieta, his army numbered no more than 3,000 men. In rapid succession, Villa's strongholds in Sonora, Ciudad Juárez, and Chihuahua fell to Obregón, and by the beginning of 1916, the Centaur of the North was reduced to guerrilla warfare.

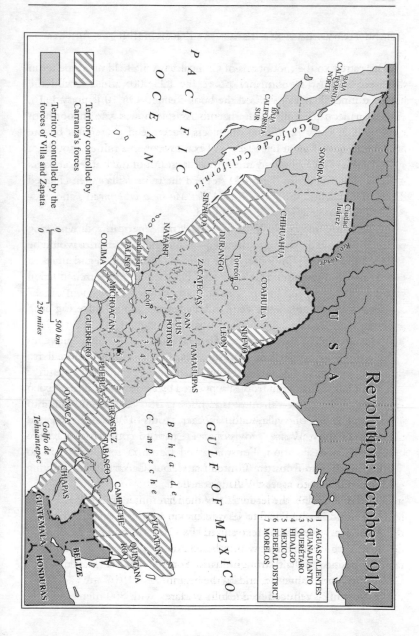

Revolution: October 1914

Territory controlled by
Carranza's forces

Territory controlled by the
forces of Villa and Zapata

PACIFIC OCEAN

Gulf of California

BAJA CALIFORNIA NORTE

BAJA CALIFORNIA SUR

SONORA

Ciudad Juárez

Rio Grande

SINALOA

CHIHUAHUA

U S A

NAYARIT

DURANGO

COAHUILA

Torreón

JALISCO

Guadalajara

ZACATECAS

León

COLIMA

MICHOACÁN

SAN LUIS POTOSI

NUEVO LEÓN

GUERRERO

PUEBLA

VERACRUZ

TAMAULIPAS

Bahía de Campeche

GULF OF MEXICO

OAXACA

TABASCO

Golfo de Tehuantepec

CHIAPAS

CAMPECHE

YUCATÁN

QUINTANA ROO

GUATEMALA

HONDURAS

BELIZE

0   250 miles

0   500 km

1 AGUASCALIENTES
2 GUANAJUATO
3 QUERÉTARO
4 HIDALGO
5 MEXICO
6 FEDERAL DISTRICT
7 MORELOS

PANCHO VILLA AND BLACKJACK PERSHING

In his retreat to the mountains of Chihuahua, Villa held up a smelter in Juárez, leaving the company poorer by $25,000, and attacked the Hearst ranch, where he killed the book-keeper. On 10 January 1916, Villa made it painfully clear that no American was safe in northern Mexico. A party of mining engineers, guaranteed protection by the Mexican government left El Paso, Texas to reopen a mine in southern Chihuahua. Two hundred and forty miles south of the border, at Santa Isabel, a barrier across the tracks stopped the train. Villa's men charged into the coaches, shouting '*Viva Villa! Muerte a los gringos!*', and executed fifteen Americans in cold blood.

Villa's next move was a surprise attack on American soil. Knowing that if he could draw American troops into Mexico, Carranza would be forced to respond. On 9 March he entered New Mexico and attacked the American garrison at Columbus, New Mexico. At 4 a.m., 360 men struck the town, and before United States cavalry drove them off, 17 citizens of Columbus were dead and the town was a smouldering heap of ashes.

Carranza immediately ordered General Plutarcho Calles to move his division to the border, and placed the garrison at Vera Cruz on alert.

On 15 March 1916, General John 'Blackjack' Pershing led a punitive force of 6,000 American troops, supported by two aircraft, into Mexico on one of the greatest manhunts in history. But Villa was nowhere to be found, and in one village after another, shouts of 'Viva Villa' greeted Pershing's army. Worse, provisions were hard to come by in a hostile country. In desperation, Funston asked Carranza for permission to bring in supplies from the United States, but Carranza was readying Mexican troops to meet the Americans.

At Parral, Villa's hometown, an American unit was attacked by the citizens, and Pershing had to send in cavalry to rescue them. When the fighting was over, forty Mexicans and two Americans were dead. At El Carrazal, the Americans were confronted by a large mob, and the troops opened fire with machine guns. When it was over, seventy-four Mexicans and twelve Americans were dead.

Meanwhile, Villa attacked Chihuahua city with 800 men, and held the town for two days before pulling back into the mountains. In November, he struck the Chinese community at Torreón, leaving a trail of blood behind him. Why Villa hated the Chinese has yet to be explained, but it is reported that he hated them even more than he did *gringos*.

Carranza ordered General Jacinto Treveño to move his army north, and a Mexican stand-off with the Americans was reached at Colonia Dublin. Any further movement south, Teveño warned Pershing, would result in war with the Mexican government.

Pershing demanded 50,000 more troops for the campaign, but Wilson had lost interest in Mexico. The campaign had cost the United States 130 million dollars to date, and pressures were building up in Washington to enter World War I. Carranza dispatched Obregón to the border to settle terms for a withdrawal with Pershing, and an agreement was reached whereby all American troops would be out of Mexico by February. The invasion, however, sapped Villa's strength by forcing him to fight on two fronts.

That month British intelligence intercepted a message from Arthur Zimmerman, the German foreign minister. The message informed Carranza that on 1 February, Germany would begin unrestricted submarine warfare in the Atlantic. Every effort would be made to keep the United States neutral, but failing to do so, Germany proposed an alliance with Mexico. The terms were very generous. The Kaiser offered joint command of the war, a common peace treaty, generous financial support, and in the event of victory, Mexico would regain its former territories in New Mexico, Arizona, and Texas. Carranza, however, had little faith that Germany could extend its power across the Atlantic, and turned down the offer.

On 28 July 1920, Villa and 758 rebels laid down their arms. The government gave each rebel a year's wages, and granted Villa a *hacienda* at Canutillo. The war, in which more than a million Mexicans lost their lives, was over.

The morning of 20 July 1923, found Pancho Villa on his way back to the *hacienda* after attending to some business in Parral. He came home unaccompanied by his usual bodyguard of fifty mounted men, and as he entered town, there were no police on duty and the military garrison was away on manoeuvres. Villa himself was at the wheel, and at a signal from a candyseller, a blast of gunfire from a house riddled the Dodge. One of the attackers rushed from the house to put a bullet in Villa's head, but the Centaur of the North was dead, his right hand frozen in the act of reaching for his pistol.

Art of the Revolution

The Revolution gave birth to an art movement in Mexico that found its greatest expression in mural painting, where it was accessible to all. The movement was not only political and social, but aroused a sense of national consciousness, which expressed itself in a variety of forms.

The movement was launched in 1922 by a group of Mexican artists inspired by new social ideals, history, and everyday life, and made possible by grants from José Vasconcelos, the Secretary of Education in the Obregón administration. From this movement, three masters of the twentieth century, ranking with the great masters of the past, would emerge.

Diego Rivera (1886–1957), began his studies in art at the early age of ten. From 1907 to 1921, he travelled through Spain, Italy, and France, where he worked with Picasso, Braque, Juan Gris, and others. He made his first contribution to contemporary art within the Cubist Movement, and its influence is clearly seen in Rivera's later murals, where depth and perspective are suppressed, and height and breadth are emphasized.

Rivera's basic motifs were the Indian and the *mestizo*, whom he painted in brown and earthen red tones, while he portrayed *criollos* and Spaniards with sharp lines and harsh colours. His themes concentrated on land distribution and agriculture, the daily life of the rural peasant, children, social issues, government oppression of the poor, and the eventual triumph of the *mestizo*.

From 1930 to 1934, he painted murals for the Museum of Modern Art in New York City, the Art Institute of Detroit, and the Museum of Modern Art in San Francisco.

For several years after 1934, Rivera concentrated on easel paintings of portraits, and water colours of Mexican life and landscapes. After

1940, however, he turned again to murals, notably for the World's Fair in San Francisco and the National Palace in Mexico City.

Rivera's vast interpretation of Mexican history is seen in the monumental stairway of the National Palace. In the lowest parts are scenes from the conquest, in the centre is the national symbol of Mexico, the eagle and the serpent, and on the highest level, the Revolution, with Zapata at the top. In lunettes at the top are other episodes in history – the Reform, Porfirio Díaz, and the Revolution. Surrounding them are scenes from the war with the United States and the execution of Maximilian. The ancient indigenous world as seen by Rivera is on the right wall, and on the left, a contemporary world in a chaotic scene with Karl Marx at the top. The mural, sadly, was never completed as a result of Rivera's death.

José Clemente Orozco (1883-1949) was born in the state of Jalisco. Both of his parents were of direct Spanish descent, and because of his ancestry and style he has often been called the Mexican Goya. The loneliness and grandeur of his works and his taste for mockery are perceived to be comparable to Goya.

He received no formal training in drawing or painting, but the experience he gained as an architectural draughtsman would contribute to his development as one of the foremost muralists of Mexico. After his first exhibition in 1915, he produced numerous murals, easel paintings, and lithographs in Mexico and the United States. His concern was with the fundamental problems of man and his social institutions, and his portrayal of these themes is forceful, expressive, passionate, and often volatile. His criticism of history had as its sole purpose the expression of reality and truth without partisanship. No artist has ever carried tragedy beyond the level of Orozco.

His brutal portrayal of a distorted Christ, God in grotesque forms, and nude Madonnas often brought the Church down upon him, and angry crowds often mutilated his frescos. One of his most famous frescos shows Cortés and Malinche naked, sitting side by side above Mexico, representing the union that created the *mestizo*. After his return from the United States, he turned to the theme of the conquest, where Cortés now appears as a violent conqueror, dressed in full armour with sword in hand.

His famed *Prometheus*, painted in 1930, is now displayed in Pomona College, California.

Alfaro David Siqueiros (1896–1974), pursued a career divided between painting and Revolutionary politics. At the age of sixteen, he joined Venustiano Carranza's forces as a drummer boy, from which he would recreate scenes of camp life, battles, and death in later life. From 1919 to 1922 he travelled and studied in Europe, and upon his return to Mexico, became a prominent leader in the Painters' Syndicate and began painting murals.

In time, Siqueiros became deeply involved in left-wing politics, spending his time organizing labour unions and attending international Communist symposiums in Moscow, Buenos Aires, Montevideo and New York. He was arrested in 1930 and 1931, and spent time in jail in Taxco, where he painted canvases and did lithographs and woodcuts. In 1960, shortly after his term as secretary of the Communist Party ended, he was again in jail on the charge of social dissolution.

Siqueiros's paintings convey violent social protest through dynamic brushwork, dramatic contrasts in light and shade, and heroic themes. His work is not so vast as that of Rivera and Orozco, but his finest achievements have their place among those of the great artists of our time in their originality and dramatic force.

His contribution to contemporary art has been a significant one. Interested in new techniques and materials, he has used as a medium pyroxylin, a compound related to gun cotton with remarkable drying properties, and other technical innovations, such as team painting and air guns. Siqueiros was also a master at easel painting, and his self-portraits have a moving quality that comes from the authority of his technique and the force of his personality.

Not all muralists of the Mexican movement were of Mexican birth. Jean Charlot was born in Paris, France, on 7 February 1898. He attended the Lycée Condorcet and the École des Beaux Artes until 1917, when he joined the French Army. He served in the army of occupation in Germany until 1920, and after a brief stay in Paris, emigrated to Mexico.

In Mexico, he joined the Painters' Syndicate and became identified with the great mural movement taking place there. Although his father

A woodcut by left-wing artist David Alfaro Siqueiros: *The peasant, the soldier, and the worker.*

was a Frenchman from Russia and sympathetic towards the Bolsheviks, Charlot was not particularly concerned with the Revolution nor with the ideology of Rivera, Siqueiros, and Orozco.

His experiments in the Cubist Movement and his acquaintance with Mexican artifacts and pre-Columbian picture manuscripts led him to create a style that was both modern and Mexican. His *Fall of Tenochtitlán* in the staircase of the National Preparatory School was the first mural of the entire group to be completed in true fresco. The use of fine greys and the transparency of his figures, as compared with other Mexican murals, is decidedly European. *The Washerwoman* and *The Pack Carriers* in the Ministry of Education, however, are scarcely distinguishable in technique and colour from the surrounding works of Rivera.

In 1926 Charlot gained the post of staff artist to Sylvanus Morley, the leader of the Carnegie expedition at Chichen Itza, where he copied

Maya frescos and bas-reliefs that could not be satisfactorily photo-graphed. On Sundays and holidays he spent his time painting everyday scenes in the Yucatán: a woman with a child at her breast or slung on her back; another washing clothes in the river, nude from the waist up; and others kneeling before the *metate* grinding maize for tortillas.

In 1929 Charlot came to the United States, where he held positions at the Art Students' League in New York, the Colorado Springs Fine Arts Center, and a number of universities. Later, he accepted a position as Professor of Art at the University of Hawaii.

Charlot has more than 36 murals to his credit, and his easel paintings appear in most major public collections. His writings list over 65 major books, portfolios, and articles, the most prominent of which are *Art from the Mayas to Disney* (1939), *Art-making from Mexico to China* (1950), and *Dance of Death* (1951).

CHAPTER FOURTEEN

1920–40: The Roots of the Modern State

The Constitution of 1917

By the late autumn of 1916, Villa's forces had been reduced to the extent that the Carranza administration was able to stabilize the civil government and give some thought to legitimizing the Revolution. Although Carranza had his own agenda for the new constitution, he found he had little support from the Constitutionalist leadership, and reluctantly called for a convention to meet in Querétaro in December, 1916.

To ensure that the débâcle of the Aguascalientes convention would not be repeated, he excluded Zapatistas and Villistas from the assembly. Unfortunately for Carranza, however, he found the Constitutionalists seldom in ideological agreement among themselves, and in the end, was forced to accept a document that was far too liberal for his liking. Unlike the Aguascalientes convention, only 30 per cent of the delegates were military men. The large majority was made up of younger men with professional titles and university educations, and the leadership of the convention was in the hands of Álavaro Obregón, who had broken with Carranza, and Francisco Mújica. Six weeks after the convention met, Mexico had a new constitution.

The Constitution of 1917 would prove to be a watershed between pre-Revolutionary Mexico and modern Mexico.

The biggest loser was the Catholic Church. All Church lands were confiscated without compensation, and all places of religious worship were now the property of the State. Since Spain had financed the construction of all religious buildings after the conquest, the State argued, they were now, by definition, government buildings. All elementary education was compulsory and secular, and churches of all creeds were prohibited from establishing schools of primary instruction. Monastic orders were banished, all ministers were required to register with the government, and none, under penalty of law, was permitted to criticize the laws of the country or its administrators. And, for the first time in history, divorce was legalized in Mexico.

New land laws virtually eliminated the *hacendados*. Legislation was enacted that limited the maximum number of acres that an individual or a corporation could hold, and the *ejidos* were declared inviolable. Subsoil minerals and petroleum rights were now the sole property of the State, and foreigners were barred from owning land within 62 miles of the frontiers or 31 miles from the sea.

On the labour front, workers were granted the rights to form unions, engage in collective bargaining, and to strike. The law established a minimum wage, an eight-hour working day, a six-day week, worker's

Venustiano Carranza, president 1915–20

compensation and sick benefits. Women were granted the same wages as men for the same work, and could not be assigned dangerous tasks. The new social programmes enacted by the architects of the constitution did not please the First Chief, and like Porfirio Díaz before him, he reacted by ignoring them.

The end for Carranza came in April 1920, when he tried to name Ignacio Bonilla, an unknown, as his successor. Álvaro Obregón pronounced against the government; Adolfo de la Huerta, the governor of Sonora, declared for an independent republic; and General Plutarco Calles mobilized an army and marched against the capital.

By May, Carranza had neither the means nor the will to resist the rebels, and on 5 May he embarked for Vera Cruz with an entourage of supporters, an armed escort, and the nation's entire treasury of gold bars in a train of sixty railway wagons. The caravan came under heavy attack before it left the outskirts of the capital, and by 14 May Carranza was forced to flee the train on horseback. On 20 May Carranza and his staff reached the village of Tlaxcalantongo, where his generals urged him to spend the night until the route north was declared safe. Shortly after 3 a.m., Calles's forces attacked the village, and Carranza's leg was broken by a bullet. Knowing the end was near, Carranza calmly put on his glasses and pressed the muzzle of his pistol to his chest.

Post-war Reconstruction.

In November 1920, Álvaro Obregón assumed the presidency of Mexico and opened a new era in Mexican politics. A moderate, his tenure of office favoured conservative compromise rather than social radicalism. He avoided outright expropriation of lands, preferring instead to let rural villages apply through the government bureaucracy for individual grants. His administration distributed almost a million hectares of land to rural communities. Although he did not enforce all the provisions of Article 123 of the Constitution, he did not oppose its most important provisions. He encouraged the formation of unions and defended the right to strike, but only if the workers belonged to CROM, the *Confederación Regional Obrera,* Luis Morones's huge union with a membership of more than a million. As a check and balance on

Morones, Obregón supported the formation of the peasant union CNC, the *Confederación Nacional Campesina*.

Without doubt, Obregón's most important appointment was that of José Vasconcelos as Minster of Public Education. Under Vasconcelos's guidance, more than a thousand rural schools were constructed between 1920 and 1924, more than had been built during the previous fifty years. By 1924, more than a thousand libraries had been established and stocked with books emphasizing Mexican culture, and government printing presses distributed cheap editions of the Classics throughout the nation. Teachers and public health workers visited rural areas, and Spanish was taught for the first time in the more remote regions of Mexico. Vasconcelos also sponsored the arts and humanities. Sponsored by his programmes, José Clemente Orozco, David Alfaro Siqueiros, Diego Rivera, and Francisco Goitia painted murals extolling the Revolution and the rise of *mestizo* power on the walls of government buildings throughout the nation.

The Obregón administration, however, failed to gain recognition from the United States. American oil lobbyists had been pressing the United States government for years to take a more active role in protecting their interests in Mexico, but received little support from the Wilson Administration. With the implementation of Article 27 of the Constitution calling for nationalization of subsoil resources, however, the threat of outright seizure of the oil fields was now a reality. The lobbyists found a friendly audience in Warren G. Harding, a conservative who believed his primary goal was to foster American investments at home and abroad, and they were able to persuade him to withhold recognition of the Obregón administration until guarantees of American interests were forthcoming. Obregón desperately needed the oil revenues from the United States, but yielding to the Americans on a constitutional issue would be political suicide at home.

The Texas Company took Obregón off the hook when it challenged the retro-active provision in Article 27 of the Constitution in Mexican courts. The Supreme Court eventually settled the issue when it ruled that the government could not seize oil lands from any company that had taken some 'positive action', such as drilling for oil or even erecting scaffolding in preparation for drilling prior to 1 May 1917.

The matter was finally settled in the spring of 1923 when commissioners from both countries met on Bucareli Street in Mexico City. Mexico ceded that Article 27 would not be retro-active, and the United States in return would grant recognition and reopen the embassy. In addition, Mexico agreed to settle claims for damages suffered by Americans during the Revolution.

The Bucareli Agreements, however, were not well received by the Nationalists. Obregón, they believed, had sold out to the American oil barons and their supporters in Congress, and looked forward to the imminent elections of 1924, when they could seat a new president. When Obregón anointed his fellow Sonoran, Plutarco Calles, for president, violence erupted across the nation.

Conservatives, *hacendados*, and prominent churchmen believed Calles to be an out-and-out radical, and initiated a move to oust Obregón. They were soon joined by the military, who were still seething under the latest force reductions, conservative Nationalists, and prominent labour leaders not associated with CROM. Leadership of the coalition fell to Adolfo de la Huerta, the Governor of Sonora.

Obregón, however, was not without resources. Although a number of officers and men deserted him, most remained loyal to the government. CROM threw its support behind Obregón, and a number of peasant organizations remained loyal to their president. Furthermore, the United States supplied war materials, and the American navy blockaded the ports of Tampico and Vera Cruz to prevent shipments of arms from reaching the rebels.

The revolt lasted no more than three months. The rebels were soundly defeated, and de la Huerta fled for the United States, leaving 7,000 men dead or dying on the battlefields of Mexico.

THE MAXIMATO

Plutarco Elías Calles won the 1924 election by a wide margin, and immediately let it be known that he would carry out the aims of the Constitution without following the path of compromise chosen by his predecessor.

His first target was the Bucareli Agreement. Upon reaching office, Calles was beset by American oil lobbyists seeking confirmation that their properties would be protected against expropriation. Instead, the Congress, at Calles's urging, enacted a new petroleum law that decreed all pre-Revolutionary land concessions null and void, and instructed all oil companies to turn in the deeds granted in perpetuity by Porfirio Díaz. The government, however, would validate the leases if the company could show it was responsive to the 'doctrine of positive acts', but the leases would be ratified for no more than fifty years.

The new law triggered another round of sabre rattling in the United States. Rockwell Sheffield, the new American ambassador, believed that Mexico was 'the second Bolshevik country on earth', a 'Soviet Mexico', an opinion fortified no doubt by Alexandra Kollontai, Mexico's first ambassador from the Soviet Union. Upon meeting Calles, her first words were 'There are no two countries in the world more alike than modern Mexico and the new Russia!'

On 10 November 1926, The *New York Times* advocated breaking off relations with Mexico. The oil situation was deteriorating, and a new international threat was evolving in Nicaragua. The United States supported the incumbent conservative Adolfo Díaz, and Mexico supported the revolutionary Augusto Sandina. Calles sent two expeditions to Nicaragua to aid Sandina's guerrillas, but Coolidge responded by landing marines in Nicaragua and ordering troop manoeuvres along the United States–Mexico border.

The situation was defused when President Calvin Coolidge recalled Sheffield and replaced him with Dwight Morrow. Morrow chose to live in a Mexican house in Cuernavaca rather than the embassy, and commissioned Diego Rivera to paint a fresco in the Palace of Cortés. His family shopped in the open market-place, and he often visited towns and rural areas to observe the impact of the Revolution on workers and peasants. When he felt comfortable with Calles, he served the *coup de grâce* by inviting his son-in-law, Charles Lindbergh, to conduct a good will tour of Mexico.

Meetings between Morrow and the *Jefe Máximo* were informal, and they often had breakfast together to discuss issues of economic development. On the oil issue, Morrow set Calles at ease by saying the issue should be determined by Mexican courts, and the United States expected no special consideration.

In 1927 the Mexican Supreme Court declared the fifty-year oil lease provision to be unconstitutional, and that foreigners who had obtained subsoil rights prior to 1917 were entitled to them in perpetuity. The official announcement of the Court's decision credited Mexico with resolving the problem, and ruled that any future controversies on this issue would be resolved in Mexican courts without interference from the United States. Calles and Morrow agreed that domestic stability, guarantees for private property, and co-operation between foreign and Mexican capital were vital for the economic growth of Mexico. To meet these objectives, the United States renegotiated Mexico's debts on more favourable terms.

The *Jefe Máximo* exerted as much pressure on the Church to conform to the provisions of the Constitution as he had on land ownership and oil rights. Whereas Obregón had adopted a *laissez-faire* attitude towards some of the more restrictive policies, Calles asked for extraordinary powers from Congress to impose even more regulations upon the clergy.

The Church had never accepted the anti-clerical Articles 3 and 130 of the Constitution, and tension between the Church and the State had been building up since 1920. The breaking point was reached on 4 February when the Archbishop of Mexico, José Mora y del Río, granted an interview with the newspaper *El Universal*. The Church, he argued, strongly opposed the anti-clerical articles of the Constitution, and Catholics could not in all good conscience accept them. Furthermore, the Catholic position was not open to negotiation.

On 2 July the new law was published. It included punishments for crimes related to worship and teaching, a requirement that all priests register before they could assume their ministry, the deportation of 200 foreign priests and nuns, the closing of 73 monasteries and convents, and secularization of all primary education. Church schools were closed, and all foreign priests were deported,

The *Jefe Máximo* did not have to wait long for the Church to retaliate. On 21 July 1926, every church in the country closed its doors. Mass was not celebrated, the rites of marriage and baptism were not performed, and the dead were buried without benefit of the last rites.

Riots broke out in the streets, and armed resistance appeared in the northern and western states by a rebel group that called themselves the Cristeros. To the cry of '*Viva Cristo Rey!*', they destroyed schools and government property, and murdered teachers, leaving their bodies covered with banners marked VCR, the Cristero battle insignia. In April, the Cristeros dynamited a train, killing more than a hundred civilians. Federal troops retaliated by murdering a priest for every teacher killed, and tortured suspected Cristeros and their families. The war raged through 13 states across the centre of Mexico for more than three years, and when it ended, more than 70,000 lives had been lost.

With the assistance of the Pope, the Cristeros reached an agreement with the government on 17 June 1929. A general amnesty was granted to Cristeros who laid down their arms; the homes of the bishops and priests were restored; and religious teaching was permitted in public schools. The Cristero revolt was over, but the Church had gained nothing. Not one of the government's laws regulating the Church was rescinded, and the government took a more aggressive course in seizing Church properties.

Calles was still occupied with the Cristeros when hopeful candidates began their campaigns for the 1928 presidential elections. The Congress had extended the presidential term to six years, and the law was changed to permit one re-election, provided it did not immediately follow the first. Callas threw his support behind Obregón, expecting him to return the favour at the end of his term. Obregón won the election by a large majority, but two weeks before his inauguration, he was assassinated at a garden banquet. A young artist sketching caricatures of the guests while they were dining gradually worked his way to the head table. He stopped to show Obregón his work, and before a stunned audience, he pulled out a pistol and fired five shots into Obregón's head.

Congress was now forced to name an interim president until elections could be held, and Calles had no difficulty in persuading the legislators to name the first of his puppet presidents, Emilio Portes Gil.

By the time the 1929 elections rolled around, Calles had formed the PNR (Partido Nacional Revolucionario) which, though its name would be changed several times, would dominate Mexican politics throughout the twentieth century.

The PNR candidate for the special election was Pascual Ortiz Rubio. The opposition candidate, running under the platform of no re-election, lost by a margin of nearly two-to-one amid rumours of election fraud. Rubio served for two years, but when Calles overruled him on several policy decisions, he tendered his resignation 'with my hands clean of blood or money'. Calles chose General Abelardo Rodriguez to serve as an administrator for the final two years of the six-year term.

The Great Depression of 1927 hit Mexico hard. Dependent upon the United States for 69 per cent of its imports and 60 per cent of its exports, the slow-down in the United States' economy was a devastating blow to that of Mexico. Unemployment tripled between 1929 and 1933, and those still employed and earning the minimum wage were unable to meet a third of their families' basic needs. Furthermore, the United States claimed that immigrant workers were taking away jobs from Americans, and deported more than 300,000 workers and their families.

The PNR, responding to the demands of radicals and Marxists, introduced a Six Year Plan that called for reducing Mexico's dependence on foreign markets, promoting agrarian reform and small businesses, and developing Mexican enterprises rather than foreign ones.

Calles chose General Lázaro Cárdenas as the PNR candidate for the presidential race of 1934, but if he believed he had found another puppet, he soon learned that he had released the tiger.

Immediately after the election, Cárdenas broke with tradition by cutting the presidential salary in half, and conducted the nation's business from his own home rather than from the presidential palace at Chapultepec Castle. He installed a telegraph line so the people could send their complaints directly to him, and opened the doors of the National Palace to every peasant and Indian who wanted to see him.

Cárdenas's credentials for the presidency were beyond reproach. During the Revolution, he had fought in the brigades of Obregón and Calles, served as the military commander of Tampico, had been elected to a term as governor of Michoacán, was Calles's secretary of war, and ultimately became president of the PNR.

Consolidation of presidential power had, throughout Mexican his-

The president who cut his salary in half: General Lázaro Cárdenas

tory, depended upon the support of the military, and Cárdenas made it his first priority to bring the army into his camp. He raised salaries and benefits, which were long overdue, cultivated promising young offi-cers, initiated an improved system of education throughout the army, and called for a full-scale reform of the military. Allies of the Sonorans were either retired or transferred from key posts, and former Villistas and Zapatistas were assigned to strategic positions. He eliminated lifetime tenure for judges, limiting them to six-year terms, and rid the legislature of Callista Senators and deputies by charging them with 'incitation to rebellion and seditious maneuvers'.

When he was confident of army support, he fired the Callistas in his cabinet, forced Callistas out of influential positions in the PNR and other key political offices, and relieved Callista generals of their com-mands.

Calles began to speak against the administration and enter into intrigues, but Cárdenas was always one step ahead. In 1936, Cárdenas arrested the *Jefe Máximo* and his supporters and hustled them aboard a aeroplane bound for the United States.

Under Cárdenas, organized labour underwent a major reorganization. The CROM group of unions was in disarray, and Cárdenas took the opportunity to rid labour of the rampant corruption of Luis Morones. Cárdenas chose the radical labour leader Vincente Lombardo Toledano to form a new national union, the *Confederación de Trabajadores* (CTM), and with subsidies from the government, the membership reached a million within two years.

Cárdenas was dedicated to land reform, but favoured collective land tenure rather than private ownership. During his term, he distributed more land to the peasants than had been distributed in all the years following the Revolution. A strike of cotton workers in the Laguna region near Torreón gave Cárdenas the opportunity to put his concept of land utilization into practice. He condemned 600,000 acres in the region, offering the 332 owners compensation with agrarian bonds, which were essentially worthless. Cárdenas then settled 31,000 families numbering 150,000 people in the Laguna to form the first State-operated farm. The Banco Nacional de Crédito Ejidal, capitalized at thirty million pesos, was created to extend farm loans for seeds, fertilizer, and farm machinery, and the Lázaro Cárdenas Dam was constructed to irrigate the entire region.

By the end of 1936, loans of 8,124,692 pesos, all secured by crops worth more than fifty million pesos, were granted to 29,690 families for the cultivation of 247,000 acres.

In the early part of 1936, the Mexican Oil Workers Union, 18,000 strong, forced the oil companies to sign a collective-bargaining agreement. The union's first demand called for a 66-million-peso package in wages and benefits. The oil companies rejected the offer and the issue was referred to the Council of Conciliation and Arbitration. Their ruling was that the seventeen British and American oil producers would have to pay 26 million pesos for wages and benefits, not the 14 million offered by the companies. After reading their report, Cárdenas summoned the American ambassador and informed him that the State would take part in all decisions regarding wages and benefits within the oil industry. Dealing with the government rather than the union was another matter for the oil companies, however, and they lost no time in raising their offer to 20 million.

In November 1937, the Standard Oil Company issued an ultimatum: 'We cannot pay and we will not pay'. Standard Oil took the risk knowing that Mexico had neither the management nor technical expertise to maintain production, nor the markets and resources available to the companies. Their calculated risk, however, backfired when the Mexican government repealed the 'doctrine of positive acts' of the Bucareli Agreement, and once again all oil leases were in jeopardy. On 15 March 1938, The government ordered the oil companies to pay the full 26.3 million pesos and hire 1,100 new employees, and after receiving no response, declared them in contempt of court. On 18 March the companies met Cárdenas and agreed to pay, but it was too late and too little. Cárdenas had reached his decision to nationalize all oil properties.

At ten o'clock that night, Cárdenas informed the nation by radio of his decision, and he received an outburst of support from every corner of Mexico as well as from a number of Latin American countries.

In the United States, on the other hand, the press was calling for Cárdenas's head, and conservative members of Congress were pressing for intervention. But Franklin Delano Roosevelt had run for election on a platform that called for non-intervention in Latin America, closing that avenue of retaliation.

Mexico agreed to pay fair compensation, but the companies boycotted oil sales to Great Britain, France, and the United States until the full indemnity was paid. This proved not to be a wise decision for the Allies – Cárdenas was forced to sell oil to the Axis powers until 1941 before he could pay off the indemnity. But Petróleos Mexicanos (PEMEX) was here to stay. With the outbreak of World War II, oil was now a strategic material, and Mexico could sell every barrel the nation could produce.

Under Cárdenas, Mexico would at last gain national unity and achieve a socialistic state that could work freely with foreign capitalism. Under his policies, Mexico would also become a haven for the persecuted of other lands, regardless of race, politics, or religion.

> There is no antipathy or prejudice in our country against any country or race in the world.... Distinctions or persecutions of any part of the population are contrary to the spirit and the laws of my government.

Among us, any North American is welcome, black or white, Jew or Catholic, all that we ask is that they obey our immigration laws.

Lázaro Cárdenas

His foreign policy was a reflection of his moral convictions. He condemned Japan's invasion of China, Hitler's *Anschluss* of Austria, and Italy's invasion of Ethiopia. Through Mexico's delegates to the Geneva Convention, he condemned the Nazi genocide against the Jews, protested against Germany's invasion of Czechoslovakia, Belgium, and Holland, and, despite Mexico's leftist leanings, Russia's invasion of Finland.

In the last two years of his administration, his policies often brought violent attacks down upon the regime, but he never took reprisals.

CHAPTER FIFTEEN

The Modern Era

As the nation prepared for the 1940 elections, it was assumed that Cárdenas would anoint Francisco Múgica, one of the more radical revolutionaries, as his successor. The prospect caused enough panic among the conservatives that they formed an opposition party, the National Action Party, (PAN) and named General Juan Andreau Almazán, a wealthy Catholic landowner, as their candidate. Cárdenas, however, surprised the electorate when he chose his Secretary of War, General Manuel Ávila Camacho, a moderate, instead.

There was little enthusiasm for Ávila Camacho even among the party leadership. He had joined the Revolution in 1914, and gradually worked his way up the ranks to become a general officer, but his military career had been somewhat colourless. He was known more as a compromiser than a field commander, and within the party, he was often referred to as the 'Unknown Soldier'.

With Ávila Camacho's election, the nation took a turn to the right as government policy became progressively more conservative. The liberal ideals of the Revolution and the rights of peasants and workers took a back seat in a thrust for modernization and industrialization.

Land redistribution slowed down as Ávila Camacho parcelled out less than a quarter of the land distributed by Cárdenas. Furthermore, the president favoured small, private ownership, and land was passed on to the heads of families rather than to the community.

On the labour front, he removed the railways from union control and sponsored legislation to prohibit 'illegal' strikes. He dismissed Vincente Lombardo Toledano, the Marxist labour leader, from the CTM and replaced him with the conservative Fidel Velásquez, who would hold the post for 56 years. During his long career, Don Fidel served as a federal senator and an adviser to eleven presidents, and many considered him to be the most powerful man in Mexico. But that power was more often exercised to help the government and the party at the expense of all other interests, including those of his own workers.

A former Mexico City baker, Velásquez rose to power in the union movement in the 1930s. A strong anti-Communist, he rewarded his friends with money and power and punished his enemies with brute force. In his early years, Velásquez was able to trade his clout for increased wages, job protection, and generous benefit programmes, although he often supported government measures limiting strikes. In the 1980s, he helped the government impose severe austerity measures that eroded workers' wages and benefits, and following the 1994 peso devaluation, supported a United States-backed rescue package that slashed real incomes by more than 20 per cent.

Mexico and World War II

Prior to Hitler's invasion of Czechoslovakia in 1939, *El Universal,* Mexico City's independent newspaper, convinced that the Munich Agreement rectified the wrongs done to Germany by the Treaty of Versailles, felt that Germany was justified in her position. After Russia and Germany signed the non-aggression pact of 19 August 1939, in which the two powers agreed to keep the peace for ten years, the Mexican left, led by Lombardo Toledano, and the Mexican right, led by Almazán, took a strong pro-German position. But when Hitler abrogated the pact and ordered the *Wehrmacht* into Russia, Ávila Camacho threw Mexico's support behind the Allies, and only a handful of Mexican fascists opposed him. On the day after the Japanese attack on Pearl Harbor, Mexico broke diplomatic relations with the Axis powers and urged all other Latin American countries to do the same.

Ávila Camacho deported all German, Italian, and Japanese diplomats from the country, and most Mexicans were satisfied that there was no need for a formal declaration of war.

But the Germans soon changed their minds. On 14 May 1942 a German submarine torpedoed a fully lit and well-identified Mexican tanker heading towards the United States. Ávila Camacho sent a demand for full indemnification and an apology from Germany, and Germany responded by torpedoing a second tanker on 24 May. The attacks cost twenty-three Mexican lives.

On 28 May Ávila Camacho formally declared war on Germany, Italy, and Japan, and Congress granted him extraordinary war powers to suspend Constitutional guarantees if he felt national security was at risk.

The government seized German, Italian, and Japanese properties, and the secret service arrested several *Gestapo* officers and rooted out agents operating covert radio stations sending instructions to German U-boats operating in the Caribbean and the Atlantic.

Mexican nationals living in the United States joined the army in exchange for promises of United States' citizenship, and with Mexican-Americans, formed a contingent of a quarter-of-a-million men. The unit lost a thousand men killed in action, 1,500 received the Purple Heart, and seventeen Mexicans and Mexican-Americans, more than any other minority ethnic group in the United States, received the Congressional Medal of Honour.

Mexico's contribution to the air war was Squadron 201, 300 Air Corps volunteers trained in the United States to fly P-47 Thunderbolts on combat missions in the Philippines and Formosa. The Aztecs flew 50 missions during the war, and lost eight men.

One of the most effective contributions Mexico made to the war effort was the *bracero* programme, conceived by Franklin D. Roosevelt and Ávila Camacho, that permitted Mexican labourers to harvest crops in the southwestern United States. The greater part of the American agricultural work-force was in the armed services, and without the *braceros,* the country was facing a prohibitive loss of crops. Under the agreement, Mexican labourers were transported across the border to harvest the crops with the proviso that they were not to displace American workers nor be used to suppress wages in the United States. The workers were provided with transport to and from their homes, and wages were set at 46 cents an hour.

During the 25 years the programme was in effect, 4,712,866 Mexicans participated in it and sent $749,900,000 to Mexico through official channels, plus an indeterminate amount to their families through the postal services.

Post-war Economy

During the war, the United States purchased large amounts of silver from Mexico to finance the war effort, as well as other strategic materials such as copper, tin, and produce. The United States also advanced loans for Mexico's industrialization, and private investors, fleeing wartime price controls and high taxes in the United States, made heavy investments in Mexico. American direct investment in Mexico rose sharply in 1946, doubled in the 1950s, and tripled in the 1960s.

Wartime shortages in the United States and Europe had deprived Mexico of its imported manufactured goods, and with the influx of new capital, businesses were created to increase production to satisfy the demand and provide a surplus for export to other Latin American countries. The government gave tax concessions to new businesses, and established the National Financiera to provide loans to industry.

To encourage Mexican investment into the growing economy, the Congress passed legislation in 1944 to allow foreign investment in the expanding industrial complex, provided Mexican capital held the majority interest in mixed ventures. Tariff protection and tax exemptions provided additional incentives, and with Don Fidel at the helm of the CTM, the wage structure of the entire nation was under tight control.

The industrialization of Mexico almost tripled the national income from 1940 to 1945, and per capita income jumped from 325 pesos to 838 pesos. While the earning power of the middle class increased substantially from the new economy, however, few of the benefits trickled down to the lower classes.

MIGUEL ALEMÁN VALDÉZ

By 1946, the PRM was no longer controlled by intellectuals, advocates of land reform, and radical labour leaders. Instead, businessmen, economists, and technicians dominated the party. To reflect the new

Miguel Alemán Valdéz, the first of Mexico's presidents who had not served in the Revolution

direction of the Revolution, the party changed its name to the Partido Revolucionario Institucional (PRI), and for the first time, nominated a civilian as its presidential candidate.

This time the '*dedazo*', the pointed finger, reached out to Miguel Alemán Valdéz, the first of Mexico's presidents who had not served in the Revolution. Elected Governor of Vera Cruz at the age of thirty-six, Alemán caught the attention of the party by reopening the churches to end twenty years of religious tension, and settling a bitter land dispute in favour of the peasants. He launched his career into national politics when he organized a bloc of governors to support Cárdenas in the nationalization of the oil companies. Ávila Camacho was sufficiently impressed to appoint him to the key cabinet post of Minister of the Interior.

With a financially stable government, Alemán was able to launch an unprecedented programme of public works. The most important of his projects was the construction of dams to reclaim agricultural land and generate sufficient electricity to satisfy the demands of Mexico's rapidly growing industrial complex. The Morelos Dam on the Colorado River near Mexicali changed seven hundred thousand acres of desert into rich vegetable farming land; the Álvaro Obregón Dam created another rich farming area in the Sonora Desert; and the Falcón project, a joint venture with the United States, brought thousands of acres of farmland under cultivation in the lower Rio Grande Valley. The most ambitious of his projects was the completion of the Miguel Alemán Dam in 1950. A series of four dams controlled the fall of the Papaloapan river on its journey from the mountains of Puebla, Oaxaca, and Vera Cruz to the Gulf of Mexico, and by 1960, 300,000 acres were reclaimed from the coastal swamplands and 50,000 kilowatts of electrical energy generated.

Alemán's other major project was the modernization of the nation's transport infrastructure. He upgraded the railway system and added to it by acquiring the last foreign-owned railway, the Southern Pacific of Mexico. The Pan American Highway now reached from the United States border to Guatemala, a major expressway connected the capital to Acapulco, and a highway across the Isthmus of Tehuantepec connected Salina Cruz on the Pacific Coast to Puerto México on the Gulf Coast.

The government also adopted an aggressive programme of oil exploration and modernization of PEMEX facilities. New pipelines were laid, new refineries were built, and more wells were drilled. By the end of the Alemán administration, the production of crude oil had doubled.

The most imposing of Alemán's projects was the construction of the National University of Mexico on the pedregal, a lava bed on the southern edge of the capital. The buildings were designed by such talented architects as Félix Candela, and the murals on the façades were created by Diego Rivera, Alfaro Siqueiros, and Juan O'Gorman. The University, originally built to hold a student body of 25,000, now accommodates 129,000 students, and their tuition costs amount to no more than a few cents per annum. Alemán considered the university to be a monument to his presidency, and commemorated it by erecting a thirty-foot statue of himself at the entrance. The statue, however, has been the target of every student demonstration, and the monument was toppled more than once during student protests.

Alemán became the first sitting president to visit the United States. The purpose of the visit was to arrange loans from the Export-Import Bank and to invite investors to participate in offshore drilling for petroleum in Vera Cruz and Tabasco. President Harry Truman reciprocated by visiting Mexico City and laying a wreath at the monument of the *Niños Héros*, the cadets who died fighting American forces at Chapultepec Castle.

Corruption had been an accepted way of life in government since Colonial days, but under the Alemán administration, it became a fine art. The long-standing practice that those in top government posts could tap the public purse without risking serious reprisal was now manifest by naked greed. Lower-rung bureaucrats had always been careful in applying the *mordida*, the 'bite', but under the Alemán administration, they threw caution to the wind. The *nouveau riches* built palatial mansions, held bacchanalian parties, and poured rivers of money into their excesses. A notorious incident occurred when the actress María Félix, on location in Michoacán, mentioned to her lover, Jorge Pasqual that the film crew had run out of ice. Pasqual, who controlled oil distribution in Mexico, responded by sending her by seaplane a refrigerator filled with such delicacies as lobster and caviar. The lady, however, had the grace to ask him if in the future, he would send sacks of maize, rice, and beans for the Indians instead of caviar and lobsters for her.

Fortunately for Alemán, former presidents are untouchable. After leaving office in 1952, he spent his retirement days travelling through Europe on his yacht with a Brazilian actress. One highly placed source in the government estimated that Alemán and his cronies had drained $800 million from the National Treasury.

Adolfo Ruiz Cortines: the Caretaker Administration

After the Alemán Administration scandals, the PRI desperately needed a candidate who could restore integrity to the party. Their choice was

Adolfo Ruiz Cortines, now in his sixty-first year, whose personal honesty and Party loyalty were beyond question.

Born in 1889, Ruiz Cortines left school early to learn book-keeping, a skill that was highly valued in Vera Cruz. He joined the Revolution, but as an army paymaster saw little if any combat. His only moment of glory came on 20 May 1920, when federal forces intercepted Carranza's train carrying the National Treasury at Aljibes, and he was charged with escorting the gold bars back to Mexico City.

In a series of articles published in the magazine *Crisol,* Ruiz Cortines was the first writer to draw public attention to the problem of Mexico's rapidly growing population. His argument that unchecked population growth could lead to serious problems for the nation, however, made him few friends in the Church.

He began his political career at the age of forty-five, and moved through a series of posts until 1944, when he was elected Governor of Vera Cruz. Later, he became Minister of the Interior in the Alemán Administration, but he managed to keep his reputation for honesty even though surrounded by naked corruption and wasteful spending. When the *dedazo* pointed towards him for the 1952 election, he celebrated in his typical manner – he took some friends to a taco stand and treated them to a movie at the Cine Metropolitan.

In an acceptance speech, it is customary for the incoming president to praise the good works of the outgoing president before presenting his programme, but Ruiz Cortines launched a fiery attack on Alemán with his first words. At the conclusion of his speech, he pointed his finger directly at Alemán and said, 'I will not permit the principles of the Revolution nor the laws that guide us to be broken.... I will be inflexible with public servants who stray from honesty and decency'.

On his first day in office, he published a complete and detailed list of his assets, which consisted of a house in Mexico City, a farm jointly owned with a friend in Vera Cruz, his savings account, his wife's 1948 Lincoln, and their furniture. His net worth came to about $34,000. He then required all public employees to do the same, warning them that they would be audited at the beginning and at the end of his Administration. He refused the customary offer of a new automobile from a local car dealership, and when his wife received 300 gifts upon her birthday, he ordered her to send everything back except those that had come from close friends. He made little progress, however, against the *mordida*, the bribes demanded by minor bureaucrats and officials who awarded government contracts, which by now had become entrenched in the system.

Ruiz Cortines initiated no new large-scale and ambitious projects as his predecessor had done, but concentrated instead upon seeing Alemán's projects through to completion and sponsoring smaller projects, such as metalling rural roads so that farmers could get their products to market.

Under his administration, the IMSS, the Instituto Mexicano de Seguro Social, was extended to cover the rural areas of Mexico. Benefits in the countryside were less than those received in urban areas, but some hundred thousand people received social security and health benefits for the first time in history.

Although Ruiz Cortinas distributed less land to peasants than either of his two predecessors, his agricultural programmes improved yields to the point that Mexico no longer had to import maize or wheat, and sugar became an export commodity.

Despite a burgeoning industrial output, labour unrest was at an all-time low. Hundreds of disputes were settled peacefully by arbitration, and only thirteen labour disputes led to a strike. A general strike, however, was narrowly averted when the government devalued the peso from 8.65 to 12.50 to the dollar.

In 1953, Ruiz Cortines pushed through a change in the Constitution that gave women the right to vote and hold elective office. Within two years, five women legislators had been elected to Congress and others had received appointments as ambassadors, magistrates, and high-level civil servants.

Dark clouds, however, were gathering on the horizon. The uncurbed population growth of the nation was troubling to politicians and sociologists alike. From 1934 to 1958, the population of Mexico had doubled from 16 million people to 32 million. Worse, the population explosion was concentrated in the cities, where the annual growth rate approached 7 per cent as compared to 3 per cent for the nation. The population of the Federal District alone increased from 3 million in 1952 to 5 million in 1958.

For the rural population, the cities were a Mecca where a better life could be found. Peasants came by the hundreds of thousands, only to be reduced to begging in the streets when they realized that factories and mills had few jobs for unskilled labour. To create jobs for the unskilled, Ruiz Cortinas was forced to use their labour with picks and shovels instead of machinery to build schools, hospitals, sewage-disposal plants, and housing.

ADOLFO LÓPEZ MATEOS – THE ORATOR

Born on 26 May 1909, the son of a dentist, the young Adolfo attended primary school on a scholarship, and in 1926, entered the Instituto Científico y Literario. He was a relatively poor student, more interested in outdoor life than in studies, and graduated only by taking special examinations. In 1925, he married Eva Sámano after a twelve-year courtship, before, during, and after which he had numerous affairs.

López Mateos had a phenomenal gift for oratory, and in a competition for public speakers sponsored by a newspaper in 1929, he won the championship of the Federal District. Later that year he would come second in another competition, but with his dramatic speech about the Spanish language he would gain the attention of the party.

> It is an idiom of bronze, a language of bells and of cannon but also a language of gold and silver, that has translated the mystical ecstasies and amorous raptures of a race.

In 1929 he went to work for the José Vasconcelas campaign against Ortiz Rubio, the puppet candidate for the presidency sponsored by Plutarco Elías Calles. It proved to be a dangerous undertaking. Assassins from the *Jefe Maximo's* PNR murdered his friend and co-worker, Germán del Campo, and he was brutally attacked and left bleeding in an alley from severe head wounds. After the elections, López Mateos fled to Guatemala to avoid persecution, and remained there until 1930, when he returned to Mexico to finish his studies in economics. Friends of his fiancée's father gained him a position with the Governor of the State of Mexico, and in 1931, he became the private secretary of Carlos Riva Palacio, a follower of the *Jefe Maximo,* and put his oratorical gifts to work for his former persecutors.

In 1941, Isidro Fabela, a Senator from the State of Mexico, took him under his wing and taught him the fine art of Mexican politics. When Fabela was appointed Ambassador to the World Court at the Hague, López Mateos, with the blessing of presidential candidate Miguel Alemán, took Fabela's seat in the Senate. In 1952, Ruiz Cortines appointed him Minister of Labor, and in 1957, he became the presidential candidate of the PRI.

The 1958 election was unique, inasmuch as it was the first time that women voted for a president. It was feared that the women would support the PAN candidate, who was endorsed by the Church, but the majority voted for López Mateos, although their vote added little to the party's overwhelming majority.

With the election of López Mateos, the government reversed the trend set by Ávila Camacho eighteen years previously and moved to the far left. López Mateos himself described his programme as 'extreme left within the Constitution', but he made it clear that there would be no place for the Communists in his administration.

His pro-labour position came as no surprise, since he held the post of Secretary of Labor during the Ruiz Cortines administration. For urban workers, the government initiated a major programme to build low-cost housing in the major industrial cities. One development in Mexico City covered a slum of 10 million square feet, provided housing for 100,000 people, and contained 13 schools, four clinics, and several nurseries. The rents were within reason – $6.00 per month for a one-bedroom unit, and $16.00 for a three-bedroom unit. A programme was also initiated to encourage new industries to locate away from the major cities, but the programme made no significant headway against the overcrowding that was strangling the urban areas.

The most serious labour problem arose when an inflationary rise of prices led to a Communist-led strike of the National Railroad, tying up the entire system with month-long work stoppages. When negotiations broke down, López Mateos lost patience and sent in the army to disband the strikers. He ordered the arrest of the Demetrio Vallejo, the Communist head of the union, 2,600 militants, and the muralist Alfaro David Siqueiros on charges of sedition.

His intervention struck a sour note with labour, but he regained his standing somewhat when he implemented an article of the Constitution that called for workers to share profits with management. As a result, the earnings of many workers increased by five to ten per cent a year.

López Mateos increased land redistribution by allotting 30 million acres to individuals and *ejidos,* more than the total distributed in the past eighteen years, and relieved land tensions in the north by clearing new lands in the forests of Quintana Roo and the Isthmus of Tehuantepec. The government also established a food distribution system to provide affordable staples for lower-income people and a market for farm produce. Health care and old age pensions were increased, and the IMSS programme for rural Mexico was expanded. The government also purchased the cinema industry, and the president decreed that ticket prices would be affordable to all.

The first foreign-policy test for López Mateo came when, in 1959, Fidel Castro overthrew the rightist government of Fulgencia Batista and established a Marxist government in Cuba. It had long been Mexico's policy to recognize all foreign governments, regardless of how they had come to power, and López Mateo refused to yield to pressure from the United States to place an embargo on Cuba and vote for Cuba's expulsion from the Organization of American States. The Mexican government condemned the invasion of the Bay of Pigs, and remained the only country in the Western Hemisphere to maintain air service and diplomatic relations with Cuba. Mexico, however, condemned the Soviet Union when they deployed ballistic missiles in Cuba, and relations with the island nation cooled considerably.

During the López Mateos administration, the PRI came under increasing criticism as a one-party democracy, a party accountable only to itself that refused to tolerate the voice of opposition. López Mateos was sensitive to the issue, and sponsored an amendment to the Constitution that allowed opposition candidates access to the lower House of Congress.

THE TLATELOLCO MASSACRE

Gustavo Díaz Ordaz had been a judge, a professor of law, a vice-rector of the University of Puebla, a federal deputy, and Secretary of the Interior in the López Mateos Administration. He was a devoted Catholic, an enemy of Communism, and a conservative. A hard-liner against labour strikes, he was López Mateos's hatchet man who put down the National Railroad strike by sending in the army, and it was Ordaz who invoked the law of 'social dissolution' that sent David Siqueiros to prison. Later, Díaz Ordaz again used military force to crush a strike of doctors and nurses. But after winning the presidential election in 1964, Díaz Ordaz pledged to carry out the liberal policies of his predecessor.

The 1968 Olympics were to be the defining moment of the Díaz Ordaz administration, a showcase for the entire nation. It was the first time in history that the International Olympic Committee had awarded the games to Latin America or to a developing country. In preparation, the city embarked upon a crash programme to build athletics facilities, housing for the Olympians, hotels for the hundreds of thousands of tourists expected, and to complete the new underground system. Critics howled that the costs were prohibitive, but the government held its ground with projections that hundreds of millions of dollars would be left behind by tourism, and help its plans for the new housing and facilities after the competitors left.

But the timing for the Olympics was not especially favourable, since the 1960s was a period of increasing unrest throughout the nation. Student strikes shut down one university after another, and the less affluent of the middle classes were beginning to join protest marches. A 1966 strike at the National University forced the rector to resign, and radical groups fought among themselves for leadership of the new movement. Violence in the streets erupted in July 1968, when a fight broke out in the streets between a college preparatory school and a vocational school. Fights were common among student groups, but this one escalated into a major riot when the mayor of the Federal District sent the *granaderos*, a paramilitary riot force, to break up the fighting. A few days later, leftist students gathered to celebrate the anniversary of the Cuban Revolution, and another major riot broke out when the *granaderos* tried to disband the assembly.

In August, representatives from the schools of higher education in the capital and schools from other major cities gathered in Mexico City to organize the National Strike Committee (CNH). Shortly afterwards, the Coalición de Maestros (Coalition of Teachers) was organized to support the students. On 4 August the CNH sent a list of six demands to the government.

1. dissolution of the *granaderos*
2. removal of the two most important police chiefs
3. respect for the autonomy of the universities
4. redress for anyone injured by the *granaderos*
5. repeal of the laws of 'social dissolution'
6. release of all political prisoners.

On 27 August the students held a massive rally in the Zócalo, shouting, 'We don't want the Olympics! We want the Revolution!' There were speeches, pictures of Che Guevara pasted on the walls, cathedral bells ringing, and the red and black flag of Cuba's Revolution draped over a lamp-post. When no dialogue with the government was forthcoming, the CNH left a team to occupy the Zócalo until their next meeting, scheduled for 1 September.

On 28 August the police, backed up by armoured cars, entered the Zócalo and moved three thousand demonstrators out into the streets. Police and students fought each other in the centre of the city until the army moved in with tanks and pushed the students back beyond the Alameda. When a small van with University identification crossed their path, the police stopped it and beat up the passengers, including the women. As daylight grew stronger, more units of police arrived, and the fighting broke out again. The army returned with fourteen tanks, and students stood fast before them while the body of protesters retreated. As the soldiers advanced, people in buildings along the way dropped rubbish, bottles, and flowerpots on them.

In the days that followed, tanks were deployed along the perimeter of the National University while masked men entered the campus and attacked students with clubs, blackjacks, and metal pipes. On 31 August 200 armed men in plain clothes attacked a preparatory school and threw the students into cattle lorries after beating them senseless. That day, the CNH asked for a dialogue with the government without police or army interference. In their statement to the president, they wrote:

Even during the celebration of the 19th Olympic Games, we pledge to sweep the streets every day ... to serve as ushers, as interpreters. ... Before being students in a struggle to achieve greater freedom and democracy, we are Mexicans.... We are not against the Olympics. We want Mexico to fulfill its Olympic commitment with dignity.

On 13 September 200,000 students marched along the Paseo Reforma in a silent protest, wearing handkerchiefs tied over their mouths while helicopters hovered overhead. On 15 September, the students celebrated Independence Day on the esplanade of University City, and three days later, the army moved in and closed down the University. The students offered no resistance, but five hundred people, including members of the faculty, were arrested.

On 2 October a week before the Olympic Games were to begin, the CNH called for an assembly in the Plaza of Three Cultures in Tlatelolco. What followed was a deliberate and well-planned attack on the students.

The morning of the day the meeting was to begin, tanks surrounded the plaza, but their presence was no surprise to the students nor of any particular concern – by now they were a familiar sight. It has never been clear how many people gathered in the square that day, but their number has been estimated at between five and ten thousand.

Mingling among the crowd were young men each wearing a white glove or a white handkerchief knotted about the left hand. At about 6.20 in the evening, helicopters began circling the plaza, and when a flare was dropped, the men wearing white gloves made a dash to the third floor of the Edificio Chihuahua and ordered the protest leaders to lie on the floor. The men were from the Battalion Olympia, the security force for the Olympics. Without warning, the helicopters and troops stationed in the upper floors of the buildings surrounding the plaza opened fire on the crowd below with heavy weapons. The crowd dashed for the safety of the streets, but soldiers moving into the plaza pushed them back into the field of fire.

To justify the attack, it had to appear than the students opened fire first. Snipers armed with .22-calibre rifles were stationed on the roofs of the surrounding buildings, and as the attack began, they fired at random into the crowd below. One of the shots struck the commander, General Hernández Toledo. With the shooting of a general with a non-military weapon, the government could now claim that the army retaliated only after being attacked by the demonstrators.

Heavy fire poured into the crowd for sixty-two minutes, then a ceasefire was called. A small tank fired a single round, and the firing began again and continued until eleven o'clock that night.

At daylight, the cover-up began. Street lights were turned off, the telephone service was cut, journalists were barred from the area, and a crew was busy spreading sawdust across the plaza floor to hide the bloodstained pavement.

How many died that night may never be known. The government admits to 43 deaths, but the *Manchester Guardian* reported 325 fatalities, a number considered closer to the truth by witnesses to the massacre. There were no bodies left to be counted or given a decent funeral – trucks hauled them away to a secret location and burned them.★

Each year on 2 October candles burn in the Plaza of Three Cultures in memory of those who died.

Surprisingly, the Olympics were relatively free from disturbance, but there were internal repercussions. The Mexican poet Octavio Paz, then Ambassador to India, resigned his post in protest and compared the massacre to the charnel houses at Tlatelolco where the Aztecs made their mass sacrifices. Lázaro Cárdenas accused the administration of betraying the Revolution by using arms against the students, and questioned the legitimacy of the PRI to represent the people.

LUIZ ECHEVERRÍA ALVAREZ

Next to the president, the most important post in the government was that of Minister of the Interior, more commonly referred to as the 'Enforcer'. Luis Echeverría served in that post for twelve years, first as Assistant Minister of the Interior under Díaz Ordaz during the López Mateos administration, then as Minister when Díaz Ordaz assumed the presidency.

Early in his term as president, Echeverría promised to end the strife between the government and the universities, but in spite of his relative anonymity, the students knew who to blame for the Tlatelolco Mas-

★ The author is indebted to Enrique Krauze, *Mexico, Biography of Power*, New York, 1997, for his detailed report of the Tlatelolco Massacre and the events that led up to it.

University City, Mexico City

sacre. He asked for a private dialogue with the student leaders to resolve their differences, but the students demanded a public one, which he declined. Student demonstrations continued, but the government's suppression, although less visible, was more covert and systematic.

The most violent incident during the Echeverría Administration occurred on 10 June 1971, Corpus Christi Thursday, when thousands of students marched in the streets to demand the release of political prisoners. Without warning, a group of thugs dressed as students charged into their midst and attacked them with martial arts batons. Bloody and beaten, the injured were seized and dragged off into a side street and hauled away in unmarked police cars and ambulances. When the assault was over, eleven students lay dead, more than 200 were wounded, and thirty-five were missing.

Echeverría appeared on television that night and announced that an immediate investigation would take place no matter where the blame might fall. Within a few days two highly placed officials, the Regent of the Federal District and the Chief of Police, resigned, but the investigation never went any further. Later in his term, Echeverría attempted to address a student convocation at the National University, but he was met with a hail of stones and driven off the campus.

Thirty years of unprecedented economic growth in Mexico ended early in the 1970s when the nation was caught in a worldwide depression. The foreign debt reached $20 billion, and government expenses exceeded income by a large margin. To offset the deficit, the government raised prices for petrol, increased fees for electrical and telephone services, printed more money, and imposed rigid price controls on all basic commodities. A 10 per cent tax was added to all luxury items, and a surcharge of 15 per cent added to restaurant and night-club bills. Inflation rose to more than 20 per cent a year, but the worst was yet to come. The peso was devalued for the first time in twenty-two years, causing a flight of capital as investors moved money into foreign investments and people rushed to exchange pesos for dollars. And with unemployment reaching new heights, a mass migration into the United States took place.

In the countryside, sporadic incidences of violence erupted, and a radical liberal movement began to hold up banks to finance the coming revolution. In the mountains of Guerrero, guerrilla forces assassinated the chief of police in Acapulco, and kidnapped a prominent senator who was a candidate for governorship of the state. A series of political kidnappings followed as the Rector of the University of Guerrero, the United States Consul General in Guadalajara, the British Honorary Consul, a wealthy Guadalajara business man, and the daughter of the Belgian Ambassador were seized. Even José Guadalupe Zuno, Echeverría's father-in-law, was held for ransom.

Troubles in the country for Echeverría continued as thousands of landless peons in Sonora invaded the rich Yaqui Valley and seized almost a quarter-of-a-million acres of privately owned land. While the issue was still under review by the Supreme Court, Echeverría took the unilateral action of declaring that the lands held by the owners exceeded Constitutional limits and granted the peasants 250,000 acres for communal development. Echeverría's decision resulted in a protest strike by businessmen, industrialists, and landowners that threatened to shut down the country.

On the international front, Echeverría toured Ecuador, Peru, Argentina, Brazil, and Venezuela to promote regional economic co-operation and to urge the lifting of the economic blockade against Cuba. He supported the admission of the People's Republic of China into the United Nations, and the following year, established diplomatic relations with China.

Echeverría's government had strong ties with the Salvador Allende administration in Chile, and the overthrow of the government and murder of Allende by the CIA-sponsored Pinochet junta outraged all of Mexico. Echeverría welcomed exiled Chilean leftists into Mexico and even found them positions in his Administration.

In 1970, Echeverría assumed the presidency of the OAS, the Organization of American States, but during his tenure, he never failed to express his dissatisfaction with the organization. In a 1974 address to the National Congress, he said, 'The OAS is more inoperative every day. It cannot achieve strength of any kind unless it carries out a basic reform of its own structure and methods and confronts the reality of political pluralism. It must not insist on remaining a theatrical backdrop for undisguisable hegemonic maneuvers.'

Echeverría also favoured Panamanian sovereignty over the canal, the drafting of a code to regulate the activities of transnational corporations, transfer of technology at a reasonable cost, and the lifting of sanctions against Cuba.

As his term drew to an end in 1976, he announced his candidacy for the post of Secretary General of the United Nations. His bid, however, met with disaster when he compared Yasser Arafat to Benito Juárez, and ordered his representative in the United Nations to cast two votes equating Zionism with racism. His speech cost Mexico untold millions of dollars when Jewish groups in the United States organized a tourist boycott of Mexico.

José López Portillo y Pacheco

In another society, López Portillo could have laid claim to the aris-tocracy. Of pure *criollo* ancestry, he claimed direct descent from the conquistadors, from those who had discovered the Philippines, and from the first settlers of Sonora. A man of moderate wealth, López Portillo found sufficient time to paint and to produce three books. The first, *Genesis and Theory of the Modern State,* was a somewhat scholarly treatise, the others novels entitled *Quetzalcoatl* and *Don Q.* In the last, he saw himself as a reincarnation of Quetzalcoatl, who would one day return to his people and redeem them from their evil ways.

López Portillo's early career in politics was not particularly noteworthy. Through three administrations he served in minor government posts, and may have spent his entire career in anonymity had it not been for his close friend, Luis Echeverría, whom he served as Minister of Finance. Three years later, the *dedazo* pointed his way, and he was elected without opposition when PAN declined to nominate a candidate.

Using his recent expertise in government finance, López Portillo reorganized the federal bureaucracy and centralized control of the budget. His appointees to high-level positions were businessmen, labour chiefs, scholars, peasant leaders, and, of course, relatives. His sister, his son, and his cousin all held important posts, and Rosa Luz Alegría, his mistress, was appointed Minister of Tourism.

López Portillo began his term as president of a bankrupt nation. Flight of capital, inability of Mexican products to compete with foreign products, government subsidies of agricultural produce, and devaluation of the peso increased the national debt to almost $50 billion by 1976. A loan of an emergency $1.2 billion by the IMF bailed López Portillo out temporarily, but restrictive guidelines were imposed upon the federal budget, trade policies, and wages. The austerity programme demanded by the IMF reduced growth of the GDP to 3 per cent a year.

But the PRI had an ace up its sleeve. Vast deposits of oil had been discovered near the Chiapas-Tabasco border in 1974, but Echeverría, wary of pressure from the United States, had been reluctant to disclose the full extent of the discovery. Oil had also been found in the floor of the Caribbean, and by 1979, offshore oil increased Mexico's estimated reserves to make it the fifth largest oil producer in the world. In June, another gusher in the Caribbean erupted and discharged 30,000 barrels of oil a day into the sea for nine months, fouling every beach from

Campeche to Texas. From 1976 to 1980, annual income from petroleum increased from $500 million to $6 billion. By 1982, proven oil reserves were estimated to be 72 billion barrels, and probable reserves between 90 and 150 billion barrels. In addition to the nation's petroleum riches, Mexico had proven natural gas reserves of 200 trillion cubic feet.

Credit was no longer a problem. The IMF and the World Bank were prepared to underwrite López Portillo's government programmes, foreign investments flowed back into Mexico, and US President Jimmy Carter paid a state visit to discuss trade agreements.

With the booming economy, López Portillo began a series of ambitious programmes for public works, industrial expansion, social welfare, and government subsidies of consumer goods. The government laid new pipelines, and built more tanker facilities and petrochemical plants. To exploit the new offshore wells, Mexico was forced to borrow more millions from overseas to pay for expensive machinery and new technologies. Debt service now reduced national income to below the cost of the government's new programmes, but Mexico was confident that rising oil prices would offset the budget deficit. Unfortunately a world glut of oil in the early 1980s caused prices to fall, and Lopez Portillo's critics began to question his strategy of modernizing the nation through capital-intensive projects and deficit financing.

Agriculture remained a continuing problem as Mexico was still dependent upon imports for basic staples. In 1980, for example, grain imports from the United States totalled 8.2 million tons, and sugar, which was once an export product, was now imported from Cuba. To reduce Mexico's dependency on imports, the government inaugurated the Sistema Alimentario Mexicano (SAM) in 1980. A programme of government subsidies, the goal was to reach an agricultural growth of 4 per cent a year and reach self-sufficiency in grain by 1985. The government gave price guarantees to growers, and agreed to compensate farmers in the event of crop failure. The scheme was amply funded by a loan of $325 million from the World Bank, but it fell far short of its goals. In the 1980s, Mexico imported 10 million tons of food annually and paid for it with petro-dollars.

With the leverage of a worldwide need for petroleum, Mexico could now afford to take a more aggressive stand in international affairs. In 1979, thousands appeared in the streets to mock Jimmy Carter when he arrived in Mexico to discuss trade controls, drug smuggling, illegal Mexican immigration, and, of course, petroleum, which was now in critical demand because of the OPEC crisis (Mexico was not a member of OPEC). López Portillo chose the occasion to remind Carter of past aggressions of the United States south of the border and its continuing lack of respect for Mexican dignity. He also refused to support the United States' boycott of the Moscow Olympics.

Mexico also took a defiant stand against the policies of the United States in the Caribbean and in Central America. The Reagan Administration was concerned about the proximity of leftist rebel activity in Nicaragua and El Salvador to the oil fields of Mexico, which Washington considered a strategic resource. If Anastasio Somoza was ousted in Nicaragua, the Administration feared the domino effect would spread Communism northwards and force the United States into a military confrontation.

On 10 March 1983, Ronald Reagan said: 'If guerrilla violence succeeds, El Salvador will join Cuba and Nicaragua for spreading fresh violence to Guatemala, Honduras, even Costa Rica. The killing will increase and so will the threat to Panama, the canal, and ultimately Mexico.' Other ultra-conservatives in the Administration and in Congress warned that the Communists were no more than a two-day drive from Harlingen, Texas, and even Hollywood got in the act by producing *Red Dawn*, a film that predicted a Communist invasion from the south.

When Somoza was overthrown by the Sandanistas, López Portillo immediately took up their cause, proclaiming their Revolution had been fought for the same freedoms for which Mexico and Cuba had shed their blood. When the last of Somoza's troops left Nicaragua, López Portillo transported the rebel leaders to Managua in the presidential jet.

The following year López Portillo joined François Mitterand of France in an offer to negotiate a truce between the right-wing ARENA government of El Salvador and the revolutionary Farabundo Martí

National Liberation Front (FMLN). López Portillo even offered the FMNL facilities in Mexico City as headquarters for their movement.

In 1981, another economic crunch began in Mexico. A worldwide glut of oil forced Mexico to cut back production and to reduce export prices by $8 a barrel. In August 1982 the international community bailed out Mexico again with a loan of $10 billion, part of which guaranteed bargain prices for gas and oil sales to the United States. In 1982, the government postponed payment on the national debt, which had risen to $80 billion, a quarter of which came from private investors. As investors and businessmen lost confidence in the economy, they began shifting assets into foreign investments and bank accounts in the United States. To stop the flight of capital, López Portillo shut down all foreign exchange houses and closed all dollar accounts in Mexico's banks.

In September 1982, in his State-of-the-Nation address, López Portillo informed a stunned populace that he had nationalized fifty-nine banks. The step was justified, he said, because Mexicans, aided by private banks, had taken more money out of the country than all the empires that preceded them.

The president did not leave office a poor man, however. During his term, he built four magnificent mansions on a hill overlooking the city. The people referred to the compound as 'Dog Hill', parodying López Portillo's promise that he would defend the peso 'like a dog'.

The Great Earthquake of 1985

The people had not forgotten the excesses of Tlatelolco and Corpus Christi, nor had they forgotten the reckless mismanagement of resources that left Mexico buried in debt when Miguel de la Madrid Hurtado assumed the presidency in 1982. Furthermore, the economic crisis had substantially weakened the popularity of the PRI and its electoral support. Wisely, de la Madrid chose not to promise the impossible in his inaugural address. Instead, he painted a grim picture of austerity that would have to be pursued if the double-digit inflation rate was to be brought under control.

Integral to his plans was a bail-out loan of $4 billion from the IMF, with restrictive clauses that required the government to curtail public spending, raise taxes, and curb imports. On his own initiative, de la Madrid eliminated new projects, sold off unprofitable State-owned enterprises, reduced federal subsidies, eliminated 50,000 federal jobs, and cut back salaries of employees with permanent positions.

Labour would also have to pay a price, even though de la Madrid's economic and political objectives ran contrary to the State's traditional pact with labour. Specifically, his objectives demanded wage freezes, cutbacks in employment, and elimination of labour conflicts. These changes, however, could not be done by fiat. They could be accomplished only if the labour pact was modified to allow the government to tighten its review of proposed strikes, prohibit strike coalitions, and alter procedures covering wage negotiations.

The government also raised prices of utilities and petrol, doubled the value-added tax, eliminated subsidies for food and transport, and abolished price controls. Again, the burden fell upon those who could least afford it.

Early in his administration, de la Madrid cracked down upon corruption among high-ranking government officials. A former director of PEMEX was convicted for embezzlement of $43 million and sent to jail for ten years, and Mexico City's Chief-of-Police was charged with fifty murders, trafficking in drugs, and extortion. In addition, an audit of his finances was conducted to determine how, on a salary of $65 per week, he managed to buy a palatial residence at the coastal resort of Zihuatanejo, a home near Mexico City housing a casino, a gymnasium, and a discothèque modelled on New York City's Studio 54.

De la Madrid, however, chose not to examine López Portillo's purchase of the 'Dog Hill' mansions during his term as president.

By 1983, de la Madrid's programme began to show promising results. Inflation fell to 80 per cent, and the trade balance showed a surplus of $12 billion. Unfortunately, the slowdown in inflation was offset by a negative 4.7 per cent growth in the NDP. Nevertheless, de la Madrid never missed an instalment on the national debt, no matter what sector of the economy it affected. By 1984, however, the peso began to fall again, and by the summer of 1985 reached 360 to the dollar.

During the morning rush-hour of 19 September 1985, a tectonic plate in the Pacific Ocean shifted, and an earthquake registering more than 8.0 on the Richter Scale shook the unstable ground beneath Mexico City, bringing down tall buildings that buried everything in their path under mountains of rubble.

The great *terremoto* caught the government unprepared, and it reacted slowly and ineffectively to the disaster. The city lacked heavy equipment to move the tons of concrete and bricks in the streets, yet made no plea for help from the international community. The Ministry of Foreign Affairs announced that there were no conditions under which they would seek aid, particularly from the United States.

Before the dust had settled, however, students from preparatory schools, the University, and Politécnico were organizing teams to remove the rubble with picks and shovels to search for survivors. People risked their lives entering crumbling buildings to search for survivors, and among those seeking for their loved ones was the great operatic tenor, Placido Domingo, fruitlessly searching for his aunt.

Aid, however, did come from the American people. Disaster specialists sent dog teams trained to sniff out people caught in the rubble, and others sent volunteers, tents, clothing, medical supplies, food, and anything else that might be needed.

The toll taken by the earthquake has never been determined. Government estimates set it at 10,000, others at 20,000, and those who dug out the dead and dying swore it exceeded more than 30,000. The cost of property damage was estimated at $4 billion.

A second disaster followed the earthquake when the bottom fell out from under the peso. By autumn 1986, the rate fell to 800 to 1 against the dollar, by January 1987 to 950 to 1, and at the end of the year, it stood at a catastrophic 2,300 to 1. When de la Madrid left office in December 1988, the national debt stood at an all-time high of $105 billion.

Carlos Salinas de Gortari

The 1988 elections were contested by all parties. Manual Clouthier, the PAN candidate, advocated closer ties with the United States, a lesser role for government in the economy, incentives for the private sector, and an end to election fraud. Cuauhtémoc Cárdenas, the son of former president Lázaro Cárdenas, who was the candidate of a coalition of leftist parties, called for greater independence from the United States, and proposed deferring the payment on the national debt.

The PRI candidate was forty-year-old Carlos Salinas de Gortari, who had earned a doctorate in economics at Harvard, and served in the de la Madrid cabinet as Secretary of Planning and Budget.

When the first election returns were announced by the Ministry of the Interior, the negligible difference between the votes for Cárdenas and Salinas stunned the PRI monitors. Unfortunately, the computer system 'crashed' before the final results were in, and when the results were tabulated electronically, Salinas was declared the winner. His opponents claimed fraud, but since the PRI controlled the election machinery, there was no way of establishing an accurate count of the vote. Salinas took possession of the records and stored them in the cellars of the Legislature, where they were burned. Later that year it was revealed that Raul Salinas, the brother of the president, arranged for the police to tap Cárdenas's telephones, and a few days before the election, Cárdenas's top aide was killed to intimidate his campaign workers. The decline of voter confidence in the PRI, however, was manifest inasmuch as Salinas received only 50 per cent of the vote, the lowest margin ever for a presidential candidate.

Cárdenas, encouraged by his performance in the election, decided a leftist party would be viable in the next election and formed the Party of Democratic Revolution (PRD).

In the state elections, however, opposition candidates broke the grip of the PRI for the first time. PAN candidate Ernesto Ruffo won the governorship of Baja California Norte, and another PAN candidate, Francisco Barrios, was elected governor of Chihuahua.

Salinas's economic reform policy was similar to that of de la Madrid, but his policies were more consistent, more extensive, and yielded better results. He privatized such major enterprises as Telemex, the telephone monopoly, the banks, and the State television station. He privatized the airlines, the highways, sugar mills, and even the cinemas. By 1994, the number of State firms had been reduced to twenty-seven. In 1990 Salinas renegotiated the foreign debt and reduced the interest and principal payments by 35 per cent. By 1992, he had balanced the budget by cutting government spending, and through an anti-inflation pact with industry and a strict wages policy, slowed down inflation. Price increases fell from 159 per cent in 1987 to less than 10 per cent in 1993.

In 1992, Salinas was granted an audience with Pope John Paul II, and for the first time in 130 years, diplomatic relations between Mexico and the Vatican were restored. Churches could now purchase property, open religious schools, and perform public celebrations.

As early as his second month in office, Salinas cracked down on the labour unions. He arrested Joaquín Hernández, the powerful leader of the Oil Workers Union – ostensibly for graft, but also for supporting Cárdenas and financing a tract relating Salinas's accidental killing of a servant when he was eight years old. The next labour leader to face arrest was Agapito González Cavazo on charges of tax evasion – one day, incidentally, before his Union of Journeymen and Industrial workers was scheduled to strike.

The *ejidos* were anathema to Salinas, and he viewed land redistribution as a dinosaur left over from the Revolution. *Ejidos*, the communal lands, made up about a quarter of Mexico's arable land, and Salinas looked upon them as unproductive and a prime example of why Mexico was not self-sufficient in food production. One had to look no further than Mexico's northern neighbour for justification of his argument. In 1978, the yield of maize in the United States was five times that of Mexico, the potato crop double, and tobacco 50 per cent greater. The primary factors for Mexico's poor production were that the size of the average farm was less than 12 acres, which prevented the use of machinery, and the *ejidos*. In 95 per cent of the *ejidos*, land was assigned to an individual to keep as long as he worked it, but without a title, he had no collateral to offer for loans or for purchasing seed.

Salinas's solution was to modify the 'untouchable' Article 27 of the Constitution. The government formulated a fast-track programme that could funnel funds directly to peasants without burdensome processing through the bureaucracy. The programme, called Solidarity, provided for private ownership of *ejido* lands, and granted titles to the peasants that allowed them to sell, mortgage, trade, or lease their lands. There had been no consultation with peasants and no national referendum.

As the economy gained steam and Salinas's stature in the world community grew, he moved to join the North American Free Trade Agreement, (NAFTA), which he believed was vital to the long-term economic health of Mexico. There would be considerable opposition from hard-line Revolutionaries, he knew, who believed that free trade would put Mexico at a disadvantage with the United States and Canada, and many were suspicious of closer ties with the Americans. To sell the idea to Mexican business as well as to his northern partners, Salinas gave a prominent role to the business community in the NAFTA negotiations. In many areas, private-sector representatives led the negotiations and planned public-relations campaigns in Mexico as well as in the United States. The signing of the agreement triggered a wave of new investments within Mexico as well as from overseas, and during June 1994, $49 billion was pumped into an economy that was growing at 3.45 per cent a year.

NAFTA and the Zapatistas

Chiapas is the most resource-rich state in Mexico. With less than 4 per cent of Mexico's population, it is the country's largest coffee exporter, the third largest maize producer, and among the top three states in exports of bananas, tobacco, and cacao. Cattle-ranching is growing at an unprecedented rate, hydro-electric power is readily available, and most important, Chiapas has some of the richest oil reserves in Mexico.

Yet 75 per cent of the state's population lives below the poverty line in deplorable conditions. Nineteen per cent of the state's economically active population have no cash income, and 39 per cent earn less than the minimum wage, some $3 a day. Three-quarters of the population are malnourished, half live in homes with dirt floors, and 30 per cent of the children do not attend school.

Ejidos count for 54 per cent of the land in Chiapas, but only 11 per cent is commercially viable. On the other 43 per cent, subsistence peasants consume most of what they produce and market less than that which is needed to obtain the basic necessities of life.

When Salinas launched his attack on the *ejidos*, he was in effect destroying the culture that had sustained the Maya peasant from time immemorial. His Solidarity Programme, which gave the peasants the right to own their land, came at a price they were unwilling to pay – it removed the provision in Article 27 that protected the *ejido* from seizure of its lands to pay off debts. Furthermore, with import duties lifted under NAFTA, the peasant could not hope to compete with the flood of cheap maize and other staple goods from the United States.

On 17 November 1993, the Congress of the United States approved the North American Free Trade Agreement, and on the morning of 1 January 1994, a clandestine organization of Maya Indians known as the Zapatista Army of National Liberation (EZLN), rebelled in Chiapas. Led by a masked man calling himself Sub-commandante Marcos, the EZLN seized six towns in Chiapas, including San Cristóbal de las Casas, the second largest city in the state. Sub-commandant Marcos was later identified as Raphael Sebastián Guillén Vincente, a Westernized *mestizo* educated in Mexico City and a former volunteer worker for the

Raphael Sebastián Guillén Vincente – 'Sub-commandante Marcos'

Sandanistas in Nicaragua – though he never confirmed his identity. Limited encounters with government forces in San Cristóbal and the surrounding areas killed 145 and wounded hundreds, but after ten days, the Zapatistas withdrew and disappeared into the Chiapas jungle.

The 12,000-man rebel army that took San Cristóbal, however, was only the tip of an iceberg that the government would have to consider. The EZLN was only the military wing of the rebels, subordinate to civilian leadership. The high command was the Clandestine Revolutionary Indigenous Committee-General Command (CCRI-CG), made up of representatives from all the Maya communities – Tzotzil, Tzeltal, Chol, Mam, Tojolobal, and Zoque. Thus for a thousand soldiers under arms, tens of thousands of villagers from the confederation stood ready to fight.

Salinas, however, had no intention of initiating another Tlatelolco public relations' disaster. He ordered the army to dislodge the Zapatistas from the cities, drive them into the jungle, and set up a perimeter of containment. Shortly afterwards, the government issued a unilateral ceasefire, and Bishop Samuel Ruiz was approved by both sides to negotiate between the government and the ELZN.

ERNESTO ZEDILLO PONCE DE LEÓN

Luis Donaldo Colosio, an economist educated at Northwestern University and a protégé of Salinas, was chosen as the PRI candidate for the presidential elections of 1994. Colosio, however, never seemed certain that he really wanted to be president. The Zapatista uprising had depressed him and caused him to reconsider Mexico's progress in human rights and the fight against poverty. Furthermore, his wife had terminal cancer, and he refused to leave her until she pressed him to accept the nomination.

On 6 March 1994, Colosio distanced himself from Salinas in a bold campaign speech. Instead of praising Salinas's accomplishments, he described Mexico as an impoverished Third-World nation and promised to separate the PRI from the government. Two weeks later, as he moved through a crowd of well-wishers in Tijuana, a single gunman, Mario Aburto Martinéz, shot him in the head. The Mexican people were never convinced that Aburto acted alone, but no evidence ever surfaced that Colosio's murder was politically motivated.

In August 1994, Ernesto Zedillo, the PRI candidate, was elected president of Mexico with a majority of 50 per cent of the national vote. The PRI maintained its strong majority in Congress, but PAN doubled its 1988 vote totals. The PRD, however, fared poorly with a total vote of only 20 per cent. The election was fairly clean, and the opposition, with the exception of the EZLN, accepted the results.

Zedillo's first year in office would prove to be a trial by fire, as economic woes were followed by a massive scandal that rocked the nation.

On 19 December, three weeks after Zedillo had been sworn in, he withdrew the Bank of Mexico's support of the peso, and the exchange rate plummeted from 3.4 to 7.0 to the dollar. Despite a $50-billion bail-out by the Clinton Administration and Zedillo's renewing wage and price controls, however, the situation continued to deteriorate.

The problem had arisen during the latter part of the Salinas Administration when foreign investments fell off due to the uncertainty of the political situation caused by the uprising in Chiapas, the assassination of Colosio, and the subsequent assassination of José Francisco Ruíz Massieu, the deputy head of the PRI. These events, coupled with the nation's growing trade deficit, caused Salinas to allocate $20 billion of the nation's international reserves to shore up the peso. Unfortunately, Salinas chose not to devalue before leaving office, leaving Zedillo to clean up the mess.

The scandal, which reached to the highest levels of government, began when the PRI reformist, José Francisco Ruíz Massieu was gunned down in the streets in September 1994. The government blamed a lone gunman, but the public, well inured to high-level politics, chose to believe that his killing was a conspiracy promoted by PRI hard-liners.

The gunman, Daniel Aguilar, was captured and claimed that PRI Congressman Manuel Munoz Rocha had ordered the hit on Massieu, but Rocha was nowhere to be found. It was rumoured that he was either hiding in Texas or dead. With Rocha's disappearance, suspicion shifted to Raul Salinas, Carlos Salinas's brother and Ruíz Massieu's brother-in-law. He was arrested and charged with being an accessory to the murder. During the investigation, Raul Salinas was found to have accumulated $200 million while in office.

Mario Ruíz Massieu, the brother of José Francisco was chosen to lead a probe into the assassination, but he quit after being accused of steering the probe away from Raul Salinas. In 1995, Ruíz Massieu was detained in Newark, N.J. while fleeing to Spain. An investigation of his finances revealed that he had deposited $9 million in cash in a Houston bank during the time he had served as a prosecutor in Mexico. The cash shipments were properly declared on Customs and IRS forms, but a United States jury confiscated $7.9 million of the funds on suspicion that it was laundered money from drug dealers. The evidence against Massieu was thin, but judges blocked four attempts by the government to deport him.

Francisca Zetina, a psychic employed by Maria Bernal, Raul Salinas's former mistress, claimed to have proof that Salinas had bludgeoned Munoz Rocha to death. Zetina led Pablo Chapa, the chief investigator of the Massieu and Colosio assassinations to Salinas's ranch, where she claimed Rocha's body was buried. Chapa triumphantly announced that Rocha's body had been found, but subsequent forensic tests proved the body to be that of Zetina's father-in-law, whose body had been dug up and planted on Salinas's ranch to frame him. Chapa went into hiding, and Zetina and Bernal were charged with obstruction of justice. The scandal sent Carlos Salinas to Ireland seeking asylum

In 1999, Raul Salinas was found guilty of the murder of José Francisco 'Pepe' Ruíz Massieu and sentenced to 50 years in prison. Six months later, a Mexican appeals court reduced his sentence to 27 years and six months.

One of the more significant social programmes furthered under the Zedillo Administration was the enfranchisement of Mexican women. While the Equal Rights Amendment languished in the United States Congress, Mexico now promises women equal job opportunities, equivalent salaries, and legal standing. Hundreds of women serve as police officers, and are considered by many to be less corruptible than their male counterparts. Ten women have been elected to the Senate, 55 to the Chamber of Deputies, and one, Socorro Díaz, has served the Chamber as its first woman president.

Overpopulation, however, still looms as Mexico's greatest problem. The population in 1944 was 22 million, and by 1998 had reached 97 million, a growth rate of 1.9 per cent annually. In 1968, the situation seemed hopeless when the Vatican banned all methods of contraception. In 1970, more than six hundred thousand Mexican women underwent illegal abortions, and thirty-two thousand died. By 1972, the situation forced the Council of Mexican Bishops to issue a pastoral letter encouraging couples to make responsible decisions about the size of their families. Government-sponsored clinics were established to offer birth-control literature, and by 1992, more than six thousand family planning centres were in operation throughout the country.

Under the Zedillo Administration, a progressive approach to family planning was implemented that focused upon everyone from elementary school students to married parents. Fifth and sixth graders were provided with explicit textbooks that taught 'how babies are made', and personal counselling in Mexico's poorest slums answered such questions as why and how to use a condom.

Government programmes run television spots on a daily basis that focus on delaying sexual relations, sterilization, and spacing of children. The spots address not only family planning but the man's role in contraception and vasectomy and communication among couples.

Mexfam, the largest non-government family planning service, works throughout the country, concentrating its efforts in slum areas. Here teenagers come from families with six-to-eight children, and receive their sex education not from their parents, but from TV, and unwed mothers in the barrios bear an estimated 372,000 children each year. Mexfam does not advocate abortion, which would put it on a collision course with the Catholic Church, but does provide information on 'emergency contraceptive pills' that may be taken within 72 hours after sex to prevent pregnancies.

The goal of government and privately funded programmes is to reach a balance between births and deaths by the year 2005, but much work is yet to be done.

1997, the Mid-term Elections

Early in his presidency, Zedillo, in view of growing public antagonism against the PRI, recognized that major changes in the political system could wait no longer. In an unprecedented move, he named independents and a member of PAN to his Cabinet, requested more participation in government from Congress, and even initiated discussions with the PRD. In the war against corruption, he forced the resignation of the entire Supreme Court, re-organized the police forces, and established a means whereby the citizenry could file complaints against corrupt officials. Among Zedillo's more important election-reform programmes was the creation of the Federal Election Institute (IFE), an autonomous government agency that supervised the voting. The agency was made independent of PRI control in 1996.

On 6 July 1997, the PRI won 239 seats in the mid-term elections, a dozen short of an overall majority. PRD won a surprising 125 seats, PAN 122, the Green Ecology Party eight, and the Worker's Party six. A coalition of the minority parties was now in a position to block government spending plans, call Cabinet members to account, and even impeach them. In the states, PAN won four additional governorships and elected a number of mayors in major cities.

The most significant victory, however, was in Mexico City, where Cuauhtémoc Cárdenas defeated Alfredo del Mazo by a majority of nearly two to one. It was the first election of a mayor since 1968, when the city expanded its boundaries and the president was given the responsibility of appointing the mayor.

Cárdenas's platform was to rid the police force of corrupt commanders, move the army out of the city, attack corruption in the highest levels of government as well as in the street, and to initiate programmes that would reduce the severe air pollution of the city.

Cárdenas's progress, however, was slow, and 15 months after the election, little had been accomplished. Among Cárdenas's many problems was the city administration, where more than two-thirds of the personnel belonged to a union controlled by the PRI. The union's employees were, by law, practically impossible to dismiss, and attempts to prosecute or discipline them were met with threats to strike and shut down the city. Compounding Cardenas's problems was the city budget. Although he controlled the federal district, the president controlled the surrounding metropolitan area and held the responsibility of allocating funds for the federal district.

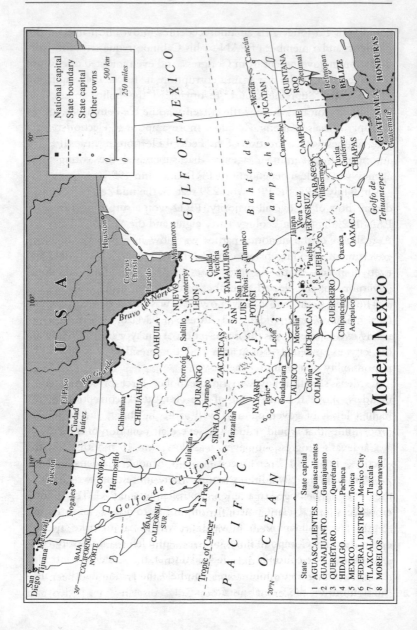

Modern Mexico

In 1999, Cuauhtémoc Cárdenas was forced to admit he lacked the power to carry out his reforms, and he submitted his resignation.

Election 2000 – the Velvet Revolution

Zedillo, as promised, forsook the *dedazo* and held an open primary to choose the presidential candidate of the PRI, breaking with seven decades of authoritarian tradition. To ensure a clean primary, the party spent $3.3 million to organize the vote, nearly as much as was spent for a presidential election. The party established 64,200 polling stations nationwide, and hired more than 450,000 people as officials and poll watchers. Any registered voter was allowed to cast a ballot, whether a member of the party or not.

Although there were instances of irregularity, such as vote-buying with handouts of food, threats, promises of government aid by the PRI, and ballots stolen and burned in polling stations, the elections were orderly overall, and no charges of fraud were filed by minority parties when Francisco Labastida won the primary.

The opposition candidates were Vincente Fox Quesada, a centre-right politician chosen by PAN, and Cuauhtémoc Cárdenas, the left-centre candidate from the PRD.

Francisco Labastida, an ex-governor of Sinaloa, was an economic conservative and a social liberal. In the Zedillo Cabinet, he had held three secretarial posts: Interior, Energy, and Agriculture. Critical of Zedillo's free-market, free-trade policies, he proposed to concentrate on supporting domestic industries rather than exports. He viewed political reform as a gradual process that would build a 'healthy closeness' of the PRI to the government, a marked departure from Zedillo's policy of a 'healthy distance' between government and the PRI. His primary advantage in gaining the presidency was the Zedillo Administration's lowering of inflation and the steady growth of the nation. His liabilities were his inability to deal with the Zapatista uprising while Secretary of the Interior, and the fact that he was the first president in 18 years who did not speak English.

Vincente Fox was a businessman and a rancher. He had been the chief executive officer of the Coca-Cola company in Mexico and

Vincente Fox, the political maverick

Central America, and had served a term as governor of Guanajuato. His primary economic goals were to develop a 'Silicon Valley of the South' in Mexico and to amend NAFTA to protect migrant workers. He proposed to withdraw the army from the Indian areas of Chiapas, and disarm the rightist military groups as well as the Zapatistas.

Political reform and corruption were major issues with Fox, but perhaps the most important feature of his platform was his proposal to transfer federal funds to municipal governments. Each year, a flat 5 per cent of the budget went to local governments which, in many cases, left little money for basic needs, such as clean water supplies, paved streets, and adequate waste-disposal facilities. Under the Fox plan, cities would now have incentives to pursue progressive economic goals, such as attracting manufacturing plants, promoting tourism, marketing local products, and other fund-raising projects.

Fox is a political maverick. In 1997, he declared his candidacy for the presidency without seeking permission from the party, and immediately set about distancing himself from the public perception of PAN as a pro-Catholic élite party. The party formally nominated him in 1998, although some of the party leaders made no attempt to show their dislike for him. He recruited several prominent leftist intellectuals to his side, and entered into an alliance with the centrist Green Ecology Party of Mexico. During the campaign, he tacitly repudiated the conservative ideology of PAN, and was outspoken in supporting abortion with no restrictions, opposed religious education in public schools, and supported gay rights. Other than the PRI political machinery, his biggest problem seemed to be the threat of Cárdenas pulling votes away from him.

Cuauhtémoc Cárdenas, the left-of-centre former mayor of Mexico City, was making his third run for the presidency. His economic programme proposed an increase of taxes on the wealthy, reduction of taxes on the poor and the middle class, and renegotiation of the foreign debt. His political-reform platform was essentially the same as that of Fox, and his position on the Chiapas uprising differed only in that he would not disarm the Zapatistas. With no chance of winning, he was criticized by the left for improving the chances for a PRI victory by failing to throw his support behind Fox.

The IRE went to great lengths to ensure a fair and honest election. With a budget of \$492 million, each of the main parties received \$118 million for campaign expenses, and the remainder went for the training of 800,000 civilian poll watchers, transparent ballot boxes, and curtained voting booths. Opposition parties sent representatives to all 113,000 polling stations; the Civic Alliance Watchdog assigned 2,000 members to monitor the election; and the Carter Center of Atlanta sent representatives to spend election day at each party's headquarters. The Grupo Reforma newspapers sent 100 reporters to remote areas of Mexico to conduct exit polls and compare them with the official tallies. Nearly all observers agreed that the election would be the fairest ever.

For the PRI, however, a victory by a narrow margin would be perceived that the election had been rigged. To improve the margin, in spite of protests by the IFE, the PRI began spending unprecedented amounts of government funds on anti-poverty programmes, subsidies for seed and equipment for farmers, and several million dollars to keep children in school and receive medical check-ups. The funds were not strictly illegal unless they were tied to votes, but, as the PRI well knew, it is out of character in rural Mexico to accept a gift without giving something in return.

In March, the nation's radio stations allocated equal time for each of the three major candidates, but as Fox began to close on Labastida in the polls, PAN and the PRD received less and less air time, while there was no change in time for the PRI. This came as no surprise to the opposition, since the government controlled all media concessions, and more importantly, government advertising was one of the media's biggest sources of income. In the final weeks of the campaign, Zedillo, in spite of IFE protests, increased government advertising for PRI programmes.

On 2 July 2000, the 71-year rule of the PRI, the longest reign of any political party in the world, came to an end with an almost overwhelming majority for the opposition. With 98 per cent of the ballots counted, Fox received 43 per cent of the vote, Labastida 36 per cent, and Cárdenas was a poor third with 16 per cent. Labastida, sensitive to the charges of fraud in the 1998 elections, however, conceded defeat long before the final tallies were counted.

But the vote was far from an endorsement of Fox. Sixty-six per cent of those who voted for him were voting for change, not for his policies, which drew only 28 per cent of the vote. The post-election analysis showed that Fox's supporters were the young, the educated, students, private-sector workers, and even government workers. Labastida's supporters were primarily the elderly, the rural sector, those with no schooling, party loyalists, and housewives.

The aftermath of the election found the PRI in disarray. The party made massive lay-offs in the central bureaucracy, and the party faithful in rural areas were frantically spending funds for government-subsidized projects before the 1 December deadline, when Fox would be inaugurated as president. Dulce Maria Sauri, the president of the PRI, resigned, and no one was eager to step forward and assume the party leadership. Even the 21 million-member PRI union, the Confederacy of Mexican Workers, abandoned the party when it backtracked on threats to hold a nationwide strike if Fox won the election.

For many, the scapegoat was Ernesto Zedillo, who had created election reforms that allowed people to cast their votes in secret, where they could vote free from coercion or fear of party bosses. But Zedillo knew that he could not delay the forces of change any longer, and if his party lost because of his actions, so be it – democracy would take its course. There was, however, no recrimination from the Mexican public – a post-election poll showed that 90 per cent of Mexicans approved of him, and were impressed with his dignified and statesman-like acceptance of his party's defeat.

The future does not look good for the PRI, since their core vote is rapidly disappearing. The elderly are dying, the illiterate are becoming more educated, and the rural population is gradually moving to the cities.

In the foreseeable future, it is expected that Fox will create an auditing agency like the Government Auditing Organization, the watchdog agency in the United States, to monitor public finances and fight corruption in the executive branch. A major overhaul of the Interior Ministry is also long overdue, since the public has had enough of its spying on citizens and political enemies, covering up crimes of ranking party members, and worse, its responsibility for the Tlatelolco Massacre.

The major questions for the future will centre on the ability of Fox to establish a stable administration. Having all but abandoned the ideology of the conservative elements of PAN, will the party be divided between Foxistas and PANistas, and leave Fox with no party machinery to support him? Will he be able to build alliances in a legislature that will be the most splintered in Mexican history? And most important, can he win over the majority that voted not for him or his ideology, but simply for a change of government?

Mexico Today

By the end of World War II, Mexico, as the only one among the Spanish-speaking nations in the Americas that had succeeded in eliminating feudalism and military coups, was ready to enter the political and economic affairs of the world at large.

Although a charter member of the United Nations, Mexico chose not to align itself with any Latin American country or any other bloc. In particular, Mexico maintained a distant but diplomatic relationship with the United States. During the 1970s and '80s, Mexico made it clear to the United States that its foreign policy would not be directed from the White House, and that Wall Street would not be permitted to weaken OPEC using Mexican Oil.

During the missile stand-off between Cuba and the United States in 1959, Mexico was the only country in the Western Hemisphere to maintain diplomatic relations with Cuba, and did not hesitate to condemn the Reagan Administration when Grenada was invaded.

During later times, Mexico hosted such world figures as Juan Carlos, the Pope, and the King of Sweden, and Mexican presidents have travelled to Europe, Asia, Africa, and South America.

To promote regional trade in the Western Hemisphere, Mexico has backed the Latin American Free Trade Association (LAFTA), the Latin American Economic System (SELA), and the North American Free Trade Association (NAFTA).

On the domestic front, the Revolution served Mexico well. Land redistribution broke the back of the *hacienda* system and rid the nation of the *rurales* and summary executions. Freedom-of-speech activists were no longer sent to prison or into exile, and a stable if not overly democratic political system had been established.

Health and welfare programmes had reduced infant mortality from 30 per 100 to 5 per 100, and life expectancy had increased from 36 to 70 years. Society now supported a large middle class that could afford houses, cars, television, mobile phones, and pay for their purchases with credit cards.

For the greater part of the population, however, the Revolution had scarcely improved their lot. The gap between the rich and poor had increased: the lowest 20 per cent shared only 3 per cent of the new wealth, while the upper 20 per cent shared 54 per cent. Illiteracy was still prevalent, wages were low, housing in short supply, and medical care in rural areas was far from adequate. By the 1980s real income had fallen as inflation outran the minimum wage.

Urbanization experienced a phenomenal increase as Mexico City and the Federal District grew from 3 million in 1950 to an estimated 20 million by the end of the twentieth century. With the increase in population and uncurbed development, the city lost much of its colonial charm to the sophistication of a Paris or New York. With urbanization came traffic so heavy that roads could not be built fast enough to accommodate it, and by the 1970s, the crisp, clean air of Mexico had become worse than the smog of Los Angeles.

In rural Mexico, the peasant still practises farming, but with plots so small he can feed no more than his own family. The *ejido* is gradually disappearing as new rules allow private ownership of communal lands, which the farmer can sell, trade, or mortgage for seeds and supplies. The rules, unfortunately, brought about armed conflict in the highlands of Chiapas, as paramilitary groups, backed by local government officials, began to attack villages loyal to the Sandanistas to force them to sell. One of Vincente Fox's first acts as President of Mexico was to purge Chiapas of corrupt government officials.

INFLUENCE FROM THE UNITED STATES

Cultural changes throughout Mexico took place as American products flooded its cities. The *supermercado* with packaged meats and TV dinners, replaced the traditional marketplace and McDonalds, Coca-Cola, Dennys, and Pizza Hut changed the eating habits of a nation. Even soccer, the national sport, is losing ground to American Football. Every Sunday, the Vaqueros de Dallas are televised in every major market as far south as conservative Oaxaca, regardless of whom the Mexican soccer team is playing.

LITERATURE

Mexican literature entered the world stage when Octavio Paz won the Nobel Prize for *El Labertino de la soledad [The Labyrinth of Solitude]* (New York, 1950). In a series of essays, Paz explores the character and culture of the Mexican, which can be extended to Latin America as a whole.

Carlos Fuentes took his place among the élite of literature with his novel *La región mas transparente [Where the Air is Clear]*. Fuentes, disillusioned with the changes brought about by the Revolution, combines a condemnation of capitalism with a critique of human nature.

Both Fuentes and Paz have taught at Cambridge University and at universities in the United States. Fuentes served Mexico as Ambassador to France, and Paz as Ambassador to India.

On the educational front, revisionist history has found its way into schoolbooks. Porfirio Díaz is seen more as a positive factor in the development of Mexico, and Emiliano Zapata has lost much of his heroic lustre. And, for the first time, the facts behind the Tlatelolco Massacre have come to light.

TOURISM

If oil is the lifeblood of the Mexican economy, then tourism is its backbone. Since the Alemán administration, tourism has been critical in obtaining foreign exchange to offset Mexico's perennial trade deficit. Mexico began a big push to attract tourists as early as 1950 by modernizing the rail system and completing the Mexico segment of the Pan-American Highway, which made possible car travel between the United State and Guatemala. By 1952, ten thousand miles of metalled roads crossed Mexico. To cater further for the motorist, the Department of Tourism established the Green Angels to provide assistance to stranded motorists, and spaced emergency roadside phones less than a mile apart along the major highways. All Green Angel vehicles can provide necessary repairs to enable a motorist to reach the nearest town. The Department of Tourism maintains offices throughout Mexico, English is spoken everywhere, and there is a favourable rate of exchange between the peso and the dollar.

With its nearly 4,000 miles of coastline on the warm waters of the Pacific Ocean, the Golfo de California, and the Caribbean, Mexico is a paradise for fishermen and -women, sun-bathers, snorkellers, and scuba divers. Those who prefer solitude to the crowded luxury resorts find no difficulty in discovering beaches far from the beaten track.

Most of Mexico's ruins are easily reached by car, and the tourist is free to explore the temples and palaces of the Maya, the Toltecs, and the ruins of as yet unknown peoples. For the adventurous, there are roads, not always in the best condition, that allow one to visit the ancient ruins of Belize and even the great Maya site of Tikal in Guatemala. In the southern highlands of Mexico, visitors are welcomed among some of the Indian groups that still worship the ancient gods of the past.

For sightseeing in the cities, the rich colonial heritage of Mexico is a feature attraction. Many churches and mansions of the past have been preserved and restored from the silver-mining regions in the north as far as the Yucatán in the south.

Epilogue

The Zapatistas

On 21 February 2001, Sub-commandante Marcos, accompanied by 23 Zapatista leaders, 1,000 supporters and nearly as many journalists, led a caravan of 100 vehicles on a 2,000-mile journey to Mexico City.

Their cause was to protest against the failure of the government to ratify the San Andreas Accords granting Indian autonomy throughout Mexico. The Accords were worked out between Zapatistas and Ernesto Zedillo in 1996, but were never sent to Congress for approval. If ratified by Congress, the Accords would give 11 million Indians, speaking 56 different languages, the right to decide their own government, control their lands, and formal recognition of their social traditions. Foremost in their demands was improvement of Indian quality of life. Ninety per cent of their communities had no sewers, 60 per cent no running water, and illiteracy hovers close to 44 per cent.

Vincente Fox submitted the Accords to Congress in the first weeks of his administration, but found difficulty in persuading his conservative PAN party to support the Zapatista demands.

In January 1994, the Zapatistas, protesting against the North American Free Trade Association (NAFTA), attacked San Cristóbal de Las Casas and several other towns in Chiapas. The revolt ran its course in 10 days, but encounters with Mexican troops had cost 145 lives. The rebels withdrew into the jungle, and government troops set up a perimeter to control the Zapatistas, where they remained isolated from mainstream Mexico until Vincente Fox was elected president.

En route to the capital, the caravan passed through 12 states, stopping at key cities to build support for indigenous rights. In Querétaro, teenagers wearing black ski masks, the signature attire of Marcos and the Zapatistas, greeted the rebels. At Actopan, a crowd waving flags emblazoned with doves welcomed them, and when they reached Toluca, just 30 miles from Mexico City, thousands greeted them with a standing ovation.

On 21 March, after laying a wreath on the grave of Emiliano Zapata, the Zapatistas marched into the Zócalo, the heart of Mexico City, where 100,000 supporters, many wearing ski masks to demonstrate solidarity, greeted them. The Zapatistas vowed that they would not leave the capital until they had met a Congressional peace commission.

In a radio address, Fox welcomed them to the political arena, and invited Marcos to the presidential palace. 'The rebel caravan could not have taken place under previous administrations', he said, 'and this march demonstrates that we already live in a mature democracy where anyone can express himself; where anyone can complain, and where anyone can shout or criticize the president.'

Marcos chose not to accept the president's invitation.

Eight days later, PAN leaders in Congress and the PRI rejected the rebels' request to address the Senate and the lower house. Diego Fernandez de Cevallos, a powerful PAN Senator, objected to many provisions of autonomy laws, and opposed the meeting on the grounds of the Zapatistas' 1994 declaration of war against Mexico. Members of Congress from leading parties also felt that the Accords needed modification, and objected to masked rebels addressing Congress from a podium reserved for heads of state.

After meeting the press, the Zapatistas posted a notice on their web site stating that they would leave the city.

Fox made a dramatic appeal for an eleventh-hour meeting with rebels, and after he agreed to transform three military bases in Chiapas into community centres and release 50 political prisoners, a compromise was reached. The rebel leaders would address an informal session of Congress.

Guerrillas wearing bandannas, sandals, army boots, baseball hats, traditional costumes, and ski masks now had their day before Congress. But it was not Marcos who addressed the assembly; it was Commandante Esther, leader of CCRI-GG, the Clandestine Revolutionary Indigenous Committee-General Command. Marcos was not present.

'Many of you thought that Sub-commandante Marcos would be the one to speak', she said. 'You see that you are wrong. Sub-commandante Marcos is just that: a sub-commandante. We're the commanders. Our warriors have done their job. Now, it is our time for respect. The person speaking before you is not the military leader of a rebel army, but the political leadership of a legitimate movement.'

The difficult task facing both parties is to reach a resolution between the aims of the San Andreas Accords and the civil rights that the Mexican Constitution guarantees its people. Among them are freedom of religion, women's rights, and property rights, which are not observed by many of the indigenous groups. Commandante Esther is well aware of the problems ahead, but asks the Congress to recognize the differences and acknowledge that her people are, after all, Mexicans. Nevertheless, a long and difficult road lies ahead.

Notes

Notes

Notes

Mexican Heads of State

The Aztec Empire

Tenoch   *no date*
Acamapichtli   *1372–1391*
Huitzilíhuitl   *1391–1415*
Chimalpopoca   *1415–1426*
Itzcoatl   *1426–1440*
Moctezuma Ilhuicamina   *1440–1468*
Axayácatl   *1468–1481*
Tizoc   *1481–1486*
Ahuitzotl   *1486–1502*
Moctezuma Xocóyotl   *1502–1520*
Cuitláhuac   *June–October, 1520*
Cuauhtémoc   *October 1520–August 1521*

New Spain

IMMEDIATE POST-CONQUEST PERIOD
Hernán Cortés   *1521–1524*
Anarchy   *1524–1526*
First *Audiencia*   *1527–1530*
Second *Audiencia*   *1530–1535*

THE VICE-REGAL PERIOD
Antonio de Mendoza   *1535–1550*
Luis de Velasco (the elder)   *1550–1564*
Gastón de Peralta   *1566–1568*
Martín Enríquez de Alamanza   *1568–1580*
Lorenzo Suárez de Mendoza   *1580–1583*
Pedro Moya de Contreras   *1584–1585*

Alvaro Manrique de Zúñiga   *1585–1590*
Luis de Velasco (the younger)   *1590–1595*
Gaspar de Zúñiga y Acevedo   *1595–1603*
Juan de Mendoza y Luna   *1603–1607*
Luis de Velasco (the younger)   *1607–1611*
Fray Garcia Guerra   *1611–1612*
Diego Fernández de Córdoba   *1612–1621*
Diego Carríllo de Mendoza y Pimentel   *1621–1624*
Rodrigo Pacheco y Osorio   *1624–1635*
Lope Díaz de Armendáriz   *1635–1640*
Diego López Pacheco Cabrera y Bobadilla   *1640–1642*
Juan de Palafox y Mendoza   *1642–1648*
Marcos de Torres y Rueda   *1648–1649*
Luis Enriquez y Guzmán   *1650–1653*
Francisco Fernández de la Cueva   *1653–1660*
Juan de Leyva y de la Cerda   *1660–1664*
Diego Osorio de Escobar y Llamas   *1664*
Antonio Sebastián de Toledo   *1664–1673*
Pedro Nuño Colón de Portugal   *1673*
Fray Payo Enríquez de Rivera   *1673–1680*
Tomás Antonio de la Cerda y Aragón   *1680–1686*
Melchor Portocarrero Lasso de la Vega   *1686–1688*
Gaspar de Sandoval Silva y Mendoza   *1688–1696*
Juan de Ortega y Montañez   *1696*
José Sarmiento Vallardes   *1696–1701*
Juan de Ortega y Montañez   *1701*
Francisco Fernández de la Cueva Enríquez   *1701–1711*
Fernando de Alencastre Nonoña y Silva   *1711–1716*
Baltasar de Zuñiga y Guzmán   *1716–1722*
Juan de Acuña   *1722–1734*
Juan Antonio Vizarrón y Eguiarreta   *1734–1740*
Pedro de Castro y Figueroa   *1740–1741*
Pedro Cebrián y Agustín   *1742–1746*
Francisco de Güemes y Horcasitas   *1747–1755*
Augustín Ahumada y Villalón   *1755–1760*
Francisco Cajigal de la Vega   *1760*
Joaquín de Monserrat   *1760–1766*
Carlos Francisco de Croix   *1766–1771*
Antonio María de Bucareli   *1771–1779*
Martín de Mayorga   *1779–1783*
Matías de Gálvez   *1783–1784*
Bernardo de Gálvez   *1785–1786*
Alonso Nuñez de Haro y Peralta   *1787*

Manuel Antonio Flores   *1787–1789*
Juan Vincente de Güemes Pacheco y Padilla   *1789–1794*
Miguel de la Grúa Talamanca y Branciforte   *1794–1798*
Miguel José de Azanaza   *1798–1800*
Félix Berenguer de Marquina   *1800–1803*
José de Iturrigaray   *1803–1808*
Pedro Garibay   *1808–1809*
Francisco Javier de Lizana y Beaumont   *1809–1810*
Francisco Javier de Venegas   *1810–1813*
Félix María Calleja del Rey   *1813–1816*
Juan Ruíz de Apodaca   *1816–1821*
Francisco Novella   *1816–1821*
Juan O'Donojú   *did not assume office*

POST-INDEPENDENCE
Emperor Augustín de Iturbide   *1822–1823*
Guadelupe Victoria   *1824–1829*
Vincente Guerrero   *1829*
Anastasio Bustamante   *1830–32, 1837–39, 1842*
Antonio López de Santa Anna   *periodically, 1833–1855*
Valentín Gómez Farías   *1833, 1834, 1847*
Nicolas Bravo   *periodically, 1839–1846*

REFORM PERIOD
Ignacio Comonfort   *1855*
Benito Juárez   *1855–1858, exiled*

CONSERVATIVE TAKE-OVER
Felix Zuloaga   *1858–1859*
Ruling Junta   *1860–64*
Emperor Maximilian von Hapsburg   *1864–1867*

LIBERAL RESTORATION
Benito Juárez   *1867–1872*

POST-REFORM PERIOD
Sebastián Lerdo de Tejada   *1872–1876*
Porfirio Díaz   *1876–1880*
Manuel González   *1880–1884*
Porfirio Díaz   *1884–1911*

REVOLUTIONARY PERIOD

Francisco León de la Barra (interim)   *1911*
Francisco Madero   *1911–1913*
Victoriano Huerta (interim)   *1913–1914*
Eulalio Gutiérrez (interim)   *1914*
Venustiano Carranza   *1915–1920*
Alvaro Obregón   *1920–1924*
Plutarco Elías Calles   *1924–1928*
Emilio Portes Gil (interim)   *1928–1930*
Pascual Ortiz Rubio   *1930–1932*
Abelardo Rodríguez (interim)   *1932–1934*
Lázaro Cárdenas   *1934–1940*

MODERN ERA

Manuel Avila Camacho   *1940–1946*
Miguel Alemán Valdés   *1946–1952*
Adolfo Ruiz Cortines   *1952–1958*
Adolfo López Mateos   *1958–1964*
Gustavo Díaz Ordaz   *1964–1970*
Luis Echeverría Alvarez   *1970–1976*
José López Portillo   *1976–1982*
Miguel de la Madrid   *1982–1988*
Carlos Salinas de Gortari   *1988–1994*
Ernesto Zedillo Ponce de León   *1994–2000*
Vincente Fox Quesada   *2000–*

Chronology of Major Events

AD810–910	Classic Maya Collapse.
AD987	Toltec migration to Chichen Itza.
1325	Mexica, later known as Aztecs, found Tenochtitlán.
1496–1502	Ahuitzotl extends Aztec Empire across Anahuac.
1502	Moctezuma Xocoyotl elected emperor.
1517	Francisco de Córdoba discovers Yucatán.
1518	Juan de Grijalva discovers Mexican mainland.
1518	Cortés lands at Vera Cruz.
1519	Cortés enters Tenochtitlán.
1520	Moctezuma Xocóyotl dies, Cuitláhuac succeeds to the throne, dies of smallpox within 80 days; Cuauhtemoc, last Aztec emperor succeeds to the throne.
1521	Fall of Tenochtitlán.
1523	Pedro de Alvarado conquers Guatemala.
1523	First Franciscans arrive in New Spain.
1525	First Dominicans arrive in New Spain.
1527	First *Audiencia* established in New Spain.
1527	Diego de Mazariegos pacifies the Chiapas Plateau.
1529	Beltran Niño de Guzmán presides over first *Audiencia*.
1530	Second *Audencia* arrives in New Spain, with Bishop Sebastian Ramírez Funleal presiding.
1531	Juan Diego has vision of the Virgin at Tepeyacac.
1535	Don Antonio de Mendoza, first viceroy of New Spain, arrives.
1535	Francisco de Montejo conquers northern Yucatán.
1536	Cabeza de Vaca reaches New Spain.
1540	Francisco Vázquez de Coronado expedition to Cibola.
1542	Juan Rodríguez de Cabrillo expedition to California.
1545	New Laws restore *encomienda*.
1546	Juan de Tolosa discovers silver in Zacatecas.
1560–1579	Northern border of New Spain reaches New Mexico.

1565	Fray Andrés de Urdañeta discovers westward passage from the Philippines.
1566	Martin de Cortés plots rebellion against the Crown.
1571	First Jesuits arrive in New Spain.
1665	Blacks and mulattos riot in Mexico City.
1759–88	Charles III overhauls the economy of New Spain.
1762	British seize Manila and Havana.
1767	Charles III expels Jesuits from New Spain.
1769	José de Galvez sends Gaspar de Porillo and Juan Bautista de Anza expeditions to California, and commissions Junípero de Serra to establish missions along the length of the state.
1804	Charles IV appropriates charitable funds of the Church to finance Spain's Wars.
1808	Napoleon marches on Spain, abducts Charles IV and places brother Joseph on throne; Charles IV abdicates throne for son, Ferdinand VII; Central Junta formed in Cadiz to resist Napoleon; New Spain divided between recognition of Junta or independence.
1810	Fray Miguel Hidalgo y Costilla and Ignacio Allende lead armed resistance against government; Rebels defeat royalist troops defending Mexico City, but Hidalgo withdraws.
1811	Rebel army defeated, Hidalgo and Allende executed
1813	José María Morelos lays siege to Mexico City, but by year's end, viceroy defeats Morelos.
1815	Morelos captured and executed.
1821	Colonel Augustín de Iturbide and Vincente Guerrero claim independence from Spain, wage successful campaign; Viceroy resigns.
1822	*Coup d'état* establishes Iturbide as Augustín I, Emperor of Mexico.
1823	Augustín I forced to resign, exiled from Mexico.
1824	Constitution of 1824 drafted, Guadelupe Victoria elected president.
1828	Manuel Gómez Pedrada elected president, forced to resign and leave country.
1829	Vincente Guerrero assumes presidency, overthrown and executed by Vice-president Anastasio Bustamante.
1829	Spanish expeditionary force invades Mexico at Tampico, defeated by General Antonio López de Santa Anna.
1833	Antonio López de Santa Anna elected president.
1834	Santa Anna switches sides, instals conservative government, declares Constitution of 1824 null and void.
1835	General Martín Perfecto de Cos, a brother-in-law of Santa

	Anna, leads peace-keeping force into Texas, is defeated in December.
1836	Santa Anna lays siege to the Alamo in February, suffers defeat at San Jacinto in April.
1836	Texas claims the Rio Grande as far as its source, incorporating thousands of square miles of Colorado and New Mexico into the Republic.
1838	*Criollos* and Maya Indians drive Mexicans from Yucatán and instal independent government.
1838–1839	The Pastry War.
1841	Yucatán government guarantees religious freedom, abolishes special privileges for clergy and military, grants full citizenship to Indians.
1844	James K. Polk advocates annexation of Texas, Oregon, and California.
1845	Texas becomes the 28th state in the Union.
1846	Polk orders General Zachary Taylor to take up a position on the Rio Grande; Mexican cavalry ambushes American patrol, killing twelve, wounding six, and capturing 63; Polk orders massive offensive against Mexico; General Stephen W. Kearny reaches Santa Fé and claims New Mexico for the United States; Captain John Charles Frémont seizes Sutter's Fort, California, and declares the state an independent republic; Yucatán reunited with Mexico; Commodore John Sloat seizes *presidio* at Monterey Bay and raises American flag.
1847	General Andrés Pico surrenders California to Major John Frémont; Santa Anna marches north with 20,000 troops, suffers defeat at Buena Vista; General Winfield Scott lands unopposed at Vera Cruz with 10,000 troops and marches to Mexico City; city falls, Santa Anna withdraws troops and renounces presidency; Treaty of Guadelupe signed by Mexico and United States.
1847–1900	Caste War of Yucatán.
1853	Gadsden Purchase approved.
1855	Santa Anna resigns presidency and goes into exile; Ignacio Comonforte becomes president.
1856	Constitution of 1857 written.
1858–1861	War of Reform.
1861	Benito Juárez elected president.
1862	France, Britain, and Spain occupy Vera Cruz; French forces defeated at Puebla.
1863	French defeat Mexican army at Puebla, Juárez moves government to San Luis Potosí.

1864	Emperor Maximilian and Carlota enter Mexico.
1867	Napoleon withdraws French forces from Mexico; Maximilian executed; Juárez elected to third term as president.
1871–1872	Juárez elected to fourth term, dies in office.
1872–1876	Sebastián Lerdo de Tejada presidency.
1876	Porfirio Díaz revolts, occupies Mexico City and seizes power.
1880	General Manuel Gonzáles elected president.
1884	Díaz re-elected, sponsors measure to eliminate restrictions on re-election.
1906–1908	Growing number of rail, mining, and industrial strikes organized by Flores Magón brothers. Díaz responds with excessive force.
1910	Díaz decides against retiring, will run for another term; Francisco I. Madero accepts nomination of Partido Liberal Mexicano (PLM) for president; Madero jailed, released on parole after election; Madero calls for national uprising on 20 November.
1911	Pasqual Orozco and Pancho Villa capture Ciudad Juárez; Díaz sues for peace and sails for Paris; Francisco Madera elected president; Emiliano Zapata rebels.
1912	General Victoriano Huerta and Pancho Villa defeat Pascual Orozco.
1913	General Manuel Mondragón, Félix Díaz, and Bernardo Reyes march on Mexico City; Madero assassinated, Victoriano Huerta assumes presidency.
1914	Huerta defeated, resigns presidency; Venustiano Carranza convenes Aguascalientes convention; Eulalio Gutiérrez chosen as provisional president; Carranza and Alvaro Obregón establish separate government in Vera Cruz.
1915	Pancho Villa and Emiliano Zapata occupy Mexico City; Obregón defeats Villa at Celaya; United States recognizes Carranza government; General Plutarco Elías Calles defeats Pancho Villa at Agua Prieto.
1916	General Pablo González defeats Emiliano Zapata; Pancho Villa attacks garrison at Columbus, New Mexico; General John Pershing enters Mexico with punitive force.
1917	Zapata forces González to withdraw to Mexico City; Pershing withdraws from Mexico; Constitution of 1917 ratified.
1919	Zapata assassinated at Anenecuilco; Pancho Villa lays down arms.
1920	General Plutarco Calles overthrows Carranza; Álvaro Obregón elected president.
1923	Pancho Villa assassinated; Bucareli Agreement signed.

1924	Plutarco Elías Calles elected president.
1926	*New York Times* advocates breaking relations with Mexico over oil crisis; Church shuts down in protest of government persecution.
1929	*Cristeros* lay down arms.
1928	Obregón assassinated.
1934	Lázaro Cárdenas elected president.
1938	Cárdenas nationalizes oil companies.
1940	Manuel Avila Camacho elected president.
1941	Start of World War II, Mexican oil a strategic material.
1942	German submarine sinks Mexican tanker, Mexico declares war on Germany.
1946	Miguel Alemán Valdéz elected president; PRM renamed *Partido Revolucionario Institucional* (PRI).
1952	Adolfo Ruiz Cortines elected president.
1953	Women given right to vote and hold elective office.
1958	Population of Mexico reaches 32 million; Adolfo López Mateos elected president; Women vote for president for the first time.
1959	Fidel Castro overthrows Fulgencia Batista in Cuba; Lopéz Mateo recognizes Castro Administration, condemns US Bay of Pigs invasion.
1964	Gustavo Díaz Ordaz elected president.
1968	International Olympic Committee awards 1968 games to Mexico; Tlateloco Massacre one week before the Olympic Games.
1970	Luis Echeverría Alvarez elected president; Mexico establishes diplomatic relations with China; Echeverría elected president of Organization of American States (OAS).
1971	Corpus Cristi attack on students; Foreign debt reaches $20 million, peso devalued.
1976	José López Portillo y Pacheco elected president; National debt reaches $50 billion.
1980	Income from oil exports reaches $6 billion.
1981	Worldwide glut of oil forces Mexico to cut prices.
1982	National debt reaches $80 billion, government postpones payments; López Portillo nationalizes banks.
1982	Miguel de la Madrid Hurtado elected president.
1985	Magnitude 8.0 earthquake strikes Mexico City.
1988	Carlos Salinas de Gortari elected president.
1992	Salinas balances budget.
1993	US Congress approves North American Free Trade Agreement (NAFTA) with Mexico.

1994   1 January Zapatista Army of National Liberation (EZLN)
            attacks San Cristóbal de Las Casas; Luis Donaldo Colosio,
            presidential candidate, assassinated; José Francisco Ruíz
            Massieu gunned down in the streets; Ernesto Zedillo Ponce
            de León elected president; Zedillo withdraws Bank of
            Mexico's support of the peso, exchange rate plummets.
1995   Mario Ruíz Massieu detained in Newark, N.J.; Raul Salinas,
            Carlos Salinas's brother, suspected of murdering José Francisco
            Ruíz Massieu; Scandal sends Carlos Salinas Gortari into exile.
1997   PRI loses majority in congress in mid-term elections.
1999   Raul Salinas found guilty, sentenced to prison; PRI declares
            open primary for presidential election.
2000   Vincente Fox Quesada elected president; PRI loses 71-year
            grip on presidency.
2001   Sub-commandante Marcos leads a caravan of 100 vehicles on
            a protest mission to Mexico City.

Further Reading

General Histories

COCKROFT, JAMES D., *Mexico: Class Formation, Capital Accumulation, and the State* (New York, 1983)

KRAUZE, ENRIQUE, *Mexico: A Biography of Power*, tr. Hank Heifitz (New York, 1997)

MEYER, MICHAEL C. and SHERMAN, WILLIAM L. *The Course of Mexican History* (New York, 1995)

MILLER, ROBERT RYAL, *Mexico: A History* (Norman, 1985)

ROSS, JOHN, *The Annexation of Mexico. From the Aztecs to the IMF* (Monroe, 1998)

SIMPSON, LESLEY BYRD, *Many Mexicos* (Berkeley, 1966)

Pre-Columbian Mexico

ADAMS, RICHARD E. W., *Prehistoric Mesoamerica* (Boston, 1977)

COE, MICHAEL, *Mexico: From the Olmecs to the Aztecs* (New York, 1994)

COE, MICHAEL, *The Maya* (New York, 1999)

COE, MICHAEL, *Breaking the Maya Code* (New York, 1992)

CULBERT, T. PATRICK, *The Lost Civilization: The Story of the Classic Maya* (New York, 1992)

DAVIS, NIGEL, *The Aztecs* (Norman, 1982)

DURAN, DIEGO, *The Aztecs*, tr. Doris Heyden (New York, 1994)

MORLEY, SYLVANUS, G. and BRAINARD, GEORGE W., *The Ancient Maya*, ed., rev. Robert J. Sharer (Stanford, 1983)

PROSKOURIAKOFF, TATIANA, *Maya History*, ed. ROSEMARY A. JOYCE (Austin, 1993)

SAHAGUN, BERNARDINO DE, Florentine Codex: *General History of the Things of New Spain*, tr. ARTHUR J. O. ANDERSON and CHARLES E. DIBBLE, 13 vols. (Salt Lake City, 1970–82)

SANDERS, WILLIAM T. and PRICE, BARBARA J., *Mesoamerica: The Evolution of a Civilization* (New York, 1968)

SCHELE, LINDA and JOYCE, ROSEMARY A., *The Blood of Kings. Dynasty and Ritual in Maya Art* (Fort Worth, 1986)
THOMPSON, J. E. S., *The Rise and Fall of Maya Civilization* (Norman, 1966)
VAILLANT, GEORGE C., *The Aztecs of Mexico* (Baltimore, 1970)
WHITECOTTON, JOSEPH W., *The Zapotecs* (Norman, 1984)

The Conquest

CORTÉS, HERNÁN, *Letters from Mexico*, tr. and ed. A. R. PAGDEN (New York, 1971)
DÍAZ, BERNAL DEL CASTILLO, *The Discovery and Conquest of Mexico*, 1517–1521, tr. A. P. MAUDSLAY (New York, 1996)
DURAN, FRAY DIEGO, *The Aztecs: The History of the Indies of New Spain*, tr. DORIS HEYDEN and FERNANDO HORCASITAS (New York, 1964)
FUENTES, PATRICIA DE, (ed.) *The Conquistadors; First-Person Accounts of the Conquest of Mexico* (New York, 1963)
GARDINER, C. HARVEY, *Naval Power in the Conquest of Mexico* (Austin, 1956)
GOMARA, FRANCISCO LÓPEZ DE., *The Life of the Conqueror by His Secretary*, tr. and ed. LESLEY BYRD SIMPSON (Berkeley, 1977)
LANDA, FRIAR DIEGO DE, *Yucatán Before and After the Conquest*, tr. WILLIAM GATES (New York, 1978)
LEON PORTILLO, MIGUEL, (ed.), *The Broken Spears: The Aztec Account of the Conquest of Mexico*, tr. LYSANDER KEMP (Boston, 1990)
PADDEN, R. C. *The Hummingbird and the Hawk* (Columbus, 1967)
PRESCOTT, WILLIAM HICKLING, *History of the Conquest of Mexico* (New York, 1998)
THOMAS, HUGH, *Conquest* (New York, 1993)

The Colonial Period

BAKEWELL, PETER J., *Silver Mining and Society in Colonial Mexico: Zacatecas, 1546–1700* (Cambridge, UK, 1971)
BENÍTEZ, FERNANDO, *The Century After Cortés*, tr. JOAN MACLEAN (Chicago, 1965)
BRICKER, VICTORIA REIFLER, 'The Caste War of Yucatán: The History of a Myth and the Myth of History', in JONES, GRANT D., *Anthropology and History in Yucatán* (Austin, 1977)
BRICKER, VICTORIA REIFLER, *The Indian King, The Indian Christ* (Austin, 1981)
CABEZA DE VACA, *Adventures in the Unknown Interior of America*, tr. CYCLONE COVEY (Albuquerque, 1990)
CHEVALIER, FRANÇOIS, *Land and Society in Colonial Mexico: The Great Hacienda*, tr. ALVIN EUSTIS, ed., LESLEY BYRD SIMPSON (Berkeley, 1963)

HANKE, LEWIS, *The Spanish Struggle for Justice in the Conquest of America* (Boston, 1965)

GIBSON, CHARLES, *Tlaxcala in the Sixteenth Century* (New Haven, 1952)

GIBSON, CHARLES, *The Aztecs Under Spanish Rule* (Stanford, 1964)

HARING, CLARENCE, *The Spanish Empire in Mexico* (New York, 1947)

POWELL, PHILIP W., *Soldiers, Indians & Silver; the Northward Advance of New Spain, 1550–1600* (Berkeley, 1952)

REED, NELSON, *The Caste War of Yucatan* (Stanford, 1964)

RICARD, ROBERT, *The Spiritual Conquest of Mexico* (Berkeley, 1966)

SIMPSON, LESLEY BYRD, *The Encomienda in New Spain* (Berkeley, 1982)

STEPHENS, JOHN L., *Incidents of Travel in Central America and Yucatan* (New York, 1969)

STEPHENS, JOHN L., *Incidents of Travel in Yucatan* (New York, 1963)

WOLF, ERIC, *Sons of the Shaking Earth* (Chicago, 1959)

From Independence to Revolution

CADENHEAD, IVIE E., Jr., *Benito Juárez* (New York, 1973)

CORTI, EGON C. *Maximilian and Charlotte of Mexico*, tr. CATHERINE A. PHILLIPS, 2 vols (New York, 1929)

HAMILL, HUGH, *The Hidalgo Revolt: A Prelude to Mexican Independence* (Gainesville, 1966)

LA PENA, JOSE ENRIQUE DE, *With Santa Anna in Texas*, tr. & ed. CARMEN PERRY (College Station, 1997)

ROBERTSON, WILLIAM S., *Iturbide of Mexico* (Durham, 1952)

ROEDER, RALPH, *Juárez and His Mexico, a Bibliographical History, 2 vols* (New York, 1947)

RUIZ, RAMÓN E., (ed.) *The Mexican war: Was it Manifest Destiny?* (New York, 1963)

SANTA ANNA, ANTONIO LÓPEZ DE, *The Eagle: The Autobiography of Santa Anna*, ed. ANN FEARS CRAWFORD, tr. SAM GUYLER and JAIME PLATÓN (Austin, 1967)

SMITH, JUSTIN H., *The War with Mexico*, 2 vols, (Gloucester, Mass, 1963)

TIMMONS, WILBERT H., *Morelos of Mexico: Priest, Soldier, Statesman* (El Paso, 1963)

Revolution to the Modern Era

BEALS, CARLETON, *Porfirio Díaz: Dictator of Mexico* (Philadelphia, 1932)

BRADDY, HALDEEN, *Pershing's Mission in Mexico* (El Paso, 1966)

BRENNAN, ANITA and LEIGHTON, GEORGE, *The Wind that Swept Mexico; The History of the Revolution, 1910–1942* (Austin, 1971)

GUZMAN, MARTÍN LUIS, *Memoirs of Pancho Villa*, tr. VIRGINIA H. TAYLOR (Austin, 1965)

KNIGHT, ALAN, *The Mexican Revolution, Vol. 1: Porfirians, Liberals, and Peasants* (New York, 1986)

MACLACHLAN, COLIN M., *Anarchism and the Mexican Revolution: The Political Trials of Ricardo Flores Magón in the United States* (Berkeley, 1991)

MEYER, MICHAEL C., *Mexican Rebel: Pascual Orozco and the Mexican Revolution, 1910–1915* (Lincoln, 1967)

WOMACK, JOHN Jr., *Zapata and the Mexican Revolution* (New York, 1968)

REED, JOHN, *Insurgent Mexico* (New York, 1969)

RUÍZ, RAMÓN EDUARDO, *The Great Rebellion, Mexico 1905–1924* (New York, 1980)

WEYL, NATHANIAL and WEYL, SYLVIA, *The Reconquest of Mexico: The Years of Lázaro Cárdenas* (New York, 1939)

The Modern Era

BRADENBURG, FRANK, *The Making of Modern Mexico* (Englewood Cliffs, N.J., 1964)

CLINE, HOWARD, *Mexico: Revolution to Evolution, 1940–1960* (New York, 1963)

HELLMAN, JUDITH ADLER, *Mexico in Crisis* (New York, 1983)

MORRIS, STEPHEN D., *Political Reformism in Mexico: An Overview of Contemporary Mexican Politics* (Boulder, 1995)

NEEDLER, MARTIN C., *Politics and Society in Mexico* (Albuquerque, 1971)

ROETT, RIORDAN, (ed.), *The Mexican Peso Crisis: International Perspectives* (Boulder, 1996)

CASTAÑEDA, JORGE G., *The Mexican Shock: Its Meaning for the U.S.* (New York, 1995)

Society and Culture

BECKER, MARJORIE, *Setting the Virgin on Fire: Lázaro Cárdenas, Michoacan Peasants, and the Redemption of the Mexican Revolution* (Berkeley, 1995)

BRENNER, ANITA, *Idols Behind Altars: the Story of the Mexican Spirit* (Boston, 1970)

CHARLOT, JEAN, *Mexican Art and the Academy of San Carlos, 1785–1915* (Austin, 1962)

CHARLOT, JEAN, *The Mexican Mural Renaissance, 1920–1925* (New Haven, 1963)

FERNANDEZ, JUSTINO, *A Guide to Mexican Art*. tr. JOSHUA C. TAYLOR (Chicago, 1969)

Folktales of Mexico, ed. and tr. AMÉRICO PAREDES (Chicago, 1970)

FOSTER, GEORGE M., *Tzintzuntzan: Mexican Peasants in a Changing World* (Boston, 1967)

LEWIS, OSCAR, *The Children of Sánchez: Autobiography of a Mexican Family* (New York, 1961)

PAZ, OCTAVIO, *The Labyrinth of Solitude: Life and Thought in Mexico*, tr. LYSANDER KEMP (New York, 1961)

PAZ, OCTAVIO, *Sor Juana. Or, The Traps of Faith*, tr. MARGARET SAYERS PEDEN (Cambridge, MA, 1988)

REED, ALMA M., *The Mexican Muralists* (New York, 1960)

ROMANUCCI-ROSS, LOLA, *Conflict, Violence, and Morality in a Mexican Village* (Palo Alto, 1973)

SIQUEIROS, DAVID ALFARO, *Art and Revolution* (London, 1975)

The Indigenous Peoples of Mexico

BLAFFLER, S. G., *The Blackman of Zinacantan* (Austin, 1972)

CANCIAN, FRANK, *Economics and Prestige in a Maya Community* (Stanford, 1965)

COLLIER, JANE FISHBURNE, *Law and Social Change in Zinacantan* (Stanford, 1973)

FABREGA, H. and SILVER, D.B., *Illness and Shamanistic Curing in Zinacantan* (Stanford, 1973)

GOSSEN, G., *Chamulas in the World of the Sun* (Cambridge, MA, 1974)

GUITERAS-HOLMES, C., *Perils of the Soul: The World View of a Tzotzil Indian* (New York, 1961)

KEARNEY, MICHAEL, *The Winds of Ixtepeji: World View and Society in a Zapotec Town* (New York, 1972)

LA FARGE, O. and BYERS, D., *The Year Bearer's People* (New Orleans, 1931)

OAKES, MAUD, *The Two Crosses of Todos Santos: Survivals of Mayan Religious Ritual* (Princeton, 1969)

MEYERHOFF, BARBARA G., *Peyote Hunt: The Sacred Journey of the Hiuchol Indians* (Ithaca, 1974)

PEARCE, KENNETH, *The View from the Top of the Temple, Ancient Maya Civilization and Modern Maya Culture* (Albuquerque, 1984)

POZAS, RICARDO, *Juan the Chamula: the Ethnological Recreation of the Life of a Mexican Indian* (Berkeley, 1962)

REDFIELD, ROBERT and ROJAS, ALFONSO VILLA, *Chan Kom: A Maya Village* (Chicago, 1967)

TEDLOCK, BARBARA, *Time and the Highland Maya* (Albuquerque, 1982)

VOGT, EVON Z., *The Zinacantecos of Mexico* (New York, 1970)

Travel

Mexico Travel Book, (AAA Publishing)

Historical Gazetteer

Numbers in bold refer to main text

CAMPECHE STATE

Campeche Francisco de Córdoba, the leader of the ill-fated expedition to Mexico of 1517, was the first Spaniard to reach the site of the modern city. The chieftain, whom he named Lázaro, welcomed the Spaniards ashore and provided them with provisions and water. Juan de Grijalva, who arrived in 1518, was not so fortunate. Squadrons of hostile warriors attacked him when he attempted to land, and in the skirmish, one Spaniard was killed, 40 were wounded, and Grijalva lost two teeth.

The colonial city was founded in 1540 by Francisco de Montejo. In the 16th and 17th centuries, the city, prosperous from the export of hardwoods and dyewoods, was repeatedly attacked by English privateers, the most notorious of whom was Sir Francis Drake. In 1686, the city fathers undertook the construction of a massive hexagonal wall with eight redoubts to protect the city. The Fuerte de San Carlos, now a handicraft centre, was built with secret underground passages to hide the women and children when enemy ships were sighted. Some of the tunnels and passageways are open to the public.

The city is now the home base of the largest Gulf-Coast shrimp fleet in Mexico, and its offshore wells a major source of petroleum.

The only major archaeological site in Campeche is **Edzna**, a Maya ceremonial centre 28 miles southeast of the city. Its dominant structure is a chambered pyramid 100 feet high, as measured from the base to the roof-comb at the summit. The temple overlooks a central plaza and a small acropolis. **7, 85, 199, 202, 203, 204, 205, 308**

CHIAPAS STATE

San Cristóbal de las Casas At the time of the conquest, Chiapas was a province of Guatemala. In 1821, the province declared its independence, and in 1824, a plebiscite declared it a state of Mexico. San Cristóbal de las Casas, the principal city of the Chiapas Plateau, was founded in 1528 by Diego de Mazariegos, who had pacified the region the previous year.

The name of the city is a combination of its patron saint, and Bartolome de Las Casas, the Dominican firebrand who spent a lifetime fighting against the *encomienda* system. Appointed the first Bishop of Chiapas in 1542 by Charles V and named Protector of the Indians, his efforts led to the enactment of the New Laws, which prohibited the enslavement of Indians. The laws, however, were not enforced, and in 1544, Las Casas resigned his bishopric and returned to Spain to continue his fight for the Indians.

San Cristóbal is one of the last major cities in Mexico that reflects the attitudes and conservatism of the early post-conquest years. The colonial heritage of the city is nowhere more evident than in its ancient churches, built by Spanish settlers in the 16th and 17th centuries, and maintained in the lavish Spanish tradition by their descendants for nearly four hundred years. Four of the churches were built between 1547 and 1587, and three more in the 17th century, all of which are still active. Each of these churches serves as a showcase for paintings, sculptures, and other priceless relics from post-conquest and early Colonial years. The oldest is a 13th century statue of the Virgin that was carved in Spain.

The major religious festival of San Cristóbal takes place in the third week of July. The fiesta begins on 17 July when townspeople climb the hill on the west side of town to the Church of San Cristóbal. Three weeks later, it ends with a procession of vehicles driving up the hill to be blessed by the Bishop. **7, 129, 199, 236, 315, 316, 317, 324, 332, 333**

Chamula The tiny hamlets surrounding San Cristóbal are home to more than 100,000 Maya Indians. Their remote ancestors, the Tzeltal, broke away from the southern lowlands in the 5th and 6th centuries to return to their ancestral home in the highlands. The migration occupied the better part of three centuries, and brought with it cultural patterns strong enough to endure for the next fourteen centuries. The principal groups are the Chamula, the Zinacanteca, and the Tzeltal. Both the Tzeltal and the Chamula fought bitter caste wars against the *criollos*; the Tzeltal rebelled in 1712, and the Chamula in 1868.

There are great similarities between the Caste War of Yucatán and the Caste War of Chamula, inasmuch as both were centred on native religious symbols. The war began on 22 December 1867, when a Chamula girl found three talking stones while tending her sheep. The Chamulas interpreted the discovery as a sign that God wanted them to rebel against the whites. The war ended on 10 October 1870, with heavy casualties on both sides.

Talking saints are still active among the highland Maya, but not in the churches, where civil and religious authorities have outlawed them.

Visitors to the highland centres are usually welcome to enter the principal churches where the Maya worship their dual gods. The Church of San Juan Bautista in Chamula is open to tourists, but only with permission of the village elders. There are no pews along the nave, and worshippers stand or kneel on a dirt floor strewn with sweet-smelling pine boughs. The ceremony is an impressive display of Catholicism merged with native religious beliefs. Holy week in Chamula reaches its climax in February with a firewalking ceremony, when the Maya purge their souls of sin.

Chamula lies seven miles northwest of San Cristóbal, and can be reached via a paved road.

Palenque One of the great Maya centres of the Classic Period (AD 300–900), Palenque lies in the tropical jungle north of the Chiapas Plateau, where the rainfall exceeds 100 inches a year.

Only a fraction of the archaeological zone has been cleared and restored; many of the ruins still lie buried in the surrounding rain forest. Extensive restoration has been done on the Palace Complex and the Temple of the Inscriptions in the plaza, and the smaller temples surrounding the plaza are in various stages of restoration. Palenque is especially noted for its bas-reliefs of figures whose facial features are uniformly 'Classic Maya'.

Élite burials, elaborate in scope, have been uncovered in a number of major and minor structures at the site. The most impressive is the Tomb of Pacal in the Temple of the Inscriptions. The tomb lies 80 feet below the floor of the temple, and a five-ton slab with elaborate carvings and inscriptions caps the monolithic sarcophagus in the burial chamber. The walls of the crypt bear stucco reliefs of the nine lords of the night and the underworld.

Despite its remote location, Palenque is easily reached by road, rail, and air.

CHIHUAHUA STATE

Chihuahua The city, founded in 1709, played a significant role in the Mexican Revolution. A twenty-eight-year-old muleteer, Pascual Orozco Jr, was the first to organize an armed force of farmers, miners, and unemployed workers in Chihuahua. With his army, some carrying nothing more than pitchforks, he attacked government forces in Cerro Prieta, Ciudad Guerrero, and other settlements.

Pancho Villa, who hid in Chihuahua after he fled from Durango, worked there as a miner, a peddler, a construction worker, and a cattle rustler. After Villa and Orozco joined forces, they attacked federal troops, cut railway and telegraph lines, and captured several key towns in the territory. Later, in a joint operation, Orozco and Villa captured Ciudad Juárez on the US border.

In April 1913, after escaping from federal prison, Villa returned to Chihuahua and formed the army that would be known as the formidable División del Norte.

Pancho Villa's 90-room mansion in Chihuahua is now a museum, where his pistols, uniforms, cartridge belt, and archives are displayed. Also on display is the bullet-riddled Dodge in which he was assassinated. Secret passages in the mansion provided Villa with means of escape through a number of exits.

Father Miguel de Costillo y

Hidalgo, the Father of the War of Independence, was tried for treason and executed before a firing squad in Chihuahua. **2, 237, 248, 263, 265, 266, 268**

GUANAJUATO STATE

Guanajuato In 1810, as the forces of Miguel Hidalgo and Ignacio Allende approached the city, the local militia prepared to defend the Spanish population in the Alhóndiga, the public granary. The militia tried to hold off the rebels from the parapets, but the defence collapsed when a young miner, protected from the fire above with a slab of stone, reached the wooden gates of the Alhóndiga and fired them. During the sack of the city, the rebels butchered more than five hundred Spaniards and a thousand Indians. When Hidalgo and Allende were captured and executed, their heads were displayed on the walls of the granary. A statue honouring the miner lies in the hills above the city.

Today the **Alhóndiga** is a museum. Regional crafts and the paintings of Chavez Morado are displayed on the lower floor. The second floor contains a *Belles-Artes* section showing works of Mexican and international artists, and the remainder is devoted to the mining industry of the region.

Guanajuato is also the birthplace of **Diego Rivera**, and his house is now a museum, where sketches of some of his earlier murals are displayed.

San Miguel de Allende The city was founded in 1540 by Fray Juan de San Miguel, who named it San Miguel el Grande. Its historical significance dates back to 1810, when Captain Ignacio Allende and Father Miguel Hidalgo y Costilla set in motion the Independence Movement that led to the overthrow of Spanish rule in Mexico.

The government has declared the town a national monument, and many of its colonial residences, including that of Ignacio Allende, have been restored. Today, San Miguel is an art centre that attracts American expatriates, artists, teachers, and writers.

The most prominent structure in the city is **La Parroquia**. In 1880, during the Francophile frenzy that took place in the Porfirio Díaz Administration, a self-taught Indian mason named Ceferino Gutiérrez undertook the task of converting an old Mexican church into a gothic cathedral. With no knowledge of French architecture, Gutiérrez, working only from postcards, built a cathedral that would do Paris proud. Each of the three main bells in the belfry has its own distinctive tone.

The tomb of Anastasio Bustamante, the conservative president of Mexico during the War of Reform, lies in the rear of the vaulted chapel.

Dolores Hidalgo The city, known as the Cradle of Independence, has been designated a national monument by the Mexican government. A statue of Hidalgo, holding the banner of the Virgin of Guadalupe high above his Indian troops, stands in the main plaza. The local museum was Hidalgo's home, where many of his personal effects, such as his eyeglasses, clothing, furniture, books, and portraits, are on display. The museum also contains pieces of the bones of Allende and Morelos. **2, 158, 160, 161, 166**

GUERRERO STATE

Acapulco   In 1491, Ahuitzotl established the first Aztec foothold on the Pacific Ocean at Acapulco. Within four years, his armies controlled the coastline as far north as the River Balsas, a distance of 180 miles.

During the Colonial Period, mule trains carried all cargo bound for the Orient overland to Acapulco. Once each year, the Manila Galleon sailed to Manila laden with silver, and returned with spices, silk, tapestries, jade carvings, ivory, gold, and rare woods. Before 1565, however, adverse trade winds forced the Galleon to return by way of the Cape of Good Hope to Mexico. With the discovery of the eastern passage in 1565, however, the new route enabled Mexico to expand trade to the East Indies and challenge the Portuguese monopoly.

In 1813, the rebel leader José María Morelos laid siege to Acapulco to disrupt Spanish shipping to Manila and the east. He captured the city, but failed to achieve his objective – the Spaniards had opened a new port at San Blas, 500 miles to the north.

Fort San Diego was built in 1616 to ward off Sir Francis Drake and other privateers, but was heavily damaged by an earthquake, Morelos's four-month siege, and a French bombardment in 1863. Today the fort is home to the **Acapulco History Museum**, where documents relating Acapulco's history from pre-

Columbian time through the War of Independence can be seen. Items from the Colonial Period of trade with the Orient, such as furniture and vases, are displayed.

The beaches of Acapulco are closer to Mexico City than any on the west coast, and when a four-lane highway was opened in 1955, tourism converted Acapulco from a backwater port city to one of the world's top resort destinations. Famous for its beaches, the area around the city offers a variety of water-related activities. The **Coyuca Lagoon** is noted for birdwatching in the mangroves, fishing for mullet and catfish, and water-skiing. The **Magic Marine World Aquarium** contains marine life exhibits, pools, water slides, snorkelling, and a school for scuba diving. Big-game fishing for marlin, sailfish, barracuda, yellowtail, and shark is also available.

The city is now a regular port of call for cruise ships from all the major lines, most of which come from Los Angeles.

Zihuatanejo   The twin resort complexes of Zihuatanejo and **Ixtapa** lie 110 miles north of Acapulco along the coast. Artifacts and stelae found near Zihuatanejo indicate that the site may have been occupied as early as 3,000 BC. The city was once a port of call for Spanish galleons, but soon found it could not compete with Acapulco for the Philippines' trade. Until the 1970s, Zihuatanejo was a backwater beach town, but with the development of Ixtapa as a major beach-resort town four miles up the coast, Zihuatanejo quickly followed suit.

The **Archaeological Museum** contains maps and murals that trace pre-Hispanic migrations into the area. Artifacts show that the region had trade relations with cultures as far away as the Olmecs of the Gulf Coast. **136, 137, 163, 164, 305**

HIDALGO STATE
Tula Site of **Tollan**, the ancient capital of the Toltecs. Founded *circa* AD 960 by Topíltzin, a priest of the Quetzalcoatl cult, Tollan's period of dominance was relatively brief, lasting only until 1156. The culture was noted for its accomplishments in painting, sculpture, and architecture. The ruins provide evidence that the Chichimecs, nomadic barbarians from the northern highlands, destroyed Tollan. **46**

JALISCO STATE
Guadalajara The city, now the capital of the state, was founded in 1530 by Nuño de Guzmán, arguably the most brutal and ruthless of the *conquistadores*. During his tenure as governor, his slaving practices were responsible for killing thousands of Indians by forcing them to carry supplies to the mines over mountainous terrain. The city was also the seat of Benito Juárez's government-in-exile for a short period during the reign of the Emperor Maximilian.

The **Palacio de Gobierno** contains a number of murals by José Clemente Orozco, who was born in Guadalajara. The themes depict the history of Mexico, and include such prominent events as Father Miguel Hidalgo's abolition of slavery in Mexico. The **Museo Clemente Orozco** is the former studio of the great muralist, where personal artifacts, such as his easel, photographs, documents, and letters, are displayed, and a mural, *Allegoría del Vino*, covers one wall.

The **Archaeological Museum** of western Mexico contains artifacts from sites in Colima, Nayarit, and Jalisco. Most of the handmade figurines date from the Classic Period (AD 300–900). The figurines include men and women in naturalistic poses, some playing flutes or beating drums, warriors brandishing war clubs, and contestants playing a ball game. Though not particularly artistic, they portray the everyday life of the ancient Mexicans in great detail. **2, 218, 220**

MEXICO CITY, THE FEDERAL DISTRICT
The Templo Mayor During the siege of Tenochtitlán, Cortés destroyed the city brick by brick and house by house to protect the Spaniards from the barrage of arrows and stones from the rooftops, and when the city fell, nothing remained but the temples. After the fall of the city, the temples were torn down to provide materials to build homes for the settlers and the cathedral. All that remain today are the ruins of the great temple, where Ahuitzotl sacrificed more than 2,000 prisoners of war in a period of four days.

Before the conquest, the temple rose 200 feet from the floor of the plaza, and on the upper platform, the temple of Huitzilopochtli, the Lord of

Creation, stood to the right, and the temple of Tlaloc, the god of rain and fertility, to the left. Current excavations show that it was built above four older and smaller temples. The ruins are located just north of the Zócalo, the central plaza of the federal district, and the National Palace.

The **Museo Templo Mayor** adjacent to the site provides a valuable historic perspective of Aztec history, and contains more than 7,000 pre-Columbian artifacts.

Several important discoveries have been found in and about the Zócalo. One of the most important finds is the circular stone disc that was dedicated to the Fifth Sun, a period beyond which the Aztecs believed that the Universe would cease to exist. A second discovery of importance is a stone tablet commemorating the dedication of the temple to the god Huitzilopochtli in 1487. Both are now in Mexico's **National Museum of Anthropology**.

Cerro de La Estrella National Park Located near Ixtapalapa, about seven miles south of Mexico City, the **Cerro de la Estrella** [Hill of the Star], is the site where the Temple of Uixachlan stood. On the summit of the temple, the new fire ceremony was observed at the closing of every 52-year cycle of the Mexican calendar. The date was of great religious significance to the Aztecs, because it was a time when the very existence of their Universe was threatened. Fires were extinguished throughout the city, and all eyes turned south as priests conducted the ceremony that would bring the heavens into har-

mony once more. When the stars were in their proper alignment, a priest kindled a fire and cast the heart of a captive into it. If the flame blossomed into a fire that could be seen from the city, the people knew that the world was safe again. Today the park is the venue for a Passion Play that is performed on Good Friday.

The crest of the hill offers a spectacular view of Mexico's great volcanoes, Popocatepetl and Ixtacci-huatl.

The Cuicuilco Pyramid The earliest of Mexico's pyramids stands on the pedregal, the ancient lava flow that is home to the National University of Mexico. Dated at approximately 600 BC, it is considered to be one of the oldest artificial structures on the North American continent. It was destroyed when the Extol volcano erupted in 150 BC.

Chapultepec Park Chapultepec Castle, built in the 1780s, lies on the site of an ancient Aztec fortress, and stelae carved with the images of Moctezuma Xocoyotl, Moctezuma Ilhuicamini, Tlacaelel, Axacayatl, and Ahuitzotl still stand on the hill.

In the mid-19th century, the castle was a military college, and when American forces invaded the capital in 1847, the cadets were pressed into combat. A statue on the palace grounds commemorates the sacrifice of the six who died in the battle.

Today the castle serves as the Museum of National History, which covers the period from the conquest to the Revolution of 1910. The primary exhibits are large paintings and statues of prominent leaders and military heroes. The furnishings of the palace are those that Maximilian and Carlota brought from Europe, and the gardens surrounding the palace were designed by Carlota.

The **Gallery of the Mexican Struggle for Liberty** is located half way up the hill. Dioramas trace Mexican history from the arrival of the Spaniards to the creation of the Constitution of 1917. Some, such as the execution of Maximilian, are presented with a great sense of drama.

The **Rufino Tamayo Museum** on the eastern boundary of the park displays a collection of this Oaxacan artist, and the works of Pablo Picasso, Joan Miró, and Salvador Dali.

The National Museum of Anthropology The exhibits in the museum cover three major eras of Mexican culture: the hunter/gatherer and early village-life period; pre-Columbian civilization; and the ethnography of the nation's indigenous groups.

Exhibits include early tools and weapons, mammoth-kill sites, artifacts from burial sites, and pottery. Most important, however, is the exhibit dealing with the development of maize, which ushered in the first civilization on the North American continent.

The pre-Columbian section of the museum is its largest, and its exhibits cover every major culture from the time of the Olmecs (1150–900 BC), to the fall of the Aztec empire in AD 1519. Some of its more noteworthy exhibits are a full-scale reproduction of the tomb of Pacal, the ruler of Palenque in the 7th century AD, a colossal stone head from the Olmec culture, and the frontal elevation of the Temple of Quetzalcoatl at Teotihuacán. There is also a large-scale model of the ceremonial plaza at Tenochtitlán prior to the arrival of the Spaniards.

Some of the more important artifacts found in the museum are the Stone of the Fifth Sun, which marked the beginning of the end of the Aztec empire, a tablet marking the dedication of the great temple, and a panel from the Temple of the Cross at Palenque. Figures, statues, and carvings are presented in rooms dedicated to the various early cultures of Mexico.

In the ethnology section, exhibits display the crafts, apparel, ritual life, and social organization of the indigenous cultures of Mexico.

The museum bookshop provides English-language guides to the museum, and a 20-minute audiovisual presentation describes the principal cultures of Mexico.

The National Palace The palace was the official residence of the Spanish viceroys from 1698 to 1821, when Augustín de Iturbide declared the nation independent of Spain. Since then, it has housed the offices of the president and other government officials.

The bell that Father Miguel de Costillo y Hidalgo rang on 15 September 1810 hangs above the entrance to the palace. On that day, the president rings the bell at exactly 11 p.m., in remembrance of the War of Independence.

The living quarters of Benito Juárez on the second floor of the palace are now a national monument. The museum contains his bedroom furniture and desk, pictures and documents dealing with his life, and his small library.

The epic murals of Diego Rivera are the chief attractions of the palace. Those on the main staircase illustrate the history of Mexico from the Aztec era to the Revolution of 1910. All the national heroes of Mexican history: Juárez, Zapata, Hidalgo, and Morelos, appear on the walls.

Rebels protesting against liberal reforms laid siege to the palace in 1913, and for 10 days, artillery exchanges destroyed many government buildings and killed hundreds of civilians.

Art Museums A number of museums featuring the works of the principal artists of the Revolution lie in the Federal District.

The **National Preparatory School** is noted for José Clemente Orozco's murals of post-Revolutionary Mexico; they portray the tragedy of war. Three floors contain paintings of colonial Mexico and works by David Alfaro Siqueiros and Fernando Leal.

The centrepiece of the **Diego Rivera Mural Museum** is his *Dream of an Afternoon in the Alameda Central*. All the historic characters: Cortés, Juárez, Santa Anna, Maximilian, Carlota, Díaz, and a host of others are portrayed. Rivera himself appears as a child, and prominent artists such as his wife, the surrealist Frida Kahlo, and José Guadelupe Posada can be seen in the mural.

The **Museum of Modern Art** is another repository for the works of Rivera, Siqueiros, Tamayo, Orozco, and other contemporary Mexican and international artists. One of Frida Kahlo's best-known surrealistic works, *The Two Fridas*, is featured.

The **Polyform Siqueiros** is dedicated to the works of the artist. His murals cover the exterior walls of the building, and his epic *March of Humanity* covers the 26,000-square-foot ceiling.

The National University of Mexico The University, the oldest in the Americas, was founded in 1553. One of the first faculty members was Cervantes de Salazar, the noted historian of the Conquest, who held the chair of Professor of Rhetoric.

Situated on an 800-acre site on the **pedregal**, it serves a student body of 300,000 students. For the visitor, the most interesting features of the campus are the murals that cover the walls of its major buildings.

The main library is a tall rectangular block covered with mosaic tile frescos on the exterior surfaces. The frescos by Juan O'Gorman present the history of Mexico from the pre-Cortesian era to the artist's interpretation of Mexico's future. One entire wall of the administration building is devoted to a Siqueiro mural that shows Mexican students returning the fruits of their labours to the nation. The mural incorporates pieces of coloured glass in a way that projects a sense of movement. A mosaic of a three-headed mask in the **School of Medicine** represents the three cultures of Mexico: Spanish, Indian, and *mestizo*. Diego Rivera's contribution is a mosaic of coloured stones with a sporting theme on the walls of the stadium. The stadium was used for a number of events in the 1968 Olympics.

Coyoacan A suburb of Mexico City, originally located on the western shore of Lake Texcoco, Coyoacán was established as the seat of the first government of New Spain by Hernán Cortés.

In the early years of the 20th century, the city became the avant-garde art centre of Mexico, and Frida Kahlo was one of the city's pre-eminent artists.

Kahlo's home is now the **Frida Kahlo Museum**, and many of her later works reflect her depression caused by poor health. She developed polio at an early age, and later suffered a bus accident, which left her in a wheelchair. The wheelchair still sits beside an easel with one of her unfinished paintings.

Her tempestuous relationship with Rivera was interrupted by an affair with Leon Trotsky, the exiled Russian revolutionary, who lived with Rivera and Kahlo for a short time. Trotsky was assassinated by one of Joseph Stalin's assassins after he moved from her house. His home, now **The Trotsky Museum**, is a short distance from Kahlo's residence. **5, 6, 198, 217, 220, 221, 223, 226, 233, 247, 250, 253, 257, 258, 260, 265, 328, 329, 332, 333**

MEXICO STATE

The Basilica de Nuestra Senora de Guadalupe The Basilica, seven miles north of central Mexico City, houses the most revered religious icon in Mexico.

The Virgin appeared to Juan Diego, newly converted Indian peasant, in December 1531 on the hill of Tepeyac, and asked him to build a church there. He took her message to Juan de Zumárraga, the Bishop of Mexico, who demanded proof of the miracle. In a second visitation, the Virgin directed Juan Diego to pick roses that were blooming on the hill and take them to the bishop. When Juan Diego opened his cape to offer the roses to the bishop, however, the roses were gone and a radiant image of the dark-skinned Virgin appeared. Zumárraga, convinced that Juan Diego had seen a miracle, ordered that a church dedicated to the Virgin of Guadalupe be built on the site where she had appeared.

Tepeyac is the site where Indians worshipped Tonantzin, the Earth goddess, in pre-Conquest times, and the Basilica is considered a symbol of the fusion of Christianity with the old gods of Mexico.

The first basilica was constructed in 1709 to display the sacred image, but the settling of the city into the unstable ground of the lake bed caused it to list to one side. The original basilica is now a museum of religious art, and a larger and more modern building now houses Juan Diego's cape.

Ixtaccíhuatl and Popocatepetl National Park

Amecameca A market town in the pass between the two great volcanoes is the gateway to the park. Ixtaccíhuatl, the Sleeping Woman, 17,343 feet high is dormant. From its appearance, some cataclysmic eruption in the prehistoric past may have blown the crest away. Popocatepetl, the Smoking Mountain, standing 17,877 feet, is still active, and the latest series of eruptions occurred as recently as 1999. Although both mountains lie in the tropical zone, snow covers both crests throughout the year.

The Aztecs believed that Popocatepetl stood between heaven and the underworld, and that its eruptions were caused by the stirring of evil kings seeking the path to eternal peace deep inside the mountain.

In November 1519, the Spaniards caught their first sight of the Valley of Mexico from Amecameca. In the distance they saw the towers of Tenochtitlán and a vast lake, with cities and towns along its shores as far as the eye could see. Cortés sent a scouting party up the slopes of Popocatepetl, but the mountain chose that particular moment to erupt. Smoke billowed from the vent, and the ground shook so violently that they were forced to descend before they were buried under a blanket of ash. After the fall of Tenochtitlán, the Spaniards mined sulphur for their gunpowder from the crater of Popocatepetl.

Today, Amecameca is host to mountain climbers ready to challenge the volcanoes. The ascent of either mountain requires two days, and mountain-climbing experience is a prerequisite. Horses and guides are available in Amecameca.

Teotihuacán The Archaeological Zone lies approximately 32 miles northeast of the Federal District. The name Teotihuacan means 'Place of the Gods', but the name given by its ancient inhabitants is unknown. Founded some time in 200 BC, the city grew to a metropolis of 200,000 people by AD 600, but by AD 750, the city was destroyed and abandoned. At the height of Teotihuacán civilization, its people dominated other cultures throughout Mexico and Central America.

Teotihuacán is the legendary site where the gods created the Fifth Sun out of the darkness. At the spring equinox, thousands of spectators pack the summit of the Temple of the Sun to celebrate the ritual.

Scale models of the archaeological zone and artifacts from the site can be seen in the small museum at the site. **4, 24–29, 70, 71, 100, 321, 323**

MICHOACÁN STATE
Morelia The city was founded in 1541 by the Viceroy Antonio de Mendoza. Named Valladolid after the Viceroy's birthplace in Spain, it was changed in 1828 to honour its most famous son, José María Morelos, the hero of the War of Independence. Other than Morelos, its only historical significance is the **Colegio de San Nicolás**, where Father Miguel Hidalgo y Costilla studied and later taught theology.

The **Morelos House Museum** was José María Morelos's residence in 1801, and was occupied by his descendants until 1910, when it became a museum. It contains some of his personal belongings, manuscripts, and exhibits of the War of Independence.

The **State Museum**, once the mansion of Mexico's first emperor, Augustín de Iturbide, houses figurines from pre-Columbian Michoacán.

The cultural side of Morelia features the **Casa de Cultura,** a building devoted to the performing arts, the internationally famous Boy's Choir, and the **Museum of Contemporary Art**. The **Convention Center** houses a planetarium, a theatre, and a greenhouse that contains more than 3,000 varieties of orchids.

Tzintzuntzan   In the early years of the sixteenth century, Tzintzuntzan was the capital of the vast Tarascan empire. By 1500, the empire encompassed all of the modern state of Michoacán and parts of states to the east and the west. At the time of the conquest, the city had a population of some 40,000, scattered about the barrios and the shores of Lake Pátzcuaro. The town had palace buildings, quarters for the wives and concubines of the emperor, residences for the élite, and homes for workers and craftsmen. Five pyramids overlooked the central plaza, and on the top of each, eternal fires were fed by the vassals of the king.

The Aztecs were never able to subjugate the Tarascan Empire. The only major confrontation with Tenochtitlán came about when Axayácatl, the sixth lord of Mexico, was humbled in the fields of Michoacán.

The end of the empire came about in 1540, when Tangaxoan surrendered to the Spaniards. They executed the ruler, stripped the priests and nobles of their rank, and reduced the city to a village.

The pyramids have been restored, and the 16th century **Convent of Santa Anna**, also restored, is now open to visitors. The church courtyard is noted for its olive trees, which were planted by the Bishop Vasco de Quiroga in defiance of the Crown's prohibition of the planting of trees in New Spain.

Concerts, performances of Spanish plays, and dramas based on the Nativity take place in Holy Week, starting on 16 December.

Lake Patzcuaro is one of the highest lakes in the country, and some 20 Indian villages lie along its shore, many accessible only by boat. The favourite catch is the *pescado blanco,* a delicate whitefish that is unique to the lake. The picturesque butterfly nets that were once used by fishermen now appear only for photographers.

The Museum of Popular Art is part of the former Colegio San Nicolas, and the ruins of a pre-Columbian town lie on the grounds. **2, 122, 164, 215, 225, 283**

MORELOS STATE

Cuernavaca   Now capital of the state, the city was once the playground of Aztec emperors. After the conquest, Cortés, now Marquis of the Valley of Oaxaca, ruled his vast estate from his palace in Cuernavaca, and during the French occupation, Maximilian and Carlota spent their summers in their home on the outskirts of the city.

Cortés's palace, located on the

main plaza, is now the **Cuauhna-huac Museum**, where exhibits show the evolution of Mexico from pre-historic times. Diego Rivera murals portray the conquest of Mexico, the War of Independence, and the Mexican revolution. **250, 251, 257**

NAYARIT STATE

San Blas The appearance of this small, unusual coastal village belies the major role it played in the East Indies trade from the 16th to the 19th centuries. During the War of Independence, when Acapulco was under siege, it handled the bulk of cargo along the west coast of Mexico. In the 18th century, the town was a ship-building centre and a port for the Spanish Fleet. The ruins of a Spanish fortress still stand on a hill over-looking the town.

Off the main artery along the Pacific Coast, **Tepic** is the nearest large town, and San Blas can be reached only by a jungle road. The main attractions are its excellent beaches and casual social life in the plaza after sunset. The jungle is a favourite spot for birdwatchers. Among the mangroves and swampy lagoons, more than 300 bird species have been identified. Motorized launches are available for tours through the area. **2, 163**

NUEVO LEÓN STATE

Monterrey On 19 September 1846, General Zachary Taylor, acting on orders from President James K. Polk, opened the Mexican–American War when he launched an attack against Monterrey. In June 1910, Francisco Madero challenged Porfirio Díaz for the presidency of Mexico, and while campaigning in Monterrey, was seized and jailed by Díaz's agents.

Today, the city is called the Pittsburgh of Mexico, a centre of steel and chemical production, commerce, and manufactured products.

The **Alfa Cultural Center** contains a fine planetarium, an IMAX theatre, and a number of exhibits pertaining to the city. The **Monterrey Museum**, once a brewery warehouse, displays early brewing equipment, regional costumes, and the works of Latin American artists. Exhibits in **The Regional Museum of Nuevo Léon** trace the development of culture and industry in the area. A display of note includes the rifles used to execute the Emperor Maximilian. **2, 191, 218, 225**

OAXACA STATE

Oaxaca The city produced two of Mexico's best-known presidents: Benito Juárez and Porfirio Díaz. Juárez, a pure-blooded Zapotec Indian, served as President of Mexico from 1861 to 1872, during the difficult years of the Wars of Reform and the French invasion. Díaz's presidency spanned 27 years, and his dictatorship brought about the Mexican Revolution in 1910.

Monte Alban, the great Zapotec centre, lies two miles from the city. The centre flourished from 400 BC to about AD 900. The reason for the collapse of Monte Alban civilization has never been determined, but it occurred in a period when the Maya abandoned their great centres in

Mexico, Guatemala, and Honduras. Portraits of early Zapotec life are seen on engraved stelae, murals on the walls of excavated tombs, and funerary urns. The Zapotecs may have been the first culture in Mesoamerica to develop a written history.

The **Rufino Tamayo Museum** of Oaxaca contains an impressive collection of artifacts from Monte Alban. **6, 29, 30, 31, 66, 215, 216, 217, 220, 228, 230, 234, 239**

PUEBLA STATE

Cholula The city lies about 90 miles from Mexico City, on a broad and fertile plain at the foot of Popocatepetl. In pre-Hispanic times, Cholula was one of the most important religious areas of Mexico, a sanctuary that drew pilgrims from every corner of Anahuac to worship at the shrine of Quetzalcoatl. The **Great Temple of Cholula** is the largest pyramid of ancient Mexico, measuring 180 feet high and covering 25 acres. Archaeologists estimate that Cholula was founded about 400 BC, and that its civilization reached its peak about AD 200, when Teotihuacán flourished. The Toltecs occupied the site about AD 1000, followed by the Aztecs *circa* 1400.

Cholula was also the site of a massacre that still lives in infamy. When Cortés billeted his army there on his way to Tenochtitlán, he felt he had reason to suspect that the Cholulans were plotting to kill the Spaniards. He assembled 2,000 porters, warriors, and nobles in the plaza, and at his signal, the Spaniards fired into the crowd.

Cholula is a city of churches, and, if one counts the nearby villages, there are 39 in all. The **Santuario los Remedios** lies on top of the Temple of Quetzalcoatl.

Puebla The capital and commercial centre of the state, Puebla lies in a valley surrounded by **Ixtaccíhuatl** and **Popocatepetl** to the west, and **Cerro de la Malinche** to the east.

On May 1862, Puebla was the site of the battle that is now commemorated by one of Mexico's most important celebrations, *Cinco de Mayo*, 5 May. Napoleon III, ambitious for territorial gains in Mexico, ordered a French expeditionary force to occupy Mexico City to secure the county for its new Emperor, Ferdinand Maximilian von Habsburg, the Archduke of Austria. The French forces, however, suffered an embarrassing defeat at Puebla by a rag-tag Mexican army. **6, 221, 247, 249**

QUERÉTARO STATE

Querétaro In 1531, the city's defenders were defeated by the Spaniards when a cross suddenly appeared in a sky darkened by a solar eclipse. A chapel was built to commemorate the miracle, and the Church undertook a massive effort to convert the Indians to Catholicism. In 1654, a monastery and a church were built on the site.

Early in the 19th century, Querétaro was the home of the Society for the Study of Fine Arts, where Father Miguel Costillo y Hidalgo and Ignacio Allende formed the plot to overthrow Spanish rule in Mexico.

In 1867, the Emperor Maximilian

set up his headquarters in Querétaro after Juárez drove him out of Mexico City. He was executed on the Hill of the Bells on 19 July 1867.

The Constitution of 1917 was drafted in Querétaro, as was The Treaty of Guadalupe, which ceded California, New Mexico, and Arizona to the United States after the Mexican-American War. The Partido Revolucionarío Instítucional (PRI), the party that would control Mexican politics until the year 2000, was organized there in 1929.

A monument to Juárez stands on top of the **Hill of the Bells**, behind a chapel erected by the Austrian government in honour of Maximilian. Photographs taken in 1867 are displayed in a small museum near the chapel. The **Museum of the Holy Virgin** contains colonial uniforms and weaponry, and the desk where the council that ordered the execution of Maximilian sat.

The **Palacio Municipal** was the seat of the Spanish governors in colonial times, and the home of *La Corregidora*, the heroine of the War of Independence. Under house arrest, she managed to warn Hidalgo and Allende that their plot to overthrow the government had been discovered. **157, 159, 219, 226, 275**

QUINTANA ROO

Cancun   On the mainland of the Yucatán Peninsula, across from the Isla Mujeres, the narrow, white-sand strip of Cancun is an island of luxury hotels and elegant apartment blocks. One of the world's most glamorous playgrounds, Cancun is the hub of a tourist industry that supports the middle class on the north coast, and provides employment for thousands of Maya Indians from the deep forest. Some of the richest archaeological sites on the Yucatán Peninsula lie within a short distance of Cancun.

The ruins of **Xel-ha** and **Tuluum**, Maya centres that are known to have been occupied as late as 1618, lie 60 miles south of the resort. Tuluum occupies a bare, windswept promontory overlooking the Caribbean, a setting with a natural beauty that has drawn visitors from all over the world.

Only the ruins of Xel-Ha remain, but some lie in a setting unrivalled among the world's antiquities. In a narrow rock-rimmed inlet, the Mexican Government established an underwater research laboratory, supported, in part, by fees collected from tourists for snorkelling and scuba-diving privileges. In the clear, blue water, among the spectacular tropical fishes of the Yucatán coast, divers can see the ruins of submerged temples in the depths below. At **Chenchomac**, further down the coast at the **Baha de Ascension**, the natives came on to the beach in 1518 to welcome the Grijalva expedition. A member of the expedition compared the city with Seville.

Cobá, an enormous site with some 6,500 known structures, lies 25 miles inland from Tuluum. The most accessible of its structures are two large pyramids, and from the summit of the largest, there is an unparalleled view of the lush tropical forest and the lakes surrounding the site. The known period of occupation of Cobá was from AD 435 to 830.

Chichen Itza, the incomparable Toltec site, lies 120 miles east of Cancun. According to legend, the city was founded by Quetzalcoatl Topilzin in AD 987, when Tezcatlipoca drove him out of Tula. The fall of Chichen Itza came about in AD 1200, when Hunac Ceel, the chieftain of Mayapán, captured the city.

Cozumel Island Juan de Grijalva made the first landing on the island in 1518. The Cortés expedition landed on Cozumel in 1519, where the *conquistadore* had the good fortune to find Jerónimo Aguilar, a survivor of a shipwreck on the Yucatán coast, whose ability to speak Chontal Maya would be instrumental in the conquest of Mexico.

Cozumel's only town, **San Miguel de Cozumel**, lies on the western coast of the island. The town is the centre of island activity with shops, restaurants, nightspots, and, unlike Cancun, budget hotels. More expensive accommodation to the north and south of San Miguel, in the hotel zones. Like Isla de Mujeres, many of the centre's streets are closed to vehicular traffic

Exhibits in The Cozumel Museum record the history of the island's culture from pre-Columbian times to the Caste War of Yucatán, when refugees from the war settled on the island.

The **Archeological Park** contains reproductions of artifacts from Olmec, Maya, Aztec, and Toltec cultures in an open park.

The **Palancar National Submarine Park** is Mexico's foremost diving area. The peak of the season is June to August, when the waters are calm and warm. A twenty-mile stretch of coral reefs offers unlimited opportunities for the diver to explore sunken shipwrecks and undersea caverns, and to observe the marine flora and fauna.

Isla de Mujeres The small island, three miles off the north coast of **Quintana Roo**, was the site of the first landing of Europeans on the North American continent. Its name was given by its discoverer, Francisco de Córdoba, who found many small figurines of females, which led him to believe that Amazons occupied the island. The figurines represent Ix Chel, the Moon Goddess and the

Goddess of Childbirth. In 1917, the Mexican government erected a monument to commemorate his discovery.

The island is only four-and-a-half miles long and half-a-mile wide. A great salt marsh lies off the northern shore, and it was once the greatest source of salt in Mexico and Central America. In pre-Conquest times, the Yucatec Maya harvested salt from the marsh and exported it as far as Xicalango, the great trading post at the Laguna de Terminos.

Early in the 19th century, the notorious pirate Jean Lafitte used the island as a rendezvous, leaving behind him a legacy of tales of buried treasure.

The south end of the island terminates in a high promontory that commands one of the most beautiful scenes in the Caribbean. Deep swells rise from a vast expanse of blue-green ocean and disintegrate over massive boulders at the base of 50-foot cliffs. At the tip of the promontory, a tiny Mayan temple perches like a lonely sentinel on the barren heights.

The island marks the northern end of the 300 mile-long barrier reef that stretches as far south as the Gulf of Honduras. Garrafon beach lies about half-a-mile south of the promontory, on the leeward side of the inland. Discovered by the French oceanographer Jacques Cousteau, Garrafon offers scuba-diving and snorkelling opportunities that rival the Great Barrier Reef of Australia. Diving equipment is available on the island. **47, 48, 49, 85**

SAN LUIS POTOSÍ STATE

San Luis Potosí The city, now the capital of the state, was founded in the 16th century as a mining centre for the rich deposits of silver located in the vicinity. It was the seat of the provisional government of Benito Juárez in 1863, and again in 1867. In 1910, Porfirio Díaz, troubled by Francisco Madero's campaign against him for the presidency, placed him under house arrest in San Luis Potosí, where he wrote the manifesto for the Mexican Revolution.

The **Museum of Culture** exhibits the works of national and regional artists. The **Regional Museum** contains artifacts and historical documents dating from the 16th century. The **Museum of Popular Art** displays crafts from the state as well as the Huastec region of northeastern Mexico. **2, 193, 221, 247**

TABASCO STATE

Villahermosa Located on the navigable Rio Grijalva, 30 miles south of the Gulf of Mexico, Villahermosa is an important distribution point for rubber, cacao, and coffee from the interior. In the 1970s, the discovery of oil fields and the development of hydro-electric power made the city a major commercial centre.

Founded in 1519 as Santa María de la Victoria, it lies near Centla where Cortés and his army, besieged by a large force of Maya warriors, would have perished but for a last-minute charge by the cavalry. The defeated chieftain, in a gesture of good will, gave Cortés 20 women,

one of whom spoke the language of Mexico.

The **Museum of Anthropology** is noted for its reproductions of the murals of Bonampak, a major Maya ceremonial centre 100 miles southwest of Palenque. The murals, with themes of war and violence, changed the commonly held view of the Maya as a peace-loving people. Among its collections of artifacts from the various cultures of Mexico, a reproduction of the Dresden Codex, one of only four that survived the Spanish occupation, is on display.

The **La Venta Museum**, an open-air park, contains 30 Olmec monuments, among which are three colossal stone heads, one of which weighs 30 tons. Other Olmec artifacts include sculptures, stelae, and a tomb. All are scattered throughout the park's tropical forest, where monkeys and deer roam freely. **92**

TLAXCALA STATE

Tlaxcala An old and traditional enemy of Moctezuma, Tlaxcala was torn between allowing the Spaniards to pass through the city on their way to Tenochtitlan or declaring war against them. Maxixca, the spokesman of the republic, swayed by Cortés's promise to aid them in their war against Mexico, favoured welcoming them into the city. Xicoténcatl, the captain-general of the republic, however, suspicious of Cortés's motives, attacked the Spaniards. Xicoténcatl was defeated, and Maxixca forged an alliance with the Spaniards that would be instrumental in the conquest.

Before departing for Mexico, Cortés held Catholic rites for the Tlaxcalans in what is now the **Ex-Convent of the Assumption**, where the original stone baptismal font can still be seen.

Later in the war, Cortés, needing armed craft to clear Lake Texcoco of Aztec war canoes, sent the shipwright Martin López to Tlaxcala to construct his brigantines. After the ships were built and tested on a nearby river, they were disassembled, and 8,000 Tlaxcalan porters transported the hull timbers, decking, and rigging across the rugged mountains to Texcoco.

The **Regional Museum of Tlaxcala** lies in the church cloister, and paintings display the history of the city from prehistoric times to the present.

The **Governor's Palace** contains murals portraying agricultural themes and the history of the people of Tlaxcala.

The **Tzilatlan** ruins lie north of Tlaxcala. Tzilatlan was one of the four provinces of the Republic of Tlaxcala at the time of the conquest, and the home of Xicotencatl. The ruins include a palace and small structures with murals that portray the republic's wars against Moctezuma.

The **Cacaxtla** ruins lie about 12 miles south of Tlaxcala. The site is a complex of courtyards, tombs, and living quarters. The murals on several of the buildings are well preserved and comparable to those in Bonampak. The largest and finest depicts two groups of warriors in combat. One group wears feathered panaches and jade jewellery, the other jaguar skins. Other murals portray themes of fertility and the rain god Tlaloc. The centre rose to prominence *circa* AD 650–900, and was abandoned about AD 1000. **62, 94, 122**

VERACRUZ STATE

Jalapa Now the capital of Veracruz, Jalapa was Cortés's first stop on his march to Tenochtitlan in 1519. He chose this difficult route across the eastern sierra to avoid the strong Aztec garrison blocking the direct route to the tableland. His course would take him through the high pass between the **Pico de Orizaba**, Mexico's highest mountain at 18,696, and the great massif of the **Cofre de Perote**, 14,049 feet above sea-level. His route from Veracruz to Tlaxcala has been carefully traced by historians, and offers a challenge to the many hikers who attempt the journey. The view along the route is well worth the effort.

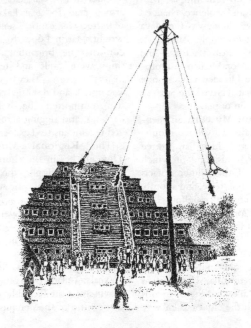

The **Museum of Anthropology**, run by the University of Veracruz, specializes in the Gulf Coast's Indian groups, such as the Totonac, Huastec, and Olmec cultures. The museum's exhibits include Olmec heads, jade figurines of the were-jaguar cult, figurines of people bearing classic Olmec features, and jewellery carved from jade and bone.

The city's cultural life includes the Jalapa Symphony Orchestra, the Ballet Folklórico Veracruzana, and stage performances in the **State Theatre**.

Papantla The city, once the capital of the ancient Totonacs, still retains elements of the culture, and many of its people still wear the costumes of their ancestors. More importantly, however, Papantla is the gateway to the ruins of **El Tajín**, the major Huastec site of the Late Classic Period (AD 600–900). The site covers about 146 acres, but outlying ruins are scattered over several thousand acres, hidden by the jungle growth of the coastal region. The primary structure is the **Pyramid of the Niches**, a six-

tiered structure with 365 niches along its sides. The number of niches is thought to signify the 365 days of the solar year. The centre was destroyed about AD 1200 by nomadic invaders from the north.

The site is famous for the ritual of the *volares* [flyers]. Four Totonac Indians, tied to ropes wound about a 100-foot pole, leap from the top and slowly descend to the ground in ever widening spirals. Their motion turns a wooden capstan at the top, where a fifth man plays a drum and a flute.

Veracruz The city is Mexico's oldest and largest port and the gateway to the interior. Cortés reached Veracruz in 1519, and established his first colony, which he named La Villa Rica de la Veracruz, at Quiahuitzlan, 30 miles north of the modern city.

Veracruz was also the site of foreign invasions into Mexico, first by the French in 1839, then by the Americans in 1847, and again by the French in 1862. During the War of Reform (1858–61), Benito Juárez established his government-in-exile at Veracruz.

The Spaniards, for lack of a safe harbour, made their first landfall on **San Juan Ulua**, a small island just off the shore of Veracruz. During the Colonial Period, they constructed a massive fortress there to protect their New World trade. The fortress is now a convention centre, connected to the city by a causeway, and the dungeons are open to the public.

The Spaniards first observed human sacrifice in Mexico on a small island offshore from Veracruz. In 1518, Juan de Grijalva discovered a temple containing the bodies of two young men who had been sacrificed not more than three days previously. He named the place the *Isla de Sacrificios*. The city's pre-Lenten *Carnaval* is now conducted on the island.

The **Museo de Arte e Historia Veracruzana** contains displays of pre-Hispanic history, and artifacts from the Mexican Revolution and the Mexican-American War.

Zempoala (Cempoala) Cortés learned of the extent and weaknesses of Moctezuma's empire from the Totonac chieftain of the city. He began the construction of Veracruz, the first Spanish settlement on the continent, 14 miles north of Cempoala. From the colony, he marched into the interior with 450 foot, 300 Cempoalan warriors, and 15 horse. To prevent word of the discovery of Moctezuma's inland empire from reaching Cuba and Spain, he scuttled his fleet in ten fathoms of water.

Later in the campaign, Cortés defeated Panfilo Narvaez at Cempoala with a surprise night attack. With less than 200 men, he captured a force of more than 800 foot and horse. **6, 7, 86, 194, 196, 204, 219, 220, 223, 226, 246, 256, 257, 277**

YUCATÁN STATE

Mérida The conquistador Francisco Montejo founded the city in 1542 on the site of **Tihu**, the ancient Mayan city he destroyed. Until recently, Mérida and the Yucatán Peninsula have been relatively isolated from mainland Mexico. The only access to the peninsula required crossing the Laguna de Terminos by ferry, and if

the water was rough, one might spend several days on **Carmen Island**. Today a road into the interior connects Villahermosa with Campeche and Mérida.

With ready access to Europe and the Gulf cities of the United States through **Progreso**, the seaport 18 miles north of the city, the culture of Mérida has a continental flavor not seen in greater Mexico. Colonial mansions along the **Paseo de Montejo**, a boulevard fashioned after the Champs Elysées, show the architectural styles of France, Italy, Spain, and Morocco. Most of the homes were built in the 19th century by settlers who grew wealthy growing henequen, a tough fibre used for making rope and coarse clothing.

Mérida is the gateway to many of the major archaeological sites of the Maya Classic Period (AD 300–900). The **Puuc Hills** sites, **Uxmal**, **Kabah**, **Sayil**, **Xlappahk**, and **Labna**, lie along a straight line 50 miles south of Mérida. **Bolonchén de Rejón**, the *cenote* where John Lloyd Stephens made his perilous descent, lies just beyond the archaeological zone and is open to tourists.

Chichen Itza, the major tourist attraction in Yucatán, is located on a major highway 65 miles east of Mérida. Its ruins are the most famous in the New World, and the name of Chichen Itza has come to be synonymous with the Maya as are the pyramids of the pharaohs with ancient Egypt. The glamour and mystique of the ruins are due, in part, to early explorers, who believed that they had at last found the lost city of Atlantis. Furthermore, intriguing and romantic tales of its mysterious sacrificial well evoked visions of depraved priests throwing young virgins to pagan gods lurking in its murky depths.

The highway divides the Toltec period (AD 987–1200), from the Maya period (AD 600–889). Distinctive differences are evident in the architecture of the two periods. The major structures built during the Maya period are the Nunnery, the Iglesia, the Red House, and the Caracol (so named by the Spaniards). The major structures built during the Toltec period are the Castillo, the Temple of the Warriors, the Ball Court, and the Temple of the Chac Mool.

The Castillo was built above an earlier temple erected *circa* AD 918. A narrow stairway ascends to the inner temple, where a throne of a snarling jaguar, painted bright red, stares wildly with its jade eyes past a reclining Chac Mool. The tourist highlight of the day occurs when a small door at the foot of the north staircase of the Castillo opens to allow visitors to climb to the throne room.

Dziblilchaltún, the huge site 20 miles north of Mérida, covers an area of 18 square miles, and shows occupation prior to 600 BC. **Izamal**, known to have been a major religious centre *circa* AD 400, is considered to be the site where the foundations of élitist Maya religious thought in the north were developed. Other ruins in the region show great antiquity. Many of them were little more than colossal mounds of rubble when John Lloyd Stephens saw them in 1841,

and have since been totally destroyed. **Mayapán** Located some 25 miles southeast of Mérida, Mayapán rose to power after Hunac Ceel, a Cocom chieftain, captured Chichen Itza in AD 1200. Hunac Ceel was also called Ah Nacxit Kukulcan, and claimed descent from Kukulcan, the Maya name for Quetzalcoatl.

Mayapán became the central government of the Yucatán, and the Cocoms maintained order and control of the peninsula by holding hostage the ruling lords of the principal cities. Their dynasty ended in AD 1450, when the Xiu family at Mani instigated an uprising among the captive Maya lords and killed all but one of the Cocoms. With the fall of the city, the last form of central government vanished in the Yucatán, leaving in its stead a number of warring, independent principalities that survived until the arrival of the Spaniards.

The power of the Cocoms was broken and Mayapán destroyed, but the city lived on in the memories of their descendants for more than a century after its destruction. Well into Colonial times, they were able to recognize their ancestral home-sites at the ruins. **7, 32, 38, 43, 44, 45, 47, 48, 49, 191, 196, 199, 202, 207, 213, 214, 253**

ZACATECAS STATE

Zacatecas The city had its beginnings in 1546, when Juanes de Tolosa found a deposit of silver so rich that within four years, foundries, churches, stores, and mansions rose at the site of the lode. By the end of the

18th century, the mines at Zacatecas and other sites in the north would produce one-fifth of the world's silver. Zacatecas continues to be a centre of silver mining in Mexico, and the 200-year-old El Bote mine is still in operation.

The **Patrino Chapel**, erected in 1728 at the top of the promontory now known as the **Cerro de la Bufa**, offers a spectacular view of the city and the surrounding mountains. The crest can be reached by a cable lift from **Cerro Grillo** and a metalled road. **The Battle of Zacatecas Museum** on the summit records Pancho Villa's capture of the city in 1914.

Zacatecas was also the home of the noted artist Francisco Goitia. **The Pedro Coronel Museum** houses the private collection of the noted Mexican artist and sculptor, and displays works by Pablo Picasso, Salvador Dali, Juan Miró, and Marc Chagall.

A lesser-known fact about Juanes de Tolosa's role in Mexican history was his marriage to Doña Leonor Cortés y Moctezuma. Doña Leonor was the issue from an affair between Cortés and Isabel, the sole surviving heir of Moctezuma. Her union with Tolosa would produce three children, Juan Cortés y Moctezuma, Leonor Cortés y Moctezuma, and Isabel Cortés Moctezuma. **2, 137, 258, 266**

BAJA, THE FORGOTTEN LAND

In 1533, mutineers on a ship owned by Hernán Cortés sought refuge on the peninsula near La Paz. Twenty Spaniards were killed by the natives, but two escaped in the ship's boat and brought word to New Spain that they had found pearls. Hernando de Grijalba led a second voyage to the peninsula, and managed to reach the narrows at the upper end of the Golfo de California, but found that the land was uninhabited and waterless. The Baja was abandoned to pirates, who raided Spanish galleons from its hidden coves and inlets.

The entire length of the Baja was opened to motorists in 1973, when the trans-peninsular highway joined Tijuana in the north to La Paz at the southern tip. The greater part of the Baja between Ensenada and La Paz is rugged and thinly populated, and travelling off the main highway is usually best done in four-wheel-drive vehicles.

Prehistoric murals of warriors, deer, and mountain goats, painted by an unknown people, cover the canyon walls of the mountains of the central Baja, and petroglyphs can be found in the caves of the mountains north of San Ignacio.

Outdoor recreation and scenery are the primary attractions for the tourist. Along both coasts, resorts cater for surfers, deep-sea anglers, surf anglers, snorkellers, sightseers, and sun-bathers. Less elegant but equally popular are the fishing villages where life is more casual, and one can find solitude on a pristine beach anywhere along the coast.

Hundreds of species of fish are found in the Pacific Ocean and the Golfo de California, and the southern tip of the peninsula is home to game fish such as marlin, sea bass, bonito,

Baja California

mahimahi, sailfish, amberjack, and yellowfin tuna. Charter boats are available at nearly every seaside town on the Baja.

Whale-watching along the Pacific coast is one of the most popular attractions of the Baja. Each year, from December to March, more than 15,000 grey whales migrate 6,000 miles from the Bering Sea to Laguna Ojo de Liebre (Scammons Lagoon), near Guerrero Negro, where females bear their young. Occasionally, a whale will swim into the shallows to scratch barnacles from its back. The Ensenada Museum of Science sponsors boat tours for whale-watching, and charter boats are available at Guerrero Negro and other points along the coast.

La Paz, on the southern tip of the peninsula, is the site where Indians killed the Spanish mutineers in 1533. The Jesuits founded a mission at La Paz in 1720, but abandoned it 30 years later when smallpox brought to New Spain by the Spaniards nearly wiped out the native population. A permanent settlement was established on the site in 1811, and in 1829, La Paz became the territorial capital.

After the mining and pearl industries petered out, La Paz became a back-water town until tourists discovered its favourable climate and its sport-fishing opportunities. La Paz maintains its Mexican character, despite the yearly influx of tourists. Many of its colonial homes and buildings are still evident, and families continue to observe the custom of parading along the *malecón* on Sunday. The La Paz museum displays dioramas, photographs of cave murals, paintings, and excavation sites.

Cabo San Lucas was a sleepy beach community until wealthy Americans began mooring their yachts in the bay in the 1950s. Now it is a port of call for cruise ships and a favoured location for the up-market tourist. High-rise hotels offer 18-hole golf courses, floodlit tennis courts, marinas, charter fishing, scuba diving, snorkelling, sailboating, fine dining, and entertainment. Apartment blocks, boutiques, and restaurants are commonplace on the hills and the waterfront, and caravan parks are available for motor homes.

Glass-bottomed boats make daily tours to view marine life, and charter boats are available for hunting the blue marlin, a year-round sport. A catch-and-release policy is observed. Charter flights are also available at Cabo for whale-watching at San Ignacio Lagoon.

For the more relaxed tourist, Loreto, Mulejé, and San Felipe offer sport fishing, surf fishing, camping, kayaking, scuba diving, and access to the unspoiled beaches along the Golfo de California. **1, 236, 248**

Glossary

Aguada Underground cisterns used to store water during the dry season

Alcalde A justice or town-council member

Audiencia A council chosen to represent the Crown in the New World

Atlatl A sling used to throw spears

Cabacera Capital of a district containing more than one town

Cabildo A municipal council

Cacique An Arawakian word given by the Spaniards to designate a leading chieftain

Calmecac A preparatory school for the instruction of male Aztec children

Calpulli The ruling council of a tribe

Caudillo Commander of an armed group

Centificos An advisory panel of lawyers and economists in the Porfirio Díaz administration

Cenote Underground wells in the Yucatán

Chacs The rain gods

Charro A Mexican cowboy

Chicle Latex of the sapodilla tree used in the manufacture of chewing gum

Chultunes Bottle-shaped receptacles carved in the bedrock used to collect water for the dry season

Cihuacoatl Aztec vice-regent; literally the 'snake woman'

Corregidor A mayor or magistrate

Criollo A person of Spanish descent born in the New World

Cuicacalco The House of Song

Dedazo A finger

Ejido A communal land grant

Encomienda A grant of native villages to an *encomendero*, who is entitled to tribute and labour in exchange for the welfare and religious instruction of the inhabitants

Escoreses Masons who follow the Scottish rite

Fueros Privileges of the military and church to try clergy and military personnel outside of civilian courts

Gauchipine   A derogatory name for Spaniards in New Spain

Hacienda   A landed estate serviced by Indian labour working for wages, but in a *de facto* feudal relationship with the *Hacendado*

Henequen   Fibre of the agave cactus

Huipile   A traditional blouse worn by Maya women

Maquahuitl   A war club studded with obsidian blades

Mestizo   A person of mixed Spanish and Indian blood

Metate   A stone used for grinding maize

Mulatto   A person of mixed Spanish and African blood

Obraje   A factory

Octli   An alcoholic drink made from the fermented juice of the maguey plant

Patronato   Patronage

Peninsulares   Spaniards

Peones   Day labourers

Pocos   Mexican polka dancers

Pulque   Alcoholic drink obtained from the maguey plant

Rancheros   Ranchers

Repartimiento   Lands given in fief to the *conquistadores*

Rurales   Law-enforcement officers used to keep peace in the countryside

Sacbes   Ancient roads built by the Maya

Siete Partidas   Laws established by Alfonso X giving the people access to the crown

Telpochcalli   School for lower–class Aztec males

Tlatoani   An Aztec ruler. Literally 'he who speaks'

Totoloque   An Aztec game played by casting markers

Ueytlatolani   The supreme Tlatoani

Vaqueros   Another term for Mexican cowboys

Xochitl   Nahuatl term for flower

Yorkinos   Masons who follow the York rite

Zambo   A person of mixed African and Indian blood

Index

Acamapichtli, 52, 53
Acapulco, 136, 137, 162, 163, 165, 305, 358
Agriculture, origins of, 15, 18; in New Spain, 144; 62% of GNP, 154, in Yucatán, 201
Aguilar, Jerónimo, 91, 92
Ahuitzotl, 64–66, 73–75
Alamo, 181–184
Alemán, Miguel Valdéz, 291; major public works programmes, 293; arranges loans from American investors, 294; corruption of administration, 294
Alhóndiga de Granaditas, 160, 162, 357
Allende, Ignacio, 157, 160, 162
Alvarado, Pedro de, 109; massacres Mexicans at festival, 111–112; besieged by Mexicans, 112; conquers Guatemala, 127–129; killed, 136
Alvarez, Juan, 217, 218
Amecameca, 56
Amélie, Carlota, 222, 223, 225
Ampudia, Pedro, 190, 191
Anahuac, 63
Ancient Man in Mexico 12–15
Art: Olmec, 21–23; Teotihuacán, 25, 27–29; Maya, 39–40; Zapotec, 30, 31; Toltec, at Chichen Itza, 47–49;

at Tula, 49–50, Aztec, 78; of Revolution, 270–74
Atzcapotzalco, 54–56
Audiencia, 140, 142, 143, 151, 156, 157, 159
Austin, Stephen, 180
Ávila Camacho, Manuel, 288; chooses to support allies in World War II, 289; 292, 298
Axayácatl, 62–64
Ay, Manuel Antonio, 203
Aztec Empire, weakness of, 121–124
Aztecs, 50–84 passim;arrival in the Valley of Mexico, 51–52; as Tepanec mercenaries, 53; overthrow Atzcapotzalco, 54–58; the empire, 58–66; their universe, 69–70, 78–79; human sacrifice, 72–75; poetry and literature, 76, 82–83; palaces and temples, 76–78; sculpture, 78; laws, 80; education, 81; marriage, 83
Aztlán, 51

Bacalar, 208, 211, 213
Baja California, 1, 236, 248, 376, 377, 378
Bajio, 2
Balam Na, 211, 212
Balsas River, 5
Barrera, José María, 208, 210

Basilica de Guadelupe, 363
Belize, 15
Benevente, Toribio de, 139
Bonampak, 40
Bourbon dynasty in New Spain, 152
Bowie, James, 181
Braceros, 290
Bravo, Nicolás, 169
Britain, 194, 220
Bucareli Agreements, 279
Buena Vista, battle of, 193
Bustamante, Carlos María de, 170, 173

Cabeza de Vaca, Álvar, Núñez, 130–135
California, 189, 191, 193, 194, 198
Calles, Plutarco Elías, 262, 263, 268, 277, 279–284 *passim*, 297
Calmecac, 58, 81
Campeche, 7, 85, 199, 202, 203, 204, 205, 308, 354
Candelaría (river), 7
Cape Corrientes, 4
Cárdenas, Cuauhtémoc, 312, 321, 323, 325
Cárdenas, Lázaro, 283, 284; on land distribution, 285; nationalizes oil resources, 286; 288, 292, 303
Carranza, Venustiana, 255, 257, 258; and Convention of Aguascalientes, 259; 260, 261, 262, 266, 268, 269, 275, 276, 277
Castro, Fidel, 299
Ceiba tree, 199, 200
Celaya, Battle of, 261, 266
Cempoala, 93, 94, 373, 374
Cenotes, 8, 10, 11
Central America, 23
Central Junta in Cádiz, 156
Cetina, José Dolores, 203
Chac Mool, 48
Chalco, 56, 122

Chalco, lake, 5, 197
Champotón, 85
Chamula, 355, 356
Chan Santa Cruz, 208, 212, 213
Chapultepec, 198, 223, 231, 283, 360
Charles II, 151, 152
Charles III, 152, 153, 156
Charles IV, abdicates in favour of Ferdinand VII, 156
Charles V, 142
Charlot, Jean, 272
Chi, Cecilio, 203, 205, 206, 208, 210
Chiapas: pacified, 129; 199, 236, 315, 316, 317, 324, 332, 333, 354, 355, 356
Chichen Itza, 47, 48, 49, 374
Chihuahua, 2, 237, 248, 263, 265, 266, 268, 356
Chilam Balam, 209
Chimalpopoca, 53, 65, 68
Cholula, 62, 94, 122, 367
Church, and the Crown, 126, 138; and the Indian, 141–142, 149; in Yucatán, 199, 200, 201; growth during Porfiriato, 240, 241; retaliation against Constitution of 1917, 281
Cíbola, Seven Cities of, 130, 135
Científicos, 234, 235, 246
Cinco de Mayo, 221, 238
Ciudad Juárez, Treaty of, 249; 253, 263, 264, 265, 266, 268
Coahuila, 2
Coatzacoalcos, 7
Cocoms, 206
Colorado, 189
Colosio, Luis Donaldo, 317, 318
Comonfort, Ignacio, 218, 219
Constitution of 1812, 164, 165
Constitution of 1824, 170, 176, 185, 201
Constitution of 1841, 202, 204

Constitution of 1857, 219, 255
Constitution of 1917, 244, 275
Coolidge, Calvin, 280
Córdoba, Francisco Fernández, 85, 354
Coronado, Francisco Vásquez de, expedition to United States, 135
Cortés, Hernán, early life, 88–89; appointed captain of third expedition, 90; sails for New Spain, 91; at Cozumel, 91; battle of Centla, 92; welcomed at San Juan Ulúa, 92, 93; demands to see Moctezuma, 93; at Cempoala, 93–94; founds Villa Rica de la Vera Cruz, 94; invokes Siete Partidas, 95; sinks fleet, 96; march to interior, 96; defeats Tlaxcalans, 98; attempts to convert Tlaxcalans, 98, 99; Cholula massacre, 99–100; enters Tenochtitlán, meets Moctezuma, 100–103; seizes Moctezuma, 105–106; defeats Pánfilo de Narváez at Cempoala, 109–111; beseiged in Tenochtitlán, 112–113; retreat from city, 113–116; march to Tlaxcala, 116–117; attacks Tenochtitlán, 118–121; captures Cuautémoc, 121;
Cortés, Martin, 88; leader of revolt, 150–151
Council of the Indies, 142
Cozumel, 85, 368, 369
Cristeros, 282
Crockett, David, 184
Cross, first speaks, 208; organization of, 210; officers of 210, 211; dictatorship of, 211; 213, last ceremony of, 214
CTM, *see* Confederación de Trabajadores, 285
Cuautémoc, 118, 120, 121

Cuba, 85, 86, 95
Cuicuilco, 24, 360
Cuitláhuac, city 56, 57
Cuitláhuac, emperor, 112; attacks Spaniards, 117; dies, 118
Culhuacán, 56, 57

Díaz Ordaz, Gustavo, 299; and the 1968 Olympics, 300
Díaz, Bernal, describes Tlatelolco, 103–105; speaks of captivity of Moctezuma, 106, 200
Díaz, Félix, 253, 254
Díaz, Juan, incites mutiny, 95, 96
Díaz, Porfirio, 221, 225, 226, 228; on democracy, 229–230; 231–236 *passim*; 239, 240, 241–248, *passim*; 249, 250, 251, 255, 256, 270, 280, 330
Dolores Hidalgo, 161, 357
Dresden Codex, 36
Durango, 2, 263

Earthquake of 1985, 311, 312
Echeverría, Luis Alvarez, 303, and riot of Cristeros, 304, 305; as president of OAS, 306, 307
Ejidos, 235, 241, 242, 258, 276, 299, 314, 315, 316, 317
El Paso, 249
Encomienda, defined, 125–26; impact of New Laws upon, 126, 148
Esther, Commandante, 334

Family planning, 320
Farías, Valentín Gómez, 170, 196
Ferdinand VII, 156, 165, 166
Flores Magón brothers, 243, 244
Freemasonry, 171
Fox, Vincente, 323, 324; elected president, 326; 327, 332, 333
Francophiles, 237–239

French invasion of Mexico, 220, 221
Freemasonry, 171
Frémont, John Charles, 193, 194
Fuentes, Carlos, 329

Gadsden Purchase, 198
Gálvez, José de, 153, 154
Golfo de California, 1, 2, 330
Goliad, execution of prisoners of war, 184–186
Gonzáles, Manuel, 239
Grijalva (river), 7, 86
Grijalva, Juan de, 85, 86, 88 87
Guadalajara, 2, 218, 220, 226, 258, 359
Guadelupe Hidalgo, Treaty of, 198
Guanajuato, 2, 158, 160, 161, 166, 357
Guatemala, 1, 7, 66
Guaymas, 2
Guerrero, 163, 358
Guererro, Vincente, 172; as president 172; assassinated, 173
Guzmán, Beltran Niño de, 143

Haciendas, 145–150, 241, 242, 276
Hermosillo, 2
Hidalgo, (state), 359
Hidalgo y Costilla, Miguel, 158–162 *passim*, size of army, 162; 224, 357
Honduras, 85
Houston, Samuel, 181, 186, 187
Huerta, Victoriano, 251, 253; as president, 254; 255, 256, 257, 258, 264
Huexotzingo, 62, 94, 122
Huitzilopochtli, 51, 52, 54

Indian nobility, post conquest, 149–150
Indians, conversion to Catholicism, 141–142

Inquisition, Holy Office of, 158, 162, 164
Isabel Cortés y Moctezuma, 114
Iturbide, Augustín de, Plan de Iguala, 165; as Augustin I, Emperor of Mexico, 165, 166, 169
Itzcoatl, 54–58, 65
Iztaccíhuatl, 367

Jalisco, 2, 218, 225, 359
Jesuits, expulsion from New Spain, 153, 154
Juárez, Benito, 213, 215–221, 224–233, *passim*

Kabah, 43
Kaminalujú, 29
Kearny, Stephen, 191, 193, 194
Kennewick man, 13

Labastida, Francisco, 323, 326
Labna, 43
Labour, peon, 241, 242, 243, 244, 255, 246, 276, 277, 278; Confederación de Trabajadores, (CTM), 285; 288, 291
Laguna de Terminos, 7
Lake Chapala, 2
Las Casas, Bartolome de, 138
Laws of Reform, 220, 224
Lee, Robert E, 196, 197
Lerdo de Tejada, Miguel, 218
Lerdo de Tejada, Sebastián, 228, 232, 233, 240
Lerma River, 2
Ley Iglesias, 218
Ley Juárez, 218
Ley Lerdo, 218
Limantour, José Ives, 235
Lopéz Mateos, Adolfo, 297, 298, housing and urban development, 298; labour problems 298, 299; supports Fidel Castro, 299

Lopéz Potillo, José, 306, 307, 308; opposes Ronald Reagan on support of Nicaragua rebels, 309; nationalizes banks, 310

Madero, Francisco, 244, 247–254 *passim*; 256, 263, 264
Madrid, Miguel de la; austerity programme of, 310, 311; earthquake disaster, 311, 312; peso plummets, 312
Maize, 16, 17, 19
Manual Nahuat, 208
Marcos, Subcommandante, 316, 332, 333, 334
Marina, Cortés's interpreter, 92
Maximilian, 213, 221, 223–227, 271
Maya Civilization, 32–45 *passim*; agriculture of, 18, 19; ceremonial centers, 33, 34, 43, 354collapse of, 43; calendar, 37, 38, 39; science, 36, 37; early settlements, 32, 33; in Guatemala, 29; at Tikal, 29, 34–36
Mayapán, 375
Mérida, 7, 202, 203, 205, 213 defences of, 206; 207, 374
Mexico City, 5, 6, 198, 217, 220–233 *passim*; 247, 250, 253, 257, 258, 260, 265, 328, 329, 332, 333, 359–363 *passim*
Mexico, 233; and the Great Depression of 1927, 283; mobilizes forces against Axis Powers, 290; the bracero programme, 290, 291; great earthquake of 1985, 311, 312; 327, 328, 330, 331
Michoacán, 2, 122, 164, 215, 225, 283, 364
Mining, 137, 138, 168
Missionaries, 125, 138, 139, 140
Moctezuma Ilhuicamina, 58–62, 65;
Moctezuma Xocóyotl, 65; elected emperor, 67–69; 88; appeases

Cortés; greets Cortés, 102–103; orders chieftains to obey Cortés, 106–107; stoned to death, 112–113; his descendants, 114; fears of omens, 123; fear of Quetzalcoatl, 123–124; descendants of, 149–150
Monte Alban, 29–32; early inhabitants 29, 30, 31; hieroglyphics, 30, 366
Montejo, Francisco de, (son) conquers Yucatán, 129
Montejo, Francisco de, (father), 95
Monterrey, 247, 366
Morelos, (State), 250, 257, 365
Morelos, José María, 162, convenes Congress of Chilpancingo, 163; 164
Morrow, Dwight, 280, 281

NAFTA, 315, 316, 324, 328, 332
Náhuatl, 139
Napoleon Bonaparte, occupies Spain, 156; defeated, 165
Napoleon III, 221, 223, 225
Nárvaez, Pánfilo de, 107–110, 130
Nayarit, 2, 163, 365, 356
Nevada de Colimo, 4
New Fire Ceremony, 70, 71, 360
New Laws, 126
New Mexico, 189, 191, 193, 198, 268, 269
New Orleans, 215, 217
Nezahualcóyotl, 54, 56; dike of, 59; 67, 238
Nezahualpilli, 67, 72, 74
Ninos Heros, 198
Novelo, Bonafacio, 204, 208, 213
Nueces River, 189
Nueva Leon, 2, 191, 218, 225, 366

Oaxaca (state), 6, 29, 66, 215, 217, 220, 228, 230, 234, 239, 366

Oaxaca, (city), 6, 216, 230
Obregón, Álvaro, 255, 257, 258, 259, 260, 261, 266, 269, 270, 275, 277, 278, 279, 281; assassination of, 282
Ocampo, Melchor, 215, 217, 218
Oil, 278, 279, 280, 281, 285, 286; discoveries of new sources, 307
Olmec civilization, 20–23
Omens in Mexico, 71, 72
Oregon, 189, 193
Orizaba, 4
Orozco, José Clemente, 271, 272, 273, 278, 359
Orozco, Pasqual, 248, 249, 253, 263, 264, 356

Palenque, 200, 356
Papaloapan River, 6
Paricutin, 5
Partido Acción Nacional (PAN), 288, 294
Partido de Revolucion Democracia, (PRD) 313
Partido Liberál Mexicano (PLM), 243, 244, 248, 291
Partido Revolucinario, Institucional, (PRI) formed, 292, 294; loses 2000 election, 326
Partido, Nacional Revolucionario, (PNR), 282, 283, 284
Pat, Jacinto, 203, 205; terms for treaty, 206; 207, 208, 210
Paz, Octavio, 303, 329
Pec, Venancio, 208, 210
Pershing, John Blackjack, 268, 269
Peto, 205, 207
Philip II, 144
Philip V, 152
Philippine Islands, 136
Pino Suárez, José María, 253, 254
Plan de Ayala, 251, 259
Plan de Ayutla, 218, 228
Plan de Potosí, 251

Plan de Guadelupe, 255
Poinsett, Joel, 171, 172
Polk, James K. 189, 190, 191, 192
Poot, Crescendio, 213, 214
Popocatepetl, 4, 367
Population: doubles to 32 million between 1934–1958, 296; reaches 97 million in 1998
Population: of Teotihuacán, 24; of Tula, 49; of Tenochtitlán, 123; distribution in Colonial period, 147, 155
Potonchán, 86
Puc, Juan de la Cruz, 209, 211
Puebla, (state), 6, 221, 247, 249, 367
Puertocarrero, Alonso de, 95
Pyramids, of Quetzalcoatl, 25; of the Sun, 27; at Tikal, 34; of the Adivino, 44

Querétaro, 219, 226, 275 367; Literary and Social Society of, 157, 159
Quetzalcoatl, 46, 47, 49, 50, 71, 88, 123, 124
Quintana Roo, 368
Quiahuitzlán, 95

Reagan, Ronald, 309
Reyes, Bernardo, 246, 251, 253, 265
Rio Grande de Santiago, 2
Rio Grande, 189, 191
Rivera, Diego, 270, 271, 272, 273, 278, 280, 357, 362
Romero, Juana Catalina, 231
Rosada, Eulogio, 203
Ruiz Cortines, Adolfo, 294; and women's right to vote, 296; 297
Rurales, 233, 234, 243, 245, 246, 254

Sacrifice, human; at Teotihuacán 27, at Chichen Itza, 49, at Tenochtitlán, 71, 72–75

Sacrificios, Isla de, 86
Sahagún, Bernardino de, 139
Salinas de Gortari, Carlos, 312; tainted election of, 313; the Zapatistas, 315–317
Salinas, Raul, 318, 319
San Andreas Accords, 332–334
San Andreas Tuxtla, 4
San Cristóbal de Las Casas, 316, 317, 332, 354, 355
San Luis Potosí, 2, 193, 221, 247, 370
San Miguel de Allende, 357
Santa Anna, Antonio López de, 169, 173–176, 180–189 *passim*, 191, 192–193, 196, 198, 201, 202, 217, 218
Sayil, 43
Scott, Winfield, 191, 194–198; 257
Silver, discovery of, 137–138; production in Colonial period, 154
Sinaloa, 225
Siqueiros, Alfaro David, 272, 273, 278 , 299, 300
Sisal, 206, 213
Slavery, abolished in New Spain, 126; 148; of Maya, 213
Sloat, John, 194
Sonora (desert), 2
Sonora, (state), 262, 266
Stephens, John Lloyd, 8, 10
Sutter's Fort, 193

Tabasco, 370, 371
Tacuba (Tlacopan), 94
Tampico, 4, 283
Tarascans, 62
Taylor, Zachary, 190, 191, 192, 193
Tehuantepec, 1, 6, 66, 230, 236
Tenochtitlán, 5, flooded, 59; 61, 62, 64, 71, 72, 73, 76, 77, 94, 100, 102, 105, 111, 118, 119, 122, 123
Teotihuacán, residential housing in, 24–25; ceremonial centre, 25–27;

mural art, 27–29; influence in Mesoamerica, 29
Tepeaca, 60
Teuhtliltl, 92
Texas, 177–181, 184, 187, 189, 193, 202, 265, 269, 308
Texcoco, city, 67, 122
Texcoco, lake, 5
Tezcatlipoca, 46
Tezozomoc, Hernando Alvarado, 54
Tezozomoc, lord of the Tepanecs, 53
Tienda del Raya, 201, 242, 246
Tikal, 33–36
Tizoc, 64, 65, 68
Tlacaelel, 54, 55
Tlacopan, 67, 122
Tlatelolco, 53, 61; merchants, 60; war with Tenochtitlán, 62–63
Tlatelolco massacre, 299–303
Tlaxcala, 62, 94, 122, 371, 372
Tlilancalqui, 88
Toltecs; origins of, 46; at Chichen Itza, 47, 48, 49; at Tula, 49, 50
Torréon. 265, 266, 269
Totonacs, 60
Travis, William, 181, 183, 186
Tula, 46; population of, 49; ceremonial centre, 49, 50; 359

Ulúa, San Juan, 86, 88, 194
United States, 189, 190, 193, 194, 198; forces in Mexico, 191; 234, 235, 244, 248, 249, 253, 262, 265, 269, 278; the Bucareli Agreement, 279; 280, 286, 288, 291, 293, 309
Urdaneta, Fray Andrés de, discovers eastward passage from the Philippines, 136–137
Usmacinta River, 7, 86
Uxmal, 43

Valladolid, sacked, 202–203; siege of, 205; 208, 213

Vallejo, Mariano Guadelupe, 194

Velásquez, Diego, governor of Cuba, 85; instructions to Cortes, 90, 91; sends Pánfilo Narváez to arrest Cortés, 107–108

Velásquez, Fidel, 288, 289, 291

Veracruz, (state), 6, 7, 372, 373, 374

Veracruz, (city), 86, 194, 196, 204, 219, 220, 223 226, 246, 256, 257, 277

Victoria, Guadelupe, 169, as president, 171

Villa, Pancho, 248, 249, 253, 255, 257, 258, 259, 260, 261, 262; defeat at Agua Prieto, 263, 264–270 *passim*; 275, 356

War of Reform, 219, 220

Wars of Independence, 156–176

Wilson, Henry Lane, 254

Wilson, Woodrow, 256, 257, 262, 266, 269

Xicalango, 60

Xicoténcatl, 96, 98

Xlappahk, 43

Xochimilco, lake, 5, 197

Yaqui Indians, 191, 255

Yucatán, 7, 191, 196, 199, 202, 207, 213, 214, 253, 374, 375

Zacatecas (state), 2, 137, 258, 266, 375, 376

Zapata, Emiliano, 248, 250, 251, 252, 254, 255, 256, 257, 258, 259, 260, 261; assassination of, 262, 271, 330, 333

Zapatistas, 315, 316, 317, 324, 325, 332, 333

Zapotecs, 60, 66, 215

Zaragoza, Ignacio, 221

Zedillo, Ernesto, 318; inherits the Salinas scandal, 318, 319, 320; forms Federal Election Institute, (IFE), 321; 326, 327, 332

Zuloaga, Félix, 219